VOICES

Essays on Canadian Families

SECOND EDITION

edited by Marion Lynn
Research Consultant

THOMSON ™

NELSON

Australia   Canada   Mexico   Singapore   Spain   United Kingdom   United States

THOMSON

NELSON

Voices: Essays on Canadian Families
Second Edition

by Marion Lynn

Editorial Director and Publisher:
Evelyn Veitch

Executive Editor:
Joanna Cotton

Acquisitions Editor:
Brad Lambertus

Marketing Manager:
Lenore Taylor

Senior Developmental Editor:
Edward Ikeda

Production Editor:
Carrie Withers

Production Coordinator:
Helen Locsin

Copy Editor:
Kelli Howey

Proofreader:
Nick Gamble

Creative Director:
Angela Cluer

Cover Design
Sue Peden

Cover Image:
Detail from Lumiere Enigmatique
by Ann McCall

Interior Design:
Peggy Rhodes

Interior Design Modifications:
Sue Peden

Compositor:
Gerry Dunn

Printer:
Transcontinental

**National Library of Canada
Cataloguing in Publication Data**

Voices: essays on Canadian
families/edited by Marion Lynn
—2nd ed.

Includes bibliographical
references.

ISBN 0-17-622315-0

Family—Canada. 2. Kinship—
Canada. I. Lynn, Marion, 1939–

HQ560.V64 2003 306.85'0971
C2002-904591-6

TABLE OF CONTENTS

PREFACE

This second edition of *Voices: Essays on Canadian Families* adheres to the principles that shaped the first edition and gave it a unique place in literature on Canadian families and kinship. The rich material presented here cuts across a variety of topics of interest to students and researchers in sociology, women's studies, and related fields. Family and kinship are analyzed from the perspectives of gender, race, sexuality, class, and culture. Ways of studying these forms of social organizations and social practices within the social science disciplines are shown to have great influence over published results. Most of the essays from the first edition have been updated and included in this edition. In order to create a slimmer volume and to include a short section on emerging issues, some of the original essays had to be left out but are available from the publishers in their original form. Some of the writers are well known for their work on families; others are just beginning to publish material from their very current and topical research. Many of the writers analyze and write about families from standpoints that are only now being given a voice in scholarly texts.

This text is intended for university and college students without an extensive background of studies in family and kinship. It will be useful as well for upper-level secondary school students as an introduction to the study of the family, and for readers interested in exploring some of the current debates in research and theory-building. It can be read as a supplement to a core text that presents basic sociological concepts or it can stand on its own as a text on families.

Although these essays inevitably apply the standard concepts and are preceded by Introductions that put them into context, they are not intended to provide a systematic or comprehensive introduction to the sociology of the family. Instead, they are meant to bring into the sociological dialogue some of the families that are often excluded—although these families may be surprisingly common in Canadian society—and to capture some of the voices that are trying to be heard.

This is a user-friendly text. Statistics, research methods, theories, and analyses are presented in language that can be understood by the beginner as well as the more sophisticated reader. The Introductions that begin each section pull out the main concepts and themes of the essays and show, as well, the intersection of family issues among the essays. Each essay opens with a list of objectives and concludes with key-term definitions and discussion questions. Readers might find it useful to approach each essay by first reviewing these three sections, using the objectives, defined key terms, and discussion questions to guide their reading. As well, instructors can use these items in assigning essay topics and exam questions.

I am appreciative to all who helped in the creation of this text. I thank Joanna Cotton, Brad Lambertus, Edward Ikeda, and Carrie Withers of Nelson Thomson Learning for providing ideas, critiques, and support in publishing this second edition. I thank the reviewers of the text for their time and thoughtful criticisms and suggestions, many of which were incorporated into the final versions. Thanks to Tracey Adams, University of Western Ontario; Tami Bereska, Grant MacEwan Community College; Jeff Braun-Jackson, Memorial University of Newfoundland; Helene Cummins, Brescia University College; Karen Kobayashi, University of British Columbia; Gillian Ranson, University of Alberta; Anna Lucy Robinson, Lambton College; Vappu Tyyskä, Ryerson University; and Victor Ujimoto, University of Guelph. It is with sadness that we give a special thank-you to the late Dr. Ellen Gee. Ellen Gee died suddenly on November 3, 2002. She was considered one of the top scholars in the sociology of family in Canada. Her contributions and her presence will be greatly missed. Most of all, I wish to thank all of the contributors for researching, writing, and editing their work and for having the insight and the vision to shape their part of a collaborative project, a project that they had to trust would do credit to their published work. Finally, I thank my own extended family, the Lynns and the Holmeses, which, in all of its diversity and richness, warmth, and wit, has provided the source of my ongoing interest in family matters.

Marion M. Lynn
Research Consultant

PART I

Diverse Family Forms

Part I of *Voices: Essays on Canadian Families* deals with diverse family forms. These essays examine different kinds of families from the point of view of their structures and role relationships—who makes up the family, how they are related to each other, and what special characteristics shape their lives as individuals and as family members.

The section begins with Donna Lero's examination of the statistically most common form of family in Canada today: the husband–wife dual-earner family (Chapter 1). Lero outlines some of the reasons that this family form has emerged as the dominant one in late 20th-century Canada. She discusses the impact that having both partners work outside the home has on family relationships, including the power dimensions that determine the sharing of domestic work. She also considers the effects of dual-earner families on the broader social system and discusses the policy implications of this significant shift in the structure of family life.

Lero ranges widely in this discussion, touching upon many different topics and themes in sociology. Her profile of dual-earner families in Canada provides an introduction to research methods—large statistical surveys as well as small-scale case studies. She shows how changes in the family and in women's paid employment are linked to both historical processes and contemporary trends and features of the broader society. Lero also isolates an important problem for detailed examination: the inequality between husbands' and wives' domestic responsibilities and career paths that emerges in most dual-earner families. Her discussion of this problem raises theoretical questions about the interrelationships of issues, ideologies, and social realities.

The issues that are touched on in this essay resonate throughout the text: the family in its social and economic context; unequal male–female power relations in the family and in society; a critique of various family ideologies; family behaviours as economic strategies and social adaptations; and the personal and social implications of coping with stress and with changed roles and responsibilities.

The next essay, by Marion Lynn, looks at single-parent families—a family form that is growing and commanding a great deal of attention in both the scholarly and the popular press (Chapter 2). Located within a framework of statistical data and background literature, this essay draws on a qualitative study of 50 women and men in single-parent families. This essay argues that although it contains features peculiar to late 20th-century Western society, the current growth in single-parent families is not inconsistent with diversity and change in family structures historically. This particular change can be understood as part of broader changes in the lives of men and women, but centrally in the lives of women.

The discussion here lists some family forms that may or may not be included in everyone's definition of *single-parent family*, including gay and lesbian families and situations where children are cared for by both their separated parents. The research study that forms the core of the essay uses a sample small enough for its subjects to be interviewed individually, unlike some of the large surveys cited in the review of the literature. The interviews were *open-ended*; that is, they allowed interviewees to discuss matters in detail and in a conversational format. The results, then, are qualitative (revealing how people think about and describe their own situation) rather than quantitative or statistical. The interviews reveal some conflicts between image and reality—again, a theme that is taken up in other essays. Notably, we see that single parenthood can be a liberating experience for women, and that a lower income need not lead to feelings of impoverishment.

Another consequence of the increase in divorce and remarriage in late 20th-century Canada is the increase in stepfamilies. Elizabeth Church criticizes the absence of literature on these families and the failure of census data to recognize stepfamilies (Chapter 3). This lack is a social fact—it shows that our society is generally not prepared to support the stepfamily as an institution or provide it with guidelines for developing. Yet, like single-parent families, stepfamilies are more consistent with historical forms of family than might initially be assumed. Until the late 19th century, it was not uncommon for at least one parent to die before the children were grown, and in England and the United States 20 to 30 percent of families were stepfamilies.

Church argues that the failure to recognize stepfamilies results partly from our discomfort with what they represent. Today, most stepfamilies result from divorce, and the social *stigma* (or negative label) that attaches to divorce carries over into the popular image of the stepfamily. In addition, because in our society *kinship* (who is defined as "family") is based on the married couple and not on the extended family (which may include, for example, grandparents or cousins), divorce causes much instability in the family unit. When stepfamilies are formed after divorce, the new roles and relationships that arise often do not fit into the neat slots we use when we imagine the "standard" nuclear family. Stepfamilies also contradict our usual assumption that a household is always a family; members of a stepfamily who live together may not consider themselves to be related, or they may consider people living in other households to be their immediate family. The stepfamily, then, represents an alternative model to the nuclear family.

Church draws on her own study of 105 stepmothers to examine some of the complexities of family, household, and kinship practices involving stepfamilies. She raises questions about definitions of nuclear family, extended family, and kinship. Like the previous essay on single-parent families, Church argues that "atypical" families—in this case stepfamilies—should not be seen as necessarily dysfunctional, inadequate, or problematic. Perhaps, she says, we should see divorce as part of the normal life cycle and no longer expect stepparents to conform to conventional parent roles. Church points out the benefits that can be derived from living in stepfamilies and suggests that we use stepfamilies as models of the fluid, non-traditional family—especially their members' freedom in choosing roles and kin. As in many of the other essays in this section, individual choice—including the way that people can control their lives by naming their own situation and thus constructing meaning—is an important theme in this essay.

What do we know about families that are not built upon the heterosexual model of marriage? The next two essays provide insight into families of lesbian women and of gay men. Rachel Epstein begins with questions that most people never have to confront, questions about authority over and responsibility for children and about the legitimacy of extended family relations (Chapter 4). She bases her analysis of lesbian families on interviews with women living as lesbian couples, as well as on her own experiences. This study is framed by a growing body of literature on lesbian families. Epstein shows how sociological research into the lesbian family is a product of lived experience. Many of the early studies were done in the context of court cases to decide the custody of children. Their aim was usually to show how well lesbian mothers and their children conformed to the heterosexual norm of the family. More recently, sympathetic writers have attempted to point out the positive differences that lesbian families can model for society as a whole.

Some of the issues raised by Epstein's research are the ways in which lesbian couples divide and share domestic and paid work, what names the children use for their two "moms," and what happens to custody arrangements if lesbian couples separate. Her exploration of some of the debates being carried on in the lesbian community—for example, whether lesbian parents can claim conventional family benefits and rights without compromising their vision of a radical alternative to the nuclear family—points out the direction that current research is taking. Often, it is lesbians themselves who are doing or suggesting the research; as we see in other essays, the "subjects" here are giving voice to their concerns, using social analysis in their own interest, acting autonomously, and making choices for themselves. Epstein sees herself as an advocate as well as a sympathetic researcher; she concludes her paper with a list of policies for the government to implement that are based on a redefinition of family.

Think of the concept *gay family* as an abstract sociological category. Now imagine what such a family might be like in real life. In Chapter 5, James Miller takes us right into the kitchen of "Panic Manor," as his "out" family calls their house, and challenges us to draw the sociological lessons from the experience. He calls this an "anti–case study," criticizing the traditional case study as an instrument of male heterosexual power, much as Epstein does. The essay is structured as a catalogue of alternative values and written as a clever, combative response to those who attempt to impose conservative values as the norm and who would prefer families like Miller's to remain invisible.

Miller presents a provocative autobiographical narrative of his own coming out as a gay father and the troubles and triumphs, griefs and joys of his complex household. He writes in the tradition of cultural studies, decoding or "reading" the social data and ideological biases that he finds present in contemporary culture and daily situations. Not surprisingly, he does not spare the writing of sociologists. These cultural representations and situations, as well as the terminology in which they are expressed, are part of a public *discourse* (a kind of conversation), which Miller as cultural critic breaks into and subverts. In a style that is heavy on satire and irony, he addresses himself to the social consciousness of the people involved in his family and of the reader, and to the ideologies of the society in which they live.

Miller does not deny the difficulties that both children and adults of families such as his face in the day-to-day world—for instance, his children having to explain to their friends that although their father is gay they "probably are not." In this revision to his original essay, he shows how his initial optimism about forming a family based on a gay partnership was tempered by the real-life difficulties of rearing adolescents and the constant need to readjust one's perceptions and structures of family. But he refuses to adopt the image of deviance, sorrow, and pessimism that he believes is associated with the case study approach frequently used to represent families that have defied heterosexism and chosen to live openly in gay or lesbian households.

An "out" lifestyle tends to focus attention on a family and its dynamics. In contrast, the disability of a parent is a personal characteristic that is seldom acknowledged as important in considering family roles and relationships. In revising the original essay written by Karen Blackford, Neita Israelite addresses this lack of recognition in her research on families that have a disabled parent (Chapter 6). This piece criticizes much of the mainstream literature that does deal with disability for presenting the stigma placed on members of these families as "natural" and the disability itself as a medical issue rather than a social issue of barriers and exclusion.

Blackford and Israelite suggest an approach that takes into account both structure and agency. In this approach, disability is dependent on the way society is structured to exclude and disadvantage those we stigmatize as disabled. Two case studies from Blackford's research indicate the degree to which children interpret their own agency in directing their lives and achieving goals: a 16-year-old boy becomes one of the caregivers in the family when his mother becomes disabled; an 11-year-old girl increases her contribution to domestic work to help ease the load of her mother when her father becomes disabled. These are designed to be case studies with a difference. Blackford calls them participatory action research: the people studied help plan the study and interpret the results. This method is intended to break down the distance between researcher and subject and, Blackford says, to promote positive social change. (It might be useful to refer to James Miller's critique of the case study and consider whether Blackford's method solves the problems he notes.) By concentrating on children of parents with disabilities, this essay helps show the social context of disability, rather than portraying it as an individual problem: how disability is worked out in social interactions, and how the family, not only the individual, can be the relevant unit in the study of disability.

This section begins with dual-earner families, a trend that is the norm for most younger families in Canada today, and ends with an analysis by Susan McDaniel of the impact of aging on family life, focusing on families in mid-life (Chapter 7). McDaniel suggests that an analysis of families by structure fails to take into account a dynamic, life-course approach. In other words, as families change during the course of their lives, they pass through different life situations and face different challenges. The same family with young children and a mother who is able to do only part-time work away from the home may in a few years have both parents in full-time paid employment. In another 15 years the mother, in addition to her own full-time career, may be caring for her parents or in-laws. A dynamic approach asks, among other things, how families move into and out of such situations and what the implications are for families and for society.

In considering the impact of mid-life and aging on the labour force, on division of labour in the household, on caregiving and emotional supports for family members, McDaniel provides an insightful critique of the literature and of policy implications. This is an increasingly relevant area given Canada's demographic patterns. McDaniel points out some contributions of feminist research to the study of the family: the recognition of unequal responsibility and power in the home; the "discovery" of unpaid, "hidden" work; the argument that what we see as natural and eternal (especially in gender relations) may have social causes.

This essay—in its approach to theory and its social data—can be compared to those by Lero and Barber (Part II), which discuss women's work inside and outside the home in different contexts and environments. McDaniel criticizes the outdated model of the family used in some policy proposals and insists on women's right to work, to benefits, and to recognition as productive members of society. She concludes that all forms of families—single-parent, stepfamilies, and common-law families—face particular challenges of balancing work and family in mid-life and recommends that more attention be devoted to families at this stage of their life course.

1

Dual-Earner Families

Donna S. Lero

Department of Family Relations and Applied Nutrition
University of Guelph

Objectives

- To provide a context for understanding the growth and current prevalence of dual-earner families.

- To provide readers with a profile of dual-earner families in Canada and to illustrate some of the differences between dual-earner and male breadwinner families.

- To help readers understand the wide diversity that exists among dual-earner families in demographic and employment characteristics, in the ways husbands and wives think about paid work and family work roles, and in the adaptations they make individually and as a couple/family to address the challenges involved in integrating work and family responsibilities along with other aspects of their lives.

- To introduce readers to the major sociological theories and perspectives that have been applied to research on dual-earner families.

- To identify the need for changes in policies and workplace practices that could reduce the difficulties many dual-earners are experiencing in combining both paid work and family roles, especially among parents of young children and those with more complex caregiving responsibilities.

INTRODUCTION

The last 30 years has been a unique period in the history of family life in Canada. Demographic, social, technological, and economic forces have interacted to produce dramatic changes both in the structure and composition of Canadian families and in the roles and relationships among family members. Today's families are smaller, more mobile, and, if there is a husband and wife,[1] in most cases both are earners with significant, continuing ties to the paid labour force, even in families with very young children. Dual-earner families, once atypical compared to male breadwinner families, are the most prevalent family form and have been for some time. In 1967, the first year for which figures are available, less than a third of husband–wife families consisted of dual earners: husbands were the sole breadwinners in 58.4 percent of these families. As shown in Figure 1.1, 30 years later in 1997 dual-earner couples accounted for 61.3 percent of all husband–wife families; in only 16.5 percent were husbands the sole earner (Statistics Canada 1999). The most recent numbers provided by Statistics Canada (2002) indicate that growth in dual-earner families is

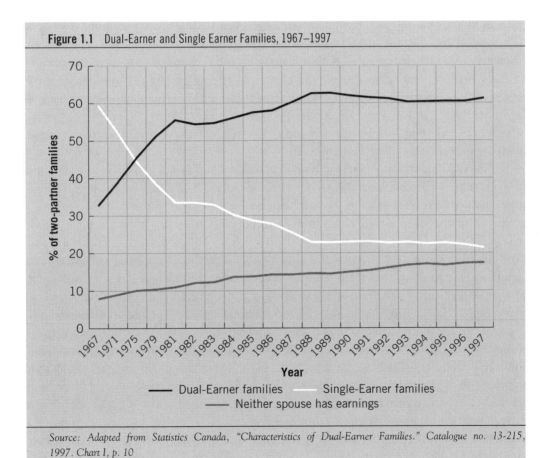

Figure 1.1 Dual-Earner and Single Earner Families, 1967–1997

Source: Adapted from Statistics Canada, "Characteristics of Dual-Earner Families." Catalogue no. 13-215, 1997. Chart 1, p. 10

continuing. In 1999, 64 percent of all husband–wife families were classified as dual-earner families. Moreover, today 73 percent of two-parent families with children are dual-earner families, in most cases with both parents employed full time (Jackson and Scott 2002).

Readers should note that the estimates presented above of the percentage of husband–wife families that are dual-earner families are based on all husband–wife families, including those in which the husband and/or wife are 65 years or older. If these percentages were calculated only for non-senior husband–wife families, the estimates would be even higher.

An interesting and not unimportant observation is that while dual earners have accounted for more than half of all husband–wife families since 1979 and more than 60 percent since 1987, dual-earner families are still often described as a newly emergent or recently developed family form and are implicitly, if not explicitly, compared to a "traditional" model of male breadwinner–wife at home families. Despite the fact that change and innovation are embraced quickly on other fronts, recognition, acceptance, and adaptations to this major change in family roles and in the composition of the labour force has been much slower—perhaps signifying the ambivalence many have experienced in accepting changes that are closely associated with traditional **gender roles** and beliefs about what is best for children. Recent attitudinal studies suggest that norms are changing, and that Canadians increasingly agree that both husbands and wives should contribute economically to the household and share the responsibilities of rearing children. Nonetheless, there remains a considerable lag between changes in attitudes and in behaviour, and a **structural lag** in developing and adopting the kinds of public policies and workplace changes that are required to support dual-earner families and reduce the amount of stress and **role overload** many are experiencing, particularly women.

Since 1980, the volume of research on dual-earner families has grown dramatically and now attracts considerable interest on the part of sociologists, psychologists, economists, feminist scholars, and policy analysts. Research studies include a wide range of topics and use a variety of methodologies that range from large population surveys to ethnographic case studies. While research on this topic could benefit from greater attention to cultural and class differences in the experiences of dual-earner families, the research has expanded quite significantly from an original focus on dual-career marriages to include a much wider range of types of dual-earner families and circumstances. Researchers today are teasing out information about how specific employment factors, personal and family circumstances, and role expectations are affecting individual behaviour and family outcomes. Among the challenges researchers and family scholars face are (1) conceptualizing and studying couples and families, rather than individuals, as the unit of analysis; (2) capturing the range of factors that impinge on dual earners and their families, including the economic, policy, and service/community context that may constrain or broaden their options; (3) obtaining and interpreting information about the meaning individuals attribute to their earning and domestic roles within their family; (4) appreciating and studying individuals in dual-earner families as active agents who employ adaptive strategies and make decisions within the limits of the options and resources available to them; and (5) recognizing the fluidity in both employment and family circumstances that many individuals experience and that colours their current actions and perspectives.

In particular, it is important to recognize that the term "dual-earner" is a fairly crude structural label that provides little detailed information about each partner's employment circumstances and adaptations to employment demands, their relative contributions to household income, or the division of household labour. The psychologist Urie Bronfenbrenner would describe the label of being a dual-earner family as little more than a "social address." To know more about dual-earner couples and families, it is important to study how they experience the complexity of the work–family interface to learn more about the factors that meaningfully distinguish among dual-earner families and to better appreciate how multiple factors and mediating processes affect them.

In order to put a human face on the numbers to follow, consider the case of an actual couple we'll call Peter and Ellen Stone. During the early years of their marriage, both Peter and Ellen were employed full time, belonging to the larger category known as "DINKs" (dual income, no kids), which ironically includes Ellen's parents as well, who are in their late fifties. After taking a slightly extended maternity leave Ellen returned to work, initially on a part-time basis. She increased her involvement to full time, but after six months was laid off from her job as a result of corporate restructuring. For a time Ellen looked for another job, working on occasion as a temporary secretary; however, it made sense to stop looking for a more permanent job when she became pregnant with their second child. Two years later, Ellen is again working part time, but hopes to gain full-time employment in her field within the next year, as she wishes to make better use of her education and talents. While Ellen and Peter recognize that her part-time status makes life at home less hectic, both are painfully aware that their financial situation is tight and not entirely secure, especially since Peter left the job he had previously and is still building up a clientele for his three-year-old business.

DUAL-EARNER FAMILIES IN CONTEXT

Historical Change in Women's Paid Employment

The growth in the number of women entering and continuing to participate in the labour force on an ongoing basis is the main storyline behind the growth of dual-earner couples.[2] While the most remarkable changes in women's and mothers' labour force participation arguably have occurred in the last 25 years, historical accounts trace a much longer and uneven transition in women's economic roles. As a variety of writers have pointed out, married women have always worked,[3] although often without being paid a monetary wage. Accounts of the history of women's involvement in the economy (Armstrong and Armstrong 1994; Krahn and Lowe 1993; Jones, Marsden, and Tepperman 1990) reveal that women's entry into and continuous participation in the paid labour force has been affected by a variety of forces that acted to push women out of, and pull women into, the paid work-force at different times. In many ways, historical patterns support an analysis of women as a "reserve army of labour" that was called upon when their involvement was necessary for the national economy or was desired in gender-segregated occupations.

In tracing the history of women's lives and changes in their economic contributions, Jones, Marsden, and Tepperman (1990) refer to three main periods. From 1871 to 1914, most Canadians lived in rural areas and depended on primary production activities such as farming, fishing, and trapping. Women's contributions to the household economy were of critical importance and included such tasks as tending livestock and the garden, making clothes, and food preparation, as well as child rearing. Moreover, women were directly involved in generating family income through the production and sale of agricultural goods in local markets. As a result, the division of labour between men and women was more fluid, with little distinction between **private and public spheres** of economic activity (household and market work).

The second main period, roughly from 1914 to 1968, was marked by extensive industrialization and an increasing division of labour between men and women. Private (home) and public (industrial work) spheres became more sharply defined, and age, sex, and class were more prominent divisions in the economy. In citing the work of historian Veronica Strong-Boag, Jones et al. note that other than during the Great Depression and the two world wars, when women entered the labour force in large numbers, and with the exception of poor women who had little choice, women's involvement in paid work "merely punctuated major life changes." Women's participation in the paid labour force was often described as peripheral to their family roles, with the bulk of their paid involvement occurring before marriage or the birth of their first child.

But this general picture belies ongoing tensions resulting from economic, political, and social forces that affected women's desire to participate in paid work, their opportunities to do so, and forceful efforts to exclude them. For example, concerns about economic security following the Depression, when men and women took whatever jobs were available, prompted union organizers and others to mobilize for better wages and working conditions so that a man's wages would be high enough to support a wife and children (a "family wage"). While the labour movement's success in that regard improved the economic circumstances of single-earner families, it was also used to justify reducing married women's involvement in paid work and produced the template for gendered and separate spheres of paid (public) and private (domestic) work (Glickman 1997). The shift from an industrial economy to a service economy and the labour shortages that occurred during the two world wars attracted many women to the office jobs that became available to them and to higher paying "men's jobs" that were vacated during the war. However, concerns about preserving sufficient numbers of well-paying jobs for men soon became evident in both postwar periods, resulting in such formal actions as legislation in 1918 that allowed the Civil Service Commission to limit job competitions on the basis of sex, and in 1921 to "prohibit married women from holding permanent posts unless they were without husbands or no other candidates were available. Such a policy, called a 'marriage bar' was common in the 1920s and 1930s" (Jones, Marsden, and Tepperman 1990, 42).

The end of the Second World War brought with it active discouragement of married women remaining in the paid labour force, the withdrawal of supportive childcare services, the introduction of a family allowance, and the baby boom. The postwar period also brought prosperity, increased consumer goods, and major expansion of the service sector in areas attractive to women. These included public-sector jobs in health, education, and social services, as well as many positions in clerical fields and in sales and retail. Although the latter categories were frequently poorly paid and nonunionized, these occupations provided many new openings to women, both part and full time.

The third period in the process of women's employment transition is described as beginning in 1968 and extending until the present day. It is characterized by the majority of women working for pay—and, as evident in the last 15 years, continuing to do so with less time out of the labour force for having and rearing children. The late 1960s was a watershed period for women and for families in many ways: birth control became widely available, the *Divorce Act* was passed, and by the end of the decade it was evident that two incomes were becoming a necessity for middle-class urban families. Moreover, jobs deemed "suitable for women" in a largely segregated market economy continued to increase as a result of expansion in government services, other service sectors, and some professions. An important legislative action was the introduction of maternity leave benefits under the *Unemployment Insurance Act* when it was amended in 1971. In 1990 and 1999, these benefits were extended (and corresponding provincial and federal labour legislation was amended), enabling those who qualify and can afford to do so to take up to a year of parental leave, and permitting fathers and adopting parents access to parental leave benefits. One of the specific goals of this legislation is to encourage new parents (mainly women) to retain a strong tie to the labour force and return to work after the period of leave and benefits. Similarly, other policies and programs (the National Child Benefit, and other reforms to Employment Insurance and to provincial social assistance programs) increasingly are designed as "active measures" to promote and reinforce ongoing ties to the labour force among all able-bodied adults. Projected serious labour shortages are expected to further increase government efforts to support the involvement of as many people as possible in the paid labour force.

As women have continued to play a more visible, now essential, role in the labour force, their contributions are even more evident, both in their families and in the Canadian economy. Women's labour force participation rates have increased steadily. Between 1976 and 2000 the number of women in the labour force grew from 3.6 million to 7.4 million; in 2001, women made up 46 percent of the Canadian workforce (Statistics Canada 2001b). Indeed, much of the employment growth that occurred in the last 15 years can be attributed to the growth in female employment, most especially among married women with young children (Statistics Canada 2000). Moreover, it is not only the number of women who are participating in the labour force that is a factor. The pattern of women's labour force attachment has also changed. Instead of women sequencing periods in and out of the workforce around family life transitions—particularly marriage, the birth of their first child, or their youngest child's entry into school—it is increasingly common for women to maintain a more or less continuous attachment to the labour force, a pattern that historically has been associated with men (Fast and Da Pont 1997; Skrypnek and Fast 1993).

It is important to underscore that the most dramatic growth in women's participation in the labour force has occurred among mothers of young children. While both married mothers and lone-parent mothers have increased their participation in the labour force, the most profound changes have occurred among married women. For example, while in 1976 fewer than 40 percent of married women with children were employed, in 2000 the percentage was more than 70 percent (see Figure 1.2). This is a very large change over a relatively short period of time. Moreover, although mothers have always been more likely to be employed once their youngest child is in school, today's married mothers typically are employed even when their children are infants and toddlers. In 2000, 70 percent of married

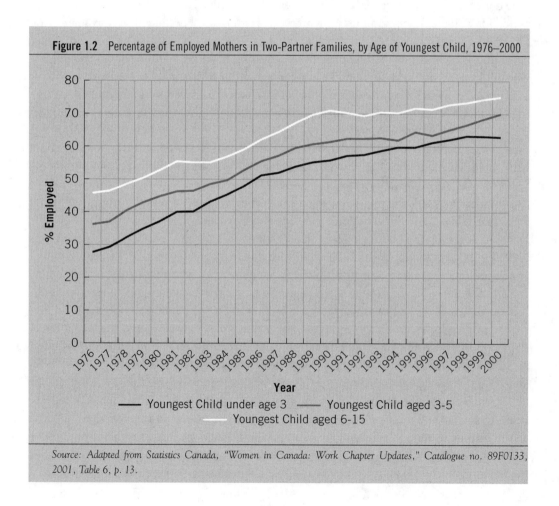

Figure 1.2 Percentage of Employed Mothers in Two-Partner Families, by Age of Youngest Child, 1976–2000

Source: Adapted from Statistics Canada, "Women in Canada: Work Chapter Updates," Catalogue no. 89F0133, 2001, Table 6, p. 13.

mothers whose youngest child was three to five years old were employed, as were almost 63 percent of married mothers with a child under the age of three (Statistics Canada 2001b). The fact that two-thirds of married mothers with preschool children are employed, most often on a full-time basis, still surprises many, particularly because it departs from gendered notions of mothers at home with their young children. It also is not well supported by family policies, employment practices, or well-developed childcare services, which one would expect to be in place to support this phenomenon.

Other Factors Affecting Women's Employment and Family Roles

In addition to the factors referred to in the preceding section that have directly affected women's access to paid work, many more forces, all intertwined, have had particular effects in the last 25 years on women and on families. All of these facilitate women's continuing involvement in the paid labour force and, hence, the tendency toward dual-earner families. Such factors include the following:

- *A rapid rise in divorce rates, a lower marriage rate, and the tendency toward later marriages.* These factors indicate that larger numbers of working-age women are spending more time outside of marriage, which requires that they be self-supporting. When married or involved in a common-law relationship, women are less likely to relinquish their economic independence or risk the loss of their job or future career prospects.

- *Low fertility rates, along with the tendency to delay marriage and child bearing.* On average, women are deferring having children until their late 20s or 30s (with some having children in their 40s). As well, women are having fewer children, apparently in part because of work demands and income insecurity (Bélanger and Ouellet 2002; Duxbury and Higgins 2001). An extended period of time before child bearing allows women to establish themselves in the paid workforce, which promotes their ongoing involvement. In addition, the period of time when mothers have young children at home is compressed, since they are likely to have only one or two children.

- *Greater access to post-secondary education.* Greater access to post-secondary education and advanced professional training has enabled women to prepare themselves for a wider variety of occupations, including higher-paying professional and managerial positions. Today's women are the most highly educated of any generation, and there are more women with university degrees than men. Both young men and women increasingly want work that can enable them to use their education, skills, and talent and contribute in a meaningful way. "Nexus generation" and younger **cohorts** (both men and women) expect to have families *and* satisfying work.

- *Changes in social attitudes toward women working outside the home, the influence of second-stage feminism, growing workplace diversity, and the demand for talent.* General attitude change and government commitments to gender equality, as found in the *Charter of Rights and Freedoms* and various international agreements, have led to increased acceptance, at least in principle, of women's rights to economic and social equality. To the extent to which this leads to increased opportunities for women and the removal of systemic barriers, it promotes men and women being involved as equal partners, both at home and in the paid workforce. Faced with an increasingly diverse workforce, a shrinking labour pool, and the need for new talent, employers are more likely to hire and promote women, providing additional opportunities and economic rewards for their participation.

- *Additional opportunities in professions and in occupations in the service sector that have traditionally been occupied mostly by women.* Women have been increasing as a proportion of managers and professionals, and making inroads even in traditional male-dominated occupations. However, there is also a continuing and strengthening demand for entrants into traditionally female-dominated occupations. These include education, health care, and services oriented to seniors, as well as other service occupations. Stronger labour market demands and more opportunities for women increase the likelihood of their participation.

The Current Context: Economic Pressures on Family Incomes

Perhaps the three factors that have been *most influential* in promoting recent increases in the number of dual-earner families, however, are economic necessity, continuing destabilizing trends in the labour market, and personal and family insecurity. These appear to have been among the most crucial factors promoting women's increased participation in the labour force. Economic pressures have resulted in many families increasing both the number of earners and the number of hours worked per week over the last two decades (Sauvé 2002a).

Economic Necessity

Two recessions—one in the 1980s and a deeper and longer recession in the early 1990s that was followed by a prolonged jobless recovery, economic restructuring, and job losses—have greatly affected the extent to which families can depend on a single earner's income to meet the basic costs of food, clothing, housing, education, and other goods and services. Men's earnings, and especially earnings of young men under age 35, have declined or been vulnerable since the 1980s (Bélanger and Ouellet 2002; Morissette 1997). The polarization in hours and earnings that distinguishes good jobs from bad jobs (the latter characterized by low-waged, insecure work with few benefits) and actual spells of unemployment appear to underlie the increasing amount of income inequality among families. Quite simply put, two incomes have become critical simply to maintain real family income and preserve family autonomy—especially in young families and those with less education or job skills. An interesting example of this point was made by the Vanier Institute of the Family (2000). Based on average family expenditures, the Vanier Institute has estimated that in 1996 a typical family with children under 15 years of age would have to work 75.4 hours per week at an average wage in order to earn enough to cover "typical" family expenses. The latter does not include putting funds aside to save for children's education, retirement years, or unforeseen circumstances. Rather than earning money for luxuries, most women in dual-earner families are working to cover essential expenses.

While some observers attribute the rise in the number of dual-earner families to increased consumerism, others have emphasized the economic vulnerability of single-earner families. Analyses of average after-tax incomes for different family types over the 1990s confirms the fact that, over the last decade, many families struggled just to live within their means as the real value of their family's income declined or barely stayed the same from year to year (Sauvé 2002b). Families with children were particularly vulnerable, and the earnings of wives were critical for many, especially between 1991 and 1996 when average incomes after taxes for families with children were lower each year.

Consequently, wives' contributions to family income have become increasingly important, not only in their actual amount and in the percentage of family income attributable to them, but also as a critically important buffer in the event of job loss or layoff. Currently, the income difference between one- and two-earner families with or without children averages about $15,000 (Statistics Canada 2001a). In 1997, wives' incomes accounted for 31.5 percent of family income in dual-earner families, up from 30.7 percent five years earlier. Moreover, the number of husband–wife families in which the wife was either the primary earner (earning more than her husband) or the sole earner also increased in the early and middle 1990s, presumably as more men experienced unemployment or lowered earnings (Crompton and Geran 1995). In 1997, the last year for which information is readily accessible, wives earned more than their husbands in 14.3 percent of dual-earner couples and were the sole earner in 4.9 percent of all husband–wife families (Statistics Canada 1999).

Even having two earners may not be sufficient to avoid poverty or economic insecurity, however, especially if either spouse has a low-paying or part-time job, or if one or both is employed for only part of the year. Thus, while having two earners may enable some families to rise to the top **income quintile** (the top 20 percent of all families), for others, both incomes are critical just to stay above the poverty line. Estimates of the number and percentage of families who are considered to be low-income are calculated both before tax and after tax. According to the National Council of Welfare, the actual poverty rate for husband–wife families with children under 18 years of age was 5.8 percent in 1999. However, if the wife's earnings had not been included in their family's income, the percentage of poor two-parent families would have been almost four times higher (21.4 percent). Similarly, the percentage of couples without children who were poor was 3.8 percent with the wife's earnings added in. Without her income, the proportion of poor families without children would have risen to 16.9 percent. Differences calculated based on after-tax income were even more dramatic. According to the National Council's report, "the rate would have been five times higher for families with children and six times higher for couples without children" (National Council of Welfare 2002). Having two incomes was particularly crucial to avoid poverty for young families, and for those with young children.[4]

Continuing Destabilizing Trends in the Labour Market

In the last two decades, a variety of factors have operated in ways that have led to higher rates of unemployment and more instability in the labour force. These factors include globalization and increasing pressures on businesses to be competitive; cuts in public service jobs at both the federal and provincial levels, along with reductions and restructuring in the health and education sectors; delayering, downsizing, and contracting out of various functions to reduce labour costs; job loss as a result of mergers among companies and the closing of others; and the expansive use of new technologies. The impacts have included considerable job displacement and an increase in the proportion of men and women in non-standard jobs (including part-time work, temporary/contingent positions, and "own account" self-employment).

While unemployment rates have fortunately been trending down in the last two to three years, and as of late 2002 the economy has been creating jobs at a record pace, the extent to which families have been affected by unemployment during the last decade is a serious issue with longer-term consequences, particularly for those who continue to experience significant job insecurity. Based on Statistics Canada figures, between 1980 and 1997 approximately one in every three families was affected by unemployment each year, as a result of at least one family member experiencing job loss and some time out of the workforce (Jackson and Scott 2002). The increasing prevalence of non-standard work arrangements is also a concern. These jobs typically are lower paying, offer little long-term financial security, and do not provide benefits to workers or to other family members.

Non-standard work among individuals in dual-earner couples is sometimes used as an option for maintaining flexibility or managing both work and family responsibilities. Women, in particular, are more likely to choose part-time work for these reasons, especially when their children are younger or there are two or more children at home. Nonetheless, whether voluntary or involuntary, non-standard jobs provide less stable family income and are more likely to be insecure. Precarious employment has been described by Jackson and Scott as a contributor to social exclusion and as a factor that inhibits parents and their children from being full participants in their communities.

Insecurity about the stability of employment and family income contributes to family stress and reinforces the importance of having both partners maintain their ties to the workforce. Limited increases in hourly earnings over the last decade (resulting in stagnant or declining real family income) also contributes both to the perceived need for two earners and for many to work longer hours than they had previously. As shown in Figure 1.3, there has been a continuing increase in the number of dual-earner families in which both husbands and wives are employed full-time, full-year, especially among parents. There has also been an increase in the proportion of men and women who are working long hours (more than 50 hours per week).

The Importance of Two Earners for Families and the Economy

In closing this section, it is important to restate that dual-earner families have evolved into the most typical family form for a variety of reasons, and in response to many factors.

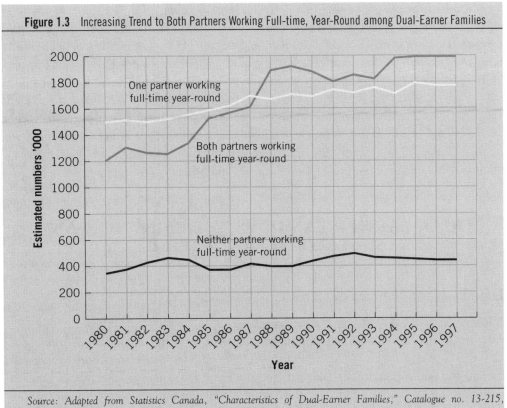

Figure 1.3   Increasing Trend to Both Partners Working Full-time, Year-Round among Dual-Earner Families

Source: Adapted from Statistics Canada, "Characteristics of Dual-Earner Families," Catalogue no. 13-215, 1997, Chart II, p. 10.

However, it is also important to note that neither an individual's nor a family's earner status is static. Over the course of even a few years, families may experience change in the employment status of one or both spouses, transitions between paid work and self-employment, and change in the number and schedule of work hours for one or both earners—either by choice or as a result of work requirements. Having two earners in the family potentially can be a source of support and stability, providing at least some protection from unexpected earnings interruptions. The central paradox is that at the same time having both spouses employed, especially on a full-time basis, can lead to additional stresses in families, particularly when there is considerable tension related to work demands, limited flexibility in work schedules, an inequitable or undesirable division of household labour, and/or limited support at home or in the community to help manage child- or elder-care responsibilities.

While I have focused mostly on the importance of two incomes for families in this section, there are other points to consider as well. As noted by the Vanier Institute of the Family (1994), "It is not just individual families that now depend on two wages. Indeed, the Canadian economy as a whole depends on the capacity of families to adapt to new realities.

The health of the private sector is sustained, in large measure, by the expenditures families make in the market place, and the public sector services on which Canadians count are paid for with the taxes contributed by both men and women" (74). Those taxes, derived mostly from employment, will be contributed by a smaller pool of working-age adults as our population ages. Beyond the economic dimension, however, Canadian society is well served when more individuals can actively contribute to a shared sense of purpose and make full use of their education, talents, and energies. For all of these reasons, it appears likely that both men and women will continue to be involved in the paid workforce for most of their lives and there will be a continuing need to address the issues that combining paid work and family responsibilities raise, both for dual earners and others.

DUAL-EARNER FAMILIES: A DEFINITION AND STATISTICAL PROFILE

Definition and Sources of Canadian Statistics

Information about dual-earner families can be gleaned from statistical profiles from large data sets, from research studies with smaller samples, and by analysis of case examples. Canadian statistics on dual-earner families are derived from census data, surveys of family income and labour patterns, and several special surveys, particularly General Social Surveys on topics such as time use and relationships with family and friends.

For some time, Statistics Canada has produced reports on the characteristics of dual-earner families based on its annual Survey of Consumer Finances. Since 1998, however, the agency has used a different survey with slightly different methods and sampling features (the Survey of Labour Income and Dynamics) to collect information about earners and family income and has not released any later reports on dual-earner families specifically. Consequently, this section relies on the latest report available, which provides information about husband–wife families for the year 1997 (Statistics Canada 1999). In this context, dual-earner families are defined as husband–wife families (married or common-law) in which both the husband and wife received wages or net income from self-employment in 1997. Data were collected in April of 1998.

Dual Earners: A Statistical Portrait

In 1997 there were an estimated 4,265,000 dual-earner families across Canada, a record number. They accounted for 61.3 percent of all husband–wife families. Only 21.4 percent of husband–wife families were classified as single-earner families (including 16.5 percent in which the husband was the sole earner and 4.9 percent in which the wife was the sole earner). In approximately 17.4 percent of husband–wife families neither spouse had earnings. The large majority of these families consisted of older couples in which the husband was at least 55 years of age, and typically 65 or older. As noted earlier, wives' earnings averaged 31.5 percent of family income in dual-earner families. Wives earned less than their husbands in 74 percent of dual-earner families, and as much or more than their husbands in 26 percent of dual-earner families. Based on calculations from the data provided, dual-earner families accounted for between 57 and 67 percent of husband–wife families in each part of the country. Approximately 57 percent of husband–wife families were dual earners in the Atlantic provinces, compared to 59 percent in Quebec and approximately 61 percent in both Ontario and British Columbia. The highest proportion of dual-earner husband–wife families was observed in the Prairie provinces (Manitoba, Saskatchewan, and Alberta), for which a combined rate of 67.2 percent pertains.

Dual-earner families are quite heterogeneous in their characteristics. They range from young childless couples to families with several children, and also include older "empty nesters" and senior couples. Voydanoff (1987) and Moen and Yu (2000) refer to the importance of understanding dual earners in different life stages (for example, young families with young children in the early career-building stage; established couples with school-age children with longer-term relationships to the labour force; "late-launching" parents who though 40 or older have young children; older couples that are shifting gears and scaling back their work involvement. It is reasonable to anticipate that couples in different life stage categories are likely to have different set of demands, resources, and experiences; however, even within these categories, couples have different levels of economic resources, different views about gender roles, and different perspectives on their desired and actual work–life experiences.

Table 1.1 and the case studies included throughout this chapter illustrate the diversity within dual-earner families, and some of the differences between dual-earner families and single-earner families in which the husband is the sole earner.

The following points can be observed:

1. The large majority of dual-earner families are made up of husbands and wives in their prime child-bearing and earning years. About 63 percent of wives in dual-earner families are 25 to 44 years of age. The largest age group for both dual-earner husbands and wives is 35 to 44 years. Compared to dual-earner couples, husbands in male breadwinner families are older, with both husbands and their wives more likely to be 55 years of age or older (see point 5 below).

2. Women in dual-earner families tend to be more highly educated when compared to women in all husband–wife families. More than half of the wives in dual-earner families (54.4 percent) had obtained a post-secondary credential—either a community college certificate or diploma or a university degree. By contrast, almost one-third of the wives in male breadwinner families had not completed high school; about 35 percent had obtained a post-secondary credential.

Table 1.1   Selected Characteristics of Dual-Earner and Husband Sole-Earner Families, 1997

Selected characteristics	Percentage of category that are dual earners	Percentage of dual-earner families	Percentage of husband sole-earner families
Age of husband			
< 25 years	76.6%	2.5	2.0
25–34	79.6%	23.0	15.8
35–44	78.4%	34.4	28.1
45–54	74.9%	27.5	23.9
55–64	45.1%	10.9	21.6
65 or older	6.9%	1.8	8.5
Age of wife			
< 25 years	73.8%	4.7	4.2
25–34	79.2%	27.4	19.5
35–44	77.7%	35.4	28.2
45–54	70.4%	24.7	23.4
55–64	32.0%	7.0	18.0
65 or older	4.0%	0.8	6.6
Education of wife			
0–8 years	22.4%	3.7	12.2
Some secondary ed	44.0%	10.7	20.5
Graduated from high school	62.3%	23.4	25.1
Some post-secondary	68.2%	7.9	7.0
Post-secondary certificate or diploma	71.9%	36.5	26.2
University degree	79.5%	17.9	8.9
Immigration status/year husband immigrated			
Husband Canadian-born	63.2%	81.5	76.4
1960 or earlier	35.3%	3.0	5.2
1961–1970	58.1%	3.7	4.2
1971–1980	71.7%	4.8	3.5
1981–1990	61.3%	4.3	6.0
1991 or later	48.7%	2.7	4.7
Presence of children			
No children in the home	50.6%	45.1	46.4
With at least one child under 6 years of age	71.3%	23.4	28.2
Children under 6 years of age only	73.5%	14.4	15.4
Children under and over 6 years of age	68.1%	9.0	12.8
Children over 6 years of age only	76.8%	31.6	25.4
Distribution in income quintiles based on all husband–wife families			
In lowest income quintile	25.0%	8.2	25
In second lowest income quintile	51.2%	16.7	25.8
In middle income quintile	67.8%	22.1	21.4
In fourth income quintile	77.3%	25.2	16.3
In highest income quintile	85.0%	27.7	11.7

Source: Adapted by D.S. Lero. Calculations based upon data presented in Statistics Canada, "Characteristics of Dual-Earner Families," Catalogue no. 13-215, 1997.

3. The presence of children in the home does not seem to distinguish between dual-earner couples and those in which the husband is the sole earner. The 45 percent of dual-earner couples without children include young couples who plan to have children, older couples who have previously raised children, and childless couples of all ages. Almost one-quarter of dual-earner families with children had at least one preschool child under six years of age; in fact, 71 percent of families with children under six years of age were dual-earner families. Male breadwinner families were slightly more likely to have children both under and over six years of age. This likely reflects the fact that mothers are less likely to be employed when there are more children at home.

4. The average income of dual-earner families in 1997 was $71,782, almost $19,000 more than the average of male breadwinner families. Moreover, families with two income earners were more likely to be in the top two income quintiles (the top 40 percent) of all husband–wife families. Fully 85 percent of families in the highest quintile benefited from both the husband's and wife's contributions. By contrast, fewer than 10 percent of husband-sole-earner families were in the top income quintile.

In addition, readers may note the following:

5. Among both husbands and wives, there are definite **cohort effects.** Of the husbands in each of the four younger age groups, roughly 75 to 80 percent were dual earners. A similar pattern is evident among wives. Thus, while young couples in which the husband is under 25 years of age constitute only a very small percentage of all dual earner families, more than three-quarters of couples with a husband under 25 are dual earners. Conversely, even though couples in which the husband is 55 to 64 make up 11 percent of dual earners, within that age cohort the proportion of dual-earner couples is much lower (45 percent) and the proportion of senior couples (based on the husband's age) who are dual earners is less than 7 percent.

6. There are some cohort effects evident among immigrants to Canada. Those who immigrated in 1960 or earlier (who are older) are less likely to be dual earners, and those who have immigrated more recently (after 1980) are also less likely to be dual earners. Among all groups, families with husbands who immigrated to Canada between 1971 and 1980 are most likely to be dual earners. Notwithstanding, it is worth observing that almost half of the husband–wife families who immigrated in the last decade (based on husband data) consist of dual-earner families.

The following additional points convey information about dual-earners' work involvement:

7. About 80 percent of husbands in dual-earner families worked full time, year round, as did close to 56 percent of their wives. In all, both the husband and wife worked full time, year round in close to half of dual-earner families (46.9 percent).

8. Just under one in five dual-earner families could be classified as dual-career families, in which both the husband and wife had a professional or managerial position. In 14 percent

of couples the husband's occupation was classified as professional or managerial, while his wife's was not; in 20 percent of couples the wife was a professional or manager; and in 47 percent of couples neither the husband nor the wife held a professional/managerial position. Couples in which both hold professional or managerial positions are most likely to be ones where both spouses work full time, and according to other research studies are more likely to experience considerable tension in managing work demands and family life if there are children at home.

Data from other sources indicate that shift work among dual-earner couples is common. In 1995, 38 percent of dual-earner couples included at least one member who worked other than a standard daytime schedule (Marshall 1998).

THEORETICAL PERSPECTIVES AND DOMINANT THEMES

Research and theorizing about dual-earner couples and work and family relationships accommodates a variety of disciplines and perspectives. The theoretical perspectives that are most often referred to in the literature include resource and social exchange theories and theories about multiple roles, including role strain and role enhancement. Another emerging line of theory development could potentially unite gender theory with a developing focus on the strategies family members and couples use to modify their roles and manage the work–family interface in keeping with their values and perceived options.

Gender-role theory and analysis features prominently in the research and discourse on dual-earner couples, since the expectation that women and men will jointly contribute to family income necessitates some redistribution of the traditional gendered division of household labour and also contributes to the expectation for greater equality in parenting/caregiving roles. Indeed, for feminists, the transformation from single-earner to dual-earner families was expected to be the catalyst for essential social change toward more egalitarian structures and family relationships (Goodnow and Bowes 1994; Lewis 1992). Instead, it appears more often the case that the "problem" of the dual-earner couple and the lack of structural change to support its effectiveness is defined as an issue of "balance" and framed as a "private trouble" rather than a public issue (Berk 1985; Spain and Bianchi 1996). Further, while there are some couples who create their own egalitarian paths, it is primarily women who accommodate to the lack of cultural and organizational supports, thereby reconstructing neotraditional gender roles.

Resource and social exchange theories derive from economic perspectives about the value of paid labour, and have been applied particularly to explain the unequal division of labour in many families. Based on earlier work by Blood and Wolfe (1960) and updated in Becker's theories of the "new home economics," a model of economic rationalism is applied that is predicated on the notion that couples will want to maximize their economic opportunities by ensuring that the partner with the highest earning capacity spends more time in paid work, while the other partner performs more unpaid work. Since earning capacity is, itself, often a product of gendered experiences, opportunities, advantages, and constraints (e.g., gendered occupational strata with lower wages paid to women, discriminatory hiring and promotion practices, and workplace ideologies and practices that are not responsive to family role obligations), this model tends to justify traditional relationships in which the lower-earning spouse (most often the woman) does more of the household work, potentially with some off-loading to others or reductions in the amount or frequency with which certain tasks are performed. It should be noted that a corollary to exchange theory is that imbalance in relative resources, such as income, education, or career opportunities, is presumed to underpin an imbalance in power relationships, as well as differential time availability. If household work is less highly valued, then the partner with more resources (and more power) does less of it. It is presumed that as women's relative contributions to household income increase, they obtain greater bargaining power and can better negotiate a more equitable distribution of household tasks. In fact, while time-use studies indicate that men are doing somewhat more of the housework and childcare than they used to, the progress toward egalitarian roles is very uneven—and appears to be influenced more by other factors (personal expectations and gender-role attitudes) than rational decision rules. Moreover, in most cases women retain the responsibility for household tasks, even when others do them (Ferree 1991; Potuchek 1992).

It is important to point out that the time husbands and wives spend in household and related tasks, and particularly with children, has become a value-laden issue within families and in our culture generally. Tensions within dual-earner couples about who does how much of what, and who has responsibility for overseeing those tasks, while inevitably affected by time demands and time availability a) are rooted in each partner's gender-role expectations, and b) increasingly reflect the fault lines in relationships. The amount and quality of family time is thus one of the key themes in current writings about dual-earner families. Moreover, expectations of at least a somewhat more equitable sharing of household tasks (redefined as *family work*) is associated with negotiations that include issues of fairness and respect. Time devoted to couple and parent–child relationships is also seen as a critical indicator of the degree of involvement and commitment one makes to family roles and obligations. As Daly (2001) has noted, both the value and meaning of family time is itself a critical factor for many individuals and families, and considerable thought and effort may be devoted to developing strategies to increase and improve the amount and quality of time available.

Role theories have become the predominant perspective in research on dual-earner couples in the last 15 to 20 years. An ongoing concern in work–family research has been the implications for individuals' mental health and the quality of family relationships of managing multiple (and sometimes competing) roles: worker, spouse, parent, caregiver. Role theorists often presume either a scarcity and conflict position or one that is more neutral or even positive about the benefits of having multiple roles. Presumptions of scarcity emphasize the finite limits of time and energy (both physical and mental) that are available to fulfill demanding multiple roles, and the potential for role strain and role conflict. Others (such as Barnett and Baruch 1985) have provided an "expansion hypothesis," suggesting that multiple roles bring a variety of rewards, potentially including increased income, greater autonomy, enhanced self-esteem, greater access to information and resources, more varied social relationships, and challenges that enhance well-being. The emphasis on balance vs. role conflict and role overload (another dominant theme) suggests a greater concern about the combination of work and family roles as a source of stress for individuals and families. And, indeed, there is reason to be concerned, given the evidence of high levels of work-related stress, role overload, and **work–life conflict** among workers in North America—especially among women and parents.

In the Canadian context, two recent studies have demonstrated that compared to the early 1990s Canadian workers are experiencing considerably more work-related stress and work–life conflict (Duxbury and Higgins 2001; MacBride-King and Bachmann 1999). Duxbury and Higgins have provided extensive information about who is most at risk of experiencing high role overload and **work–family conflic**t and under what conditions. Among employees categorized by family types, 62 to 65 percent of parents in dual-earner families and single parents (all employed full time) reported high role overload; among women, those employed in professional and managerial positions were particularly likely to report high levels of work–life conflict and job stress. High role overload and work–family interference are significantly related to employees' job stress, job satisfaction, organizational commitment, and absenteeism, and also are correlated with family outcomes. The latter include a higher incidence of work demands negatively affecting time with their spouse, perceived poor quality of couple and family relationships, lower levels of family satisfaction, and a greater tendency to miss family activities due to work.

These findings are consistent with other studies, including research on time use. Canadian General Social Survey data on time use and perceived time stress indicate that between 1992 and 1998 there were significant increases in the proportion of dual-earner parents and single parents who reported feeling severe time stress. These parents reported that they did not have enough time to do all that they needed to accomplish, felt constantly under stress, and had insufficient time with family and friends. Many report cutting back on sleep as a primary strategy for dealing with time conflicts and indicated that they were dissatisfied with the amount of stress and imbalance between work and family responsibilities (Daly 2000).

In the research referred to above and in much of the published work–family research, *role strain* and *role conflict* refer to conflict between paid work and family roles experienced by individuals that arises as a consequence of high work demands, little control, and limited support at work, and is especially prevalent among those with greater family demands—which most often means women and parents of younger children. As well, there is a growing proportion of the workforce that is involved in providing care or support to an older parent, or to an ill or disabled child, spouse, or other family member. In the face of these challenges, both men and women try to reduce some of the pressure and stress they are under. Gender roles reappear in the individual and family strategies that are often used for this purpose. In particular, it is often women who cut back on work time, forgo career opportunities, or take a period of unpaid leave or exit from the workforce to address major caregiving responsibilities.

The most recent theoretical development in dual-earner research is one that focuses on individual and family strategies as active efforts to "construct and modify roles, resources and relationships" in order to reduce stress or enable a more harmonious integration of work and family/life roles (Becker and Moen 1999; Moen and Yu 2000). There are many examples of family strategies. Some involve modifications of work involvement or work hours (such as stepping back from a fast-track career path, changing jobs, reducing work hours, negotiating more flexible hours, or rearranging shifts). Apparently, one of the major reasons some women shift from being a paid worker to being self-employed (particularly if working from home) is the presumption that self-employment will allow more control over work hours and an easier balance of work and family life (Hughes 1999). Among dual-career couples, some of the strategies Moen and Yu have identified are taking active steps to maximize both partners' careers, putting both careers on the back burner, agreeing to have one spouse be committed to a career while the other downshifts to having "a job," and planning a longer term of turn-taking where first one spouse's career has priority, then the other.

One particular strategy some families use is *off-shifting*, which involves maintaining two full-time jobs (or one full-time and one part-time job), but arranging schedules so that one partner begins work early in the day and finishes earlier, while the other begins work later, perhaps working an evening or night shift. There is some evidence that this pattern is appealing to families who want to share childcare—or need to, either because it is unaffordable or difficult to sustain. Two recent studies of parents of children with disabilities indicate that some parents may adopt this strategy as a way to ensure that their child receives stable, consistent care and support (Irwin and Lero 1997; Lewis, Kagan, and Heaton 2000).

The following quote from a father, a postal worker who works a night shift, describes off-shifting with his wife as follows:

> It's not just a matter of working opposite shifts. It's a matter of my daughter's needs. So I work nights, and then get my daughter ready for school after my wife has left for work. It takes a long time to feed her and dress her because of her cerebral palsy. Then, after school, which ends at 2:30, she really requires a lot of tutoring and extra help from me if she's going to keep up at all. I never get enough sleep. (Irwin and Lero 1997, 81)

This father's comments speak directly to the fact that work scheduling is part of a complex pattern that includes parenting, marital roles, and the personal health and well-being of each family member. In writing about off-shifting as a family strategy, I have described it as both a blessing and a curse. Some parents see it as a desirable (or necessary) way to maintain their involvement in their children's daily life on an intimate basis and to reduce the stress that might otherwise result if they relied on others to provide the care, services, and level of support that they do. Some also see this method as a way of maintaining flexibility to respond to changing or unexpected circumstances, such as doctor's appointments and so on. Yet there are downsides to off-shifting; it in effect results in serial single parenting for many, and little if any couple or whole-family time. In addition to the physical and logistical drawbacks to shift work, Presser (2000) has noted the connection between non-standard work schedules and marital instability, a serious concern.

In ending this section, it is important to contextualize what might otherwise be a focus on private strategies to address some of the stresses faced by dual-earner couples and families. As Moen and Yu note, strategies and work conditions are gendered, and many couples, despite contemporary egalitarian ideals, are adopting what may be termed a neo-traditional model that may become the "de facto typical family of the 21st century." This neo-traditional model involves women scaling back their career aspirations and work hours (and hence their earnings and pension contributions) and redefining their role as secondary or supplementary providers "by choice," in order to ensure a better balance and quality of family life within a societal context that does not facilitate an easy integration of full-time work for both partners along with family care responsibilities.[5] It should be noted here that this option is one that presumes an adequate and stable income will be maintained—a presumption that may be challenged if trends toward more precarious employment continue. Having women scale back their work hours and career aspirations is described by Figart and Mutari (1998) as reflecting both socialization and structural forces that perpetuate gendered strategies.

CONCLUSION

This chapter has described the phenomenal growth in dual-earner families and the reasons that have propelled women into the labour force. Economic, labour market, and demographic influences are continuing to play a major role in creating and maintaining a high demand for women's labour. Along with the ongoing globalization of markets and new technologies, these influences also shape the nature of working conditions (including increasing rates of non-standard or precarious employment and considerable volatility in the labour force). To meet basic family needs and provide some degree of income security, families increasingly rely on two income earners employed full time. Dramatic changes have occurred in women's roles and in families to accommodate those demands and those needs.

Yet other changes that would support greater economic and social equality for women and provide more security and less stress for women and men with family responsibilities have not yet occurred. This "structural lag" means that the policies, programs, and workplace responses that are required to support a more egalitarian social structure are missing. The consequences are reflected in the studies that consistently show high rates of role overload and stress among individuals and in couples that are employed full-time in increasingly demanding jobs who have significant family responsibilities. How do families adapt in circumstances that are created by these disjunctures? One way is to develop private individual and family strategies to optimize the circumstances in which they might continue as dual-earner families; another is to revert to one-earner status, with its consequent effects. In both cases, it is left to individual couples to negotiate earning and caring roles among themselves—and to experiment with efforts to modify work demands among employers and workplaces that vary greatly in their receptiveness and capacity to respond to employees' needs and preferences.

The task of creating more supportive structural arrangements for dual-earner families remains. Necessary changes include the development and implementation of public policies that would explicitly respect the rights of workers to a variety of options for harmonizing work and family responsibilities; changes in tax policies that disadvantage families in which there is a considerable difference in earnings between the husband and wife; changes in employment insurance to include higher levels of benefits for those taking maternity, parental, and (not yet available) family care leave; extending EI coverage to self-employed individuals and others who are excluded; the development of new policies to provide additional economic security to non-standard workers; significant increases to the National Child Benefit; a national childcare and after-school program that would enable all children to benefit at affordable levels for families; and a range of services to better support home care, health care, and special service needs for seniors and the disabled.

Significant changes in the workplace would also be required, including a change in ideology to better support the needs of working parents and others with family-care responsibilities. As one example, Denmark and Australia have recently passed legislation requiring employers to make every reasonable effort to accommodate the work schedule requests of employees with family responsibilities. This includes requests for reduced work hours and for more flexible scheduling options. In closing, one can note that progress toward achieving structural and ideological changes that would better support dual-earner families is far more difficult in the absence of a coherent family policy framework that could address the diverse needs of families across the life span. Nevertheless, there are many steps that can be taken now that would greatly benefit dual-earner families and Canadian society.

NOTES

1. Dual-earner families include common-law partners, but for the sake of simplicity and congruence with findings cited from research studies only the terms *husbands* and *wives* will be used. Same-sex couples, who may have similar economic and social experiences, are typically not included in the literature or statistics on dual-earner families.

2. Labour force participation rates for married men aged 25 to 54 have been and remain consistently high. Men aged 55 to 64 may choose or be pushed into early retirement, depending on their personal circumstances and economic conditions. There is some evidence that the proportion of employed men remaining in the workforce beyond their 65th birthday is rising.

3. Readers should be aware of the fact that discourse that dichotomizes activities as work or non-work, or paid and unpaid work, is, itself, a reflection of cultural biases. The

challenge of managing or integrating both paid work and unpaid family work, in particular, is the central issue or "problem" referred to in much of the literature on work–family conflict. It is also reflected in discussions about the division of household labour, another potentially contentious subject for dual-earner couples. Because this chapter is based on families in which both partners in a family are employed, I have followed the convention of using the word *work* to refer to paid activities.

4. An additional point related to having both husbands and wives employed is the opportunity to realize and increase pension income, whether through contributions to an employer-provided pension plan, through contributions to an RRSP, or as a result of higher CPP contributions. The lack of sufficient pension income and savings from employment over the years has been noted as a major contributor to poverty in seniors, especially among women.

5. The emphasis on neotraditional strategies does not suggest that other couples won't employ other strategies, including ones in which traditional gender roles are reversed or there is a true and equal sharing of earning and caring. But the research clearly demonstrates that, given current circumstances, the former predominates as the most common adaptation evident across the population of dual-earner families.

KEY TERMS

Cohort: A group of people who are of the same age at the same time or who share the timing of a particular experience. *Age cohorts* were born the same year or the same decade. People who immigrated to Canada in the 1990s would be an *experience cohort*.

Cohort effect: The effect that being born at different points in time has on different cohorts. Individuals who were 25 in 1995 are likely to have different labour-force experiences than individuals who were 25 in 1975.

Gender role: Attitudes and behaviour patterns said to be created and reinforced by the social system and social expectations; gender roles are divided into roles assumed to be appropriate for males and those assumed appropriate for females.

Income quintile: A quintile is a fifth. Income quintiles refer to five equal parts; in this case, families are divided into those in the lowest 20 percent based on their family income, those in the next 20 percent, and so forth. The *highest income quintile* refers to families in the top 20 percent of all families with respect to family income.

Public/private sphere: Terms used to distinguish between behavioural patterns that are typically associated with public roles, including occupational roles, as compared to private roles that are maintained within an individual family.

Role overload: Overload exists when the total demands on one's time and energy associated with the prescribed activities in multiple roles are too great to perform the roles adequately or comfortably.

Structural lag: A term that indicates that people's behaviour or attitudes have changed in ways that are not yet reflected in public policies, institutional practices, or legislation.

Work–life or work–family conflict: Conflict that occurs because of competing demands on an individual's time, energy, and commitments. This conflict may result from competing demands (see *role overload*, above), or scheduling interference (e.g., not being able to participate in a family activity because of work scheduling or overtime). Work–life conflict extends beyond family activities and time with family members to include other activities or personal interests, such as conflict between one's work and doing school tasks, or participating in a volunteer capacity.

DISCUSSION QUESTIONS

1. What appear to be the most important factors that explain, or are associated with, married/partnered women's involvement in the labour force?
2. What factors are currently affecting families in ways that encourage or reinforce dual-earner families—even among families with young children?
3. How would you answer these two questions:
   a) What do dual earners look like?
   b) How are dual-earner families different from families in which the husband is the sole earner?
4. How do dual-earner couples with children manage work, family, and childcare responsibilities? What strategies do they use? What supports are important? How well do you think they are supported currently? Explain the basis for your answer.
5. To what extent would you say dual-earner couples are egalitarian?
6. Based on this essay and your own experiences, what seem to be the most important factors affecting the division of household (or family) work and responsibility for children among dual-earner families?
7. How has your own experience affected your attitudes about men's and women's roles? Your view of dual-earner families? Your own preferences and expectations with regard to your current or future roles as an earner and family member?

REFERENCES

Armstrong, Pat, and Hugh Armstrong. 1994. *The Double Ghetto: Canadian Women and Their Segregated Work*, 3rd ed. Toronto: McClelland & Stewart.

Barnett, Rosalind, and G. Baruch. 1985. "Women's Involvement in Multiple Roles and Psychological Distress." *Journal of Personality and Social Psychology* 49: 135–145.

Becker, Gary. 1981. *A Treatise on the American Family*. Cambridge, MA: Harvard University Press.

Becker, Penny E., and Phyllis Moen. 1999. "Scaling Back: Dual-earner Couples' Work-family Strategies." *Journal of Marriage and the Family* 61: 995–1007.

Bélanger, Alain, and Geneviève Ouellet. 2002. "A Comparative Study of Recent Trends in Canadian and American Fertility, 1980–1999." In A. Bélanger, ed., *Report on the Demographic Situation in Canada 2001: Current Demographic Analysis*. Ministry of Industry. Statistics Canada, Catalogue no. 91-209-XPE.

Berk, Sara. 1985. *The Gender Factory: The Apportionment of Work in American Households*. New York: Plenum Press.

Blood, R., and D. Wolfe. 1960. *Husbands and Wives: The Dynamics of Married Living*. Glencoe, IL: The Free Press.

Crompton, Susan, and Leslie Geran. 1995. "Women as Main Wage-earners." *Perspectives on Labour and Income*. Statistics Canada, Catalogue 75-001E. (Winter): 26–29.

Daly, Kerry. 2000. *It Keeps Getting Faster: Changing Patterns of Time in Families*. Ottawa: Vanier Institute of the Family. Available at <www.vifamily.ca>.

Daly, Kerry. 2001. "Deconstructing Family Time: From Ideology to Lived Experience." *Journal of Marriage and Family* 63: 283–294.

Duxbury, Linda, and Chris Higgins. 2001. *Work-life Balance in the New Millennium: Where Are We? Where Do We Need to Go?* CPRN Discussion Paper No. W-12. Ottawa: Canadian Policy Research Networks. Available at <www.cprn.org>.

Fast, Janet, and Morena Da Pont. 1997. "Changes in Women's Work Continuity." *Canadian Social Trends*. Statistics Canada. Catalogue no. 11-008-XPE. (Autumn): 2–7.

Ferree, M.M. 1991. "The Gender Division of Labor in Two-Earner Marriages: Dimensions of Variability and Change." *Journal of Family Issues* 12: 158–80.

Figart, Deborah, and Ellen Mutari. 1998. "Degendering Work Time in Comparative Perspective: Alternative Policy Frameworks." *Review of Social Economy* 56: 460–480.

Glickman, Lawrence. 1997. *A Living Wage: American Workers and the Making of Consumer Society*. Ithaca, NY: Cornell University Press.

Goodnow, Jacqueline, and Jennifer Bowes. 1994. *Men, Women and Household Work*. Melbourne: Oxford University Press.

Hughes, Karen. 1999. *Gender and Self-employment in Canada: Assessing Trends and Policy Implications*. Ottawa: Canadian Policy Research Networks.

Irwin, Sharon, and Donna Lero. 1997. *In Our Way: Child Care Barriers to Full Workforce Participation Experienced by Parents of Children with Special Needs—And Potential Remedies*. Cape Breton, NS: Breton Books.

Jackson, Andrew, and Katherine Scott. 2002. *Does Work Include Children? The Effects of the Labour Market on Family Income, Time and Stress*. Toronto: Laidlaw Foundation. One of a series of working papers on social inclusion. Available at <www.laidlawfoundation.org>.

Jones, Charles, Lorna Marsden, and Lorne Tepperman. 1990. *Lives of Their Own*. Toronto: Oxford University Press.

Krahn, Harvey J., and Graham S. Lowe. 1993. *Work, Industry and Canadian Society*, 2nd ed. Scarborough: Nelson Canada.

Lewis, Suzan. 1992. "Introduction." In S. Lewis, D.N. Izraeli, and H. Hootsmans, eds., *Dual-Earner Families: International Perspectives*. London: Sage.

Lewis, Suzan, Carolyn Kagan, and Patricia Heaton. 2000. "Dual-earner Parents with Disabled Children: Family Patterns for Working and Caring." *Journal of Family Issues* 21: 1031–1060.

MacBride-King, Judith, and Kim Bachmann. 1999. *Is Work-life Balance Still an Issue for Canadians and their Employers? You Bet It Is*. Ottawa: Conference Board of Canada.

Marshall, Katherine. 1998. "Couples Working Shift." *Perspectives on Labour and Income*. Statistics Canada, Catalogue 75-001E (Autumn): 9–14.

Moen, Phyllis, and Yan Yu. 2000. "Effective Work/life Strategies: Working Couples, Work Conditions, Gender, and Life Quality." *Social Problems* 47: 291–326.

Morissette, René. 1997. "Declining Earnings of Young Men." *Canadian Social Trends*. Statistics Canada, Catalogue no 11-008XPE. (Autumn): 8–12.

National Council of Welfare. 2002. *Poverty Profile, 1999*. Ottawa: National Council of Welfare.

Potuchek, Jean L. 1992. "Employed Wives' Orientations to Breadwinning: A Gender Theory Analysis." *Journal of Marriage and the Family* 54: 548–558.

Presser, Harriet. 2000. "Nonstandard Work Schedules and Marital Instability." *Journal of Marriage and the Family, 62*: 93–110.

Sauvé, Roger. 2002a. *Connections: Tracking the Links between Jobs and Family*. Ottawa: Vanier Institute of the Family. Available at <www.vifamily.ca>.

Sauvé, Roger. 2002b. *The Current State of Canadian Family Finances: 2001 Report*. Ottawa: Vanier Institute of the Family. Available at <www.vifamily.ca>.

Skrypnek, B.J., and Janet Fast. 1993. "Trends in Canadian Women's Labour Force Behaviour: Implications for Government and Corporate Policy." In *Papers on Economic Equality Prepared for the Economic Equality Workshop*. Ottawa, 29–30 November 1993. Ottawa: Status of Women Canada.

Spain, D., and S. Bianchi. 1996. *Balancing Act*. New York: Russell Sage Foundation.

Statistics Canada. 1999. *Characteristics of Dual-earner Families, 1997*. Catalogue no. 13–213. Ottawa: Minister of Industry.

Statistics Canada. 2000. *Women in Canada, 2000: A Gender-based Statistical Report*. Catalogue no. 89-503-XPE. Ottawa: Minister of Industry.

Statistics Canada. 2001a. *Income in Canada, 1999*. Catalogue no. 75-202-XIE. Ottawa: Minister of Industry.

Statistics Canada. 2001b. *Women in Canada: Work Chapter Updates*. Catalogue no. 89F0133XIE. Ottawa: Minister of Industry.

Statistics Canada. 2002. "Distribution and Average Income of Husband-wife Families by Number of Earners." Available at <www.statcan.ca/>.

Vanier Institute of the Family. 1994. *Profiling Canada's Families*. Ottawa: Vanier Institute of the Family.

Vanier Institute of the Family. 2000. *Profiling Canada's Families II*. Ottawa: Vanier Institute of the Family.

Voydanoff, Pat. 1987. *Work and Family Life*. Newbury Park, CA: Sage.

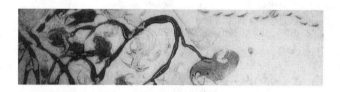

2

Single-Parent Families

Marion M. Lynn
Research Consultant

Objectives

- To introduce historical and current profiles of single-parent families in Canada, examining how these families represent both new and not-so-new forms of cohabiting and raising children.

- To point out some of the strains and stresses in marriage and family that lead to the decision not to marry, or to separate, and to form single-parent families.

- To illustrate the complexities and diversities that exist in families in which the parents of the children do not share a household.

- To examine the degree to which women are influenced by the lives of their mothers and men are influenced by the lives of their fathers as they form their own family relationships.

- To inquire as to the degree to which increases in single-parent families are related to women's determination to engage in relationships based on equality and to establish choice in their lives.

- To suggest that men play a larger and more supportive role as single-parent fathers than is commonly perceived.

INTRODUCTION

> It was amazing once I got my affairs in order and got my apartment. It was like the clouds parted and the sun came out. It was so amazing. I think it was the best thing I ever did for myself. Through that whole marriage I don't think I had this much self-esteem. Everybody says, Oh, it's a tragedy. It's not a tragedy. It's a growing thing. It probably could have happened sooner. I'm glad it didn't happen later. I probably would have been a wreck. (A separated, single-parent mother of two)

One of the most significant changes in Canadian families over the past three decades is the increase in **single-parent families**. This form of family has been the focus of attention in the popular media, in academic research studies, and in government policy debates. Popular television shows present illustrations of single parenting. In *Judging Amy*, a divorced woman (a judge) and her daughter live with her mother (a social worker), creating an extended-kin family/household of two professional women and a child. In *The Practice*, an unmarried woman (a lawyer) chooses to have a child outside of marriage—and goes to court to prevent the biological father from sharing custody of the child. She insists on her right to be a single parent, as she originally intended. Academic and social researchers have explored issues such as reasons for divorce; the increasing number of children born and reared outside of marriage; the impact on children of growing up without a father as head of the household; and the ways in which families based on single parents challenge the definition of family (Hudson and Galaway 1993). The attention governments pay to single-parent families is evident in numerous reports issued by Statistics Canada and published in *Canadian Social Trends* and *Perspectives*, for example, and by the Vanier Institute of the Family in its journal, *Transitions*.

In spite of all of this attention, there are still many gaps in our understanding of these families. The quotation at the beginning of this essay provides one example of the complexities in understanding this family form. This woman describes the experience of separating from her husband and establishing a single-parent household in terms such as "amazing," "the clouds parting," and "the sun coming out." She views this move as an experience of growth rather than as a tragedy, as the best thing she ever did for herself, and as a chance to gain self-esteem and to avoid being turned into a "wreck." This woman's voice represents an attitude to being in a single-parent family that emerges on the part of many of the women and some of the men whom I have interviewed in a study on separation, divorce, and single parenting, the findings of which are presented in this chapter.

This attitude of choosing to live on one's own to rear children, rather than with a spouse or partner, raises a number of questions that explore what it is in a two-parent family/household that could turn a woman into a "wreck" and what it is about single parenting that could add to a woman's self-esteem. It is an approach to single parenting that emerges from a number of sources. In her research and analysis, Carolyne Gorlick suggests that rather than deviance, marital separation can be seen as "an opportunity for personal growth" on a number of levels: for a healthy remarriage for both partners; a relief for children from a conflict-ridden family; an escape for women from abuse and violence; and a resistance on the part of women to living in oppressive and domineering social institutions (2000, 262). Many clients at a counselling centre for families describe separation as a new beginning, individual members constructing their new families in different ways (Freeman 1999).

There is a decidedly negative attitude toward divorce and single-parent families expressed by neo-conservatives and the far right. This attitude is illustrated by David Frum's reference to divorce and children born outside of marriage as the most important social problem faced by Canada, and his argument that, in order to revitalize the institution of marriage, we must ensure that "laws and customs favour marriage over all other ways of life" (Gorlick 2000, 261). In contrast to this approach is one found in Newfoundland, where the Minister of the Department of Human Resources and Employment supports the Single Parent Association of Newfoundland in celebrating a Single Parent Family Week, and states that it is important to publicly acknowledge the extra effort and work in raising children on the part of single parents as sole caregivers for their families (Kelloway and Walton 1998). Kissman and Allen note the importance of talking to the women who head families in order to counteract negative stereotypes. Reframing stories and emphasizing problem-solving strategies that enhance strengths empower these women and present them as active agents, rather than passive victims, in their family forms (1993).

The purpose of this chapter is to demonstrate that current parenting and household arrangements defined as single-parent families are complex, contradictory, and difficult to categorize. People tend to respond to single-parent families as though they are radically new, a significant break from the past; yet they are found as a family form throughout 20th-century Canada. Various problems are associated with living in a family with only one parent present, yet some people appear to consider it preferable to living in a two-parent family. My research replicates the work of others showing that many children whose parents live in separate households are still spending time with and being cared for by both parents on a weekly basis. They are not really being single-parented; they have not lost one of their parents. Although statistics show that women suffer severe economic losses when living in single-parent families, some studies suggest that, while there is less family money available, women have more money at their disposal than they had within a marriage. As well, research shows that it is primarily women who are opting for single parenthood instead of heterosexual marriage. This chapter attempts to unravel the apparent contradictions among some of these issues surrounding single-parent families.

CURRENT ISSUES

Historical Overview and Current Growth

Single-parent families have been increasing in Canada over the past two decades at a rate three times that of husband–wife families. According to 1996 Canadian census data, 14.5 percent of all families in Canada are single-parent families (Statistics Canada 1996). These vary from highs of 18.6 in Nunavut, 16.5 in the Yukon, and 15.9 in Quebec to lows of 13.2 percent in Newfoundland and 12.9 percent in Alberta. Eighty-three percent of these families are headed by women and 61 percent of them are living below the poverty level (Statistics Canada 1996).

However, single-parent families are not a new phenomenon in Canada. As Marcil-Gratton (1993, 73) remarks, "families built around the enduring relationship of a man and a woman have been disintegrating from the beginnings of time, leaving one parent to take responsibility." In 1931, 13.6 percent of all families were headed by a single parent, higher than the 12 percent recorded for 1986 and virtually the same as in June 1991, only to be surpassed in the 1996 census (McKie 1993, 60; Statistics Canada 1996). The vast majority of single-parent families in the 1930s resulted from the death of a parent or the separation of family members during the hard economic times of the Depression. There were few divorces, and most women who had children outside of marriage either gave them up for adoption or had them reared by their own **extended family**. Between the 1940s and mid-1960s single-parent families declined to a low of 8 percent, and since then have been rising steadily (see Table 2.1). Statscan reports that figures from the year 2000 confirm the continuence of annual increases in the divorce rate (Walton 2002).

Statistics capture those numbers of people living in particular forms of family only at the moment of the survey. **Longitudinal studies** (which study the same people over time), such as Statistics Canada's Family History Survey (1989) and Canada's National Longitudinal Survey of Children and Youth, which began in 1994–95 on a cross-section of 22,831 children between 0 and 11 years old, provide a fuller picture (Cheal et al. 1997). As other researchers have noted, longitudinal studies suggest that the numbers reflected at any

Table 2.1 Single-Parent Families in Canada

	Overall (%)	Male-headed (%)	Female-headed (%)
1941	13.6	26.0	73.0
1966	8.2	19.2	80.8
1986	12.7	17.8	82.2
1991	14.0	18.0	82.0
1996	14.5	17.0	83.0

Sources: McKie 1993, 55–60. Statistics Canada 1996.

one time represent merely a fraction of the total numbers of men, women and children who have spent some part of their life cycle in single-parent families. It is possible that up to one-third of all mothers in Canada will be single parents at some stage of their lives (McKie 1993, 60; Marcil-Gratton 1993, 74).

Complexity and Diversity

There are as many complexities and diversities among single-parent families as there are among two-parent families. Nancy Dowd (1997) predicts that 70 percent of children in the United States will spend part of their lives in single-parent-family households (viii). She suggests that the single-parent family as a model is developing and imperfect, and needs to be looked at carefully in order to be understood (112). In place of marriage, single-parent families tend to develop models of support and networking that include extended family, kin and non-kin, and paid and unpaid help, viewing children as part of a community, valued and cared for and about.

Kissman and Allen (1993) argue that there are such variations—depending on class, gender, race, ethnicity, age, and life cycle—that no one set of policy interventions or ways of measuring well-being and quality of life in single-parent families can be adhered to. The particularity of life cycle, for example, demonstrates that teenage never-married mothers and their infants have needs that are entirely different from those of older divorced mothers with adolescents. Single-parent fathers may be better off financially, but have fewer skills for childcare and for combining domestic and paid work. Emerging forms of parenting—gay, lesbian, foster parenting alone, never-married mothers—all outside the norm of the hetero-sexual marriage and all part of the diverse group categorized as single-parent families, represent forms of family that have been even more marginalized than others, and frequently surrounded by silence.

Since the 1970s, the *Charter of Rights and Freedoms* and the *Human Rights Act* have provided protection from discrimination by the state based on sexual orientation. In Quebec and Ontario, the provincial legislatures adopted omnibus legislation in 1999, effecting near-comprehensive reform to equalize the rights and responsibilities of same-sex and hetero-sexual unmarried partners. Alimony, child support, child custody, visitation, and adoption laws have been modified and amended to treat lesbian and gay parents equally. Research to date concludes that lesbian and gay families parent children as well as any others (American Civil Liberties Union 1999; American Psychological Association 1995).

Another source of diversity found in single-parent families emerges from ethnocultural membership and experience, sometimes indicating historical continuity in that particular cultural group. A history of single-parent families indicates a common response to economic and political conditions outside the control of the particular families and cultural groups as well, and can shed insight into the growth of this family form. Two case studies illustrate the importance of considering both culture and class in analyzing the difference in prevalence rates among different communities. These variables should be taken into account in policy development and implementation regarding single-parent families.

Miller and Browning (2000) look at ways in which black women in the United States have created an alternative family form of single parenting as a consequence of structural constraints that exclude black men from the marriage market. In 1960, 65 percent of black women between 30 and 34 were married; this figure changed to 39 percent in 1990. Never-married women rose from 10 percent to 35 percent. Less than half of black families comprise married couples. This is partly due to the replacement of fairly lucrative blue-collar jobs by low-paying service jobs, and to the high rate of criminal incarceration of men who might be potential mates. In 1995, for example, 32 percent of black men between the ages of 20 and 29 were in jail or on probation or parole (341). Women become involved with men who engage in criminal activities. They also settle for a "piece of a man," who fathers their child, provides intimacy and support on a part-time basis, may be involved with other women, or may be in jail (342). A choice that may superficially appear to be irrational or the behaviour of a victim on further study can be shown to be a rational, carefully considered choice on the part of a woman who knows her alternatives in the real world.

A second illustration of the impact of ethnocultural membership on the establishment of single-parent families comes from a study of Aboriginal single mothers in Canada. This study, drawing on 1996 census data, suggests that these families experience "triple jeopardy" because they are women, Aboriginal, and headed by lone parents (Hull 2001, 5–6). Single-mother Aboriginal families grew from 20 percent in 1981 to 23 percent in 1996, whereas the rest of single-mother families in Canada grew from 9 percent to 12 percent. Twenty-eight percent of Registered Indian families are single-mother-led with children 15 and under, whereas 16 percent of non-Aboriginal families are. Like women in the black American communities, Canadian Aboriginal women who are single parents have particular characteristics. They are more likely than others to have migrated from one community to another. These women are more likely to live in urban than rural areas, and therefore be living off the reserve.

When comparing Aboriginal single-mother families with those in the rest of the Canadian population, a number of differences emerge, all of which are characteristics that make single parenting more difficult. These Aboriginal mothers are younger and have more children than non-Aboriginal single mothers. However, this picture may not be all negative, and needs further consideration about support systems and about how their lives change over time. For example, unlike the general Canadian population, single motherhood among Aboriginals increases with educational level, and single-mother Aboriginals are more likely to be in school full time, especially the older ones. For those living on-reserve and in rural areas the labour market participation is better and they have higher marketable skills. Because they are younger, they are more likely to experience change over a period of time, perhaps moving into education and into communities where their skills are marketable and they have a support system.

Another very important form of complexity and diversity involves the post-separation role of the father, either as lone head of the family or as a key player in the lives of single-mother families. Although they are frequently left out of the discussion, fathers are not as absent as statistics would indicate. Marcil-Gratton points out that for children born outside of a marital union, about half of the parents had lived together. Birth records show that in 73 percent of the cases where they had lived together and in 40 percent of the cases where they had not lived together, the father puts his name on the birth certificate (Marcil-Gratton 1999).

Gorlick and Pomfret state that, while official figures indicate that about 70 percent of mothers and 10 percent of fathers have sole custody and another 20 percent share custody of children, children in fact move back and forth between parents and households at different stages of their lives and for different periods of time. Children have more agency over how they adapt to separation and divorce than might initially appear (1999). And fathers have more ongoing interaction over the years than might be assumed from official statistics and analyses. Also, although deadbeat dads are a primary reason for poverty of single mothers, many men do pay support. Almost half of court-ordered support is paid on time, and another third is paid although late; three-quarters of out-of-court settlements are adhered to (Gorlick 2000, 267).

The number of lone-father families has increased significantly in recent years. Lone fathers are now younger and more likely to have become lone fathers through marital break-down. Lone-father families are a distinctive group located in between the disadvantaged status of female lone-parent families and the more secure situation of most two-parent families. Although their incomes are lower and poverty rates higher than two-parent families, they do not experience the extreme financial problems of lone-mother families. In relative terms, their income levels have declined in recent years and they are now at a substantially higher risk of living in poverty. Lone fathers are, though, significantly more likely to be in the labour force than their female counterparts, perhaps because they receive more support from others that facilitates balancing employment and parenting. Lone-father families are more likely to reside with others (McQuillan and Belle 2001).

Economic Realities

Socioeconomic status is another dimension that distinguishes single-parent families from two-parent families, and distinguishes them from each other. Fifty-six percent of female lone-parent families are poor, compared with 24 percent of male lone-parent families (Vanier Institute of the Family 2001 "Family Facts"). In general, women-headed single-parent families are living in poverty at an ever-growing rate. In 1999 the average total income for two-parent families with children under 18 was $72,910, and for single-parent families was $30,470. Of the latter, male-headed families had income of $45,829 and female-headed families had income of $27,571 (Statistics Canada 2001).

Depending on the number of children, a single mother increases the risk of falling below the low-income measures and remaining there for five to seven years out of ten, compared with a married woman in a low-income family whose risk is three to four years living in poverty (Laroche 1998). However, although there is more likelihood of children being poor if they live in single-parent families, the proportion of children in low-income families in Canada has remained stable over the past two decades. This is due primarily to increased government transfers as employment income fell among the young and marginally employed, and to people having fewer children and having them later in life (Picot and Myles 1996).

As pointed out by a number of researchers, it is important to indicate the length of time after separation in looking at poverty in single-parent families. One study shows that, although women experience a considerable loss in family income in the first year following separation, five years later they have recovered a large part of their loss and have a family income only 5 percent ($1,000) lower than when they were married (Galarneau and Sturrock 1997). In looking at family income it is important to acknowledge that a family without a man excludes a major consumer of the family income.

An important American study that includes data from Australia, Canada, and France concludes that a combination of non-means-tested income from the state that supplements earnings, income from the market, and support from noncustodial fathers is more likely to lessen the incidence of poverty among single-mother families than reliance on any single source of income. A policy-development approach that attends to a combination of means to assist these families with supportive benefits, education and employment opportunities, community support, and insistence on father support could go a long way to eliminate poverty in single-parent families (Nichols-Casebolt and Krysik 1997).

In all of these research studies it must be kept in mind that there are a number of social, political, and economic factors contributing to the poverty of women and children. Poverty in single-parent families emerges from poverty of women and children in two-parent families and from inequities in marriage, an institution that can be shown to benefit men economically more than it does women. Poverty also emerges from women's second-class status in the labour force and from the exclusion of women from policy-making centres, such as those that regulate minimum wage, maternity leave, equal pay, accessible childcare, affordable housing, transfer payments, and family law.

It must also be kept in mind that most people move into and exit from temporary situations of poverty. Carolyne Gorlick has published some challenging material that looks at steps in the life course of women who are single parents on social assistance, arguing that a great deal of diversity exists among this group, and that following them over a period of time indicates agency on their part, persistent ability to manage, and determination to overcome barriers and problems. Most of these women are on assistance for a short period of time, usually less than three years, and many of them complete their education and move into full-time employment (2000).

Impact on Children

Including children born to common-law or **cohabiting** parents, as well as mothers living on their own, almost 30 percent of Canadian children are currently born outside of marriage and fewer numbers of their parents are marrying after their birth. In Quebec equal numbers of children are born to married and unmarried parents, but the separation of the common-law union in the early years of parenthood is less likely to occur than in the country as a whole (37 percent versus 47 percent) and than in Ontario, where 61 percent of common-law unions end before the child's sixth birthday (Marcil-Gratton 1999).

The average age at which children live with only one parent is getting younger. In the early 1980s, 10 percent of children were living with one parent by age 10; by the early 1990s, 15 percent were living with one parent at age 2. This is primarily due to increasing break-ups early in a marriage. This stage for children does not necessarily last, as they are likely to move into stepfamilies, which is the case with 60 percent of those whose parents had separated by their tenth birthday during the 1980s (Marcil-Gratton 1999).

In comparing children from separated/divorced families with those from two-parent intact-marriage families, there is an assumption that the previous family functioning of these children was the same as the latter group. To do a valid comparison, the functioning of the marriages/families would have to be the same. The former group of children would have to be compared with those who have remained in conflict-ridden, hostile, or broken-down relationship marriages, in order to determine the impact of separation and divorce on their well-being. Recent research findings corroborate this observation. "Virtually all studies to date overstate the potential divorce effects by limiting the scope of predivorce information....the impact of divorce is likely to be highly contingent on timing of divorce, the gender of the child, and the domain of behavior." The authors conclude that failing to evaluate such predivorce information "can only provide crude and often misleading conclusions about how marital dissolution affects children's well-being in later life" (Furstenberg and Kiernan 2001, 455).

Most studies to date regarding the impact of divorce on the well-being of children are positive in their outlook.

> Findings indicate that overall, more than two-thirds of children living with both parents and living in post-divorce custody arrangements are reported as well-adjusted, exhibiting no problems at all. Importantly, and contrary to popular assumptions, children living in some form of post-divorce custody are only slightly more likely to exhibit one or more problems than children living with both parents. (Haddad 1998, 3)

Rhonda Freeman summarizes recent research developments on how children experience divorce, noting that it is not a one-time event but a developmental process. The consequences for children depend upon a number of factors during this process. These include parental conflict, the economic resources available for raising children, parenting capacity, parent/child relationships, and the divorce environment. The natural resilience of children and the degree to which the process successfully evolves determine whether or not, and the degree to which, children are placed at risk (1999).

The role of fathers, as either custodial or noncustodial parent, is important. The ongoing involvement of fathers in their children's lives along with low conflict and a reasonable relationship between the parents appear to have a strong impact on the academic performance and future well-being of the child and to determine the risk of psychological problems and delinquency (Pluviati 1996).

A number of recent studies have taken a close look at the well-being of children from various family forms (Lipman et al. 1998; Ross et al. 1998a, b, c). Most children in Canada are doing well if they live with parents who score high on positive interaction and consistent parenting, have good relationships with siblings, have good friends outside the family, live in a family that receives community and kin support and encouragement, and have parents with good mental and physical health. These conditions are mediated by family form, but not necessarily determined by it. Most children in Canada from single-parent families are part of this group that is doing well. The greatest risk factors for single-parent families are low social support, family dysfunction, and parental depression. All of these are associated with low income and all can be alleviated by help in the other areas. As well, these conditions change as the children grow up and are only temporarily in high-risk situations.

Although lone-mother families are poorer and the children are at risk of having more difficulties in the behavioural, emotional, social, and academic spheres, this status on its own acts as a weak predictor of all child difficulties. The strength of the link between lone-mother status and negative child outcomes generally decreases when sociodemographic and personal variables are factored into the model predicting child outcome. Children from lone-mother families probably develop difficulties for the same reason that children from two-parent families develop difficulties.

A recent study conducted on 178 university students in social science courses compared the level of adjustment and adaptive coping ability between those who came from a separated/divorced family and those who came from a family where there had not been a separation or divorce, using validated tools that measure these characteristics against everyday hassles. This study shows no difference in the level of adjustment or adaptive coping ability between the two groups, indicating almost identical scores. This is an important study: rather than seeking out children of separated and divorced families and testing them on adjustment and coping ability, they are part of a wider social group and are asked the same questions as the other students. Although this is a group that is specific in terms of academic success, socioeconomic status cannot be measured by attendance at university, as many students from poor families attend university, relying on student loans and their own employment to finance their post-secondary education (Smith and Kohn 2002).

A STUDY OF SINGLE PARENTS

The following presentation comes from a qualitative study of 34 women and 16 men who were single parents at the time of the interviews. The children in some of these families were grown, but were still very much engaged in their parents' lives. This was a very diverse group, most having been legally married, some common-law; some had children outside of a conjugal union, and there was a self-identified lesbian, a self-identified gay man, and a man who was fathering a foster son on his own. Both men and women who identified themselves as single parents were included, regardless of the custody or living arrangements that had been made for the children. This study supports the literature indicating that, in spite of what the courts decide, men, women, and children frequently make their own living arrangements in single-parent families. As one man explains: *"I left and six weeks later my daughter arrived at my door … She wanted to live with me."*

The ages of the participants ranged from 21 to 68, with almost half the group in their 40s. Some were students; the occupations and incomes of others ranged from top administrative positions to teachers and clerical workers. Thirteen out of the fifty were born outside of Canada. As a group they represent 11 different ethnocultural communities including francophone, West Indian, and Ojibway. In this study, my goal was to uncover not only a description of how people in single-parent families managed their daily lives, but also how they arrived there.

Personal History of Family

When we discuss people currently living in single-parent families, it is commonly assumed that everyone came from a two-parent, **nuclear family** household that was happy and stable. This is far from the case. In her article "One Hundred Years of Families," Anne Milan (2000) describes a number of exceptions to what we think of as traditional families in Canada's past, including those who never married, lone parents, childless couples, and common-law unions. Although formal marital dissolution was difficult to obtain up until the last quarter-century, significant numbers of families nonetheless broke up due to abandonment, desertion, or death of one of the spouses. During the Depression of the 1930s, both marriage and birth rates decreased significantly, with 20 percent of women having no children. Both world wars played havoc with families, many of them being fractured and many living in extended-kin households.

In the group of 50 people who participated in my study, 19 (38 percent) had spent some part of their growing-up years living in a single-parent-family household, in families that existed between the 1930s and the 1980s. The reasons these families became one-parent include death of a parent, and separation resulting from immigration, economic hardship, unemployment, alcoholism, violence, and general marital discord. However, most of those interviewed remember their lives as relatively comfortable and happy, apparently with no more problems than children who grew up in two-parent families. One man describes his early years as follows:

> We spent the war years that way like everybody else did, effectively a separated family. I felt much closer to my grandmother than I did to my mother, very close to my grandparents. We were a working-class family; I never felt deprived or poor. We lived in a nice old house on a nice old street and I was perfectly happy.

On the other hand, many of the women with whom I spoke whose parents had always lived together believe that their mothers' lives—and in some ways their fathers' lives—had been disappointing, lonely, and in some cases brutal. One of the ways of compensating was with misuse of drugs and alcohol; some were under psychiatric care.

My mother's life has been quite a tragedy; being dominated and controlled and abused was a pattern that I know was in her early years. She thought the husband she married was better than she; this gave him wonderful control over her. He had affairs for an entire six-year period, and was abusive. He was always in control of the money; he never shelled out for clothes or shoes or anything. My mother clothed and raised three of us on what she could squeeze out of the grocery money.

On the whole, both female and male participants perceived their parents' marriage and family as benefiting their fathers more than their mothers. One woman in my study describes the restrictions of her mother's marriage and its costs.

My mother had several nervous breakdowns as I was growing up. She was a head nurse when she got married, a very competent person who had grown up in a home with a single mother who was a nurse. When Dad came back from the War, she got married and had kids; you were not meant to work and I know she missed it. She never felt good about herself. But Dad would not have approved. It just wasn't done.

Many of these women view their mothers' lives as not something they wanted, or intended, to reproduce. As one woman explains:

My whole childhood, with my father and the salary he was bringing home and his control over everything, just rose up in my throat as it were. And I said to my husband, "You will never be in a position to 'give me'—as you call it—money."

The men in this study tended to bring to their marriage a different vision of their family history and their memories of their parents' lives, a vision that places their fathers in the centre and is much less critical of the marriage. As one man explains:

Both of my parents were university educated. My father was a professional, an oral surgeon, and my mother studied something administrative. I've no idea exactly what it was, but I remember her indicating that she did graduate from somewhere. She was a housewife with a lot of help. My father's was the only career. My father was the breadwinner.

Several men were vague about their mothers' lives: "*Mom stayed home, was a housewife, I guess. Dad was away most of the time.*" Many of the women, on the other hand, presented a much more complex vision of the work their parents had done.

My father wasn't home a lot. He worked in restaurants; he owned restaurants. But he hung around the Legion a lot. My father didn't manage money very well, so my mother went back to work in the restaurants.

This brief profile of the family history of these women and men indicates the diversity and complexity of their original family structures and roles of their parents, and the critical view of the lives of many of the mothers, particularly on the part of the women.

Marital Dissolution

The strains in the marriages of those interviewed centred mainly around four issues: paid and domestic work; childbirth and rearing; sexuality; and control and violence. As each one of these is examined in detail, it becomes clear how their intersection could create a very difficult family life and a shaky marriage, and could lead people to consider alternatives.

Paid and Domestic Work

Examination of contemporary families uncovers the tremendous strain and resentment created in marriages by an unfair distribution of domestic tasks (Eichler 1997; Hochschild 1989, 1997; Luxton 1990). As Eichler (1997, 60) states, with the economic contribution made by women in today's families "the division of labour is greatly out of kilter." Hochschild's original study shows that only 20 percent of couples shared tasks equally; in the other families the women worked "a second shift" of up to 15 hours per week over and above what their husbands contributed (1989, 3–4). Her follow-up study shows that women in the labour force preferred work to being at home, where they felt they were faced with endless thankless tasks (1997). Statistics Canada's *General Social Survey* (1992) indicates that women who are employed full time spend twice as much time per day as their husbands on childcare and three times as much time on routine daily tasks, including maintenance and repairs. According to a recent *Work-Life Compendium 2001* (Johnson, Lero & Rooney, 2001), conflict between work and personal lives is increasing, with women reporting higher levels than men and spending more time on domestic work and childcare—in addition to elder care, furthering their education and training, and community responsibilities.

Many of the women and men I interviewed grew up in households where their mothers were main wage earners and, in some cases, the only wage earner. However, the men who participated in my study tended to bring to their own marriages the view of their fathers as the one with the career, the head of the household, seldom taking any responsibility for household work. And they seemed to repeat this division of labour, putting their careers first even though their wives were either in the labour force or trying to remain in it. In retrospect, some of the men understood this. As one man explains:

> Deterioration probably happened when my career interrupted a happy home life; we moved a great deal. I'm very career-oriented. My wife had been in a teaching career and of course that was interrupted, which was very frustrating; the children came in close intervals and I was away a lot. My career ruined a very good marriage.

Women also experienced confusion around gender consciousness and their actual gender relations. For example, on the basis of her mother's advice not to be economically dependent on a man, one woman went into marriage convinced she could have *"a wonderful relationship and a career."* Instead she found that she had two children, a full-time job, was responsible for all the housework, and did her husband's books for his business: *"that was the problem with my marriage—I was doing all the work."* She noted that her life was easier as a single parent.

> I remember being married and having two small children and working full-time, and if we did go anywhere I had to do all the preparation. Get the kids ready, pack the car. I look at that now and I think—how could you let yourself be treated that way? I had to make it so there was no effort for him. It's actually easier now.

Lesbian and gay partnerships are not immune to these strains. A lesbian woman talked about giving up her work to move to a different part of the province for her partner, and the difficulties that emerged as a consequence. A gay man talked about doing the bulk of the housework and childcare so that his partner could establish himself professionally.

Childbirth and Child Rearing

Sharing work and economic resources is presumably one of the major functions of marriage. Having and raising children is another. However, many of these women and men indicate that their relationships with their partners shifted dramatically with the birth of their children. The interviews uncovered surprisingly consistent references to the problems created by pregnancy and child rearing. Almost half of the women who had been married were disappointed because their husbands became withdrawn and uneasy when they were pregnant and when their children were born. One woman explains that the birth of a child elicited "*no joy*" from her husband. Others said that "*he started acting strange,*" or became "*like a crazy man.*" The following comment is typical of those made by several women:

> We had our first child and it was really at that point that things very clearly weren't right for the two of us. I thought, ah, this man didn't want a baby. I forced him into it; it was all my idea and it's all my fault; he's not a happy man and it's all my fault. And then I had another child—again my idea. So again I went through the guilt.

Although many of the men in the study spoke with delight and affection about having and rearing children, they also acknowledge the impact it had on their relationships with their wives. One man notes that it was originally "*a good marriage because we did not have any children.*" Another expresses the feeling that "*she went from being my exclusive property to being very much involved with her son; any wise man understands that's the way it's going to be.*"

Not all of these men adapted easily to the role of breadwinner in the family. One man describes how he felt as the sole wage earner in his family.

> I really sacrificed plenty to be the sole wage earner, really went through about seven of the most miserable years I'd ever experienced. It was awful, inhumane, and I was trapped because I was the sole support for the family.

Sexuality

In this study, lack of satisfactory sexual relations was a central point of contention for over a third of the men and women in legal and common-law marriages. Some women state that there was hardly ever any sex in their marriage, and they wondered why: Was their husband gay? Was there something unappealing about them? Men talk about their wives' lack of interest in sex, the fact that some of the women had been sexually abused or raped and were unable to enjoy sex. One man describes a very long marriage that was mostly celibate. Another claims that men of his generation believed that having sex was "like going to the theatre": if it happened once a month you were supposed to be grateful. Some of the women connect the loss of a good sex life to their partner's abhorrence of their body when they became pregnant.

> Part of it was the dichotomy between the virgin and the whore; I was desirable when I wasn't pregnant, but as soon as I became pregnant I became untouchable.

The fact that I was pregnant made him regard me as "mother" rather than "lover".... He said it was as if it was almost incestuous.

Several of these women and men had sexual relationships outside of their marriages. Their attitude to this was interesting in that no one considers these affairs as the reason for the breakdown of the marriage. In some cases the affairs and sexual liaisons were treated in a slightly cavalier manner; in other cases they were perceived as a consequence of other problems, rather than as a contributing factor. And for some people, monogamous marriage did not appear to fit their value system. As two men describe it:

Was I faithful? No, but there weren't any serious relationships. I wouldn't call it faithful, but I wouldn't call it indiscriminate either.

We didn't argue in particular, had no great arguments. But it was just like two solitudes. Of course, I wound up having affairs with various people over the last ten years.

Women also had affairs:

I had drifted into a very, very passionate affair. It was only a few months, and very limited, but it was also very strong. Even so, I did not think that was any reason to break up a marriage. I mean, I understood it for what it was.

It is difficult to pin down the extent to which the lack of satisfaction or commitment to their sexual lives contributed to, or occurred in response to, other strains in the marriages. But most people insist that it was a central factor in the demise of their relationships.

Control and Violence

Violence is an integral part of many marriage and family relationships today, as it has been in the past. More than 25 percent of these women and men who went through a separation, 11 in all, report some form of violence by the man against the woman or against his children during the relationship. The forms this violence toward the women took include being punched in the face, hit with a frying pan, and brutally raped. In most of these cases the violence occurred only once, and took place shortly before the separation. One pattern of marital violence is that of men who become abusive as the woman tries to move out of the relationship (Crawford and Gartner 1992).

A number of women and men also acknowledge verbal and psychological abuse, threats, or potential for violent acts, as well as controlling behaviours that left the women timid and unsure of themselves. The man's domination appears to have been used to keep the woman feeling powerless, fearful, and always on edge. One woman describes the effect of this as *"feeling about one inch high"*—all of her self-confidence gone. The control over women's lives took diverse forms. One woman was not allowed to have any friends or to go anywhere, including to church. Two other women were told how to dress and when to speak. Another woman was not able to listen to classical music; her husband would turn it off when he entered the house.

The three men who describe their own potential violence put it very graphically: *"You grit your teeth and you clench your fist and you walk away"*; *"A guy gets mad, he gets mad...has a few drinks...the front door's locked so he puts his fist through the glass."* Three women describe how their husbands threatened the children in order to control their behaviour, two with a knife and the other by disappearing with his small daughter for four days.

As with some of their families of origin, violence and abuse are found latent or manifest in many of the marriages and families entered into by the participants. Like the other strains in their relationships, the abusive behaviour formed part of a continuum along which the ties that keep a marriage and family together weaken and break.

Daily Lives of Single Parents

Separation and Divorce

Studies indicate that the particular ways in which separation and divorce are handled are very important for the well-being of all family members, especially children. For the people in this study, the process of separating was difficult, painful, and costly at some level for most of those involved. At the same time, it was experienced as liberating and a relief from tension, fear, boredom, and disappointment. These realities reflect the complex feelings reported in the literature on separation and divorce (Sev'er 1992; Gorlick 2000).

The degree to which the difficulties overwhelmed the positive aspects of life as a single parent depends on a number of factors. The oldest woman in my study had perhaps the most difficult time, retraining and returning to work after years as a homemaker because she had very little legal, economic, or social support. However, she left a disappointing and abusive marriage and reared five children at a time when divorce and "latchkey kids" were not common phenomena. She bought her own house: *"Nobody would rent to me with five kids, so I had to buy."* She saw her sons graduate from university and her daughters establish their own businesses. Looking back on the entire experience, she commented: *"He got all the money; I got the reason to live."*

As the social and economic systems have opened up for women over the past 25 years, life as a single parent has become in many ways more manageable. Most of the women in their 30s and 40s were already educated and established in relatively well-paying jobs that could support them and their children. And the younger women, although temporarily on social assistance and poor, were training for fairly decent jobs and careers in journalism, computer technology, and nursing. As indicated in the literature, current or potential economic independence provides a woman not only with financial resources to manage single parenting, but also it gives her an identity and a location outside of marriage and motherhood.

The break-up of lesbian and gay partnerships can be devastating, and there is no public acknowledgement of this. For example, a gay man in this study lived with his partner for 15 years, helping to raise his partner's biological daughter, sharing in everything from school trips to hair-washing, dental appointments, cooking, cleaning, and laundry. When the two men separated he went through the difficult situation of feeling like a parent who has lost custody and lost contact, because he had neither legal nor socially acknowledged rights to this child.

When we broke up, after having helped care for her since she was five, it was *fait accompli*. I wasn't supposed to get anything out of it. I couldn't visit her even on Sundays. I had no rights to a relationship with her.

The five young women in this study, all in their 20s, who had children without being married or living with the child's father, represent the kinds of choices now possible for parenting. Abortion was considered and rejected by all of these young women, as was marriage to the father of the baby. As one young woman put it when considering marriage to her child's father, *"two wrongs don't make a right."* Another stated that she was *"calling the shots."*

Support Systems

However, as the literature shows, some of the young men who are fathers to these children are very involved in parenting. One young woman had set out to get pregnant without any concern for the father's support or participation; he became so attached to the child that he requested and was given legal joint custody. They are now co-parenting their son. Most of these women have a great deal of daily support from their own family, as well as from the family of the baby's father. Some are temporarily on family benefits and in subsidized housing, others are partly self-supporting, some with help from family. This combination of public and family support will enable them to become economically self-sufficient and support themselves and their children.

One of the men who had sole custody found being a single parent too much. *"No man should have to do this by himself; it is just crazy. This does not come naturally for a man to do this at all."* However, other men who had joint custody saw advantages to single parenting and found the times with their children delightful.

I enjoyed it. It was the only time I got to see my kids. They were very good times. Most of them were very good times. Now there were bad weekends—you get bad weekends any time. But you make pizza and throw the cheese around the kitchen and that kind of stuff. And you can do what you want. That's the nice thing about being a single parent. You can handle any situation your own way. You don't have to say "Dear, what do you think about...? could we do this? have I got the right idea here?" No, you don't. You don't have to go through that nonsense.

The man who had raised a foster son for about 15 years is now a "foster-grandfather," helping to care for his foster son's daughter, creating a supportive, extended family out of this unusual origin.

We have family gatherings with my brother and sisters, nieces and nephews, and me, my son, and now his little daughter; it is lovely, like a real family gathering. He gave me a mug from his daughter saying "I Love You Grandpa." It was so important because it was like a validation of the fact that I am his "father" and his daughter's "grandfather." It was the most important thing for me.

It is important to acknowledge the need for social and community support. For many women, their work colleagues were an important source of support. One young woman describes the lifeline they provided one very difficult Christmas.

I couldn't afford to pay daycare, the Hydro was after me, everybody was after me for money I didn't have. I didn't have anything for Christmas. My supervisor phoned me to come in to work. They had two big boxes of presents wrapped up for my daughter and an envelope with $320 in it. Every year they collect for a charity, and that year they gave it all to me. It was the nicest thing anyone ever did for me.

The other sources of the support that is essential for men and women who are single parenting are their own parents and siblings. In this study, mothers in particular provided moral support, daycare, space in their homes, and money, for both the men and the women. The parents of several women helped them in a number of practical ways, including one or more of the following: they paid for their divorce, took them and their children into their home, gave them the first and last month's rent, found apartments for them, or loaned them down payments for a house. Very few men or women were given the impression that they had "made their bed and could lie in it." In some ways it seemed as though their parents, especially their mothers, were very willing to help them leave a bad situation and have a chance at a different life, a chance these mothers never had.

My mother was my godsend. I'd phone her in an anxiety attack and she would talk me through it. She's been through it herself, although not for the same reasons. She was my lifeline; without her I could not have done it.

Children are cared for in a variety of ways in these single-parent families, including accessible daycare and help from other family members. This extended-family care included weekends and evenings as well as weekdays. One young woman said that between both grandparents wanting her little boy on the weekends she had to vie for her own share of time with him.

About half of the women reported resistance on the part of their children's fathers to pay support money or to take an active role in the children's care. There were some cases in which the fathers did not participate either economically or socially in parenting their children; for some people, bitter disputes and court cases about the separation continued for years. However a number of fathers were trying to do their best in sharing the work of single parenting, taking a much more active role in economic, emotional, and physical care of their children than is commonly perceived. In some cases the father either had sole custody or had one or more children living with him for months or years at a time. As some of the children got older, they often decided to switch homes and live with their father rather than their mother—sometimes because there was a problem with the mother, it better suited their schooling, or they wanted to establish a closer relationship with him. Children and adolescents took agency in their choices of homes.

Access to affordable housing is frequently a barrier for single-parent families. However, housing was seldom noted as a problem for the people in this study. Some of the women who were students lived in subsidized housing, in apartments that were bright, spacious, and nicely furnished. They considered this subsidized housing, along with family benefits, a temporary way to the economic independence they would achieve when they completed college. A surprising number of women owned their own homes. Of those employed, 14 out of the 20 women were homeowners (70 percent), compared with 11 of the 15 men who were employed (73 percent). In addition to the employed women, one woman who was a student owned her own home; she was 33 at the time of the study, had two children, and was graduating at the top of her class in a business program.

One woman's path to home ownership shows what women who are single parents can accomplish. When she first separated with two small children and no support from their father, she lived with her mother and stepfather. She soon got on family benefits, into subsidized housing, and back to college to retrain. After two years of college, she graduated in May, started a good job in June, and bought a townhouse in July. A car was to be next on her list.

Economics

Although poverty is one of the main concerns of single-parent mothers, poverty is a relative concept. One woman describes her status as *"without money, but not poor, not in a city which offers such choices of activities for free, and with friends and family who provide such joy."* Women in this study who were living on less than $10,000 per year as students state that they do not feel particularly deprived. In some cases they share housing, and in others have housing subsidies. When they went through lean times they had help from families, work colleagues, and friends, as well as from government transfer programs. Their lives are not easy, but they demonstrate real resourcefulness. One woman lives in a basement apartment in her grandmother's house in exchange for helping with cleaning and shopping. Another cleans for her sister in exchange for her sister buying her the week's supply of groceries. One woman talks about months of eating macaroni and cheese as she paid off her ex-husband's debts, but even that gave her a feeling of competence: *"I still keep the Kraft Dinner in the cupboard, and if I had to, I could do it again."*

Studies of family finances demonstrate that money is not necessarily distributed evenly or fairly within a family or household. To have some control over distribution of family resources is a very important aspect of wealth or poverty. One woman described her ex-husband as a *"financial maniac."* Another talked about making financial decisions on her own.

> Well, this is my own, thank God! To be in charge of everything that belongs to you! When I was with my ex-husband, I worked and paid the bills and everything, but I wasn't in charge—he had the final say; even if it was good or bad, it was his decision. We'd talk about it, yes, but once he'd made up his mind, that was it. Now I can ask people's opinion about the right thing to do, but the final decision is still mine.

This is not to minimize the hardships of women facing poverty as single parents, but rather to highlight the resourcefulness of many of the women forced to survive under difficult circumstances. This importance of the relative nature and perception of poverty is validated in a study conducted in Britain, "Being Poor: Perceptions and Coping Strategies of Lone Mothers" (Graham 1987). Over 50 percent of the women in Graham's study said they were better off than when they were married, and an additional 11 percent said they were about the same, in spite of the fact that their family income was substantially reduced. They had less money, but more control over it. They economized primarily on meals, which was no sacrifice because it had been their husbands who had insisted upon, and consumed, expensive food. Food consumption in families is commonly distributed along lines of age and gender, with men getting the most expensive dishes and women and children the cheapest (Charles and Kerr 1987). In my study, as well as others, some women indicate that they quite enjoy a different way of shopping and cooking; they control their resources and work within their existing economic constraints. It gives them a feeling of freedom and empowerment, and an enhanced sense of self.

CONCLUSION

Along with the pain and disappointment of lost relationships—as one man put it, "*heartbreak, heartache, trauma and all the rest*"—life in a single-parent family brings with it opportunities for change and growth, and for freedom from the restrictions of the heterosexual nuclear family based on marriage. The narratives uncovered by the study presented here, tentative and unrepresentative as they might be, provide a picture of single parenting that is seldom seen. They suggest that single-parent families are much like two-parent families: there are problems with money, lack of time, and loneliness; and there are the stresses and joys of raising children. Despite their problems, these families can be viewed as representing a stage of one's life or as a preference to marriage, rather than as a failure or a disaster. This profile portrays single-parent families as a viable alternative to other ways of carving out a life for oneself and one's children. It does not mean that these men and women will never again enter a marriage or a live-in relationship. Sometimes they will establish gay and lesbian families; sometimes they will parent other people's biological children. But in Canada there is a continuing increase in divorce, cohabiting instead of marriage, having children without a spouse or live-in partner, and various other household and family arrangements. The definition of family both in government policies and in scholarly studies must take various types of families into account, in all their complexities and diversities.

KEY TERMS

Cohabiting: Two adults living together as though married without being legally married.

Extended family: A family in which kin who are not part of the nuclear family share the same household—for example, grandparents, sisters or brothers of the parents, cousins, nieces, or nephews.

Longitudinal study: Research that follows the same individuals through various life stages over a period of time.

Nuclear family: A family in which only two generations, comprising the mother and father and their children, live in a household.

Single-parent family: A family in which only one parent of the child or children lives in the household in which the child or children are being raised.

DISCUSSION QUESTIONS

1. Most of the literature on single-parent families presents them as poor, lonely, and marginalized. Discuss the ways in which the material in this chapter challenges that view.
2. Analyze the various situations that tended to result in the demise of the marriages and relationships of the people in this study. How might they have been kept intact?
3. What were the characteristics of their parents' marriages that might have contributed to the decisions of the men and women in this study not to marry or to leave a marriage or relationship?
4. Discuss the various strategies used by these single parents to manage their daily lives. Is there a difference between how the women manage and how the men manage?
5. Men are frequently ignored in the literature on single-parent families. What are some of the experiences of single parenting expressed by men in this study?
6. If one of your friends were deciding whether to parent without a live-in partner, what advice would you give to her or him? What information would help the person make this decision?

REFERENCES

American Civil Liberties Union. 1999. "Overview of Lesbian and Gay Parenting, Adoption and Foster Care." ACLU Fact Sheet.

American Psychological Association. 1995. "Lesbian and Gay Parenting: A Resource for Psychologists." *Issues in Gay and Lesbian Adoption: Proceedings of the Fourth Annual Pierce-Warwick Adoption Symposium.* District of Columbia: Child Welfare League of America.

Charles, Nicola, and Marion Kerr. 1987. "Just the Way It Is: Gender and Age Differences in Family and Food Consumption." In Julia Brannen and Gail Wilson, eds., *Give and Take in Families: Studies in Resource Distribution.* London: Allen & Unwin.

Cheal, David, et al. 1997. "Canadian Children in the 1990s: Selected Findings of the National Longitudinal Survey of Children and Youth." *Canadian Social Trends.* Spring 1997. Ottawa: Statistics Canada—Catalogue 11-008-XPE.

Crawford, Maria, and Rosemary Gartner. 1992. *Women Killing.* Oshawa: Women We Honour Action Committee.

Dowd, Nancy E. 1997. *In Defense of Single-Parent Families.* New York: New York University Press.

Eichler, Margrit. 1997. *Family Shifts: Families, Policies, and Gender Equity.* Toronto: Oxford University Press.

Freeman, Rhonda. 1999. "When Parents Part: Helping Children Adjust." In "Lone Parents and Their Children." *Transition Magazine.* Spring 1999. Vol. 29 No. 1. Ottawa: Vanier Institute of the Family.

Furstenberg, Frank F., and Kathleen E. Kiernan. May 2001. "Delayed Parental Divorce: How Much Do Children Benefit?" *Journal of Marriage and Family* 63: 446–457.

Galarneau, Diane, and Jim Sturrock. Summer 1997. "Family Income after Separation." *Perspectives.* Statistics Canada—Catalogue no. 75-001-XPE.

Gorlick, Carolyne A. 2000. "Divorce: Options Available, Constraints Forced, Pathways Taken." In Nancy Mandell and Ann Duffy, eds., *Canadian Families: Diversity, Conflict, and Change,* 2nd ed. Toronto: Harcourt Canada.

Gorlick, Carolyne, and Alan Pomfret. 1999. "Shifting Sands: How Families Move In and Out of Lone Parenting." *Transition Magazine*. Spring 1999. Vol. 29, No. 1. Ottawa: Vanier Institute of the Family.

Graham, Hilary. 1987. "Being Poor: Perceptions and Coping Strategies of Lone Mothers." In Julia Brannen and Gail Wilson, eds., *Give and Take in Families: Studies in Resource Distribution*. London: Allen & Unwin.

Haddad, Tony. 1998. "Custody Arrangements and the Development of Emotional or Behavioural Problems in Children." Working Paper W-98-9E. Applied Research Branch, Human Resources and Development Canada.

Hochschild, Arlie. 1989. *The Second Shift*. New York: Avon Books.

Hochschild, Arlie Russell. 1997. *The Time Bind: When Work Becomes Home and Home Becomes Work*. New York: Metropolitan Books.

Hudson, Joe, and Burt Galaway, eds. 1993. *Single Parent Families: Perspectives on Research and Policy*. Toronto: Thomson Educational Publishing.

Hull, Jeremy. 2001. "Aboriginal Single Mothers in Canada, 1996: A Statistical Profile." Winnipeg: Prologica Research Inc. Ottawa: Indian Affairs and Northern Development Canada. Catalogue No. R2–164/1996.

Johnson, Karen, Donna Lero, and Jennifer Rooney. 2001. *Work-Life Compendium 2001: 150 Canadian Statistics on Work, Family and Well-Being*. Ottawa: Human Resources Development Canada Women's Bureau.

Kelloway, Karen, and Yvette Walton. 1998. "Single Parent Family Week Recognized." St. John's, NF: Human Resources and Employment.

Kissman, Kris, and Jo Ann Allen. 1993. *Single Parent Families*. Newbury Park, CA: Sage Publications.

Laroche, Mireille. Autumn 1998. *Canadian Social Trends*. Statistics Canada—Catalogue No. 11-008-XPE. Ottawa: Supply and Services Canada.

Lipman, Ellen L., Michael H. Boyle, Martin D. Dooley, and David R. Offord. October 1998. "Children and Lone-Mother Families: An Investigation of Factors Influencing Child Well-Being." W-98-11E. [First Internet Edition, 1998.] Ottawa: Human Resources Development Canada.

Luxton, Meg. 1990. "Two Hands for the Clock." In Luxton et al., *Through the Kitchen Window: The Politics of Home and Family*. Toronto: Garamond Press.

Marcil-Gratton, Nicole. 1993. "Growing Up with a Single Parent, a Transitional Experience? Some Demographic Measurements." In J. Hudson and B. Galaway, eds., *Single Parent Families: Perspectives on Research and Policy*. Toronto: Thomson Educational Publishing.

Marcil-Gratton, Nicole. 1999. "Growing Up with Mom and Dad? Canadian Children Experience Shifting Family Structures." *Transition Magazine*. Spring 1999. Vol. 29 No. 1. Ottawa: Vanier Institute of the Family.

McKie, Craig. 1993. "An Overview of Lone Parenthood in Canada." In J. Hudson and B. Galaway, eds., *Single Parent Families: Perspectives on Research and Policy*. Toronto: Thomson Educational Publishing, Inc.

McQuillan, Kevin, and Marilyn Belle. 2001. "Lone-Father Families in Canada, 1971–1996." *Canadian Studies in Population 28* (1), 67–88.

Milan, Anne. Spring 2000. "One Hundred Years of Families." *Perspectives*. Statistics Canada—Catalogue No. 11-008. Ottawa: Supply and Services Canada.

Miller, R. Robin and Sandra Lee Browning. 2000. "Sharing a Man: Insights from Research." *Journal of Comparative Family Studies 31*, 3 (Summer): 339–346.

Nichols-Casebolt, Ann, and Judy Krysik. 1997. "The Economic Well-Being of Never- and Ever-Married Single Mother Families: A Cross-National Comparison." *Journal of Social Service Research 23* (1): 19–40.

Picot, Garnett, and John Myles. Autumn 1996. "Children in Low-Income Families." *Canadian Social Trends*. Statistics Canada—Catalogue 11-008-XPE. Ottawa: Supply and Services Canada.

Pluviati, Olga. 1996. "Consequences to Society Correlated with an Increase in Children from Single-Parent Families." Prepared by Praxis Research Associates Social Science Consultants. Submitted to Entraide Pères-Enfants Séparés. Hull, Québec.

Ross, David P., Paul A. Roberts, and Katherine Scott. 1998a. "Comparing Children in Lone-Parent Families: Differences and Similarities." Paper prepared for Investing in Children: A National Research Conference. 1998.

Ross, David P., Paul A. Roberts, and Katherine Scott. 1998b. "Mediating Factors in Child Development Outcomes: Children in Lone-Parent Families." W-98-8E. Ottawa: Human Resources Development Canada.

Ross, David P., Paul A. Roberts, and Katherine Scott. 1998c. "Variations in Child Development Outcomes Among Children Living in Lone-Parent Families." W-98-7E. Ottawa: Human Resources Development Canada.

Sev'er, Aysan. 1992. *Women and Divorce in Canada*. Toronto: Canadian Scholars' Press.

Smith, Melanie, and Paul Kohn. 2002. "Divorce, Hassles, and Coping Adaptiveness." Toronto: York University. Unpublished paper.

Statistics Canada. 1989. Family History Survey. Catalogue no. 89-509. Ottawa: Supply and Services Canada.

Statistics Canada. 1992. Canadian General Social Survey. Ottawa: Supply and Services Canada.

Statistics Canada. 1996. Health Indicators: Lone-parent Families as a Proportion of All Census Families Living in Private Households, Canada, Provinces, Territories and Health Regions, 1996. Catalogue no. 82-221-XIE. Ottawa: Supply and Services Canada.

Statistics Canada. 2001. Income in Canada 1999. Catalogue no. 75-202-XPE. Ottawa: Minster of Industry, 2001.

Vanier Institute of the Family. 2001. "Family Facts." Ottawa: The Vanier Institute of the Family.

Walton, Dawn. "Divorce Rate Up Slightly, Statscan Says." *The Globe and Mail*. December 3, 2002. P.A4.

3

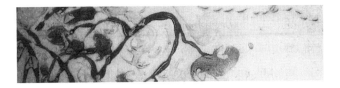

Kinship and Stepfamilies

Elizabeth Church

University Counselling Centre
Memorial University of Newfoundland

Objectives

- To explore the complexities and dynamics of stepfamilies.

- To examine how stepfamilies may differ from nondivorced, nuclear families.

- To introduce terminology and concepts relating to the study of kinship.

- To provide a review of recent research on stepfamilies.

INTRODUCTION

The number of stepfamilies in North America has rapidly increased over the last 30 years. In the United States, half of all current marriages are remarriages for at least one of the partners; one-third of American children will live in a stepfamily at some point before they become adults, while 40 percent of adult women will be part of a stepfamily (Coleman, Ganong, and Fine 2000). The numbers are less dramatic in Canada, where the rates of divorce and remarriage are lower. Nevertheless, by the early 1990s only about one-third of Canadian children were born into "traditional" families where there were two married parents who had not lived together prior to marriage (Juby, Marcil-Gratton, and Le Bourdais 2001). Twenty-six percent of men and 15 percent of women who had been married more than once identified themselves as stepparents (Ram 1990). The 1994–95 National Longitudinal Survey of Children and Youth, which looked at the family histories of 22,831 Canadian children, found that 8.6 percent of Canadian children under age 12 lived in a stepfamily (Marcil-Gratton 1998). The actual number of stepfamilies may also be under-reported because researchers often only count families where couples are legally remarried, while the reality is that couples with children are increasingly cohabiting without marriage (Bumpass, Raley, and Sweet 1995; Coleman, Ganong, and Fine 2000; Juby, Marcil-Gratton, and Le Bourdais 2001; Vanier Institute 1994).

Despite the huge number of stepfamilies in North America today, they still lack recognition and legitimacy. Even in the last Canadian census, in 2001, stepfamilies were not formally counted. Respondents were required to list their stepsons and stepdaughters as "sons" and "daughters" (Statistics Canada 2001; Statistics Canada 1996), thus masking their true status as stepfamilies. Although the traditional **nuclear family,** where children live with their two married parents, now represents a minority of Canadian families, it still dominates as the ideal for how families "should" be. Other kinds of families, such as lone-parent families and stepfamilies, are considered less valuable. The tendency to label the stepfamily as "dysfunctional," "inadequate," or "problematic" because it varies in some ways from the nuclear has been called the **deficit-comparison model** (Ganong and Coleman 1984). Compared with biological parents, stepparents and lone parents are viewed negatively (Coleman and Ganong 1995). Even in the professional literature on families, where one might expect a balanced view of stepfamilies, writers often concentrate on the problematic aspects (Coleman, Ganong, and Goodwin 1994).

Another indication that stepfamilies are not fully accepted is that there is no consensus about what to call a family where at least some of its members were part of an earlier family. *Stepfamily* is the most commonly used term. If you look in many dictionaries, however, you will see that this word is not listed. At least 23 names have been used to describe stepfamilies: for example, reconstituted families, blended families, remarried families, binuclear families (Schlesinger 1983). Each of these represents an attempt to define stepfamilies more precisely, but none really captures their complexity. For example, the term **binuclear family** (Ahrons and Wallisch 1987) was developed to reflect how, after divorce, one family now lives in two households. Yet, in remarriages where both members of the couple have children from previous relationships, the family may spread across three households. Even when there is a commonly accepted word, like *stepmother* or *stepchild*, it often has negative connotations. Everyone is familiar with the cruel and wicked stepmothers of fairy tales, and the word *stepchild* is commonly used to denote neglect or abuse. This stigmatizing and the lack of agreement about what to call stepfamilies highlights their ambiguous presence in our society. Andrew Cherlin (Cherlin 1985; Cherlin and Furstenberg 1994) has argued that stepfamilies are "incompletely institutionalized," by which he means there are few guidelines and norms to help them know how to interact and develop. He maintains that stepfamily stress can be attributed in part to the lack of societal support.

Even to talk about "the stepfamily" is misleading. There are many different types of stepfamilies, each with a distinct structure. We need to consider at least two main variables: one, residence (where the children live); and two, relationship (whose children are whose: either one partner has children from previous relationships or both do, and/or they may have mutual children from this relationship). Since women are most often awarded custody of their children (Ram 1990), the most common type of stepfamily is the **stepfather stepfamily,** where a stepfather lives with a woman and her children from a prior relationship. A family where children live with their father and stepmother is called a **stepmother stepfamily.** As joint custody becomes more frequent (Maccoby and Mnookin 1992), stepfamilies where children move between two main residences have become more prevalent. The **complex stepfamily,** where both partners in the couple have children from previous relationships, is another form. If a couple in a complex stepfamily has a mutual child, this family will include siblings, **stepsiblings** (siblings through marriage), and **half siblings** (siblings sharing a biological tie through one parent). These children may live with one parent full time, may live primarily with one parent but visit another on weekends, may split their week between parents, or may have worked out some other arrangement for sharing their time. If we consider all possible residential arrangements for children, there are 30 different types of stepfamilies (Ganong and Coleman 1994). Each of these stepfamilies may interact very differently.

The age of children at the time a stepfamily joins together also affects its development. Some studies show that a stepfamily where the children were young at the time of their parent's remarriage tends to act like a nondivorced, nuclear family (Burgoyne and Clark 1984). Early adolescence seems to be a particularly difficult time for children to have their parents remarry or re-partner. In a longitudinal study (studying the same people over time) of divorce and remarriage, Mavis Hetherington (Hetherington and Jodl 1993) found that early adolescent children had the most difficulty adjusting to their parents' re-partnering and that their relationships with stepparents were more conflicted. Adolescent children tend to become more distant and disengaged from their biological and stepparents (Hetherington and Jodl 1993) and to leave home earlier than adolescents from nondivorced families (White 1993).

There has been an explosion of research on stepfamilies since 1980, and particularly in the last ten years (Coleman, Ganong, and Fine 2000; Ganong and Coleman 1994).

Stepfather stepfamilies, where the children live full time with their mother and stepfather, have been the most studied. Although the focus on these types of families may be because they are the most common form, they also most closely resemble the nuclear, nondivorced family. I believe that the failure to validate the presence and complexity of stepfamilies in our society results in part from our discomfort with what they represent. In this chapter, I explore some of the reasons for this uneasiness and at the same time outline some of the structures and processes that characterize stepfamilies.

DIVORCE AND REMARRIAGE

Although there has been a recent rapid increase in the number of stepfamilies in North America, historically there were about as many stepfamilies as there are now. Historians and scholars (Gordon 1978; Ihinger-Tallman and Pasley 1987; Stone 1977) estimate that between the 16th and 19th centuries in England and the United States about 20 to 30 percent of families were stepfamilies. The anomalous period in terms of the numbers of stepfamilies is thus the time from about the end of the 19th century, when maternal mortality rates decreased, to about 30 years ago when divorce rates rose.

The main difference between stepfamilies then and now is that the earlier ones were formed as the result of the death of a parent. Today's come about primarily through divorce. In the United States, it was only by the 1950s that stepfamilies created by divorce became more prevalent (Ihinger-Tallman and Pasley 1987). In Canada, the divorce rate rose significantly between 1972 and 1976 following the 1968 *Divorce Act*, which made divorce more easily accessible in all provinces (Dumas and Péron 1992). Since then, the number of stepfamilies in Canada has also increased.

There is little research comparing stepfamilies following the death of a parent and those as a consequence of divorce, even though there are obvious structural differences. In a stepfamily formed after the death of a parent, the children generally live with the surviving parent and the stepparent and there is only one household. When both parents are living, there are usually two households, and the children may move from one to the other. Household boundaries with the latter group are often more permeable than those formed after death. In her study of 60 Canadian adolescents living in stepfamilies, Penny Gross (1985) found that a third had changed residence at least once. In my study of stepmothers, 35 percent of the stepmothers had had at least one stepchild move in or out of their residence at least once. For example, when one stepmother, Amy (all the names and some details have been changed in this example and any other references to stepmothers in my study), started living with Peter, his three children (Eric, Rebecca, and Melanie) lived with their mother and her new husband and visited their father on weekends (the "traditional" arrangement for stepfamilies). When Eric was 14, he decided he wanted to live with his father and moved in with Amy and Peter. Rebecca was having problems with her stepfather so she moved in as well, but returned to her mother's house after two years. None of these changes was recorded through the courts, so that Peter's ex-wife was still legally recognized as the custodial parent (the one with custody of the children). Each move made significant changes in each household. Amy, for example, had initially expected that she would have fun and relaxed weekend visits with her stepchildren. Instead, she found herself disciplining two teenagers as well as cooking and cleaning for them.

Even with the prevalence of divorce, it still carries a *stigma,* or negative label. When college students rated hypothetical situations about parents and children from intact nuclear families, single-parent families, and stepfamilies, they considered children from divorced families less stable and secure than children from nondivorced, nuclear families (Coleman and Ganong 1987). The popular press also emphasizes the negative aspects of divorce. Expressions such as "broken home" are still common, and studies showing that divorce has a harmful effect on children are given a lot of attention in the media (Whitehead 1993). Divorce is expected to cause problems. This attitude may be in part because society is still generally oriented toward first marriages, where there is only one household and the family configuration is constant. Any departure is seen as deviant or harmful.

Another way to conceptualize divorce is to recognize it as a normal part of many people's lives. For many, divorce is part of a developmental life cycle. In the United States, "serial marriage," where people marry and divorce a number of times, has become increasingly common (Coleman, Ganong, and Fine 2000). Some writers (Stone 1977) speculate that there is a natural duration to marriages. Now that people are living longer, divorce has become the way to maintain that length. Seeing divorce as a part of life for many people is not to deny that divorce and remarriage can cause significant upheaval in people's lives. Both can be painful and difficult events with long-term effects. It is not all bad news, however. In a review of research on the effects of divorce on children, Amato (2000) found that, while children with divorced parents score lower than children with married parents on measures such as academic success, psychological adjustment, and social competence, the differences are fairly small. In assessing the impact of parental divorce on children, we need to consider multiple factors such as conflict between the parents, post-divorce economic hardship, and support from peers, and not assume that divorce is the main variable.

In North America, although women remarry less often than men, both men and women remarry frequently and fairly quickly after divorce. In Canada it is estimated that 76 percent of men and 44 percent of women who divorce will remarry (Ram 1990), and 75 percent of them will do so within three years of divorce. In the United States, half the men and women remarry within three years of their divorce, and 84 percent of men and 75 percent of women eventually remarry (Cherlin 1988). Women's and men's rates of remarriage are linked with their economic status. Following divorce, the standard of living for many women and children drops (and child-support payments do not make up the difference), while on average most men's standards of living increase (Maccoby and Mnookin 1992). After remarriage, most women's financial situations improve, while men's worsen (Ganong and Coleman 1994). Women who are highly educated and financially and occupationally independent tend to remarry less often, while the opposite pattern occurs with men, so that high-income men remarry more frequently than low-income men (Crosbie-Burnett, Skyles, and Becker-Haven 1988; Ihinger-Tallman and Pasley 1987). It may be that some women remarry to get themselves out of difficult economic circumstances.

KINSHIP

In our society, *kinship*—family relations—is based on the *marital dyad,* or married couple (Firth 1956; Johnson 1988; Mead 1970; Schneider 1980). In other societies kinship may be established by the relationship between brothers and sisters or the links to the wife's or husband's family. If a marriage ends in a society where kinship links are through brothers and sisters, kinship bonds are often strengthened rather than weakened (Johnson 1988). In our society, however, the breakup of a marriage can cause a great deal of instability. Without an extended family to act as a support, divorce may lead to a situation where people feel they are floating around without an anchor. The emphasis on the marital relationship and the lack of an extended-kin network may also account for some of the effects of divorce on children, because children may also lose their family through their parents' separation. Margaret Mead, an anthropologist who was herself a stepmother, made these observations about the American family:

> We are a society in which the union of a male and female institutes a new social unit... Neither the father's kin nor the mother's kin have any legal responsibility for the children, as long as the parents are alive... Each American child learns, early and in terror, that his [sic] whole security depends on that single set of parents who, more often than not, are arguing furiously in the next room over some detail in their lives. A desperate demand upon the permanence and all-satisfyingness of monogamous marriage is set up in the cradle. (Mead 1970, 113)

Because we do not have a strong extended-family structure, we depend heavily on the marital relationship to provide support and nurturance for children. When the marital relationship collapses, this causes more chaos than might occur in an extended-kin network.

One reason for the high rate of remarriage in our society may be that men and women lose their family through divorce and thus seek to fill this vacuum quickly. Johnson (1988) found that women who became closer to their parents after divorce—that is, created a new kin network with their parents—were less apt to remarry, while men and women who decreased contact with their parents tended to become involved in relationships more frequently and faster.

Generally, the remarried couple forms the centre of a new stepfamily. This emphasis on the marital couple does not work as neatly in the stepfamily, however, as it does in the nuclear, nondivorced family. Relationships predating the marriage, such as the parent–child relationship, may be stronger than the newly married dyad's bond. People not living with the new family, such as nonresidential parents, will usually have an impact on the stepfamily.

People in stepfamilies may also have diverse ideas about what it means to be part of this kind of family. In my study of 104 stepmothers, I discovered that these women conceptualized *kinship*—whom they considered part of their family—in five distinct ways (Church 1999b). One group was what I called *nuclear stepmothers*. These women adopted the nuclear family as their model for the stepfamily. They defined their family as themselves, their partners, stepchildren, and biological children. They often wanted to sever contact with nonresidential family members, such as ex-spouses and in-laws. All assumed a mother role with their stepchildren, which led them to feel in competition with their stepchildren's mother. A second group was the *extended stepmothers*. They also considered their stepchildren kin, but did not view themselves as a mother. Their view of kinship was elastic and they welcomed remarriage as an opportunity to expand their network of connections. In describing their families, they often included extended kin, such as their ex-partner or their partner's ex-wife's family. The *couple stepmothers*, by contrast, focused on their relationship with their partner and saw this as the centre of the stepfamily. They did not consider their stepchildren part of their family, as they believed their stepchildren already had enough parenting from their biological parents. Their ideal relationship was to be a friend to their stepchildren. A fourth group was the *biological stepmothers*, who divided family along biological lines. They saw two families living in the same house: the stepmother and her children as one family and her partner and his children as the other. Finally, there were the *no-family stepmothers*. They felt alone in the situation and regarded themselves as outsiders to the stepfamily, which they considered their partner and his children. They were the most unhappy stepmothers and generally had very poor relationships with their stepchildren. Of course, I was talking to only one member of the stepfamily. It is probable that others, such as biological parents and stepchildren, have a different perspective on their family.

MULTIPLICITY OF ROLES IN STEPFAMILIES

The number and variety of relationships are much greater in stepfamilies than in nuclear, nondivorced families. In order to give an idea of how relationships multiply in stepfamilies, let me give you an example of one stepmother from my study. Her story is typical of many others. Hazel was originally married to Kurt, with whom she had two children: Alice and Bob. Within this family, Hazel had three different relationships: as a wife to Kurt, a mother to her daughter Alice, and a mother to her son Bob. After nine years of marriage, she and Kurt separated. Two years later she met George, who had been married to Laura and had two children, Kathleen and Noel. Hazel and George formed what is called a *complex stepfamily*, because both brought children from a previous relationship. Hazel's ex-husband Kurt subsequently married Ann, and they had a daughter, Elizabeth, and a son, Jesse. George's ex-partner Laura met Ravi and they began living together. It may help to chart all these relationships on a genogram (see Figure 3.1). A **genogram** is a graphic way to represent family relations and is an easy way to grasp the relationships in a family structure as complicated as this one. It is often used to trace families back through generations. (For more information about how to construct genograms, see Monica McGoldrick and Randy Gerson's [1985] book.)

As a result of living with George, the number of Hazel's kin relationships has radically increased. She now has nine (instead of three): with her current partner, George; with her former husband, Kurt; with her daughter, Alice; with her son, Bob; with her stepdaughter, Kathleen; with her stepson, Noel; with her partner's ex-wife, Laura; with her ex-husband's current wife, Ann; and with her partner's ex-wife's current partner, Ravi. Similarly, Hazel's daughter Alice has also tripled the number of kinship links she had in her original family. In charting this family, I have stayed within two generations and have not even considered the mushrooming of other extended kin. Alice, for example, has acquired two more sets of grandparents as the result of her parents' new relationships. The multiplication of potential relationships in stepfamilies is staggering.

One sign that we, as a society, have not acknowledged the complexities of stepfamilies is that we have no terms for some of the relationships. Hazel, for example, has no names for three of her nine roles. She can call herself a partner, an ex-wife, a mother, and a step-mother, but what does she call herself in relation to her partner's ex-wife Laura; her ex-husband's current wife Ann; and her partner's ex-wife's current partner Ravi? Lacking a way to describe these relationships may leave people unprepared to deal with them. In my study, many stepmothers said they had no idea of the complications that the new stepfamily would bring. While they had recognized they were adding their partner and his children to their lives, they usually did not anticipate the impact of their partner's ex-wife, or their partner's ex-wife's current partner. In Hazel's case, she and Ann (her ex-husband's current wife) have worked together to develop a homework schedule for Alice, who has school difficulties. In

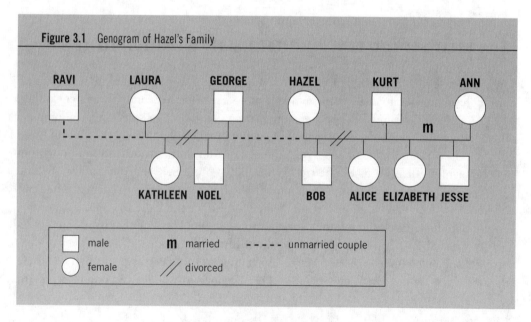

Figure 3.1 Genogram of Hazel's Family

order to plan last summer's vacations, she had to work around many people's work schedules—including Ravi's (her partner's ex-wife's current partner), whom she has rarely met.

There are few societal models for the multiplicity of relationships created by stepfamilies. Members of stepfamilies often struggle with how to act and interact with these new people. From the start, Hazel was very uncomfortable with the constant presence of Laura, her partner's ex-wife, in her life:

> When I first started living with George, Laura would come over after school to visit with the children [Hazel's stepchildren, Kathleen and Noel] during the times the children were living with us. I felt really uncomfortable about having in her in the house when I wasn't home, but I didn't think I could say anything because she and George had had this arrangement before I came on the scene. But I would sit at work imagining that she was going through my kitchen cupboards, and it bothered me so much that George told Laura he didn't want her in the house unless we were there. So then she got mad and refused to come into the house at all and would stay in the car and honk the horn for Kathleen and Noel to come out. They got angry with me and told their father that I was unreasonable ... I ended up feeling like the wicked stepmother.

One way some people deal with the ambiguity of relationships in stepfamilies is to exclude nonresidential members. Following divorce, nonresidential parents often lose contact with their children. Frank Furstenberg (1988) found that 44 percent of children had no communication with their nonresidential parent in the previous year, while 21 percent visited their nonresidential parent less than once a week. The 35 percent of nonresidential parents who saw their children more than once a week tended to have more recreational than instrumental contact; that is, they were more likely to take their children to the movies than help them with their homework. There are multiple reasons why nonresidential parents do not maintain their connection with their children. Some nonresidential parents in Furstenberg's study said they felt "awkward" visiting their children, or that it was too "emotionally painful." Our model of kinship, where so much hinges on the marital relationship, may contribute to this awkwardness. When a marriage ends and one parent, usually the father, moves out, he has to renegotiate a new relationship with his children, one not based on day-to-day living. Since we have few models for how nonresidential kin can be involved with children in an "instrumental" way, these parents may be unsure how to establish a new footing with their children.

As well, if the residential parent—usually the mother—wants to recreate a nuclear family, she may perceive the nonresidential parent as intrusive. Similar to my finding that some stepmothers attempt to recreate a nuclear family, Burgoyne and Clark (1984) found that over half the families they interviewed tried to forge a nuclear, nondivorced family. These stepfamilies usually wanted the nonresidential parent out of the picture. If your ideal is the nuclear family, you may not see a way to incorporate the new family relations that spring up with remarriage. One solution is to cut off people outside the household.

With joint custody, however, it becomes more difficult to maintain the fiction that a stepfamily can be a nuclear family. When children move regularly between two households, how do we decide which is their "primary" house and who is the residential and who the nonresidential parent? As the number of joint custody situations increases in Canada, and kin do not disappear after divorce and remarriage, a new model of the extended family may emerge.

THE ASSUMPTION THAT HOUSEHOLD EQUALS FAMILY

In our society we tend to merge the concepts of household and family. If we see a man and a woman living in the same house with children, we assume that these individuals are a family. This equating of household with family is very much tied to our ideology about kinship (Rapp 1992), which is dominated by the ideal of the nuclear family. This equation does not hold true for the stepfamily in at least three ways: (1) members of stepfamilies who live together may not feel related; (2) people in stepfamilies use a variety of criteria, in addition to household ties, to determine who is part of their family; and (3) household boundaries in stepfamilies are more fluid than they are in nuclear families.

1. *Members of stepfamilies who live together may not feel related.* The relationship of stepparent and stepchild is that of in-laws: they are related by marriage. In our society in-laws, or **affines**, do not usually live in the same household (Bohannan 1984). We do not generally expect that people will love, or even like, their in-laws—the popularity of mother-in-law jokes bears witness to this. We do expect, however, that residential stepparents, just because they live with someone who has children, will take on a parental role with their stepchildren. Just as we may not like or love in-laws who live outside the household, there is no reason to assume we will like or love the ones we live with. Researchers (Furstenberg 1987; Hetherington and Clingempeel 1992) have found that children in stepfamilies were less likely to feel close to stepparents or to want to be like them when they grew up. This is not to say that all stepparent–stepchild relationships are negative. The majority of stepchildren in Furstenberg's study expressed "benign" if "distant" feelings about their stepparents. What Furstenberg's study demonstrates is that just because stepparents and stepchildren live in the same household, we cannot assume that they will have a close relationship.

In my study of stepmothers, even those stepmothers who got along well with their stepchildren saw significant differences between their relationships with biological children and stepchildren. Often they described themselves "walking on eggshells" with their stepchildren, while they felt more "natural" with their biological children. Gina has been a stepmother for 13 years and is very close with her stepdaughter, Jane, but there is a reserve in her relationship with Jane that has never existed with her biological daughter:

> I still don't think of her [the stepdaughter] as a daughter. I still think of her as a stepdaughter. I've only known her since she was a teenager, while with my daughter who's three and a half I have a completely different relationship. I have a completely organic kind of relationship

that grew from the ground up. We will have a history, and I know everything about her and she knows everything about me, and I'm completely comfortable with her. To this day I don't feel like that about Jane.

The barrier of not having a common history was a frequent theme in my study. In stepfamilies, some people share a history while others do not. This can lead to people feeling like outsiders. To return to Hazel (whose family was charted on the genogram), her struggles with her partner's ex-wife Laura stem in part from joining a family that already has its own patterns. When George and Laura separated, he kept the family house and Laura found another place. Hazel and her children later moved into George's house. One reason Laura felt comfortable rummaging through Hazel's kitchen cupboards is that this was once her kitchen. For Hazel, however, Laura's presence was an unwelcome symbol of Laura's history with George.

One consequence of assuming that a household equals a family is that a stepfamily is regarded as a full-fledged family from the moment the couple marries (here again is the tyranny of the ideology of the marital couple). The assumption is that members instantly feel part of a family. Unlike a nondivorced family, which typically starts with the couple having time alone together and then has nine months of pregnancy to adjust to the idea of becoming parents, a stepfamily couple immediately plunges into life with children. Although stepfamilies may look like instant families, most go through a developmental process to become a family. Becoming an integrated stepfamily takes time. Some families take about 2 to 4 years (Visher and Visher 1988), others as long as 12 years, while some stepfamilies never jell as a family (Papernow 1993).

One factor affecting the development of the stepfamily is that, for some of its members, the stepfamily is their third type of family structure. Initially, they were part of a nuclear never-divorced family, then they were in a single-parent family, and now they are in a stepfamily. Not all people in stepfamilies go through this sequence (some exceptions are stepparents who do not have children from a prior relationship, and parents and children who were always in single-parent families), but the majority of members in new stepfamilies have experienced these three types of families. In the example that was charted on the genogram, Hazel was first part of a nuclear family with her husband Kurt and two children, then she formed a single-parent family, and now she has become part of a stepfamily with her new partner George and his children. Each of these types of families tend to have different patterns of interacting, which means members of a new stepfamily have to learn the "rules" of stepfamily life.

This means there has also been the loss of two earlier families. These events are often painful for children, who have little choice about their parents separating and re-partnering. Although there has been a great deal of attention to the effects of divorce on children (the loss of the original nuclear family) (Amato 2000; Hetherington 1987; Hetherington and Aratesh 1988), there has been less research on the effects of ending a single-parent family (Hetherington and Jodl 1993). Children and parents in single-parent families often develop very close bonds, and children may feel pushed aside when their parents become involved in a new adult relationship (Martin and Martin 1992; Visher and Visher 1988).

Forming a new stepfamily also often means bringing together families with different traditions and ways of behaving, from the kinds of foods eaten to how children are disciplined, how birthdays are celebrated, or even which television shows are watched. These patterns derive from cultural and religious backgrounds, experience in one's own family of origin, and the individual family's development over time. In general, remarried couples are less similar to each other in demographics—age, education, religion—than first-married couples (Ganong and Coleman 1994), so a remarrying couple may be bringing together two quite dissimilar families.

Building a stepfamily often means integrating differences and evolving new rules and rituals. This can be a slow process. One stepmother in my study, Angie, had children from her previous marriage, as did her husband, Ernesto. When they tried to decorate their first Christmas tree, the two sets of stepsiblings ended up squabbling about whose decorations would go on the tree. Angie's solution was to have two trees, one for each family:

> The first couple of years after we got married, we had two Christmas trees, one in the living room and one in the rec room. Once they [Angie's biological children and stepchildren] got older, I could say to them, "It's really a big hassle," but the first couple of years, there was so much decoration and everybody wanted everything: my kids wanted this because we had always had it on our tree, and the other ones wanted that because they had it on their tree.

Eventually the family was ready to share a Christmas tree, but the children needed the transitional time in order to feel their own Christmas traditions would be preserved.

2. People in stepfamilies use a variety of criteria, in addition to household ties, in deciding who is part of their family. Stepfamilies are spread over at least two households. People may feel stronger ties to people living outside their household than to those with whom they live. A child may live with her mother and stepfather, and this will be called her family, but her strongest attachment may be to her father whom she visits on weekends. In the National Survey on Children done in the United States, children were asked: "When you think of your family, who do you include?" A third of children in stepfamilies did not mention a stepparent, while only 10 percent left out a parent, even if that parent was absent or saw the child infrequently (Whitehead 1993). For some people in stepfamilies, the biological bond takes precedence over the household bond. In the nondivorced family these two bonds are not at odds, because the household contains biologically related kin. In the stepfamily, in-laws live with one another and biologically related kin live apart.

Who, then, is the stepfamily? Many writers about stepfamilies include only those families where the children live full time, not recognizing the strong loyalties between nonresidential parents and children. The reckoning about who is part of a stepfamily depends on who is talking. When I charted Hazel and her family on the genogram, I focused on only one dimension: the relationships among the various kin. Let us now add another dimension: their households (see Figure 3.2). Bob lives with his mother, Hazel, and his stepfather,

George, while his sister Alice lives with her father, Kurt, her stepmother, Ann, and her half siblings Elizabeth and Jesse. George's two children from his previous marriage, Kathleen and Noel, live half time with him and their stepmother, Hazel, and half time with their mother, Laura, and her partner, Ravi. We can add this dimension to the genogram by enclosing households within dotted lines.

When I asked Hazel whom she considered part of her family, she included her two biological children, her current partner, George, and her stepchildren, Kathleen and Noel, but she did not mention Kurt, her ex-husband. By contrast, if I had asked her son Bob who his family was, he probably would have included Kurt, who is his father, as well as his mother and his sister Alice. He might also have mentioned his stepfather (George), depending on his relationship with him. Bob's sister, Alice, might also count her stepmother, Ann, her half sister, Elizabeth, and her half brother, Jesse, because she lives with them. Thus, each of them would draw their family differently. If I had asked Hazel, Bob, and Alice whom they considered their family when they were still part of their original nuclear family, they all would have probably listed the same people.

In her study of 60 Canadian adolescents living in stepfamilies, Penny Gross (1985) asked them who was part of their family. Based on their answers, she developed a typology of four ways of defining remarried families. The most common type was *retention*, where the adolescents included both the residential and nonresidential biological parent but excluded stepparents. The second type was *substitution*, where the nonresidential biological parent was excluded and a residential stepparent replaced that parent. In the third type, *reduction*, one residential parent was omitted and a stepparent was not added in, and in the fourth type, *augmentation*, the adolescents included both biological parents and at least one step-

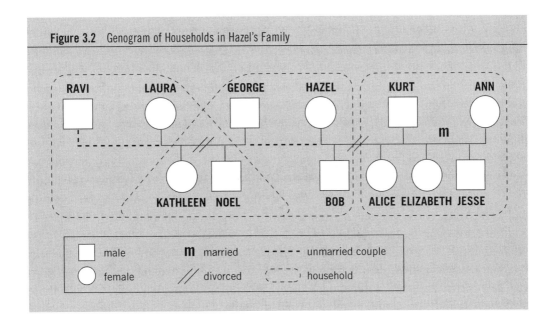

Figure 3.2   Genogram of Households in Hazel's Family

parent (usually the residential one) as part of their family. When Gross looked at how the adolescents determined who was part of their family, she found they used four dimensions: *procreative*, based on blood or biological ties; *residential*, who they lived with; *emotional*, who they felt close to; and *social*, who they interacted with or spent time with. Thus, people in stepfamilies use a variety of criteria to decide whom they consider kin. Gross attended only to the parental level. The adolescents in her study also inherited lots of other kin through remarriage, such as stepsiblings, half siblings, step-grandparents, and step-uncles and -aunts.

There is also a large degree of choice in deciding who is part of one's family. In my study stepmothers often picked and chose whom they considered relations. Often they felt related to those people whom they liked or to whom they felt close. Paula, for example, had children from her previous marriage, as did her current husband, Barry. Both her parents and Barry's parents had disapproved of their remarriage and refused to acknowledge their respective step-grandchildren. Through her stepchildren, Paula got to know Barry's ex-wife's parents (her stepchildren's maternal grandparents), who were very encouraging of Paula's efforts to create a new family life for the two sets of children. They invited Paula and Barry and the children to spend summer vacations at their cottage and became so close to all the children that Paula's children started calling them "Grandma" and "Grandpa," even though there are no biological or legal ties. Paula now considers her husband's ex-wife's parents kin because they supported her when her own family did not.

Some writers (Popenoe 1993; Whitehead 1993) see the looser ties in stepfamilies as negative and harmful to children. Rather than considering the advantages of an extended-kin network, they focus on how the stepfamily is, to its detriment, not like the nuclear family. When we think about stepfamilies, we need to think more expansively. Although few would deny that becoming part of a stepfamily can create stresses (and I will discuss some of them in the next section), there are also potential benefits—for instance, that remarriage may increase the number of people who care for the children.

3. *Household boundaries in stepfamilies are flexible.* Boundaries are more fluid in stepfamilies and stepfamilies tend to be less cohesive than nondivorced families (Visher and Visher 1988). There are a number of reasons for this. First, children move around more. They may move between households weekly or biweekly, or they may make more permanent moves—for example, when a child changes his or her principal residence to live with the other parent. It is not always clear who is, and is not, part of the household.

Second, adolescents from stepfamilies are more likely to leave home earlier and live on their own than adolescents from nondivorced families (White 1993; White and Booth 1985). It is unclear from these studies whether the adolescents left on their own or were encouraged to leave, but it appears that looser structures in stepfamilies mean that adolescents become independent more quickly.

Third, the boundaries between people tend to be fuzzier in stepfamilies. Who one is in relation to others in a stepfamily is often unclear. My daughter may marry a man with two children so that I am now a step-grandmother. What should my relationship be with these children? Should I act like a grandmother? A friendly, concerned adult? An uninvolved, distant adult? Each decision I make will affect other relationships. If I give my step-grandchildren birthday presents, will their maternal grandparents feel usurped? Will my biological grandchildren feel jealous? Will my daughter feel I am slighting her children? On the other hand, if I don't give them presents, will my son-in-law be upset?

Although the flexibility of boundaries in stepfamilies may give members of the stepfamily more freedom and choice, it also can lead to less stability and more stress. The divorce rate for remarriages is higher than for first marriages (Cherlin and Furstenberg 1994; Ganong and Coleman 1994; White and Booth 1985). The reasons for this are still not completely clear. Some researchers have found that remarriages with stepchildren living in the household are more likely than those without stepchildren to end in divorce, and that the presence of stepchildren placed strain on the marital relationship (Hobart and Brown 1988; White and Booth 1985). Other studies have not shown this effect (Ganong and Coleman 1994). It may be that the presence of children creates problems for only some stepfamilies. The looser boundaries in stepfamilies may also lead some to resolve conflict by changing the composition of the family and dissolving the marriage.

How then are children living in stepfamilies affected by decreased stability and cohesiveness? The popular opinion (Whitehead 1993) is that stepfamilies are negative environments for children. The research findings are more complex, however. In their thorough review of recent research on stepfamilies, Coleman, Ganong, and Fine (2000) found that, while stepchildren were generally at greater risk of problems such as lower school achievement and depression than were children living with two biological parents, the differences between the two groups were small. There is no simple answer to the question about the effect of remarriage on children. Multiple factors must be considered: for example, the age and sex of the children at the time of divorce and remarriage, the stepfamily's financial situation, the type of parenting, the complexity of the stepfamily, and so on. In their longitudinal studies on children's development in remarried families, Hetherington and her colleagues (Hetherington and Jodl 1993) found that about one-quarter to about one-third of children in stepfamilies experienced serious emotional and behavioural problems, compared to about one in ten children in nondivorced families. The longer the children lived in their stepfamilies, the smaller the number with serious problems. It appears that, after an initial difficult adjustment period, most children do fine in stepfamilies (Hetherington and Aratesh 1988; Hetherington and Jodl 1993).

STEPPARENT AND GENDER ROLES

Just as stepfamilies are expected to function like nondivorced families, so too are stepparents expected to take on the role of parents. Not only is this imposed from without, but stepparents themselves often believe that they should be parents to their stepchildren. As part of my interviews with stepmothers, I asked them to define a "good stepmother" (Church 1994). The majority believed a good stepmother should act and feel exactly the same as a good mother. That is, they collapsed together the roles of mother and stepmother. This ideal often created a conflict for them, however, because in their daily life they rarely could act as a mother to their stepchildren.

There are a number of reasons why stepparents cannot, and perhaps should not, attempt to be parents, particularly at the beginning. First, the biological parents are often already involved in the children's lives and may resent what they see as the stepparents' interference. Second, children often do not want a replacement parent and will reject stepparents if they try to discipline or direct them. Third, especially at the beginning, stepparents are the "outsiders" (Smith 1990) to the family and need to take time to find a way in. Fourth, stepparents' traditions and expectations about families may be quite different from, and conflict with, patterns and rules already present in the stepfamily. And fifth, stepparents have no legal status in relation to their stepchildren. This lack underlines their tenuous position in the stepfamily. In most places in North America, for instance, stepparents cannot sign a medical release form if a stepchild needs emergency medical help.

Although step-parenting is often difficult for both men and women, stepmothers seem to find it more stressful than do stepfathers (Ahrons and Wallisch 1987; Ambert 1986; Santrock and Sitterle 1987). This gender differential is very much tied to our differing expectations about how men and women should act in families. Stepmothers are more likely to take on the household work than are stepfathers (Ambert 1986; Coleman, Ganong, and Fine 2000). Even though they are not the biological parent, stepmothers often have primary responsibility for the household tasks and childcare (Ganong and Coleman 1994), become the mediator for family relationships (McGoldrick 1989), and expect themselves to be more involved than do stepfathers (Crosbie-Burnett, Skyles, and Becker-Haven 1988).

Stepparents' difficulties in defining their place in the stepfamily mirror the dilemma faced by the stepfamily as a whole. Just as paradigms for stepfamilies are based on non-divorced families, models for stepparents are often derived from the biological parent role. And, some stepmothers believe that if they cannot achieve being the good mother, then they must be a wicked stepmother (Church 1999a; Morrison and Thompson-Guppy 1985). Smith (1990) found that the more flexibly and broadly stepmothers conceptualized their role, the more satisfied they were. It may be that, just as we need to broaden our thinking about stepfamilies, stepparents may benefit from a more expansive understanding of their relationships with stepchildren.

CLASS, ETHNICITY, AND SEXUALITY

One major limitation to the research on stepfamilies is that it has focused primarily on white, middle-class, heterosexual, married families with a residential mother and stepfather. Although we know that couples with lower socioeconomic status divorce more frequently than those with higher socioeconomic status (Ganong and Coleman 1994; Stone 1990), we know very little about how different economic situations affect the dynamics and development in stepfamilies. Research on nondivorced North American families has shown that the working class, middle class, and upper class define kinship in distinctive ways (Schneider and Smith 1973). It makes sense that stepfamilies from different classes will vary as well. Similarly for cultural background—little attention has been paid to how cultural factors play a role in stepfamilies, yet they likely are significant. One of the stepmothers in my study was from India, as was her partner. She said that her stepchildren easily accepted her presence, because they were surrounded by quasi-kin:

> In India it's different. Like everybody's relative is called an aunt or an uncle. "Uncle" doesn't just mean the mother's brother or father's brother. You could call even a close friend of your parents "Auntie." And if someone was your father's aunt or your mother's uncle, they would be like grandparents.

If stepfamilies are somewhat invisible, in our society gay and lesbian stepfamilies are almost completely unseen. Gay and lesbian stepfamilies are often reluctant to identify themselves publicly because of possible discrimination. In the United States, the majority of lesbian families with children are formed after one or both of the partners leave a heterosexual relationship in which they have had children and then start a new lesbian partnership (this pattern is changing somewhat as alternative insemination is becoming more common) (Hare and Richards 1993). That is, lesbian families are often stepfamilies. There is some evidence to show that nonbiological parents act more like stepparents with children from a previous relationship and more like biological parents with children born in the current relationship. Even when they take on a parental role with their stepchildren, many gay and lesbian stepparents feel they are given even less recognition and support for their work than are heterosexual stepparents (Miller 1989).

CONCLUSION

As long as we continue to hold up nuclear nondivorced families as the ideal for families, we do a disservice to stepfamilies as well as to other kinds of families. When nuclear families are the sole model, stepfamilies look dysfunctional. As we have seen, there are stresses associated with being part of a stepfamily. The initial adjustment is often very difficult and remarried couples are more likely to separate than never-divorced couples. I believe that part of the stress in stepfamilies results from the lack of positive models. People of stepfamilies rely on structures and norms derived from nondivorced families that are often inappropriate.

If we accept stepfamilies as distinct, viable forms of families, we may also expand many of our received notions about families. The fluidity of movement between households, the large extended-kin network, and the multiplicity of roles in the stepfamily mean that a group of people can be a family without being bound by household limits, biological ties, or traditional parental and gender roles. As well as potentially creating a less stable situation, the stepfamily can also offer more choice of kin and greater freedom in defining roles. Perhaps, rather than nuclear families always setting norms for stepfamilies, we can turn our thinking around and use stepfamilies to help challenge some of our unexamined beliefs about how families should act.

KEY TERMS

Affine: Kin who are related through marriage: for example, parents-in-law and daughter-in-law.

Binuclear family: A family that lives in two residences as the result of the separation or divorce of a couple.

Complex stepfamily: A stepfamily where both people in the couple have children from previous relationships.

Deficit-comparison model: Assumption in theory and research that stepfamilies will operate at a disadvantage in comparison to nuclear families.

Genogram: A visual format for constructing a family tree that illustrates information about family relationships.

Half sibling: A brother or sister with whom a biological tie is shared through one parent, but not through the other.

Nuclear family: A family in which a first-married, heterosexual couple lives together with their mutual biological children.

Stepfather stepfamily: A stepfamily where the stepparent is a man who lives with a woman and her biological children.

Stepmother stepfamily: A stepfamily where the stepparent is a woman who lives with a man and his biological children.

Stepsibling: A daughter or son of one's stepparent. Stepsiblings are related by marriage but share no biological tie.

DISCUSSION QUESTIONS

1. What are some of the factors that differentiate stepfamilies from nondivorced families?
2. How do contemporary stepfamilies differ from those of earlier times?
3. What are some societal beliefs and myths we have about stepfamilies? Why might these have arisen?
4. What are some of the reasons contributing to the comparative invisibility of stepfamilies in our society?
5. Why, in general, do women find it more stressful to be a stepparent than do men?

REFERENCES

Ahrons, C.R., and L. Wallisch. 1987. "Parenting in the Bi-nuclear Age: Relationships between Biological and Stepparents." In K. Pasley and M. Ihinger-Tallman, eds., *Remarriage and Stepparenting: Current Research and Theory*. New York: Guilford Press.

Amato, P. 2000. "The Consequences of Divorce for Adults and Children." *Journal of Marriage and the Family 62*: 1269–1287.

Ambert, A.-M. 1986. "Being a Stepparent: Live-in and Visiting Stepchildren." *Journal of Marriage and the Family 48*: 795–804.

Bohannan, P. 1984. "Stepparenthood: A New and Old Experience." In R. Cohen, B. Cohler, and S. Weissman, eds., *Parenthood: A Psychodynamic Perspective*. New York: Guilford Press.

Bumpass, L., K. Raley, and J. Sweet. 1995. "The Changing Character of Stepfamilies: The Implications of Cohabitation and Nonmarital Childbearing." *Demography 32*: 425–436.

Burgoyne, J., and D. Clark. 1984. *Making a Go of It: A Study of Stepfamilies in Sheffield*. London: Routledge & Kegan Paul.

Cherlin, A. 1985. "Remarriage as an Incomplete Institution." In J. Henslin, ed., *Marriage and Family in a Changing Society*, 2nd ed. New York: The Free Press.

Cherlin, A., ed. 1988. *The Changing American Family and Public Policy*. Washington, DC: Urban Institute Press.

Cherlin, A., and F. Furstenberg. 1994. "Stepfamilies in the United States: A Reconsideration." *Annual Review of Sociology 20*: 359–381.

Church, E. 1994. "What Is a Good Stepmother?" Paper presented at the annual conference of the National Council on Family Relations, Minneapolis, MN.

Church, E. 1999a. "Stepmothers as Anti-mothers: Witches or Heroines?" Paper presented at the Conference on Mothers and Education: Issues and Directions for Maternal Pedagogy, St. Catharines, ON.

Church, E. 1999b. "Who Are the People in Your Family? Stepmothers' Diverse Notions of Kinship." *Journal of Divorce and Remarriage 30*: 83–105.

Coleman, M., and L. Ganong. 1995. "Insiders' and Outsiders' Beliefs about Stepfamilies: Assessment and Implications for Practice." In D. Huntley ed., *Understanding Stepfamilies: Implications for Assessment and Treatment* (pp. 101–112). Alexandria, VA: American Counseling Association.

Coleman, M., and L. Ganong. 1987. "The Cultural Stereotyping of Stepfamilies." In K. Pasley and M. Ihinger-Tallman, eds., *Remarriage and Stepparenting: Current Research and Theory*. New York: Guilford Press.

Coleman, M., L. Ganong, and M. Fine. 2000. "Reinvestigating Remarriage: Another Decade of Progress." *Journal of Marriage and the Family 62*: 1288–1307.

Coleman, M., L. Ganong, and C. Goodwin. 1994. "The Presentation of Stepfamilies in Marriage and Family Textbooks." *Family Relations 43*: 289–297.

Crosbie-Burnett, M., A. Skyles, and J. Becker-Haven. 1988. "Exploring Stepfamilies from a Feminist Perspective." In S. Dornbusch and M. Strober, eds., *Feminism, Children and the New Families*. New York: Guilford Press.

Dumas, J., and Y. Péron. 1992. *Marriage and Conjugal Life in Canada: Current Demographic Analysis*. Ottawa: Statistics Canada.

Firth, R. 1956. *Two Studies of Kinship in London*. London: Athlone Press.

Furstenberg, F. 1987. "The New Extended Family." In K. Pasley and M. Ihinger-Tallman, eds., *Remarriage and Stepparenting: Current Research and Theory*. New York: Guilford Press.

Furstenberg, F. 1988. "Childcare after Divorce and Remarriage." In M. Hetherington and J. Aratesh, eds., *Impact of Divorce, Single Parenting, and Stepparenting on Children*. Hillsdale, NJ: Erlbaum.

Ganong, L., and M. Coleman. 1984. "The Effects of Remarriage on Children: A Review of the Empirical Literature." *Family Relations 33*: 389–496.

Ganong, L., and M. Coleman. 1994. *Remarried Family Relationships*. Thousand Oaks, CA: Sage.

Gordon, M., ed. 1978. *The American Family in Social-Historical Perspective*, 2nd ed. New York: St. Martin's Press.

Gross, P. 1985. "Kinship Structures in Remarriage Families." Unpublished doctoral dissertation. Toronto: University of Toronto.

Hare, J., and L. Richards. 1993. "Children Raised by Lesbian Couples: Does Context of Birth Affect Father and Partner Involvement?" *Family Relations 42*: 249–55.

Hetherington, E.M. 1987. "Family Relations Six Years after Divorce." In K. Pasley and M. Ihinger-Tallman, eds., *Remarriage and Stepparenting: Current Research and Theory*. New York: Guilford Press.

Hetherington, E.M., and J. Aratesh. eds. 1988. *Impact of Divorce, Single Parenting and Stepparenting on Children*. Hillsdale, NJ: Erlbaum.

Hetherington, E.M., and W. Clingempeel. 1992. "Coping with Marital Transitions: A Family Systems Perspective." *Monographs of the Society for Research in Child Development 57*.

Hetherington, E.M., and K.M. Jodl. 1993. "Stepfamilies as Settings for Child Development." Paper presented at the National Symposium on Stepfamilies, Pennsylvania State University, University Park.

Hobart, C., and D. Brown. 1988. "Effect of Prior Marriage Children on Adjustment in Remarriage: A Canadian Study." *Journal of Comparative Family Studies 19*: 381–96.

Ihinger-Tallman, M., and K. Pasley. 1987. "Divorce and Remarriage in the American Family: A Historical Review." In K. Pasley and M. Ihinger-Tallman, eds., *Remarriage and Stepparenting: Current Research and Theory*. New York: Guilford Press.

Johnson, C.L. 1988. *Ex Familia: Grandparents, Parents and Children Adjust to Divorce*. New Brunswick, NJ: Rutgers University Press.

Juby, H., N. Marcil-Gratton, and C. Le Bourdais. 2001. *A Step Further in Family Life: The Emergence of the Blended Family. Report on the Demographic Situation in Canada 2000*. Statistics Canada.

Maccoby, E., and R. Mnookin. 1992. *Dividing the Child: Social and Legal Dilemmas of Custody*. Cambridge, MA: Harvard University Press.

Marcil-Gratton, N. 1998. "Growing up with Mom and Dad? The Intricate Family Life Courses of Canadian Children." Statistics Canada, Catalogue 89-566-XIE.

Martin, D., and M. Martin. 1992. *Stepfamilies in Therapy: Understanding Systems, Assessment and Intervention*. San Francisco: Jossey-Bass.

McGoldrick, M. 1989. "Women through the Family Life Cycle." In M. McGoldrick, C. Anderson, and F. Walsh, eds., *Women in Families: A Framework for Family Therapy*. New York: Norton.

McGoldrick, M., and R. Gerson. 1985. *Genograms in Family Assessment*. New York: Norton.

Mead, M. 1970. "Anomalies in American Postdivorce Relationships." In P. Bohannan, ed., *Divorce and After*. New York: Doubleday.

Miller, C. 1989. "Lesbian Stepfamilies and the Myth of Biological Motherhood." In N. Bauer Maglin and N. Schneidewind, eds., *Women and Stepfamilies: Voices of Anger and Love*. Philadelphia: Temple University Press.

Morrison, K., and A. Thompson-Guppy. 1985. "Cinderella's Stepmother Syndrome." *Canadian Journal of Psychiatry 30*: 521–29.

Papernow, P. 1993. *Becoming a Stepfamily*. San Francisco: Jossey-Bass.

Popenoe, D. 1993. "The Evolution of Marriage and the Problem of Stepfamilies." Paper presented at the National Symposium on Stepfamilies, Pennsylvania State University, University Park.

Ram, B. 1990. *New Trends in the Family: Demographic Facts and Features*. Ottawa: Statistics Canada.

Rapp, R. 1992. "Family and Class in Contemporary America: Notes toward an Understanding of Ideology." In B. Thorne and M. Yalom, eds., *Rethinking the Family: Some Feminist Questions*, rev. ed. Boston: Northeastern University Press.

Santrock, J., and K. Sitterle. 1987. "Parent-Child Relationships in Stepmother Families." In K. Pasley and M. Ihinger-Tallman, eds., *Remarriage and Stepparenting: Current Research and Theory*. New York: Guilford Press.

Schlesinger, B. 1983. *Remarriage: A Review and Annotated Bibliography*. Chicago: CPL Biographies.

Schneider, D. 1980. *American Kinship: A Cultural Account*, 2nd ed. Chicago: University of Chicago Press.

Schneider, D., and R. Smith. 1973. *Class Differences and Sex Roles in American Kinship and Family Structure*. Englewood Cliffs, NJ: Prentice Hall.

Smith, D. 1990. *Stepmothering*. Hertfordshire, England: Harvester Wheatsheaf.

Statistics Canada. 2001. "Census Questions 2001." Statistics Canada.

Statistics Canada. 1996. "Census 1996: Questions and Reasons Why Questions Were Asked." Statistics Canada.

Stone, L. 1977. *The Family, Sex and Marriage in England 1500–1800*. London: Weidenfeld and Nicolson.

Stone, L. 1990. *Road to Divorce: England 1530–1987*. Oxford: Oxford University Press.

Vanier Institute of the Family. 1994. *Profiling Canada's Families*. Ottawa: Vanier Institute of the Family.

Visher, E.B., and J.S. Visher. 1988. *Old Loyalties, New Ties: Therapeutic Strategies with Stepfamilies*. New York: Brunner/Mazel.

White, L. 1993. Stepfamilies over the Life Course: Social Support. Paper presented at the National Symposium on Stepfamilies, Pennsylvania State University, University Park.

White, L., and A. Booth. 1985. "The Quality and Stability of Remarriages: The Role of Stepchildren." *American Sociological Review* 50: 689–98.

Whitehead, B.D. 1993. "Dan Quayle Was Right." *The Atlantic Monthly* (April): 47–84.

4

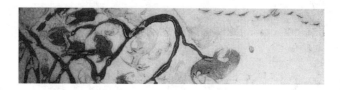

Lesbian Families

Rachel Epstein

PhD Candidate, Faculty of Education, York University
Coordinator, LGBT Parenting Network, David Kelley Services,
Family Service Association of Toronto

Objectives

- To review the research and writing that has been done on lesbian mothers.

- To explore the challenges lesbian families pose to the conventional (male bread-winner/female homemaker) model of the nuclear family.

- To consider the societal forces that undermine these challenges.

- To suggest policy changes that would acknowledge the needs and experiences of lesbian families.

INTRODUCTION

Imagine:

- You have to explain over and over again how your child was conceived.

- You are repeatedly asked in public settings whether you are a "real" parent.

- Your child cannot play with his/her friend from school because the friend's parents are disgusted by your relationship with your partner.

- You are visited by a worker from the Children's Aid Society who has been called by your neighbour complaining that you are an unfit mother.

- Your child is in a medical emergency and you are not allowed to make decisions about the care she/he is to receive.

- Your child's teacher will not speak to you about your child's progress at school.

- Your in-laws will not recognize you as a legitimate parent of their grandchild.

- You are forced to constantly defend your right and your ability to be a parent.

Lesbians raising children is not a new phenomenon. Sandra Pollack and Jeanne Vaughn, in the introduction to their 1987 lesbian parenting anthology, *Politics of the Heart*, remind us that

> there have always been lesbians who were mothers, lesbians who struggled with the decision to have children, lesbians who have gotten pregnant against their will, lesbians who have adopted and/or been foster parents, lesbians who have had children in heterosexual marriages, lesbians who have raised the children of relatives and friends, lesbians who have lost their children, who have had their children taken from them, or who have felt the necessity to give them up, lesbians who have been open, and lesbians who have hidden their lifestyles from their children. (12)

While lesbians have always parented children, these have usually been children born in the context of heterosexual marriages or relationships. It is only relatively recently that lesbians in increasing numbers are choosing to give birth to or adopt children in the context of their identity as lesbians. This essay explores some of the issues facing lesbian couples who have chosen to have and raise children in the context of same-sex relationships. It explores the ways that lesbian families challenge the gendered parenting roles traditional to a conventional model of the **nuclear family**. These challenges are undermined, however, by the **homophobia** (fear of homosexuals) and **heterosexism** (assumption that everyone is, and should be, heterosexual) encountered by lesbian parents generally, and particularly by the lack of societal recognition of the nonbiological lesbian parent. The existence of lesbian families points to the need for redefinitions of family and parenting. These new definitions need to be reflected in policy and in law.

WHAT HAS BEEN WRITTEN ABOUT
LESBIAN MOTHERS?

Lesbianism and motherhood have, for the most part, been seen as contradictory terms. Motherhood is usually defined as taking place in the context of heterosexual relationships, and sexual preference is viewed by many people as immutable—that is, unalterable. If these assumptions are held to be true, then how can lesbians be mothers? Pollack (1990, 182) points out that

> early research on sexual practices, etiology and "cures," combined with a view of sexual preference as immutable, defined the lesbian mother out of existence. Before 1970, lesbian mothers were virtually invisible in the research on homosexuality, in the early research in Women's Studies, and in the literature on mothering.

Although lesbian mothers have always existed, their presence became more visible in the 1970s and 1980s as more and more women chose to publicly claim their identities as both lesbian and mother. Unfortunately, the context in which this claiming of identity often took place was the courtroom, when a lesbian mother was faced with a custody battle and the threat of losing her children. Although the 1990s and 2000s are witnessing a slow shift toward legal decisions that recognize the legitimacy of lesbian motherhood, in the 1970s and 1980s it was common for courts to conclude that a woman was an unfit mother if she was a lesbian (Pollack 1990).

These decisions were, and in some cases continue to be, based on a number of assumptions: (1) that lesbian sexuality is immoral, and that lesbians are promiscuous, sexually maladjusted, and likely to sexually harm children; (2) that children raised in lesbian homes will develop inappropriate **gender identities** and **gender role concepts** and **behaviours**, and may themselves develop a homosexual orientation; (3) that healthy child development requires the presence and availability of biological fathers as "male role models"; and (4) that children raised in lesbian homes will be socially stigmatized (given a negative label) and subjected to ridicule, teasing, and hostility from their peers.

Understandably, much of the early research on lesbian mothers was designed to refute these inaccurate assumptions, and to assist lesbian mothers and their lawyers in developing arguments aimed at allowing mothers to maintain custody of their children.

Several studies comparing lesbian and heterosexual mothers and their children concluded that there is virtually no difference among the children with regard to gender identity, gender role behaviour, psychopathology, or homosexual orientation (Kirkpatrick 1976; Kirkpatrick, Smith, and Roy 1981; Golombok, Spencer, and Rutter 1983; Mandel, Hotvedt, and Green 1979; Hoeffer 1981).

In North America the overwhelming majority of child sexual abusers are heterosexual men. Eighty-five percent of sexual molestation is perpetrated by men who are heterosexually oriented. Women, both lesbian and heterosexual, rarely abuse children sexually (Badgley et al. 1984, cited in O'Brien and Weir 1995, 128–29).

Response from lesbian mothers to the "lack of male role model" argument is varied. Some point out the large numbers of children who have unknown, absent (physically or psychically), or abusive fathers. A 1981 study (Kirkpatrick, Smith, and Roy) comparing lesbian mothers to heterosexual single mothers found the lesbians to be more concerned with providing opportunities for their children to develop ongoing relationships with men. The study also indicated that lesbian mothers had more adult male family friends and included male relatives more often in their children's activities than did heterosexual mothers.

A more complex argument points out the problematic assumption that, simply due to biological sex, mothers and fathers provide their children with essentially different experiences. As one woman I interviewed said:

> Max regards my friend Cynthia as his best male role model. If you think of role modelling in terms of behaviours and attitudes, then Cynthia is indeed quite a lovely role model in that she's vigorous and protective and powerful and tender, and likes things like trucks....To detach certain kinds of behaviours that are seen as "masculine" from what you've got between your legs allows for far more openness and range in deciding how you are going to grow up into a human being.

The argument that lesbians should not have children because of the social stigmatization they will experience is refuted by the findings that the general psychological well-being of children in lesbian and gay households matches that of heterosexual and control match groups (Bozett 1987; Gibbs 1989; Golombok, Spencer, and Rutter 1983; Kirkpatrick, Smith, and Roy 1981). More important, however, is that this argument is similar to suggesting that people of colour, Jews, disabled people, or any group that experiences **systemic oppression** should not have children because of the potential emotional damage to the children. This is a dangerous argument whose logical extension is that only people from relatively powerful social groups should have children (O'Brien and Weir 1995, 129). As Stacey and Biblarz (2001) put it, "If social prejudice were grounds for restricting rights to parent, a limited pool of adults would qualify" (178).

Most of the early research, because it was attempting to counter homophobia, focused on the ways that lesbian mothers are similar to or the same as heterosexual mothers. In the late 1980s several writers pointed out some of the difficulties and dangers of this perspective, and the potential value of looking at the ways that lesbian families are different from other families; they suggested that this difference might be a positive or radical influence on individual children and on the society as a whole. Pollack (1990) points out the dangers of suggesting that "lesbian mothers are just like other mothers":

> Research which focuses on the ways lesbians and their children resemble heterosexual mothers and their children may be important as part of custody courtroom strategy, but it negates the healthy and positive characteristics unique to lesbian parenting ... and it obscures the radical alternative lesbian lives can model. (182)

More recent writings have begun to explore this "radical alternative" and to debate the ways that lesbian families do or do not challenge the status quo. Some argue that the powerful institution of motherhood is not necessarily transformed just because lesbians are doing it. For example, Nancy Polikoff (1987a, 49, 54) suggests that lesbians are not immune to the culture of "**compulsory motherhood**":

> We were girls before we were aware lesbians, and we were raised by families that expected us to become mothers. We read the same books and saw the same movies as our heterosexual sisters. And today we live in the same world, one which purports to value motherhood above anything else a woman can do.... Motherhood is an institution. It functions as an integral part of patriarchal society to maintain and promote patriarchy. Our lesbianism does not negate or transform the institution of motherhood. Motherhood, like marriage, is too loaded with this patriarchal history and function to be an entirely different phenomenon just because lesbians are doing it.

Ellen Lewin draws similar conclusions in her 1993 book *Lesbian Mothers*, and in a 1995 article analyzes the contradictory nature of lesbian mothering, positioning lesbian mothers as both "inside" and "outside" the institution of motherhood, as both resisting and accommodating it. Kath Weston (1991) grapples with similar questions when she asks whether "gay families" are essentially assimilationist or progressive. The assimilation argument contends that the establishment of "gay families" allows lesbians and gay men to fit more comfortably into a predominantly heterosexual society as opposed to challenging the heterosexual society's family norms.

In a discussion of the progressive nature of gay families, Weston draws attention to gender and power dynamics in lesbian households. This is one of several themes that recur in writings about the challenges lesbian motherhood poses to the dominant gender order and to familial **ideology** and practice. Other themes include the possibilities for less gender conformist behaviour in children and a greater awareness of and openness to social diversity observed in children growing up in lesbian homes.

Audre Lorde (1987) writes about what it means to be the child of a lesbian of colour:

> There are certain basic requirements of any child—food, clothing, shelter, love. So what makes our children different: We do. Gays and Lesbians of Color are different because we are embattled by reason of our sexuality and our Color, and if there is any lesson we must teach our children, it is that difference is a creative force for change, that survival and struggle for the future is not a theoretical issue. It is the very texture of our lives.... (313)

Baba Copper (1987) also stresses the radical potential of lesbian motherhood, particularly when lesbians are mothering daughters. She believes that lesbian mothers, instead of teaching their daughters to dislike and compete with other women, can teach them to bond with other women and to resist patriarchal conformity. Wells (1997) argues that, unlike what she refers to as "patriarchal families," lesbian co-mother families rear sons to experience rather than repress emotions and instill in daughters a sense of their potential rather than of limits imposed by gender.

The organization of households that operate with an absence of heterosexual gender dynamics has been the source of much research interest. In her Lesbian Household Project, Gillian Dunne investigated divisions of labour between 37 lesbian couples with dependent children and 10 without children. Based on this research, Dunne argues that lesbian motherhood, because of the absence of gender difference as a structuring principle, poses a fundamental challenge to the foundation of the gender order. She concurs with Polikoff and Lewin that motherhood both makes lesbian lives intelligible to those who otherwise cannot relate, *and* that lesbian motherhood redefines the boundaries, content, and meaning of motherhood. In the lesbian couples she studied, "mothering was usually carried out in a context where they experienced a great deal of practical and emotional support from partners, where routine domestic responsibilities were fairly evenly shared, and where there was a mutual recognition of a woman's right to financial independence" (2000).

To Dunne, the more egalitarian approaches to financing and caring for children she witnessed were indicative of the ways lesbian motherhood can transform some of the more negative consequences often associated with motherhood in heterosexual contexts. Her work echoes that of Miriam Johnson (1988), who argues that the separation of the roles of "mother" and "wife" is a necessary component of women's liberation. While Johnson sees mothering as a potentially powerful and transformative force, she views the role of "wife" as a central tenet of a system of male dominance. While heterosexual relations are not innately oppressive, the institution of marriage as constituted under North American capitalism—and its corollaries, compulsory heterosexuality and notions of femininity—create and reinforce a system of male domination and women's subordination and dependence. Johnson argues that an end to "wifing" could create a basis for egalitarian heterosexual relationships. Dunne believes there is much to be learned from the more egalitarian experiences of lesbian mothers, that domestic equality requires a more balanced approach to the allocation of time between the home and the workplace, and that this involves men and women joining together in the struggle to transform the organization of paid employment (1998).

A fascinating 2001 study echoes Dunne's work and enriches the discussion regarding the difference sexual orientation of parents makes. University of California sociologists Stacey and Biblarz surveyed 21 studies of the children of lesbians, conducted between 1981 and 1998. They explore the heterosexism inherent in most research on lesbian families, resulting in differences regarding children's gender and sexual preferences and behaviour being downplayed in favour of the "no difference, same as" argument. "Because anti-gay scholars seek evidence of harm, sympathetic researchers defensively stress its absence" (160). This downplay of differences means the loss of some stimulating theoretical explorations. To Stacey and Biblarz:

> Planned lesbigay parenthood offers a veritable "social laboratory" of family diversity in which scholars could fruitfully examine not only the acquisition of sexual and gender identity, but the relative effects on children of the gender and number of their parents as well as of the implication of diverse biosocial routes to parenthood. (179)

From their survey of research, they also conclude that the children of lesbians differ in "modest but interesting ways" from children with straight parents. They attribute some of these differences to the ways that gender and sexual orientation interact to create new kinds of family structures and processes. Some differences they highlight are:

- Children with lesbian moms exhibit an increased awareness and empathy toward social difference and tend to describe themselves in ways that indicate higher self-esteem and better mental health than do the children of other moms.

- Children of lesbians appear less traditionally gender-typed. For example, lesbians' daughters may be more than twice as likely to aspire to nontraditional jobs, and lesbians' sons are less aggressive than those raised by heterosexual mothers.

- Two women co-parenting may create a synergistic energy pattern that brings more egalitarian, compatible, shared parenting and time spent with children, greater understanding of children, and closeness and communication between parents and children. (175)

Their most controversial finding, though of no surprise if one imagines growing up in a household open to sexual difference, is that young adults with lesbian moms are more likely to have "homoerotic" experiences, yet are no more likely to identify as gay or lesbian. Despite this "reassuring" conclusion, the study may well be—and, in fact, has been—used to fuel arguments against lesbian and gay parenting, based on the culturally dominant presumption that it is better for children to grow up to be heterosexual. (In Nebraska the study was selectively cited as evidence against second-parent lesbian adoption.)

This kind of argument clearly illustrates the tensions and contradictions facing lesbians in their struggles to have, adopt, and maintain access to children. The 1990s and early 2000s have witnessed a wave of political activism aimed at securing legal rights and spousal benefits that recognize lesbian and gay relationships and the rights of lesbians and gays to parent. In these struggles we are repeatedly put in the defensive position of having to argue that we are "the same as," "just as good parents as," heterosexuals—that our children will grow up with "appropriate" gender identities and behaviours, and be no more likely than anyone else to become homosexual themselves. Acknowledgment and appreciation of the ways lesbian (or gay) families might be unique and different from heterosexual families are backgrounded, in favour of arguments more likely to successfully convince judges and policy makers of our adequacy as parents.

Although lesbian mothers in Canada are currently experiencing more wins than losses in the courts, David Rayside (2002) points out that even into the 1990s Canadian lesbian custody claimants were faring better if they could convince judges that they were discreet about their homosexuality, that they would avoid exposing their children to gay/lesbian lifestyles, and that they would endeavour to raise them as "normally" as possible.

In parts of the United States homosexuality continues to be grounds to deny custody to lesbian and/or gay parents. In a 2002 Alabama decision a lesbian mother was denied custody of her children even though the courts had previously found the father's disciplinary regime to be equivalent to violence. In the judgment, the Chief Justice wrote that the mother's relationship made her an unfit mother and that homosexuality is "abhorrent, immoral, detestable, a crime in Alabama, a crime against nature, an inherent evil, and an act so heinous that it defies one's ability to describe it" (CLGRO Newsclippings on Adoption and Parenting Issues).

While a ruling such as this would undoubtedly not be made in Canada, lesbians facing court decisions regarding access to their children continue to fear reprisals. Although there is a move in Canadian courts and legislatures toward recognition of same-sex families, lesbian parents continue to live in a social environment in which half the population believes they should be denied parenting rights (Leger poll 2001, CLGRO Newsclippings). Research on same-sex parenting rides the tension between proving our "sameness" in order to fuel arguments that support our right to parent, and recognizing the interesting and illuminating questions same-sex parenting could address in a climate that did not require defensiveness.

LESBIANS CHOOSING CHILDREN

North America is experiencing a lesbian baby boom as more and more lesbians choose, as lesbians, to become parents. Statistics are very difficult to generate when it comes to establishing how many lesbian or gay parents there are in Canada. One survey of lesbians and gay men in major American cities, sponsored in 2000 by the Kaiser Foundation, revealed that 11 percent had children in the home (Rayside 2002, 11). Stacy and Biblarz (2001) estimate that somewhere between 1 percent and 12 percent of all children ages 19 and under in the United States have a lesbigay parent. There is no reason to believe that these numbers would be substantially different in Canada.

A lesbian choosing to have a child faces a complex set of issues and decisions. She needs to decide whether she wants to attempt to adopt or to get pregnant and give birth. If she is trying to biologically bear a child she must choose **alternative insemination** or sexual relations as a means to get pregnant; she has to weigh the pros and the cons of a known versus an unknown **sperm donor**; and she has to decide what criteria are important to her when selecting donors and what legal or other arrangements she wants to make with the donor.

She also has to make decisions about the organization of the family she wants to parent within. Some lesbians are choosing to single-parent, some are parenting in couples, and others are developing more innovative parenting models. These include inclusion of a known sperm donor as a parent figure or co-parenting with one or more other people, often other lesbians or gay men.

This essay looks particularly at the experiences of lesbians who are co-parenting in couples. It is designed to explore the following questions: How are lesbian parents defining and living out their parenting roles? What does it mean to have two mothers? Are their roles the same and equal? If not, how do people negotiate the differences? What is the impact of the lack of societal recognition of the nonbiological mother? How do family, friends, and the larger society support or not support the choices that lesbians make regarding parenting? Are lesbians challenging and/or recreating the conventional model of the nuclear family in the families they are creating?

The Interviews

In 1992 I interviewed three lesbian couples (six individual interviews) who had had one or more children as a couple. Although I continue to use these six interviews as the basis of this essay, I have supplemented that material with quotes from later interviews conducted in the context of other research projects. The original six interviewees range in age from 29 to 50, three self-identify as working class, three as middle class, two as "WASP," one as assimilated francophone, one as culturally Canadian, racially African, one as South Asian/Black, and one as African/English/French/Portuguese/Jewish. The interviewees are all from within a particular subsection (feminist, activist) of a broader "lesbian community." As such they cannot be considered representative of all lesbians or lesbian parents. A more random sampling would be difficult to locate given that lesbians are self-identified and given the reluctance on the part of some lesbians to publicly identify themselves, particularly for the purposes of a research project.

Nor is a sample of three couples large enough to allow broad generalizations about lesbian parents. However, here I would draw on the work of Dorothy Smith (1990), who insists that "any story bears traces of the social relations in which it is embedded" (217). Smith addresses the issue of representativeness in this way:

> Taking the standpoint of women means relying on women's experience. This is what I've done here. There's no sample, no attempt to generalize in the ordinary sense. I do not argue that the few instances I avail myself of are representative or typical. I'm proceeding in a different way, from the assumption that any such story bears ineluctable traces of the social organization and relations that are integral to the sequences of action it retails. (217)

The stories told by the lesbian mothers below can be seen as a series of narratives that shed light on the social processes by which particular forms of family and motherhood are valorized and normalized, while others are delegitimized. While parenting small children can sometimes result in a withdrawal from active political life, the issues raised by lesbian parenting put lesbian parents right in the middle of current theoretical and strategic debates being waged within LGBT communities and in the larger political arena.

Challenging the Nuclear Family

When I refer to the conventional, or male breadwinner/female homemaker, model of the nuclear family I am referring to a model that consists of a heterosexual married couple with one or more children who are genetically related to the parents. The woman and children are economically dependent on the man; he is the primary breadwinner, she the primary caretaker of physical and emotional needs. The children are the property of the parents, and the parents have authority over the children. All of these roles are considered "natural." This is the ideological model upon which most social policy related to the family is based; it does not necessarily describe what North American families actually look like.

There are countless groups of people whose lived experience challenges this model. In many working-class traditions women have always contributed to family income; the incidence of single mothers continues to rise in North America; many heterosexuals are committed to changing gender-prescribed parenting, economic, and emotional roles; and many people have parenting relationships with children to whom they are not biologically related. Some of these challenges are chosen; others stem from economic or social necessity.

Lesbian families also pose a fundamental challenge to this family model. The existence of lesbian couples who insist on their right to have children together, and on the nonbiological parent's role as a mother, challenges the family model based on heterosexuality, marriage, and biologically related children. Lesbian families also challenge the male/female roles prescribed by the conventional model and offer alternative visions of parenting roles and division of labour within a family.

Division of Labour and Parenting Roles

Stacey and Biblarz (2001) suggest that the interaction of gender and sexual orientation in lesbian families can result in family structures and processes characterized by a more egalitarian division of childcare, greater parental compatibility, and more closeness and communication between parents and children. Dunne (2000, 25) similarly concludes that lesbian parenting households fundamentally challenge a historically entrenched gender order, "redefining the meaning and content of motherhood, extending its boundaries to incorporate the activities that are usually dichotomized as mother and father." As Deb, one of the women I interviewed, said, "We're not modelling male–female power dynamics, we're modelling women doing everything that needs to be done in order to maintain life. So I think it's very different."

Contrary to the gender-prescribed roles explicit in the conventional model, lesbian parenting roles seem to be based on each woman's personality, likes and dislikes, and style. One parent may be the "funny" parent, the other more serious; one does sports with the kids, the other pushes academics; one is more easygoing, the other more hard line; one does outdoor activities, the other is a homebody and cooks and sews with the kids; one does shopping, the other artwork; one is very playful with the kids, the other stresses practical things like storytelling and reading; one does more communication and emotional caretaking, the other teaches technical skills like guitar playing and how to use tools. The challenge to gender-defined roles is profound. Tasks are allocated according to interest, ability, and the need to get things done: "We both do laundry, we both cook, we both clean. We don't have roles aside from who we are as different people" (Sarah 1996).

Without romanticizing, idealizing, or essentializing lesbian experience (and without assuming that lesbians never fight about housework), it does seem to be the case that the gendered dynamics built into heterosexual households are challenged when both parents are women. Similarly, the division of labour within lesbian households (i.e., who stays home with children, who goes to work) is not based on the presumed economic dependence of a woman on a man, but rather on which partner can get work, who can generate more income, and the desires of each partner. All the women I interviewed described a similar negotiation process leading to decisions about who would work at home and who would go out to work.

> A lot of those decisions came from Eli. She put out that she would like to stay home. I was fine with that because I wanted to go back to work. I know with having children how expensive it is and I wanted the children to have more choices. (Fay)

> It was always going to be 50–50 in terms of who did the work. Who went out and had a job would depend on what opportunities came up for us. (Deb)

These decisions are not always easy to make, and each location (at home, in the work-force) brings with it different fears, feelings, and resentments.

> I won't sit here and say there's no resentment; of course there is. I mean you've [she indicates her partner] talked to real grown-up people all day, that actually have opinions and feelings. And then she turns around and says to me, "But you watched Elvira walk first and you listened to her first whatever" ... so trying to not get the "grass is greener" syndrome, realizing there are many flaws being out there and there are many flaws being in here. (Eli)

For these couples, what differs from what might be the expected norm in heterosexual relationships is that there is flexibility in terms of who does what. If one partner expresses distress about the work she is doing, there is room for negotiation and change.

> I clearly remember the day when I said to Barb, "The flags are starting to fly, Barb, I gotta get out of here. I've talked baby babble for a year and a half now, I don't know what it's like to socialize with adults, I've got to get out." *So that was the end of that phase.* (Anne) [emphasis mine]

While gendered parenting dynamics seem less prescribed and less pervasive in lesbian households, much more salient are the dynamics between biological and nonbiological parents.

Couple Dynamics

The nonbiological, or social, mother in a lesbian parenting dyad challenges conventional definitions of "parent" and "family," and often bears the brunt of the invisibility accorded lesbian mothers generally. As Sally Crawford (1987, 205) points out:

> No matter how strong her presence and involvement in the family ... it is she who disappears, it is she who is disenfranchised—by the school, by both families of origin, by the outside world, sometimes (even more painfully) by the children or by friends in the lesbian network who do not see her as a parent nor understand the unique pressures of her position in the family.

Like an adoptive parent or a biological father, a nonbiological lesbian parent is parenting a child she did not give birth to. But unlike an adoptive parent, she must establish her own identity and role as a parent alongside another parent who has a biological connection to the child(ren). And unlike a biological father, she has grown up as a woman in a society that views motherhood as the ultimate goal and fulfillment for women, and that assumes one mother per family. Relations between lesbian co-mothers and their children are complex, and sometimes feelings of exclusion are part of the mix for nonbiological mothers. A nonbiological lesbian mother, unlike a father in a heterosexual relationship, doesn't have a defined role in helping her partner get pregnant.

> Anne was really feeling like "I want to be the one to get you pregnant. I want to have a role in this." But she didn't have that role, and that was really hard for her. (Barb)

Benkov (1994, 149) cites a typical example of a nonbiological mother's experience:

> One evening when Kelly (child) became unusually fussy, Andrea tried everything she could think of to comfort her—all to no avail. When Jane walked into the room, Kelly immediately calmed down. Jealousy swept over Andrea like a wave of nausea. Taking her by surprise, it jarred her into realizing that her lifelong fantasies of motherhood hadn't prepared her for this emotional configuration. She was supposed to be the reassuring presence, the one who sang her children to sleep. Standing in the kitchen watching Kelly nuzzle against Jane's breast, Andrea felt superfluous, like a loose thread dangling from an otherwise perfect dress.

Two factors often cited as contributing to each woman's bonding with the child(ren) are breastfeeding and time spent caring for the child(ren). The period of breastfeeding is the period where the difference between the biological and nonbiological parent is most marked. A breastfeeding infant is much more dependent on and tied to its biological mother than on anyone else. Nobody else can meet its physiological or nurturing needs as fully. This can result in feelings of jealousy and exclusion on the part of the nonbiological parent.

> From the day she was born Marie hated the bottle. So Anne was tied to her. This caused conflict between Anne and I because I could not comfort Marie. I wanted to feed her. It caused conflict too between me and Marie at times because I'd think, "Does she love me?" (Barb)

Some couples attempt to compensate for this difference by making the nonbiological mother the "at-home" parent who spends more time with the kid(s).

> At four months she stopped breastfeeding and went to her new job and I was full-time at-home mom. So whatever bonding stuff around breastfeeding I might have been worried about was obviously easily compensated for by the fact that I was doing hours and hours with them. (Anne)

Other strategies include forgoing nursing altogether, weaning at an agreed-upon age, combining nursing with bottle feeding, or sharing parenting during the early months or after the baby is weaned. The negotiations lesbian parents engage in around their relationships to their children can be influenced by a complex set of factors, including financial considerations (who can get work, etc.), beliefs about the significance of biology in social relationships; ideas about and desires to challenge (or not) traditional family norms; potential fears on the part of nonbiological parents about bonding with children to whom they have no legal rights; relationships to sperm donors or fathers; each woman's level of desire to be pregnant and to parent; and each woman's personality, parenting style, and intra-psychic history (Epstein 1995).

One choice the lesbian nonbiological parent has that fathers share but rarely exercise is the option to actually suckle the babies they did not give birth to. A 2002 issue of *And*

Baby: Redefining Modern Parenting, a glossy U.S.–based magazine that celebrates GLBT, single, and alternative parents, includes an article entitled "Nursing for Non-bio Moms." While it can take a great deal of effort to actually produce milk, suckling for comfort is easy to do.

> I suckled my first-born for the first month and a half. Comfort suckling, they call it. Instead of using a pacifier she would do that. (Eli)

While it is now possible in many provinces for nonbiological lesbian parents to adopt their children, access to this right is not universal across Canada, and for some the legal fees involved are prohibitive. This means that many nonbiological parents continue to feel insecure about their parenting status and aware of the power of the biological parent to grant or take away their right to mother.

> The most difficult thing is always feeling insecure, always feeling like he could be taken away from me, he could decide to deny me totally. Somebody else could take him from me. People could deny me access to him. I don't have any legal right to be his parent. It permeates everything really. Even if it's not happening actually, it's always a fear. (Anna 1995)

Yet despite the insecurity that comes with their role, and in the face of a society that often delegitimizes and renders invisible their existence, nonbiological parents commit themselves emotionally, financially, and practically to their children.

> I can't imagine that I would love the kids more if I was biologically related to them. I can't imagine loving them more than I do. (Lorraine 1995)

> It's a different love, but it's as big a love, or as love a love. Marie (biological child) and I are forced on each other in a physical way. Conversely with Karl (nonbiological child) there's a different, deep, sort of philosophical part of the love. (Anne)

Names

> Loving in defiance of cultural norms, lesbians and gay men must name their relationships in a world that does not support their existence. (Benkov 1994, 168)

Language is a powerful force in naming, defining, and resisting cultural norms. Lesbian parents are faced with complicated choices regarding what language to use to describe relationships to children. Existing conventions in the dominant culture do not adequately reflect lesbian and gay families, and underlying different choices regarding language are assumptions about how we define our families. Issues of naming are particularly significant for the nonbiological parent, as she defies traditional categories and is more vulnerable to being delegitimized by language. The two most important choices lesbian parents must make are what their children will call each parent, and the surname they give to their children.

The women I interviewed had made a variety of choices regarding what their children called them, each choice reflecting important elements of their views on mothering. Particularly central to decisions about naming are women's views on the biological versus social nature of mothering. Those who view mothering as primarily socially constructed seem more likely to have their children refer to both partners with some sort of "mommyism."

We both wanted some form of mommyism, and not first names. I ended up believing in the theory that the kid would pick for himself. And now they do. And they have different names for different situations. It's like "Mommm" [an urgent appeal] does a certain job, and "Where's Anne!" does another, but mostly it's Mommy Anne and Mama Barb. (Anne)

She's always referred to both of us as her mom, or "my moms." (Deb)

One couple, clear in their conscious intent to challenge the traditional social construction of motherhood, chose to be two "parents," not "Mommys" at all. Another non-biological parent, strong in her belief in the special and unique relationship between a biological mother and her child, does not want to be "Mom," and instead chose "Bun," a nickname that originated with her partner. Some women, concerned about their children's confusion in calling both women "Mom," have chosen another term for mother, often from their own cultural heritage or language; for example, Mom and Ima (Hebrew for mother). Some choose a term that to them denotes a special relationship but that is not a recognizable "mother" term. Jan Clausen's family calls her a "flommy" (1987, 333).

Choices about surnames have equally powerful implications. A child's surname can mask the true nature of their family's structure, or it can announce to the world the existence of "two-mother" families. Choices can include simply using the biological mother's name, using both women's surnames without hyphenation, or using both with a hyphen. One family I interviewed is changing both partners' and their two children's names to a hyphenated version of both partners' surnames. In cases where there is a known father or sperm donor, decisions have to be made as to whether to include his surname in the child's name.

Although issues of language and naming are extremely important, for most nonbiological parents the nature and strength of the relationships they develop with their children override their concerns and anxieties about naming.

When Paula was pregnant I was very much concerned with what my role was going to be. We'd have conversations about "Would she call me Mommy?" For a while that was really important to me. I was still pretty unclear where I was gonna sit ... After Sarah was born it took me two days, three days maybe, before I was completely confident that that little baby knew I was on the team. I lost all that paranoia really quickly, it just seemed so obvious. We're the ones with her, we're the ones hanging out, we're the ones giving her stuff. We're the ones who are on her side. (Rebecca 1995)

Homophobia and Heterosexism

Institutionalized homophobia and heterosexism embedded in the society and encountered in the behaviours of family, friends, and institutions undermine lesbian families.

Family: "My Daughter's Friend's Daughter"

All the women I interviewed spoke about ongoing struggles with family members, particularly parents, to get them to recognize the legitimacy of the nonbiological parent and to consider themselves grandparents to the children their daughters' partners gave birth to.

This struggle for recognition can have a history in the family's refusal to recognize or accept the initial lesbian relationship, let alone the children that become a part of it. "My daughter's friend's daughter" is how one lesbian's mother identifies the child her daughter is parenting but did not give birth to. Embedded in this is her refusal to legitimate her daughter's primary relationship and role as a parent. Another woman described being referred to in a joking manner by her partner's family as the "aunt" or "live-in nanny."

The homophobic behaviours of family members range from extreme acts of exclusion, almost akin to "disowning," to much more subtle forms of showing preference for biological links—taking one child out but not the other, forgetting a birthday, writing to one but not the other, refusing to recognize a nonbiological grandchild in public.

While some women describe receiving tremendous amounts of support for the families they create from their own families of origin, most have at least one story of rejection. The stories range from mild to extreme, from small daily occurrences that undermine the non-biological parent's status as "mother" to very frightening threats that involved the potential loss of a child.

> I remember one time he was crying and I was holding him and Sonia's (birth mother's) mother took him out of my arms and said "Oh, go to your Mommy" and handed him to Sonia. (Anna 1995)

> After Laura's (birth mother's) car accident, her mother called her up and said that if she (Laura) ever died, she'd make sure I never got my hands on Max. (Roni 1995)

Rejection by biological family is a contributing factor in the establishment by many lesbians of what might be called an "extended family by choice"—a supportive network of people who act as family to one another. The establishment of family ties not based in biology challenges conventional notions of family.

> I'm not a nuclear family because I have many extended people, many extensions in my family. I know that our children will be able to turn to many people in our community because we have established the bonds for them. (Eli)

Friends: "How Can a Kid Have Two Moms?"

Although it is less frequent and less threatening, lesbian parents also run into confusion and homophobia from peers who do not understand or accept the family forms they are creating. Sometimes friends just can't understand and accept the concept of two women parenting together and will confer true "mother" status only on the biological parent. They might allude to the birth mother as the "mother," direct questions about the child(ren) to her, and generally take her more seriously as a parent.

> When I talk about Elvira being my daughter, my straight friends say, "But no, she's Fay's daughter." They have to make it very clear that she's Fay's biological daughter. (Eli)

> Sometimes they talk to Marie about immunization and things like that. They try and understand it but habit makes them allude to the mother, right, the biological mother. (Kathy 1995)

Institutions: "Talk to Me Like I'm His Mom"

Lesbian parents, like all parents, have to deal with institutions such as hospitals, daycares, and schools. This means having to make choices about how and with whom to be **out** and when to intervene on behalf of one's kids.

While ability and desire to be out varies depending on context, many lesbian mothers endorse a philosophical stance that views secret-keeping negatively and coming out as positive role modelling for children. Based on this, many choose to be very out in dealing with institutions in order to instill confidence, not fear, in their children.

> Oh, everybody knows that we're two moms. We've always been open. Our feeling is that we're much safer being out than being in the closet. Because we'd be acting like we had something to hide and that message comes across to our kids, like "Don't talk about this," or "Don't talk about that." I don't want to instill any fear. I want my kids to be confident in who they are and in our family, and that means that we have to be, too. (Barb)

But being out means encountering and dealing with homophobic responses, which can vary in their intensity from mildly annoying to extremely serious. Before, during, and after her child's birth, the nonbiological parent often has to fight to be recognized:

> She (birth mother) had a post-partum hemorrhage after he was born. That was terrible. I had to drive her down to the hospital, and then I couldn't park the car so I let her off and went running all over the place trying to find a parking space. I arrived and told them who I was and everything. They were laughing and nudging each other and they wouldn't let me go in. I had to sit out there for an hour and I didn't know whether she was O.K. or bleeding to death. (Lorraine 1995)

Schools are a major institution that lesbian mothers and their children have to confront. (For a fuller discussion, see Epstein, 1998; Letts and Sears, 1999; Casper and Schultz, 1999.) The privileging of heterosexuality and heterosexual family structures manifests itself in a multitude of blatant and subtle ways in daily school life:

- The erasure of anything but depictions of heterosexual family life in curriculum materials.
- Non-acknowledgment of the nonbiological lesbian parent in school forms, for inclusion in parent–teacher interviews, and as a potential participant in school activities and outings.
- Lack of visibility of other than heterosexual teachers and administrators.
- Denial of the reality of children's family structures.
- Rejection by friends and/or the parents of friends.
- Lack of support from the school for children and their parents who are dealing with the impact of homophobia and heterosexism.

Lesbian parents talk about feeling that they are being viewed through a lens that foregrounds their lesbianism, and that attributes any problems their children experience at school, or any non-conforming behaviours on the part of their children, as stemming from the sexual orientation of the parents. Some, conscious of the tendency for their behaviour to be viewed as "lesbian behaviour," are reluctant to make waves, fearing that it will have negative repercussions for their children. While many have had positive experiences with individual teachers, they also describe their parenting status as being tolerated but not acknowledged in the classroom.

Kids of lesbians have to learn to deal with homophobic reactions from classmates, teachers, and others, and parents have to figure out when and how to intervene on behalf of children. One couple's strategy is to encourage their kids to do well academically so that at least they can't be "gotten" in that area.

> Even though the kids tell him he's going to burn in hell because he believes in Nature instead of God and that his mothers are faggots ... in that environment he's still strong because they still have to come to him for the answers, because they don't know and he does. (Anne)

Lesbian parents also recount the benefits and positive ideas, attitudes, and skills their children develop from their experiences at school. These include skills in negotiating difficult situations and sophisticated understandings of the dynamics of oppression, of gender, and of complex political issues.

The homophobia and heterosexism encountered by lesbian parents, and particularly the powerful lack of validation of the nonbiological parent, can lead to doubts on the part of lesbian parents and their children about the legitimacy of their families. The pressure of always having to defend your right to parent can undermine your confidence in your role. Phyllis Burke (1993, 33) writes:

> Everything was fine as long as I stayed in the house. The moment I went outside, to the supermarket or playground, I became self-conscious. I could not for a single moment forget that I was assumed to be straight, and Jesse's birth mother. In some ways, I felt as if I were passing for his parent, since I had no legal connection to him. I was an imposter in my own heart.

Children, too, are vulnerable to external pressures.

> Sometimes someone will say in front of the kids, "So you're Karl's mom, and you're Marie's mom." That's really the hardest, because you have to watch them go through learning people's rather heartbreaking confusion, and maybe it [makes] them a little bit doubtful. "Are ... are ... aren't you my mom? What do you mean I'm yours, she's hers?" (Anne)

New Developments, New Debates

The late 1990s and early 2000s have seen dramatic shifts in the Canadian landscape regarding same-sex relationship and parenting rights. In 1995, Ontario changed the definition of spouse in the *Child and Family Services Act* to include same-sex couples, thus making possible second-parent adoptions (allowing nonbiological parents to adopt their partner's biological children). In 1998 British Columbia became the first province to grant same-sex couples most of the same privileges as heterosexual couples, including the right to "stranger" adoption (adoption of a child neither member of a couple is related to). In 1996 an Ontario judge, based on the landmark *M v H* case, ruled the *Ontario Family Law Act* unconstitutional in its exclusion of same-sex couples, and in 1999 Ontario passed Bill 5, an act to amend certain provincial statutes to reflect the new category "same-sex partner." In 2002 Quebec passed the most comprehensive legislation to date by creating a civil union status that accords the rights and responsibilities of married heterosexual couples to same-sex and opposite-sex unmarried couples. Currently, British Columbia, Saskatchewan, Nova Scotia, Ontario, and Quebec have laws in place that recognize same-sex relationships. Same-sex couples can legally adopt in British Columbia, Saskatchewan, Ontario, Quebec, and Nova Scotia, and similar legislation is expected imminently in Manitoba, Newfoundland, and the Northwest Territories. Even conservative Alberta has made second-parent same-sex adoption possible. In 2001, lesbian parents in British Columbia won the right to have both parents registered on a child's birth certificate, removing the need for (and cost of) second-parent adoption. Most recently, in July 2002, a three-judge panel of the Ontario Superior Court ruled that granting marriage licences only to heterosexual couples violates Canada's *Charter of Rights and Freedoms*. The Quebec Superior Court followed suit in September 2002, and a similar decision is expected in British Columbia. The Ontario decision gave the federal government two years to extend marriage rights to same-sex couples. The federal government has since launched an appeal of the Ontario decision and will likely do the same in Quebec and B.C. A parliamentary committee has also been struck on the issue of same-sex marriage, and it will hold hearings across the country.

The reasons for this attention to same-sex family issues probably involve the convergence of several factors. Over the last 20 years, lesbians and gay men in increasing numbers have pursued the creation of families that include children, often involving challenges to legal and political processes that would deny them this right. Activist movements have embraced these challenges, and parenting issues generally, particularly because anti-gay sentiment is often focused on the dangers to children that homosexuality poses. Anita Bryant's 1970s anti-gay crusade, with "Save Our Children" as its slogan, epitomizes the fear-mongering approach often adopted by right-wing opponents to lesbian and gay rights. Public opinion polls consistently indicate that it is gay and lesbian contact with children that provokes the most fear and anxiety in the general public. This being true, it is difficult for lesbian and gay movements to ignore these issues, as their opponents place them at the fore of political struggles.

As well, the recognition of same-sex families is consistent with state moves towards **privatization** of responsibility for its citizens. In other words, governments are concerned to lessen dependency on state welfare, and to increasingly put the responsibility for the support of children (and other dependants) in the hands of individuals within private households. Recognition of more people as "parents" means less reliance on state welfare systems (Rayside 2002).

Within lesbian and gay communities, the movement to secure legal rights and spousal benefits for same-sex relationships, and particularly the right to marry, has been a source of intense debate. Once again we are faced with the question of whether to argue that "we are the same" as heterosexuals in order to gain equal rights, or whether to embrace a more radical view of families that acknowledges and appreciates the ways we are different and to fight for rights and benefits that take into account the differences.

Suzanna Danuta Walters (2001), in a thoughtful essay on same-sex marriage, addresses this tension. Walters recognizes the legitimacy of the equality/civil rights issue and that there is no justification to deny one group of people access to a practice or institution that is available to others. The exclusion of lesbians and gay men from marriage leaves them socially disenfranchised, economically discriminated against, and denied access to a fundamental social institution.

On the other hand, Walters raises important questions about the impact of pursuing marriage as a road to gay/lesbian liberation. She is concerned that marriage "reinforces structural inequalities within families ... privileging state-regulated, long-term pairing over other forms of intimacy and connectedness" (348). Lesbians and gay men, often due to rejection by families of origin, have a history of creating intricate networks of friends, lovers, and ex-lovers that serve as "family." We are also developing new kinds of parenting structures by sometimes choosing to parent together and by creating families with more than two parents of a variety of sexes, genders, and sexual orientations. Walters is concerned that the legalization of same-sex marriage will set up a hierarchy of intimacy that values long-term, monogamous, cohabiting commitment and devalues other ways of being sexual, loving, and nurturing. She cites some of the conservative proponents of same-sex marriage who argue that marriage will "civilize" or "tame" the wild desires of homosexuals, forcing them into committed, monogamous relationships.

Walters ends by raising questions about the conflation of *partnering* (a presumably sexual relationship between consenting adults) and *parenting* (a relationship of profound structural dependency). Citing the work of feminist legal theorist Martha Fineman (1995), and echoing Johnson's suggestion that "wife" be separated from "mother," she suggests that in order to create a less gendered social order a distinction should be made between peer relations (partnering) and relations of dependency (parenting). This could have significant implications for the structuring of social policy:

> Perhaps gays would do better to support legislation that removes marriage as a legal and economic category, while at the same time creating frameworks to socially, legally and economically support relations of real dependency: parent to child, caretaker to caretakee, able-bodied to the disabled they care for, etc. (FN 9, 356)

In the 1995 decision that granted lesbian couples in Ontario the right to second-parent adoption, the presiding judge had to first change the definition of spouse to include same-sex couples in order to grant nonbiological parents the right to adopt. The decision, while clearly a landmark victory resulting in increased security for lesbian families, had embedded in it the assumption that the only legitimate context in which to raise children is a two-person, spousal relationship. Nonbiological parents could not adopt the children they were raising until they were recognized as their partners' spouses.

The downside of this is the reinforcement of traditional nuclear family structures; the upside is that the redefinition of spouse carries with it other benefits that many lesbian couples desire. Once again the complexity of these issues is apparent. Countless lesbian couples and their children both require and desire the economic and social benefits that spousal recognition brings. On the other hand, spousal recognition values certain family forms over others, and legitimizes those lesbian families that most closely resemble the heterosexual nuclear family.

Terry Bogis (2001), director of Centre Kids, the family program of the Lesbian and Gay Community Services Center in New York, raises some important class issues in relation to lesbian and gay parenting generally, and particularly in relation to second-parent adoption. While recognizing the tremendous boon it has been to nonbiological lesbian parents to become legally recognized as parents, the process is time-consuming, intrusive, and costly—sometimes prohibitively so. At the same time, courts are beginning to use the fact that nonbiological parents have not pursued second-parent adoption as grounds for dismissing custody claims when couples break up. In other words, nonbiological parents unable to afford the financial costs of second-parent adoption, or those who resent the elaborate and costly process required in order to adopt their own children, run the risk of losing custody of and/or access to those children.

Another crucial piece in debates about the family and same-sex relationships is the critical response to feminist critiques of the family that have come from women of colour. For example, Patricia Hill Collins (1994) suggests that for black women the key struggle is not about internal family dynamics or against male domination in the family, but rather "the locus of conflict lies outside the household, as women and their families engage in collective effort to create and maintain family life in the face of forces that undermine family integrity (47) … women of colour are concerned with their power and powerlessness within an array of social institutions that frame their lives" (53).

Collins' analysis of the family as a site of survival and resistance in the context of a hostile external world offers another lens through which to view lesbian motherhood. Collins argues that the struggles for control over their own bodies in order to choose whether to become mothers, *and* the process of keeping wanted children, are more salient issues for black women than "maternal isolation with one's children within an allegedly private nuclear family." Black women have been penalized and discouraged from having children through a range of institutional policies and practices including sterilization abuse and punitive social welfare policies.

Similarly, lesbians have historically been denied the right to have children. They have engaged in a struggle for reproductive freedom in order to secure this right, a right which is still not guaranteed. As recently as the early 1990s, a survey conducted for the Royal Commission on New Reproductive Technologies found that 76 percent of medical practitioners would refuse donor insemination to women even in a stable lesbian relationship (Rayside 2002, 41). Separation from wanted children through the loss of custody battles is at the heart of some of the most significant and painful struggles lesbian mothers have had to wage. And lesbian mothering experiences are framed by social institutions that deny their existence. Without conflating lesbian motherhood and black motherhood, or suggesting that they are mutually exclusive, it might be fair to suggest that mothering in the context of a community or culture that is generally devalued by dominant social norms might mean that internal familial power struggles and negotiations take a back seat to the need to have the family provide a source of strength, affirmation, and resistance.

While the debate regarding same-sex marriage rages hotly in lesbian and gay communities, the debate is not so evident when it comes to parenting rights, perhaps because the stakes are so high. Parenting issues are raised because of individual cases where parents stand to lose the right to have, legally parent, or maintain access to children. Because claimants are so vulnerable, "there is no other issue area in the politics of sexual diversity where there are greater pressures for challenges to be framed in safe and respectable terms" (Rayside, 2002, 56). Which brings us back again to the pressure on lesbian and gay parents to frame their claims in ways that minimize the threat to the existing order. The question then becomes this: Does the necessity of framing claims in this way negate the radical nature of lesbian parenting and the challenges lesbian families pose to conventional notions of family? As Walters puts it:

> Is it possible that the creation of gay families through marriage (or commitment ceremonies) and the raising of children is the *least* challenging aspect of gay and lesbian life? Is the formation of gay families the nail in the assimilationist coffin, linking gays irrevocably with mainstream heterosexuality? Or do these moves shake up heterosexual dominance like nothing else, permanently altering the very definitions of family? (2001, 353)

Certainly most people engaged with these issues agree that given the context in which lesbian and gay families live, they can never be simple replicas of heterosexual families. Dunne (2000) and Stacey and Biblarz (2001) make convincing arguments for the ways that lesbian parenting households quite profoundly shake up the dominant gender order, and even Walters concedes that "the creation of gay and lesbian families does pose a fundamental challenge to traditional family values" (353). Rayside points out how the social, economic, and political changes that gave rise to second-wave feminism have had significant impact on how we think about and practise intimate relations, and argues that families that consist of two parents of the same sex cannot help but continue to undermine traditional family ideology. He suggests that it is possible for same-sex parents to argue their parenting claims in conventional ways, while continuing to organize their parenting lives in unconventional ways.

The radical impact of same-sex parenting will probably become clearer over the coming years as lesbians and gay men continue to have and raise children. In the meantime most lesbian and gay parents live their lives unconcerned with the radical nature of their family practices. In a series of focus groups held recently in Toronto, LGBT parents were asked about the kinds of resources, information, and support they would find useful. Above all else, people want to know how to meet and connect with other LGBT parents. They want to talk to other parents about what's happening with their kids in daycares and schools;

about how to equip their kids with the skills they need to deal with homophobia and heterosexism; about issues of race, language, culture, and class in LGBT families; about parenting teenagers; about dynamics between nonbiological and biological parents; about sexuality and relationships and parenting; about how to deal with the pressures they feel to conform and have their children conform to traditional gender norms.

LGBT parents, like most parents, want the best for their children. While their existence may shake up gender norms and challenge definitions of family, this is not why people choose to parent.

SUPPORTING LESBIAN FAMILIES: POLICY PROPOSALS

Public policy that takes into account the specific needs of lesbian parents and lesbian families needs to begin with a redefinition of family by which the defining characteristic becomes emotional or social relationships and not biology. Specific policy implications based on such a redefinition should include:

- Establishment of women-centred, women-controlled, government-subsidized sperm banks, accessible to any woman requiring the service.

- Granting, from birth, legal parenting status to nonbiological parents based on the act of parenting.

- Legalization of second-parent adoptions (same-sex or otherwise) in cases where the biological parent is still alive and actively parenting.

- Legal reforms allowing parents to assign any surname they choose to their children.

- In cases of child-custody disputes, the requirement that the "best interests of the child" be based on relevant criteria such as caring environment and safety and stability, and not on racist, sexist, heterosexist, or ableist (discriminating on the basis of perceived disability) notions.

- Reorganization of work to account for the responsibilities of parents. This would include paid parental leave for anybody involved in the parenting of a child, followed by the possibility of part-time employment without the risk of a loss of seniority, promotion possibilities, and so on.

- Universal, affordable, and accessible childcare available on a part-time or full-time basis. The affordability should not be dependent on low wage rates for childcare workers.

- Re-evaluation of the housing needs of different family forms, and government-sponsored renovations and building initiatives to accommodate these needs.

- Requirements that daycares and schools have curriculum and materials that reflect alternative family forms, including lesbian, gay, bisexual, transgender, and transsexual families.

- Public education programs to be carried out in all government and private institutions. Programs should address the viability and positive nature of a variety of family forms, and deal specifically with homophobia and heterosexism.

For more information about the LGBT Parenting Network, David Kelley Services, Family Service Association of Toronto contact (416) 595-0307, ext. 270; 355 Church St., Toronto, Ontario M5B 1Z8; rachelep@fsatoronto.com. Visit the Family Pride Canada Web site at http://familypride.uwo.ca.

KEY TERMS

Alternative insemination: A simple procedure involving the introduction of semen into a woman's vaginal canal for the purpose of achieving pregnancy.

Compulsory motherhood: The ideological belief that women are unfulfilled or inadequate unless they are mothers, and that motherhood should be valued above anything else a woman can do.

Gender identity: Self-labelling as either "male" or "female."

Gender role behaviour: Behaviour believed to be appropriate for each gender (male or female).

Gender role concept: A set of beliefs that assigns a specific identity and range of acceptable behaviours to each gender.

Heterosexism: The assumption that everyone is and should be heterosexual and that heterosexuality is the only normal form of sexual expression for mature, responsible human beings.

Homophobia: Irrational fear and hatred of homosexuals.

Ideology (or dominant ideology): A set of ideas and daily practices that produce acceptance of existing power relations as "natural."

Nuclear family: A family unit consisting of a man and a woman who are legally married and their children.

Out, as in "coming out": Making public one's identity as a lesbian or gay man.

Privatization: The relegation of women to the "private" sphere of home and family; the transfer of the responsibility for the provision of goods or services from the state or public domain to private companies or households.

Sperm donor: A man who agrees to donate his semen for the purposes of alternative insemination.

Systemic oppression: The conditions and experience of subordination and injustice, supported by societal institutions.

DISCUSSION QUESTIONS

1. What are some of the important issues being raised by people doing research and writing about lesbian families?

2. How are lesbians who are choosing to have children challenging the conventional model of the nuclear family?
3. What societal forces are undermining this challenge?
4. What sorts of legal, social, and institutional changes need to take place in order for lesbian families to be fully recognized as legitimate families?
5. What are some of the issues raised in debates about same-sex marriage? What do you think about these issues? How does the debate differ within lesbian and gay communities, and in the larger community?
6. How can and does society benefit from the existence of lesbian families?
7. What kinds of actions can you take in your life to support lesbian families?

REFERENCES

Alpert, H., ed. 1988. *We Are Everywhere: Writings By and About Lesbian Parents*. Freedom, CA: Crossing Press.

And Baby: Redefining Modern Parenting. July/August, 2002. New York: Out of the Box Publishing.

Arnup, K. (ed.) 1995. *Lesbian Parenting: Living with Pride and Prejudice*. Charlottetown, P.E.I.: Gynergy Books.

Arnup, K. 1989. "'Mothers Just Like Others': Lesbians, Divorce, and Child Custody in Canada." *Canadian Journal of Women and the Law* 3(1): 18–32.

Badgley, R., et al. 1984. *Report of the Committee on Sexual Offenses Against Children and Youths*. Ottawa: Ministries of Justice and Attorney General and Supply and Services.

Benkov, L. 1994. *Reinventing the Family: The Emerging Story of Lesbian and Gay Parents*. New York: Crown Publishers.

Bogis, T. 2001. "Affording Our Families: Class Issues in Family Formation." In M. Bernstein and R. Reimann, eds., *Queer Families, Queer Politics: Challenging Culture and the State*. New York: Columbia University Press.

Bozett, F. 1987. "Children of Gay Fathers." In F. Bozett, ed., *Gay and Lesbian Parents*. New York: Praeger.

Burke, P. 1993. *Family Values: Two Moms and Their Son*. New York: Random House.

Casper, V. and Schultz, S. 1999. *Gay Parents/Straight Schools: Building Communication and Trust*. New York: Teachers College Press.

Clausen, J. 1987. "To Live Outside the Law You Must Be Honest: A Flommy Looks at Lesbian Parenting." In S. Pollack and J. Vaughn, eds. *Politics of the Heart*. New York: Firebrand.

Coalition for Lesbian and Gay Rights in Ontario (CLGRO). Newsclippings on Adoption and Parenting Issues, October 1989–May 2002.

Collins, P.H. 1994. "Shifting the Center: Race, Class and Feminist Theorizing About Motherhood." In E.N. Glenn, G. Chang, and L.R. Forcey, eds. *Mothering: Ideology, Experience and Agency*. New York: Routledge.

Copper, B. 1987. "The Radical Potential in Lesbian Mothering of Daughters." In S. Pollack and J. Vaughan, eds., *Politics of the Heart*. New York: Firebrand.

Crawford, S. 1987. "Lesbian Families: Psychosocial Stress and the Family-Building Process." In Boston Lesbian Psychologies Collective, ed., *Lesbian Psychologies*. Chicago: University of Illinois Press.

Dalton, S. 2001. "Protecting Our Parent–Child Relationships: Understanding the Strengths and Weaknesses of Second-Parent Adoption." In M. Bernstein and R. Reimann, eds. *Queer Families, Queer Politics: Challenging Culture and the State*. New York: Columbia University Press.

Day, D. 1990. "Lesbian/Mother." In S. Stone, ed., *Lesbians in Canada*. Toronto: Between the Lines.

DiLapi, E.M. 1989. "Lesbian Mothers and the Motherhood Hierarchy." *Journal of Homosexuality* 18(1/2): 101–21.

Dunne, G. 1998. "Pioneers Behind Our Own Front Doors: New Models for the Organisation of Work in Partnership." *Journal of Work, Employment and Society 12: 6*.

Dunne, G. 2000. "Opting into Motherhood: Lesbians Blurring the Boundaries and Transforming the Meaning of Parenthood." *Journal of Gender and Society 14: 1*.

Epstein, R. 1995. "Flommies, Imas and Mamas: Exploring the Experience of Nonbiological Lesbian Parents." Presented at the 1995 Annual Conference of the Canadian Sociology and Anthropology Association.

Epstein, R. 1996. "Transforming Motherhood: Lesbian and Heterosexual Feminist Mothers." Presented at the 1996 Annual Conference of the Canadian Sociology and Anthropology Association.

Epstein, R. 1996b "Lesbian Parenting: Grounding Our Theory." *Canadian Women's Studies 16: 2*.

Epstein, R. 1998. "Parent Night Will Never Be the Same: Lesbian Families Challenge the Public School System." *Our Schools, Our Selves 9: 1*.

Epstein, R. 2002. "Butches with Babies: Reconfiguring Gender and Motherhood." *Journal of Lesbian Studies 6: 2*.

Fineman, M. 1995. *The Neutered Mother, the Sexual Family, and Other Twentieth-Century Tragedies*. New York: Routledge.

Gibbs, E.D. 1989. "Psychosocial Development of Children Raised by Lesbian Mothers: A Review of Research." In E.D. Rothblum and E. Cole, eds., *Lesbianism: Affirming Non-Traditional Roles*. New York: Haworth.

Golombok, S., A. Spencer, and M. Rutter. 1983. "Children in Lesbian and Single-Parent Households: Psychosexual and Psychiatric Appraisal." *Journal of Child Psychology and Psychiatry 24*: 551–72.

Gross, W.L. 1986. "Judging the Best Interests of the Child: Child Custody and the Homosexual Parent." *Canadian Journal of Women and the Law 1(2)*: 505–31.

Hanscombe, G.E., and J. Forster. 1982. *Rocking the Cradle: Lesbian Mothers, a Challenge in Family Living*. Boston, MA: Alyson.

Harding, S. 1987. "Introduction: Is There a Feminist Method?" in S. Harding (ed.) *Feminism and Methodology*. Milton Keynes: Open University Press.

Herman, D. 1990. "Are We Family? Lesbian Rights and Women's Liberation." *Osgoode Hall Law Journal 28 (4)*: 789–815.

Hoeffer, B. 1981. "Child's Acquisition of Sex-Role in Lesbian Mother Families." *American Journal of Orthopsychiatry 51*: 536–44.

Hotvedt, M.E., and J.B. Mandel. 1982. "Children of Lesbian Mothers." In W. Paul, ed., *Homosexuality*. Beverly Hills: Sage.

Hunter, N.D., and N.D. Polikoff. 1976. "Custody Rights of Lesbian Mothers: Legal Theory and Litigation Strategy." *Buffalo Law Review 25 (3)*: 691–733.

Johnson, M. 1988. *Strong Mothers, Weak Wives*. Berkeley: University of California Press.

Journal of the Association for Research on Mothering: Special issue on lesbian mothering. 1999. *1: 2*.

Khayatt, D. 1992. *Lesbian Teachers: An Invisible Presence*. Albany: State University of New York Press.

Kirkpatrick, M. 1976. "A New Look at Lesbian Mothers." *Human Behaviour 36*: 60–61.

Kirkpatrick, M., C. Smith, and R. Roy. 1981. "Lesbian Mothers and Their Children." *American Journal of Orthopsychiatry 51*: 545–51.

Kranz, K.C. and J.C. Daniluk. 2002. "We've Come a Long Way Baby … Or Have We? Contextualizing Lesbian Motherhood in North America." *Journal of the Association for Research on Mothering 4: 1*.

Letts, W. and Sears, J. 1999. *Queering Elementary Education*. Lanham: Rowman & Littlefield Publishers.

Lewin, E. 1984. "Lesbianism and Motherhood: Implications for Child Custody." In T. Darty and S. Potter, eds., *Women-Identified Women*. Mayfield, CA: Mayfield.

Lewin, E. 1993. *Lesbian Mothers: Accounts of Gender in American Culture*. Ithaca: Cornell University Press.

Lewin, E. 1995. "On the Outside Looking In: The Politics of Lesbian Motherhood." In F. Ginsburg and R. Rapp, eds., *Conceiving the New World Order*. Berkeley: University of California Press.

Lewin, E., and T. Lyons. 1982. "Everything in Its Place: The Coexistence of Lesbianism and Motherhood. In W. Paul, ed., *Homosexuality*. Beverly Hills: Sage.

Lorde, A. 1987. "Turning the Beat Around: Lesbian Parenting 1986." In S. Pollack and J. Vaughn, eds., *Politics of the Heart*. New York: Firebrand.

Mandel, J., M. Hotvedt, and R. Green. 1979. "The Lesbian Parent: Comparison of Heterosexual and Homosexual Mothers and Children." Paper presented to the American Psychological Association, New York.

Mandel, J., M. Hotvedt, and R. Green. 1980. "Entrance into Therapy: Presenting Complaints and Goals of Homosexual and Heterosexual Single Mothers." Paper presented to the American Orthopsychiatric Association, New York.

Mossop, B. 1993. "Brian Mossop Responds." *Xtra* (19 March): 29.

Nelson, F. 1996. *Lesbian Motherhood: An Exploration of Canadian Lesbian Families*. Toronto: University of Toronto Press.

O'Brien, C., and L. Weir. 1995. "Lesbians and Gay Men Inside and Outside Families." In N. Mandel and A. Duffy, eds., *Canadian Families: Diversity, Conflict and Change*. Toronto: Harcourt, Brace.

Pies, C. 1988. *Considering Parenthood*. San Francisco: Spinsters/Aunt Lute.

Polikoff, N. 1987a. "Lesbians Choosing Children: The Personal Is Political." In S. Pollack and J. Vaughn, eds., *Politics of the Heart*. New York: Firebrand.

Polikoff, N. 1987b. "Lesbian Mothers, Lesbian Families: Legal Obstacles, Legal Challenges." In S. Pollack and J. Vaughn, eds., *Politics of the Heart*. New York: Firebrand.

Pollack, S. 1990. "Lesbian Parents: Claiming Our Visibility." In S.P. Knowles and E. Cole, eds., *Woman-Defined Motherhood*. New York: Haworth.

Pollack, S., and J. Vaughn. 1987. *Politics of the Heart: A Lesbian Parenting Anthology*. New York: Firebrand.

Rayside, D. 2002. "The Politics of Lesbian and Gay Parenting in Canada and the United States." Presented at the 2002 Annual Meeting of the Canadian Political Science Association.

Ricard, N. 2001. Maternités Lesbiennes. Montreal: Editions du remeu-menage.

Riddle, D. 1978. "Relating to Children: Gays as Role Models." *Journal of Social Issues 34:* 39–50.

Smart, C. 1984. *The Ties That Bind: Law, Marriage and the Reproduction of Patriarchal Relations*. London: Routledge & Kegan Paul.

Smith, D. 1990. *The Conceptual Practice of Power: A Feminist Sociology of Knowledge*. Toronto: University of Toronto Press.

Stacey, J., and T.J. Biblarz. 2001. "(How) Does the Sexual Orientation of Parents Matter?" *American Sociological Review 66:* 159–183.

Stone, S.D. 1990. "Lesbian Mothers Organizing." In S.D. Stone, ed., *Lesbians in Canada*. Toronto: Between the Lines.

Toevs, K. and S. Brill. 2002. *The Essential Guide to Lesbian Conception, Pregnancy and Birth*. Los Angeles, CA: Alyson.

Van Every, Jo. 1991. "Who Is 'The Family'? The Assumptions of British Social Policy." Revised version of paper presented at the Canadian Sociology and Anthropology Association Annual Conference, Queen's University, Kingston, ON, June 1–4.

Van Every, Jo. 1995. *Heterosexual Women Changing the Family: Refusing to be a 'Wife'!* London: Taylor & Francis.

Walters, S.D. 2001. "Take My Domestic Partner, Please: Gays and Marriage in the Era of the Visible." In M. Bernstein and R. Reimann, eds., *Queer Families, Queer Politics: Challenging Culture and the State*. New York: Columbia University Press.

Wells, J. 1997. *Lesbians Raising Sons*. Los Angeles: Alyson Books.

Weston, K. 1991. *Families We Choose: Lesbian, Gays, Kinship*. New York: Columbia University Press.

Out Family Values

James Miller

Faculty of Arts
University of Western Ontario

Objectives

- To envision a new kind of family that openly defies the supposedly "natural" opposition of heterosexuality to homosexuality.

- To distinguish the experimental organization of such a family from the traditional nuclear model prescribed by the advocates of conservative "family values."

- To define the radical values of such a family in relation to the evolving agendas of liberation for gays and lesbians in the post-Stonewall era (since 1969).

- To determine the necessary social, psychological, political, and legal conditions for the formation of such a family in contemporary Canadian society.

- To affirm the lively social reality (rather than the limp theoretical possibility) of such a family by illustrating its ups and downs in the evolution of the author's household.

- To challenge the current sociological impulse to impose the traditional narrative structure of the "case study" on the flexible dynamics of nontraditional families.

INTRODUCTION

This chapter is an updated version of the essay I contributed to the first edition of this volume (published in 1996). To the original "Out Family Values" piece, which appears here in condensed form, I have added a coda entitled "Panic Manor Revisited" in which the story of my family has been extended into the new century. Though much of the personal narrative in the original essay is now historical, I have chosen to retain the present tense in it for stylistic reasons. Hence, in the sections of the chapter preceding the coda, time-identifiers such as "now" refer to 1995, when I wrote the first draft of the essay under the idealizing spell of the Modernist Myth of Gay Liberation. In my new revisionist "now" (it's late 2002 as I write this) I'm a thoroughly Postmodern Parent — emotionally fragmented, self-deconstructing, queerly nostalgic, suspicious of my own counterdiscourses, and deeply tanned by the fallout from Nuclear Family Meltdown.

The family I live in as a father is also the family I live **out** in as a gay man. I call it an "out family" for three reasons: its openness to homosexual membership; its opposition to **heterosexist** conformity (the prejudicial assumption of heterosexuality as normal and proper); and its overtness within the contemporary lesbian and gay movement.

Mine is a family that opens out, steps out, and stands out. It opens out to people traditionally excluded from the charmed circle of the Home; it steps out beyond the polite and policed borders of the Normal; and it stands out as a clear new possibility on the horizon of what used to be called—in the heady days following Pierre Trudeau's decriminalization of **homosexuality** in Canada (1969)—the Just Society. Against the drone of current conservative rhetoric urging decent citizens to protect "family values" from homefront activists like me, I shall try to spell out here the distinctive qualities that my family has discovered in itself to meet the challenges of living in a pervasively **homophobic** culture that would rather we closed down, stepped in, and stood back.

So hear me out. Try to ignore the interference booming in over the System. The qualities I encourage in my family are not domestic virtues in the old passive Victorian sense. They are newly tested activist values empowering us to break silences in social spaces where the dominant **discourse** of family life normally goes without saying.

VALUE #1: BRAZENNESS

The most obvious reason for outing my family by name is also the first in a historical sense: when I came out to my children at the inauguration of our **post-nuclear** household in January of 1990, they immediately wanted to know whether they were gay, too. Not necessarily, I told them, trying to allay their time-honoured fears without compromising my newfound sense of pride. Yet was I not outing them by outing myself? For better or worse, I realized, my **uncloseted** gayness was bound to be socially projected onto all who lived with me. Whatever my children's sexual orientations might be, their close association with me would effectively **gay** them in the eyes of straight society and **queer** their cultural outlook. So look out, I warned them, the World likes to see things straight.

They have taken my warning to heart by setting the record straight about me and them ("Our dad's gay, but we're probably not") for any curious soul who comes into our domestic space, which is a zone of riotous free speech. The casually stated fact of my gay pride is the very opposite of a family secret. It's also no secret in my family (as visitors who examine the AIDS posters in my dining room soon discover) that everyone's sexuality is to be acknowledged and celebrated among us, whatever it should happen to be, whenever it should be declared, no bones about it, hurrah. If you can't handle that collective hurrah, you're going to have trouble meeting us even halfway. We're likely to scare you off with our outspokenness on safer sex issues and same-sex spousal benefits and sexy French men's underwear—anything goes in conversations at our dinner table—for speaking "out" on any subject under the sun is our familiar idiom.

My second reason for declaring my family "out" is to acknowledge our pioneering adventure beyond the pale of long-established social discourses and religious doctrines concerning family life. An out family must learn to speak about itself in unaccustomed ways, develop its own outlandish frontier lingo, for its members are always proudly, if at times also painfully, aware of their strategic positioning outside the nostalgically normative vision of **heterosexual** monogamy. That doesn't mean we consider ourselves exiles from the Good Life or pitiful victims of the homophobic rhetoric of the Family Coalition Party, the Community of Concern, or the folksy Falwells on Vision TV. On the contrary, my out family bravely resists the exclusionary pressures of heterosexist institutions and their defenders simply by existing as such, by brazenly occupying hallowed spaces like "family rooms" and "family cottages" and even "family restaurants" where we're not supposed to exist.

Our presence on the social map, incongruous as it may seem to our detractors, is unignorable now. If we're not easily placed in the nostalgic neighbourhoods defended by the advocates of mainstream family values, then so much the better for us: our critical distance from their restrictive norms I regard as a position of clarifying otherness and liberating strength.

My third and most insistent reason for using the term **out family** is to mark out my little cadre of significant others as a relatively new social possibility within the diversity of "alternative" living arrangements developed by gay men and lesbians over the past few decades. It's easy enough to see how my particular family stands out against the fantasy backdrop of what the straight press likes to call the General Public: we're an annoyingly real exception to the pseudo-Christian rule that God, in whose Public Eye I am a very abomination and my parenthood a persistent grain of sand, smiles only on the offspring of Real Women and the home life of Republican Bubbas.

Harder for "society" to discern is the distinctiveness of our peculiar home life within gay communities—our queerness within queer cultures. An out family may throw a smart dinner party or two, but it's not quite the same scene aesthetically as the "artists' colonies" of the sixties. The Vissi d'Arte imperative usually gives way to the domestic demands of diaper-changing or bedtime storytelling on the daily priorities list.

An out family may march together on Lesbian and Gay Pride Day (as ours brazenly does) amid the drag queens and leatherfolk and **dykes,** but home territory for the partici-pants in such a family outing is likely to be many city blocks away from the seventies-style communes in the "Gay Ghetto" where the marches commenced and still ritually return. The public schools are better in the suburbs, after all, and Daddy's special friend teaches in them now.

An out family may own a private place in the country, like our lesbian feminist neigh-bours (who've just had a new son); but "Moon Cottage," as their retreat is called, is very far from being an exclusively woman's space like many of the radicalesbian collective farms founded around the turn of the eighties in pastoral defiance of the greedy imperialist patri-archy. Fairies have definitely been spotted at the bottom of their garden. A year ago they celebrated the birthday of their *toujours gai* friend David by inviting my kids and a host of other out family friends to the Moon on gossamer wings. It was just one of those things.

Out families invariably have an interest in queer politics, though we rarely belong to street-savvy outculture cadres like Queer Nation. I like to think of us as belonging to a more dispersed and informal network of flaming heretics that might be called "Generation Q." Of course our revolutionary leaders on the Pampers-versus-Huggies front are out to engender radical awareness of sexism and homophobia—not to mention racism, anti-Semitism, puni-tive censorship, AIDS discrimination, cutbacks in arts funding, you name it. But the pre-vailing ethos of Generation Q is not utopian and our political agenda is not separatist.

We're quite likely to live down the street from your Mum and Dad, who are in for a sur-prise when they find out who's just bought the old Stanford place. What would dear old Mrs. Stanford have made of that loud rainbow flag in the bay window of her weathered yellow-brick Victorian, or that triangular bed of hot pink impatiens planted in the front yard where her bridal-wreath spireas used to be? Our heraldic imagery, the public affirmation of our social **coming out,** is being displayed on the home front now as casually as that fraying Canadian flag raised proudly over Great Uncle Douglas's front porch. We're here, we're queer, and we're buying real estate in decent neighbourhoods with mature lots.

VALUE #2: PERVERSITY

By the mid-eighties the most popular term in North American gayspeak for a congerie of close friends linked by a shared queer history and the hope of an uncloseted social future was the **chosen family.** Still implicit in this proud polemical phrase and its ethical consort "chosen lifestyle" (both of which remained current, half-jokingly, in the outspeak of the Gay Nineties) is a serious critique of the heterosexual "birth family" or "family of origin" that gays and lesbians belong to by blood or adoption, not by personal choice, just like all our supposedly well-adjusted straight siblings. Unlike them, however, we have often been excluded socially or rejected psychologically or even banished physically—literally thrust out of the nest—for no other reason than our supposedly "perverted" sexual orientation.

Perverse (in the sense of "stubborn") we may well be in our choice of friends, lovers, and families, but we strongly reject the "perverted" label. Perversity is what we show in our determined opposition to the public charge of "perversion"—an old-fashioned theological term with psychiatric and even legal applications implying a devious and certainly shameful departure from some sort of divinely prescribed route toward maturity, sanity, or salvation.

Our parents' generation and their parents' generation tended to equate homosexuality with barrenness, death of the family line, and even demonic hostility to the whole procreative enterprise ordained by the Creator. Now don't get me wrong: as a gay father I'm no Enemy of Life. Birth and I go way back. I've personally attended my own and three other happy births without gnashing my teeth or cursing the Creator, probably because the triumphant process of giving birth reminds me of coming out. Both are fruitful. Both are multiplying.

Latent in the idea of the chosen family, I suspect, is a compensatory **homosexist** disdain for the lost family of origin. With a certain taste for malicious delight the shamefully excluded have shamelessly delighted in the thought that their straight siblings are now stuck with the Old Folks at Home in an endlessly dull round of tailgate lunches and birthday dinners and midnight masses while the Chosen are free to taste the sovereign joys of child-free living in the Big City. Much gay fiction represents the chosen family in this glowing hedonistic light even today, two decades into the AIDS epidemic, when gay guys and their girlfriends no longer easily perceive themselves as a chic clique of free spirits dashing their way through the complications of that hilarious screwball comedy known as Postmodern Life.[1]

After the shakedown of the early eighties, when many people with AIDS found out with a shock who their true friends and relations were after disclosing their diagnosis, the chosen family in many instances has soberly evolved into a support group or buddy network for the sick and dying. The perversity of our friendships, their stubborn toughness, has paid off in adversity. The catastrophic momentum of the AIDS crisis has thrust birth families and chosen families into each other's arms—if it has not severed their ties forever in the acrimonious aftershocks of death. In any event, the old divides between blood kin and kindred spirits are no longer so easily mapped on the social landscape or so blithely ignored in the bleak ironies of the epidemic as some still wish they were.[2]

Even in the good old days before AIDS, chosen families could and of course did include children—voluntary sterility having never been a prerequisite for admission to the gay and lesbian movement. I suspect that more than a few chosen families in the late seventies rejoiced in the patter of little feet about their well-appointed condos and goddess-blessed communes not only for the usual proud parental reasons but also for the defiant pleasure of proving wrong the hateful rhetoric of Florida beauty queen Anita Bryant and her homophobic cohorts in the Save Our Children campaign.[3]

That campaign has never ended, though Bryant herself has mellowed enough with age to soften her hard-line stance on the demonic impact of homosexuality on "real family" values. In the late eighties, for instance, Margaret Thatcher's Tories effectively out-Bryanted

Bryant by passing legislation in the British Parliament to prevent the funding of progressive educational efforts to broaden the social concept of family to include and hence (oh horrors!) to validate and condone the new gay/lesbian category of chosen family—or "pretended family," as worthy members of Mrs. Thatcher's government preferred to call it with a sneer.[4]

In a rigorous metaphysical effort to deny the reality and erase even the conceptual possibility of procreative homosexuality on the home front, politicians everywhere are priding themselves on their defence of the family against admittedly imaginary foes. Not even former U.S. vice-president Dan Quayle's backfiring attack on the fictional family of television's Murphy Brown, whose straight identity remains miraculously uncompromised by her overt sympathy with gay and lesbian single parents, has induced the Moral Majoritarians to abandon their holy war against us. War was openly declared on us again at the 1992 Republican Convention by former Nixon speechwriter and would-be presidential candidate Pat Buchanan. Meanwhile, imaginary parents are tucking their pretend kiddies into bed and wondering how they'll pay the very real taxes required to support a public education system that denies their family's existence.

Even so-called liberals are apt to join the campaign to Save Our Children when push comes to shove. In June 1994 Lyn McLeod, leader of the Ontario Liberal Party, helped to defeat an NDP-proposed piece of legislation (Bill 167) that would have legalized the adoption of children by same-sex couples and mandated same-sex spousal benefits throughout the province. Even though this bill was in perfect accordance with the antidiscrimination clause on sexual orientation in the *Ontario Human Rights Code*, it was deemed too "controversial" and too "radical" for the General Public, whose voice McLeod claimed to have heeded in her caring, motherly way. Apparently her conscience—not to be confused with her sense of political expediency—instructed her that the "public" was not ready to accept the idea of children raised by gay or lesbian couples because it could not stomach the thought that gays and lesbians could form couples at all in the "normal" sense. It takes a delicate conscience indeed to save our children from unthinkable thoughts.

Is an out family the same as a chosen family? From the magisterially objective viewpoint of conservative backbenchers, there can be no serious political doubt that an out family is just as imaginary as a chosen or "pretended" family: both represent a demonic parody of the divinely ordained mom-and-pop operation that would mysteriously collapse without the blessing of pro-family governments.

From my militantly subjective viewpoint, however, an out family is different from a chosen family in one crucial sociological respect. In so far as the latter has been defiantly construed as a social alternative to the restrictively heterosexist 1950s-style nuclear families from which the first generation of proudly self-identified gays and lesbians sprang, its members remain bonded as friends, lovers, and ex-lovers through a shared sense of personal oppression and collective liberation. Where the long-term presence of offspring with at least one homosexual parent is not necessary or even commonly expected in a chosen family, *an out family has the next generation at its very core.*

The irreducible minimum for an out family, as far as membership goes, is one resolutely uncloseted gay or lesbian parent and one child over whom the parent has either full or shared legal custody. Whether the parent is one of the child's progenitors (biological parents) or an adoptive guardian is irrelevant to the structural definition of an out family, as I construe and experience it, though the history of its founding (or what's made of that history within and beyond the parent–child relationship) is rarely insignificant in the social and psychological interaction of its members.

VALUE #3: FLEXIBILITY

If resisting the glacial grind of heterosexist culture were the be-all and end-all of out family life, that life would be irredeemably dreary in its ideological obsessiveness and hopelessly rigid in its stance of nonconformity—doomed, in fact, to crack up and be crushed under momentous forces beyond its control. A certain comic flexibility is therefore needed to beat the grind, to take the critical pressure off, to ease the erosive friction with the world. That's where the chosen family enters the out family picture, changing it from a satiric parody of *Father Knows Best* into a workable social reality that can sustain long-term resistance to the forces pitted against it. If out parents have no network of lovers, ex-lovers, friends, or relatives to call upon for support and shelter at the start of their counter-familialist histories, they soon find one. Or one finds them.

In my case I had an unacknowledged chosen family around me before my kids and I went through the purgative fires of Nuclear Family Meltdown. It included my wife, of all people, though I had to go through the bitter flames of coming out to discover that fact in all its astonishing sweetness. Also numbered among the Chosen are several friends of the family who may enter our house without invitation and vacuum it without offence. (The vacuum cleaner is ready whenever they are, but they usually opt for dinner and conversation.) Often found dining and conversing at our table are "Uncle" David, whose famous social skills have endeared him to my kids; my graduate student, Jennifer, who often abandons tins of brownies on our doorstep as if they were in need of a good home; my trusty babysitter, Melvina, who is the chief enforcement officer of David's etiquette laws; our fairy godmother, Linda, who was a rock singer in the swinging sixties and now teaches art therapy; and my kids' best friend and teenage role model Tomak, who can swing a baseball bat with one hand and play Chopin preludes with the other. Most out parents find their core relationships with their children loosened up, extended, supplemented, protected, complicated, and in many striking and subtle ways transformed by the blending of their lives with the lives of their chosen family.

If there's one SUFFICIENT CONDITION for the genesis and determination of an out family, I would say it is this: the legally sanctioned and publicly acknowledged foundation of a household in which at least one out gay or lesbian parent lives with at least one blood-related or adopted child in a mutually sustained relationship of love, trust, and care with every expectation of remaining thus bonded for life.

That may be the be-all of it, rock bottom, but not the end-all. No out family I know of (including my own) is as demographically tight or as airlessly self-contained as this condition permits, though I'm quite prepared to imagine such a household existing somewhere out there, enjoying both a local habitation and a name, persisting over many years with something like a bright future. In reality—my reality, anyway—there's likely to be more than one child in the picture, more than one blood relative, more than one loving caregiver, more than one friend of the family who's an ex-lover of your current lover, more than one kind of family impinging on the daily operations of the household, and more than one kind of sustained relationship linking the members of the family in a dynamically complex yet cheerfully loose web of rivalries and alliances.

When I consider from a political angle all the forces that shape and sustain the queer history of my household, I'm convinced that the early and ongoing integration of a chosen family into post-nuclear out family dynamics is a NECESSARY CONDITION for its survival as a workable social organization within the heterosexist hegemony of the General Public. To resist all the externally promoted and at times internally accepted narratives of doom and disruption that threaten not only its definition and private solidarity but also our visibility and public existence, an out family like mine needs all the chosen family help it can get.

In fact, five years into the history of "Panic Manor," as my household is affectionately known, I can say without hesitation that the blessed absence of panic at the core of my post-nuclear identity as Gay Dad (a potential disaster site if ever there was one in the eyes of the General Public) is due not only to my brave brood's willingness to take on the role of "out kids" but also to my chosen family's concerted efforts to provide a nurturing matrix for our blended destinies. There's much to be said for hanging out (and loose) with us.

At Panic Manor we are all aware in our own ways, children as well as adults, that ours is not only a new family for us personally but also a new kind of family for our sociological context. Panic Manor is deviously and paradoxically situated on a sedately maple-shaded street in the "Old North" section of London, Ontario, a white, professional, middle-class haven where the rotting of gourmet compost in green plastic bins is matched in excitement only by the ripening of life insurance policies in the town's many corporate vaults. We sometimes call it "Laudanum, Ontario," in view of its many soporific attractions: Storybook Gardens, the Children's Museum, the Victoria Park Children's Festival....

You can easily fall asleep here counting the allegorical sites of intense bourgeois nostalgia for the tight security and enforced innocence of 19th-century childhood. It's truly a "great place to raise kids," as my central-casting WASP real estate agent tellingly informed me in 1985 when I moved my unexploded nuclear family out from Boston. (Just how far out that would be we hadn't a clue at the time.) When we first drove into town, *Twilight Zone* music ringing eerily in our ears, my wife and I could have sworn that we had stepped back into one of those hyperreal illustrations of home life in the Dick-and-Jane readers from our youth. Welcome to the sleepy capital of Straight Family Values.

Unlike our straight neighbours out parents don't have a 1950s, or for that matter an 1850s, to model our visions of domestic bliss upon—except ironically. We have to make our values up as we go along, mapping out a cultural frontier and carving out a social space for families like ours in the future even as we measure day by day our political and personal distances from family life in the past.

A space for such a loose improvisatory household as mine would hardly have been conceivable until 1969, when the **Stonewall riots** initiated the gay liberation movement in North America. I was 18 then, a freshman at Glendon College in Toronto, and virginally self-destined for the closet of heterosexual monogamy. Ten years later I was married, and ten years after that unmarried. According to the prevailing wisdom of the talk shows, my decade in the matrimonial closet should have been a period of intense mental agony and physical self-abuse as I struggled desperately with the vile erotic urges beneath my hypocritical social mask. Sorry, Geraldo. It was an economically tumultuous but on the whole triumphant period in which my wife Melissa and I rejoiced in the feminist-approved "natural" births of our three supernaturally gifted offspring—Sabrina (1981) and the twins Alice and William (1985)—while we busied ourselves in true eighties fashion with the fine points of gender-neutral parenting on an assistant professor's salary.

In 1985, moving from Harvard, I accepted a tenured position as Faculty of Arts Professor at the University of Western Ontario. With job security attained and a mortgage swiftly approved for our (irony of ironies) Victorian house, I was smugly certain that all was well on the home front and would remain so for ever and ever, amen. I had swallowed the laudanum and was drifting into sweet untroubled dreams of rocking Swing-O-Matics, Home-and-School Association meetings, Easter egg hunts in crocusy backyards, yearly pilgrimages to Storybook Gardens, and cute guys in spandex.

When my closet blew, its cellophane walls were blasted off in all directions by the internal pressures of my emergent gay identity combined with the external force of my wife's unflinchingly courageous will to face facts and the vast historical momentum of the AIDS epidemic. I had gone about coming out in a thoroughly academic way, at first absent-mindedly, at length bloody-mindedly, by offering an arts course on the cultural impact of AIDS in the fall of 1988. A year later my public life as an AIDS activist exploded the straight mould of my private life, and the result was a liberating rush of creative and critical energies on every level of my existence. It wasn't academic consciousness-raising about patriarchy and its discontents that battered my heart and sought to make me new at this time. It was a force closer to erotic joy. I look back on that sexual push toward self-knowledge as my "outscape" into the alternative universe of the **gaytriarchy.**

Ironically, my faithful tour of duty in traditional married life had shielded me from the "outside" threat of HIV infection even as it exposed me to the "inside" effects of cultural activism. Little did I realize when I came out on my rebirthday (October 12, 1989)—headlong, howling, and happier than the talk shows ever permit the General Public to imagine in their cathartic unmasking of the Homo Hubby—that it was to be a family outing, too. Our destination this time, however, was not the familiar realm of Storybook Gardens. When I came out to my kids, informing them in my best gender-neutral terms that Mummy was moving out to find selfhood and Daddy having found it was going to look after them in the true anarcho-democratic spirit of Panic Manor, they looked at me and then at each other with a wild surmise as if I had just announced a package tour by tornado to the Wonderful World of Oz.

VALUE #4: COURAGE

Now, five years later, my kids and I are still amazed that we managed to land safely on the other side: imagine waking up one fine morning to discover that your father is really the Cowardly Lion and the Yellow Brick Road begins at the end of your driveway. Courage is something we have learned to share: it certainly didn't come from me alone.

Try explaining homophobia to your school friends, for instance, when its manifestations are rather less obvious (though no less hurtful) than the interventions of the Wicked Witch of the West. Of course I urge my kids to question their friends' reflexively heterosexist assumptions about family, even as I encourage them to cherish their memories of a time when we too were living together in a household haplessly modelled after those nostalgic illustrations of straight white family life that still adorn the prescriptive pages of their school readers.

What you're really learning to read from these readers, I tell them in a fit of dinner-table **semiotics,** is the inscription of heterosexism and homophobia on the unwritten constitution of patriarchal culture. They grimace at me over their beet greens. I insist they eat their greens now, or it's no President's Choice Key Lime Pie for dessert.

"And I don't want any more lip out of you," I scold them, all the while delighting in their courageous lippiness. It's so *out* of them. They proceed to accuse me of systemic patriarchal oppression and threaten eating disorders in later life.

I counter by appealing to feminist precedent. Look, I tell them, look in your own family at Mummy's self-assertive reaction to propaganda of this sort. Melissa, too, decided to have a go at liberation in her own right: she's now pursuing a double career as a novelist on the cutting edge of the Canadian literary scene and a public relations officer at a large real estate concern. Not for her a comfy life of dishing out storebought sweets ad nauseam in a kitchen decorated in early-fifties theme wallpaper, the kind that shows multitudes of merry wives waving little pots and pans out of spotlessly clean windows. Gone with the Windex.

Melissa's departure from that baleful scene of domestic bliss has not meant her exclusion from our persistently sweet-toothed family, I'm glad to say. Since we agreed upon joint custody of the children in our very amicable divorce, she has regularly released them from the dictatorship of the four food groups by supplementing their diets with home-baked fudge brownies, pig-outs at a Chinese buffet, and forbidden delights from Merla Mae's Old-Fashioned Ice Cream Store. Free by mutual agreement to establish her own schedule of visits with the children each week, she has interpreted the "generous access" clause in our custody arrangements to mean (currently) a Wednesday night supper with each child individually on a rotating basis and a Saturday afternoon excursion with all three to her new condo in South London where she and her new husband Ken are converting the basement into a playroom plus bedroom for future sleep-overs. This schedule is not fixed in concrete.

It evolves with the changing demands of her dual career, her aerobic exercise regimen, and her new life with Ken. A former hockey player and rock-band drummer, Ken tends to keep his distance from the Panic Manor scene.

Melissa, on the other hand, retains her key to Panic Manor and with it her active membership in the **post-nuclear extended family** evolving out of our old life together. To the chorus of well-meaning friends, puzzled relatives, and disapproving gossips who have pumped her for some socially acceptable reason for her "abandonment" of the kids—"How could that woman just up and leave her babies with that man? Doesn't she know they'll turn out gay? It's a crying shame! It's a sin!"—she offers the simple jaw-locking explanation that she's a Bad Mom. Lots of courage in that, kids.

VALUE #5: PRIDE

No one appreciates the religious implications of familialist icons such as the Dick-and-Jane households portrayed in elementary-school readers, and the reconstructed nuclear families perpetually celebrated in the heternormative endings of Hollywood movies, more deeply than John, my lover of five years. As the eldest son of Italian immigrants who have prospered in Canada without sacrificing their Old World allegiance to Catholicism, John (or "Gianni," as he was baptized) venerates *La Famiglia* in a way that baffles the Compleat Anglo in me. Where I retain a fuzzy nostalgic regard for the family circle as an ideal of moral solidarity against the forces of discord threatening the Queen's yuletide vision of the Family of Man—gay liberation, believe me, can't dispel all fantasies cherished from childhood—he regards *La Famiglia* as a tough, adaptable instrument for social and economic survival in the Fallen World.

To the usual Catholic evidence for our fallen condition—lust of the flesh, lust of the eyes, and pride of life—John's parents add Canadian winters, Protestant church decor, and the vitamin-enriched Wonder Bread eaten by *mangia-cakes* (as they call us Anglos when we're not feasting on Angel Food made from a mix). Homosexuality doesn't make their list of postlapsarian evils because, according to John, neither Mamma nor Papa has any idea of it: it simply doesn't figure as a concept in their mental universe. As a result, neither John nor his younger brother (who's also gay) has come out to them, or feels inclined to broaden their Catholic perspectives on human sexuality any time soon.

Carmen, the elder of John's two sisters, is in on the secret, however, and agrees with her brothers' assessment of the futility of trying to explain gay identity to their tradition-bound parents. As the closest of John's relatives in age and outlook, she has helped him over many years in his diplomatic efforts to keep his two lives (and now his two families) in separate universes. She's also helped me understand the mysterious Other World of Italian family values—from which she has placed herself at a certain safe distance through her own matrimonial alliance with a WASP black sheep. Her debunking response to Anglo-Canadian prudery as well as to Italo-Canadian piety has made Sharing the Secret more of an amusing family game than an agonizing defence strategy.

Sharing the Secret allows them to distinguish their liberalized North American attitudes toward sex and marriage from the conservative mindset of their parents' immigrant generation without compelling them to renounce the survivalist value system of the Catholic family, to which they owe not a little of their present social and spiritual stability. Having welcomed me into their long-term confidence, John and Carmen expect me to keep the Secret too, and I do, out of respect for their particularly fractious family history and the strong peace-preserving impulse of Italian *cortesia*.

Yet they both know that I am at odds politically and spiritually with the self-censoring pressures of the closet, which I don't enjoy sustaining or reinforcing by my own acts of silence however courteous and socially expedient. Coming out to your parents is not the easiest thing in the world to do, I realize. Well do I remember my own mother's response to my first awkward profession of gay pride to her—it was over a crackly phone line to St. John's on Christmas Day 1989. "I'm ... a homo, Mom!" I stammered. "Merry Christmas!" Several seconds of very long distance silence followed before she retorted defensively: "Well, I suppose you blame ME for this!" I didn't, of course, but when I tried to swing into my cheery rendition of "I gotta be me!" in my proudest gay-affirming voice, she angrily hung up—and didn't speak to me for a year.

Her anger was rooted, I sensed, in a deep resentment at the still depressingly popular Freudian myth that male homosexuality is the result of Bad (that is, powerful) Moms abnormally arresting the "normal" Oedipal development of their sons. Before she could speak to me again—without fear that I was the one harbouring resentment—she had to reject the misogyny as well as the homophobia latent in the myth of maternal blame.

That took some time, and with the help of my brother and two sisters, all of whom were very accepting of my change-of-life from the word go, my mother broke her self-imposed silence and called me up the next Christmas to ask how her grandchildren were doing. We've made great progress together since then. "There's nothing the Queen of England hasn't suffered these past few years that I haven't gone through, too!" she now jokes, referring, no doubt, to the royal embarrassment over Prince Edward's rumoured closetry as well as to the marital woes of his three straight siblings.

Since my father died in 1983, I can only imagine how he would have taken the news of my coming out. Hard, I think, since he once told me as a teenager back in the sixties never to use the word *gay* unadvisedly since it had been "ruined by queers." Still, that was the sixties. He was not an unreasonable sort. As a stalwart Newfoundlander from Trinity Bay, he was nothing if not adaptable to sudden changes in the winds.

It grieves me that I can't get to know John's parents, as he has recently got to know my mother (shamelessly getting on her good side with his excellent pesto sauce and his "Mamma mia" routine) or as I got to know Melissa's wonderful and still supportive folks from North Carolina. I have met my Italian "out-laws" only once, at their daughter's bacchanalian wedding reception, where John presented me to them simply as "a friend of the bride." The multi-layered ironies were thicker than her wedding cake. It was a time for smiles, but I smile uneasily at the memory of it now because Mamma and Papa still don't know the truth about their firstborn son—not to mention their second son, who was at the reception with his unflappably campy African-American lover from New York. Yet both John and his brother showed uninhibited pride of life at this party, the truth be damned. So why must I be hung up on sober truth-telling when, in their story, things are working out just fine? Perhaps they're right to go with the flow, I tell myself, at least when the flow is pleasantly intoxicating and isn't doing anyone any harm. The truth that makes John such a large part in my bacchanals after divorce can wait for the Day of Reckoning.

Till then I shall remain quietly irked by the thought that the Panic Manor crew cannot visit "Southfork," as John wryly calls his family's farm, after J.R.'s ranch on the 1980s soap opera *Dallas*, except when his mother and father are safely away visiting their numerous relatives in Ottawa or Montreal. The pastoral opposite of Panic Manor, Southfork is a heroic recreation of Southern Italy complete with fig trees, rosemary bushes, apricot orchards, grapevines, and vast *verdura* gardens flourishing on the dourly Protestant flatlands of Southern Ontario.

What really pains me when I consider that Southfork might as well be located in Kingdom Come—not that Southern Ontario is that far from the end of the world as we know it—is the dreary thought that the closet is socially inescapable even for someone who fancies himself wholly free of it. Someone like me: an all-outer with "Silence Equals Death" tattooed on his brain.

John rightly deplores any sign of an "outer-than-thou" smugness in my occasionally critical attitude to his decision not to disclose his sexual identity to his parents. I trust he'll break the news when the time is right. He alone can judge when. In the meantime, social forces beyond the merely reflexive good-will of courtesy are at work to knit our divergent families together despite the divisive impact of the Secret. His sister-in-the-know has welcomed my children into her heart like an aunt, which is how they now regard her, and we are all looking forward to the arrival of her first child in the new year. Panic Manor has not been slow in according her expanding household full membership privileges in the out family universe.

Outness, I've come to realize, is not an absolute state of public exposure or an immutable condition of personal freedom attained through a mystical transcendence of the closet. Rather, it is a culturally relative and personally variable engagement with the closet as it adversely affects the lives of gays and straights alike. My out family, for one, tends to experience outness as a collective resistance to the fluctuating forces of Catholic dogmatism, Evangelical **familialism,** and allied social movements that seek to restrict or even to eliminate gayspace. As such, its intensity varies a good deal from person to person and from place to place and even from year to year. John (who's 36 now) came out to himself at the astonishing age of 7—decades before I was capable of taking the same small but momentous step toward self-affirmation in a straight world. He also came out to his university friends eight years before my closet blew. Yet his degree of outness in the workplace is considerably weaker than mine owing to the considerably stronger mobilization and enforcement of Catholic moralism in the educational system that employs him.

Though the closet persists for him in the house of his earthly no less than his heavenly father, John does not hesitate to identify himself as a proud gay man in all other significant contexts of his life. His practical accommodations with the closeting pressures of the Real World (including the occasional efforts on his mother's part to fix him up with a *paesana* (a fellow Italian) from Mississauga—"Such a nice girrla!") are bound at times to clash directly or indirectly with my perversely theoretical commitment to fighting closetry on all its many fronts.

His current job in the separate schools, for instance, requires him to use the usual range of "educational materials" that insidiously promote the unquestioned family values of the "dominant culture." I urge him to enlighten his little charges by exposing the heterosexist bias of their textbooks, all implicit primers in vicious Vaticanized homophobia; but he just laughs at my crypto-Protestant zeal to reform the world and calmly refuses to provoke the wrath of the Catholic School Board. He has a point. He doesn't want to lose his job merely to advance my political agenda. I counter by wondering aloud how even his highly refined sense of religious absurdity can bear the intense irony of his professional admiration for the Board's Family Life program, which either vilifies or annihilates his existence as a gay man. He declares that I don't know what I'm talking about. The Family Life program is not only remarkably liberal, all things considered, but its prevailing spirit of inquiry is bravely poised to confront the moral complexity of major social questions routinely begged or blanded over by comparable programs in the godless Public Board.

Thus does the Reformation break out in the dialectical hubbub of Panic Manor only to be met, with equal and opposite force, by the trumpets of the Counter-Reformation. Thank heavens my children are not bothered by our religious wars: they steadfastly retain a romantic allegiance to Presocratic paganism.

VALUE #6: ESPRIT

Reflecting on the various faiths at work and at war in our lives, I am reminded of two further conditions for the survival of an out family on the battlefield of contemporary identity politics. These conditions are neither sufficient nor necessary for its legal formation and composite structure but pertain rather to the gradual development of its distinctive esprit de corps and so might be considered "spiritual" prerequisites for its continuation.

First, every member of an out family must be prepared to share in one way or another the daily experience of outness or closetedness shaping the deepest political and spiritual convictions of fellow members. One need not be self-identified as a gay or lesbian to experience the joys and jeers that come with the territory. My children, for instance, must live with the living out of my visibility as a gay activist even in kidspaces where I seldom venture: when classmates make homophobic remarks at them in the schoolyard at recess—"We don't want you on the team because you're a **fag** like your dad" was an exclusionary insult recently hurled at my son like a cruel curveball—they have to deal with the consequences of my outness on their own turf and in their own way.

All I can do on the home front is to suggest various strategies for coping with homophobic backlash deflected to them. They can empower themselves by naming the prejudice ("Ever hear of homophobia, butt-head?"); they can disarm their taunters with snappy remarks of their own ("Didn't you know I just got traded from the Toronto Blue Gays?"); they can challenge the assumptions underlying the prejudicial comment ("Come on, just because my dad's gay doesn't mean I am, and even if I turn out to be gay, what difference would that make to my pitching arm?"); they can proudly turn their backs on intransigent detractors ("Too bad, guys, you could have won with my famous fastball"); or they can appeal to their teacher for intervention if the bullying gets nasty ("Mrs. Lane, Matt's threatening to bash me if I don't leave the playground!"). Though I tell myself that children who have the gumption to name and challenge prejudices from an early age grow up with a heightened sensitivity to the treatment of all minorities in our society, I know that in the short run surviving the Darwinian conflicts in the playground can be tough going when you're only 8. Fortunately, my 9-year-olds have their intimidating 13-year-old sister (a feminist lawyer in the making) as an advocate in the field.

Occasionally the conformist pressure of the General Public gets the better of them, and they find the gumption to lash back at me. Why did you have to turn out gay, Daddy? Why can't we be normal for a change? Do you have to wear your leather pants to the school concert? It's your fault Matt can't come to our house for the play rehearsal: his parents won't let him near Panic Manor because they think you'll molest him. For my part I must live with their censoring or closeting responses to me—which must be gotten off their chests from time to time—just as John must live with their periodic resentment of his intimate association with me in the house their mother left. Though assured that none of us will ever out him to the unsuspecting members of *La Famiglia*, John must also reckon with the benign but insistent pressure of our collective hope that his parents will one day know him as he truly is. Then, perhaps, his two social universes will cheerfully overlap—at least on festive occasions—even if chances are slim that they'll merge eternally into One Big Happy Family.

Hence the second of the two spiritual conditions for the thriving of an out family in the Real World: each member must be prepared to accept the relative degree of outness achieved, or closetedness tolerated, by every other member without presuming that outness is an absolute state of personal perfection or closetedness an irrevocable sign of political failure. A loving regard for the whys and wherefores of anyone's personal negotiations with the closet, however, does not preclude an ardent desire that all participants in out family life be encouraged through engagement with its values to maximize their resistance to the closeting narratives of heterosexist culture.

VALUE #7: QUEERNESS

Implicit in even the most liberal case study of a family history or individual life to illustrate a problematic case of "nonconformity" or "deviance from the social norm" is a condescending solicitude on the part of the narrating expert, whose external and thus seemingly objective testimony seeks to contain the subjects of the study within a wholly imaginary zone of controlling observation. If you find yourself the subject of a case study, you obviously need help from the narrator who's taken up (and taken over) your story. Merely by assuming a commanding viewpoint, the expert witness latently justifies a need for critical intervention by the "higher" authorities in charge of the case. These may be benevolent therapists or antagonistic lawyers, sensitive clergy or implacable cops, depending on the narrator's institutional affiliations. A case in medical terms calls for a cure; in legal terms, for a conviction; in religious terms, for a conversion; in therapeutic terms, for a collapse; in political terms, for a commission to study its harmful impact on the General Public.

Against all such constraining views of our life John frequently cites the opening lines of a speech on rodents delivered by his friend Mark ages ago in Grade 7: "Do YOU live in a hole? Do YOU live in a hole? Groundhogs do!" Various versions of this arresting intro now circulate in Panic Manor, but the queerest is this: "Do YOU live in a case study? Do YOU live in a case study? Gay dads do!"

Most case studies of homosexuals are reflexively designed to console the worried guardians of the General Public through expert testimony that the case under observation is the exception that proves the rule—the queer exception that proves this or that straight rule about marital concord, family solidarity, social order, moral hygiene, or whatever. Perhaps that's why very out gay fathers like me are virtually unheard of, and our outrageously real families unheard from, in the highly evolved "nonfiction" literature that currently lays claim to social-scientific, therapeutic, medical, or legal authority in the contentious field of family studies. That's not to say that gay fathers have been deviously ignored or despotically censored out of such literature in recent years. Far from it: the specimen count of Toms and Dicks and Harrys (not their real names, of course) who've confessed their matrimonial sins to scrupulously objective analysts is surprisingly high in recent mainstream commentary on the habits and habitats of the Domestic Homosexual.

For a good cry—make that a good laugh—I recommend the tragicomic chapter "Family Configurations" in *Gay Fathers* (1990) by Robert L. Barret and Bryan E. Robinson.[5] Under such a title such a pairing of names is bound to raise eyebrows. Are Barret and Robinson lovers? Are they fathers? Do they live together with their kids? Where do they position themselves relative to their male subjects—politically among them, socially above them, intellectually beyond them? Who are these men that they should study me?

Their tactful back-page bios identify them as professors of "counselor education" and "child and family development" at the University of North Carolina at Charlotte. Barret, a psychologist in private practice, owns up to being a father, or as the bio puts it in the occluded style of a winning career résumé, "His interest in fathering can be seen in his relationships with his three daughters and two sons-in-law, as well as in his professional writing" (facing p. 196). What about his interest in gay fathering? Has he come out to his three daughters? Neither he nor his co-author 'fesses up to a more than "professional" interest in the subject at hand, or allays queer suspicions by claiming to be straight Good Ole Boys

118

who've somehow strayed into alien psychosocial terrain without a map but with plenty of sympathy for the poor sods they find in family limbo.

Instead, they turn the serenely impersonal face of Social Science (from which shines the unblinking Public Eye) toward the darkness of gay fatherhood, and there, lurking with all the other skeletons in the seemingly narrow closet of heterosexual monogamy, their research discloses what all the tabloids have been exposing for years: a vast underworld of homosexuals in married drag subverting the Establishment they desperately want to join. The buried lives Barret and Robinson exhume are offered up to fellow psychologists and family counsellors for dissecting inspection in a series of gothic tales from the family crypt: "The Case of Sam"; "The Case of Colin"; "The Case of Phillip"; "The Case of Will: A Bisexual Father with AIDS"; and, my personal favourite, "The Case of Brad: An Establishment Gay Father with AIDS."

From the scandalous dish coolly served up as scientific data in their casebooks Barret and Robinson have managed to abstract a typology of gay father plot-lines—the messy details of so many messed-up lives—which the Public Eye can find miraculously reduced to the synchronic stillness of eight prototypical "Gay Father Family Configurations." This North Carolinian guide to Jesse Helms's worst nightmares stretches across two pages in the form of a master diagram possessing the weird clarity of a football coach's gameplan or a necromancer's chart of mutant crystal formations. All hopes of finding my proper place in society as an Establishment Gay Father without AIDS fades whenever I scan the neat array of genograms or family options charted for me by my expert overseers. My out family just doesn't fit in. Panic Manor falls out of sight somewhere between Type 5, "Joint-Custody, Single Gay Fathers" (see Figure 5.1) and Type 6, "Gay Father Stepfamilies" (see Figure 5.2)

In our Family Configuration the Mother and the Homosexual Partner cheerfully co-exist without cohabitation. The schematic reduction of complex social and psychological relationships to double-headed arrows shafted by three kinds of lines (broken, unbroken, and dottily dashed) betrays the professional counsellors' latent familialist desire to pin down the fluidly anarchic syndicality of our lives; to target our points of defiant extrusion from the closely monitored and tightly controlled system of respectable family relationships; and to fix our shifting allegiances and agendas into an institutionally determined and therefore readable format for various experts to use in "understanding us" so that our lives may no longer be an embarrassing mystery to the Establishment but an opportunity for its guardians to test their professional powers of crisis management.

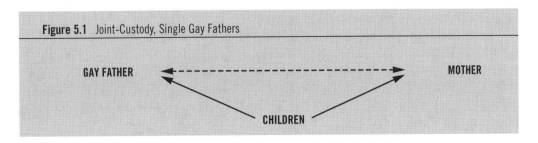

Figure 5.1 Joint-Custody, Single Gay Fathers

GAY FATHER — — — — — — — — → MOTHER

CHILDREN

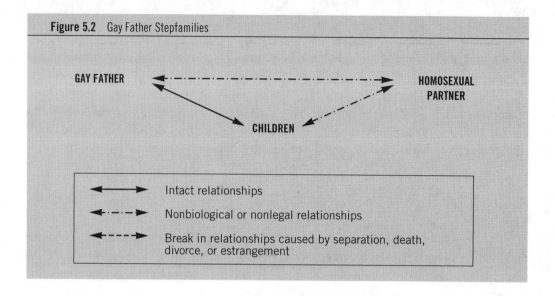

Figure 5.2 Gay Father Stepfamilies

GAY FATHER ←·–·–·–·–·–·–·–·–·–·→ HOMOSEXUAL PARTNER

CHILDREN

←——————→ Intact relationships

←–·–·–·→ Nonbiological or nonlegal relationships

←– – – –→ Break in relationships caused by separation, death, divorce, or estrangement

The heraldry of familialist privilege can be clearly read in the legend of conjunctive and disjunctive symbols accompanying the chart of the Eight Types (of which only two are reproduced here). The arrows with unbroken straight lines represent "Intact Relationships," namely those precious vestiges of straight family life that managed to survive the firestorm of Daddy's coming out. Notice how the Gay Father in both configurations has no chosen family members around to help him out: they evidently melted away in the nuclear ruins. Notice also how the Mother may still have an intact relationship with the Children in Type 5, while the Homosexual Partner manages only a nervous wavy line in his "Nonbiological or Nonlegal Relationships" with the kids in Type 6. Why the Homosexual Partner's relationship with the Gay Father is similarly squiggled in as nonlegal (illegal?) and, by implication, not intact (ruined or ruinous?) is left unanswered, perhaps because the answer goes without saying: the Straight Fathers Who Know Best view such connections through the corrective lens of the Public Eye as inherently weak, unstable, tempestuous, nausea-inducing. If you're connected to someone by a broken straight line, like Mother and Gay Father in Type 5, you're facing a dreaded "Break in Relationships Caused by Separation, Death, Divorce, or Estrangement." Encoded in the legend of the Eight Types is the fatalistic narrative of family breakdown dear to the hearts of marriage counsellors, divorce lawyers, evangelical preachers, and public health officials.

To counter the depressing impact of this narrative, I encourage my Homosexual Partner as well as my Children and their Mother to regard the post-nuclear extension of our family from a comic perspective as a wild and creative outgrowth rather than a tragic disintegration and destruction of what we once were. Family Breakout rather than Family Breakdown: get the picture? If you don't, then see Figure 5.3 for a clarification of my counterdiscursive vision of the family configuration at Panic Manor.

Figure 5.3 Panic Manor Family Configuration

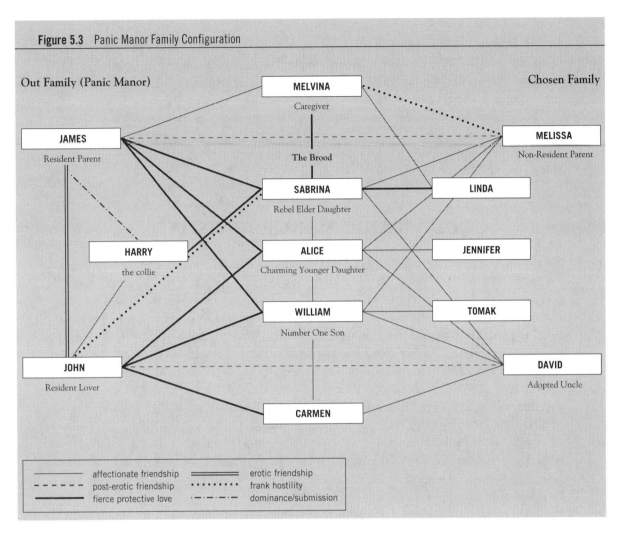

Out Family (Panic Manor)

Chosen Family

MELVINA
Caregiver

The Brood

JAMES
Resident Parent

MELISSA
Non-Resident Parent

SABRINA
Rebel Elder Daughter

LINDA

HARRY
the collie

ALICE
Charming Younger Daughter

JENNIFER

WILLIAM
Number One Son

TOMAK

JOHN
Resident Lover

DAVID
Adopted Uncle

CARMEN

————	affectionate friendship	════	erotic friendship
– – – –	post-erotic friendship	• • • • •	frank hostility
▬▬▬▬	fierce protective love	–·–·–	dominance/submission

No diagram, of course, can ever capture the feel of out family life or still its liveliness. How can I schematize sublime cultural epiphanies like the moment when Sabrina and her classmates sang "We Are the Safe Kids, We Are the Straight Kids!" in the anti-drug climax of their school play? How can I measure the gale-force of our laughter when John and I cracked up over this heterosexist anthem—to Sabrina's chagrin—while all the other parents in the audience stared at us in bewilderment? How can I graph the seismic ironies of the evening Alice tactfully informed Jennifer (who was babysitting) that if she was looking for a husband at our house she was "barking up the wrong tree"? How can I draw connecting arrows through William's heart, and through Melissa's, for all the nights he woke up at three in the morning to mourn her absence? How can I plot the twists and turns in the intense power struggle that broke out this summer between Sabrina and John after four years of resenting each other's purported "control" over me? How can I diagram the revival of

Linda's potently post-Christian godmother role in the dynamics of family disputes? How can I chart the subtle redistribution of parental authority at Panic Manor under the unruly rule of the gaytriarchy? How can I reduce to a simple line the enormous debate Sabrina and I had (and still have) over the homophobic representation of lesbians as child-eating raptors in the "same-sex environment" of *Jurassic Park*?

I can't, without bearing false witness to myself and my family. So that's why I won't have us treated as a case and our history closeted up in a case study of how and why a tragically Broken Family has absented itself from the happy throngs in Storybook Gardens. Consider this a proud outline of our presence in the Real World.

CODA: PANIC MANOR REVISITED

Six tumultuous years have passed since I first attempted to fit the idiosyncratic structure and expansive dynamics of Panic Manor into a diagram (see Figure 5.3). Only one family member has died in the interim—Harry the collie, who succumbed to canine lupus in 1996. His successor, a golden retriever named Manfred, is renowned throughout our neighbourhood for his sweet disposition and serene temperament. Though he has never formally come out to us, we strongly suspect that he is gay. Queer theorists would call him an "assimilationist." He just wants to fit in, and will do almost anything to please us. My three kids grew up with him, and despite the rough times we've been through lately, nothing ever seems to rub him the wrong way. My partner John calls him an *alma santa* ("saintly soul") for reminding us that peace can return even to Panic Manor.

I still live at Panic Manor, though the family structure I conceived there has collapsed with the apocalyptic finality of the World Trade Center towers. Looking back on that diagram, I feel unnerved beyond nostalgia. It's like gazing at the outlines of the twin towers cast by klieg lights into the night sky above Ground Zero.

Miraculously John and I have held together with a Whitmanesque "adhesiveness," having survived two family crises prompted by the urgent unhappiness of my elder daughter Sabrina. The first crisis coincided with her emotionally difficult transition to high school. Anyone who heard her practising alone in her room for hours on her electric bass guitar could tell that she was going to shake the foundations of Panic Manor in one way or another. When her midterm math grade fell below expectations, she informed her mother Melissa and her godmother Linda that she was in deep distress. Their timely support, plus a series of father–daughter therapy sessions at Family Service London, got her through a winter of discontent in which her frank hostility toward John and her volcanic anger at me were acknowledged as a serious problem affecting all members of the family.

To ease tensions, John moved out of Panic Manor for a few weeks in February of 1996 while Melissa mustered her reserves of good will and worked out a *modus vivendi* with me. By the time I found out about the math grade—three months later—Sabrina's problems at school seemed trivial in comparison with the *Sturm und Drang* stirred up by her rebellion at home. Manfred was bought for her as a peace offering and, as a further gesture of good will, as if to strengthen the blood ties linking us, Melissa adopted Manfred's charming brother Buddy. (Though neutered, Buddy has obligingly assumed a straight identity in harmony with his domestic environment.) Though Sabrina condemned us for trying to "bribe" her with a new pet, Panic Manor was soon vibrating again with the sound of her bass guitar and her roiling discontents appeared to be displaced once again into music. Deeply nostalgic for the period of her life when she lived in a "normal" family, she developed a passion for the rock groups of the 1980s. She was still very angry with me for forcing her to live under the much-altered conditions of the 1990s, and at herself too, I suspect, for failing to get what she seems to have wanted most: apologetic assurance of (and exclusive rights to) her father's love.

She very nearly succeeded in eliminating her rival during the second crisis, which coincided with her emotionally difficult transition to university. On December 20, 2000, midway through her freshman year at Western, she issued me an ultimatum. "Either John leaves Panic Manor or I quit university," she boldly declared over coffee at a campus café. Since her mother and I had just paid a hefty tuition installment the week before, I anxiously dithered for a few days and then decided to call her bluff. I opted to remain with my partner, and she promptly fled to Melissa's house and severed all ties with Panic Manor. True to her word, she quit university within a year.

In a fit of Wagnerian solipsism, I was inclined to see myself as a small-town version of the doomed sky-god Wotan attempting to deal with his fiercely recalcitrant daughter, the Valkyrie Brünnhilde. For some reason I had failed her love test and was to be punished for it. She, in turn, had failed my loyalty test and was to be banished for it. An opera buff, John tartly refers to this period in our lives as "Daughterdämmerung."

Queer theorists wisely warn us not to mistake our quaint constructs of "The Family" with what's really cooking beneath the surface of day-to-day family life, and though I tend to heed their warning academically, emotionally it's another story. My investment of hope and trust in the domestic experiment I was privately imposing on my children, my partner, my ex-wife, and my friends made me altogether too proud of its public blueprint. With the blindness of wishful thinking—that common parental failing to which idealistic gaytriarchs are peculiarly prone—I fondly believed that the diagram of my family possessed both the descriptive stability of an accurate social portrait and the prescriptive force of an emergent social model.

It possessed neither.

I've read enough long Russian novels to know that *even the happiest families change dramatically over time—usually for the worse.* Children grow up. Marriages break down. Feuds boil over. Friendships go under. Money runs out. Panic sets in. Like Prince André's crotchety old father in Tolstoy's *War and Peace*, I vainly clung to the rationalist assumption that the ethical design of my household—the diagram of my heart's home—would surely withstand the worst the unenlightened world had to offer. Visions of a brave new millennium could go up in smoke, and still my counterdiscursive diagram of Panic Manor would persist in the pages of this anthology, proclaiming the invincible perversity and brave realization of my ideals. Nothing in my literary background, however, prepared me for the explosive convergence of external heterosexist pressures and internal psychosexual conflicts that blew the experiment at Panic Manor to smithereens.

The external pressures arose quite suddenly—and strangely in tandem with our internal conflicts. In 1995, when I was drafting the first version of "Out Family Values," the gay community in London Ontario found itself under attack from two municipal leaders: an evangelical mayor who refused to grant a proclamation recognizing Gay Pride on the grounds that the God from whom she derived her "moral authority" forbade her to condone homosexuality; and a crusading police chief who whipped up a moral panic over pedophilia (that old standby of homophobic demagogues) after his officers supposedly discovered a "kiddie porn ring" operating in the heart of town.[6]

By March of 1995, the London kiddie-porn righ had been exposed as a myth by Toronto-based investigative journalists Gerald Hannon and Joseph Couture. In November of 1997, London's heterosexual majority voted their passively aggressive mayor Dianne Haskett back into office with a resounding show of support for her conservative stance on homosexuality—even though, a few short weeks before the election, she and her council had been found guilty of discrimination against the gay community and fined $10,000 by an Ontario government arbitrator.

I strongly suspect that my eldest daughter's rebellious anger at the radical nonconformity of Panic Manor was exacerbated by the circumambient moral turmoil of the city during her teen years. What I blithely defined as the salient values of the Out Family—brazenness, perversity, esprit, pride—she was compelled to live out, in earnest, against a social backdrop that reinforced her raging sense of having been betrayed by her parents, especially by her queer father, who had thrust her into a culturally discordant living arrangement that could at best be no more than a poor substitute for what mainstream society privileged as a "real" (i.e., nuclear) family. When she was 13, I recall, she put her foot down and absolutely refused to join me and her siblings in the Gay Pride March in Toronto, hitherto an annual family "outing." That was in 1994—about the time John and I began to wonder whether she was on the verge of coming out. And come out she did, four years later, in the emotional buildup to Daughterdämmerung.

Compared to, say, a Baptist minister's happy home, Panic Manor would seem to be an ideal place for a queer teen to come out in. Or so one might suppose. Ironically, for *my* queer teen, it appears to have been the *Twilight Zone*—an unsettling parody of the *Father Knows Best* world for which she passionately yearned with the frustrated conservatism of a refugee exiled from a fabled homeland taken over by an alien dictatorial power. No wonder she had difficulty fashioning her puckish version of lesbian identity within the male-dominated domain of Panic Manor. She needed her mother's heterosexually stabilized world against which to perceive and play out her own impetuous queerness, and to that other world, as Puck would say, she was to go "faster than a Tartar's bow."

Her difficult going opened up a kind of inter-familial "wormhole" through which her brother William swiftly followed at the age of 16. A straight arrow, he too felt the strong gravitational pull of his mother's alternative universe, and after many years of distancing himself from her, he was determined to rediscover who she had become on the other side of a wrenching divorce and in the happy wake of a second marriage. He moved into her house in June of 2001 and effectively cut off communication with Panic Manor until the following December.

These sudden changes in our custodial relations precipitated a surprising resurgence of divorce-era emotions in my ex and me—bitterness, anger, confusion, frustration, contempt, sorrow—which took expression in a series of what I came to call "hit-and-run e-mails." In one of these communications, demonstrating that vividness of expression for which she has received several literary prizes for fiction, she angrily compared my partner to a "vulture" circling around a corpse—namely me, presumably because I had "died" to her as a straight husband. Here was a homegrown example of what the 19th-century gay poet Gerard Manley Hopkins called "carrion comfort": a morbid aching despair that Melissa (like Hopkins, a Catholic convert during her university days) no doubt keenly felt at the time of my coming out in the late 1980s and had done her diplomatic best to bury during the 1990s. The raw detritus that came up our psychic drains in the aftermath of Daughterdämmerung was not pleasant for either of us, but its release was purgative. We're still friends, though on a rather distant footing. Today our communications are largely limited to unemotional e-mails about dentist bills and dogsitting arrangements. Canine comfort is strong on both sides.

Ironically, the contentious breakup of Panic Manor has resulted in the reconstruction of two rather conventional-looking nuclear families (see Figure 5.4) along the lines approved by middle-class marriage counsellors who urge divorced parents with joint custody over their children to find nice new partners and move on with their professional lives. A certain degree of social and psychological polarization is inevitable with this familial mitosis. At present, my younger daughter Alice, who has stayed with John and me through all these changes, finds herself in the position of chief mediator between the gaytriarchal and matriarchal universes. It is not an easy role to play at the tender age of 17, but she is a force of social concord and steps back and forth across the fault lines between the two households with grace and courage. Through her encouragement William is no longer a stranger to our house, and his identification with his mother's world, he now knows, does not require a rejection of his father's. Through the twins comes frequent word of their sister's doings, and I am glad to hear that she has recently found a worthy girlfriend, Sarah, whom we look forward to meeting someday.

Looking on the bright side, my partner and I often reflect on the one Out Family value that has truly come through for us, and that is flexibility. Gloria Gaynor's disco hit "I Will Survive" is now the official anthem of the new Panic Manor that we're building on the ruins of the old. That the collective life of the Out Family *has* survived we attribute to its strategic open-endedness, its adaptability to new circumstances, its out-and-out refusal to cave in to the ideological pressures of heterosexism and homophobia. The kinship-structure of the Out Family may be reduced these days at the level of parent–child relations, but its dynamically filiating design has not ceased to expand along the multiple levels of friendship. Six friends

Figure 5.4 Panic Manor Reconstruction

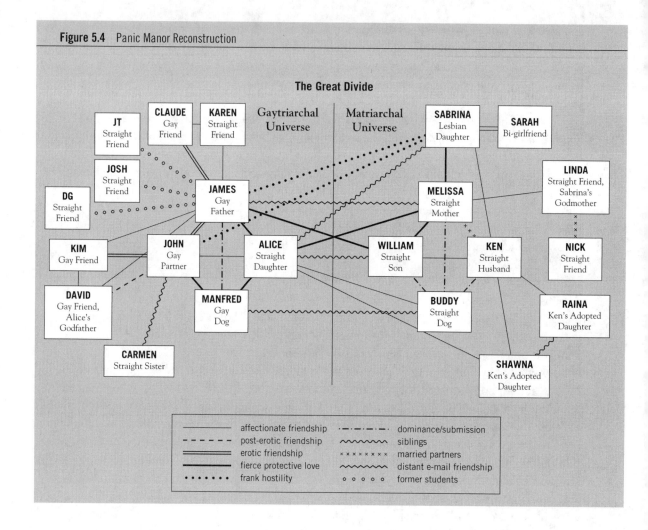

have been given new keys to our house in recognition of their principled support for its values and amicable engagement with its continuation. Four of these new members live out of town: Claude and JT in Toronto; Josh in Denver; and DG in Bangkok. The remaining two live in London and often join us for dinner. Kim is an oil painter who has recently completed exquisite portraits of Alice and Manfred, which proudly hang in our living room. Karen, a representative of the straight but not narrow community and possibly a sister from a previous life, helped me found the Pride Library at the UWO Research Facility for Gay and Lesbian Studies in 1997. A recent graduate of Western's Library Science program, she has also designed an exciting new Web site for LGBT families in Canada (http://familypride.uwo.ca)—a project made possible by a grant from the Counselling Foundation of Canada. As director of the Family Pride Canada project, I have also closely collaborated with Rachel Epstein at the Family Service Association in Toronto. Together,

Rachel and I hope to help other queer parents and their allies find the resources they need, and the peer support they seek, to face the challenges of raising Out Families of their own.

In the continuation of our Out Family, John and I have come to recognize the operation of a new value with a rather old-fashioned name: *perseverance*. We found our own way through the severity of internal rebellion and external *realpolitik*—we persevered—because we never lost our belief that we were doing the best job we could by raising three kids in a progressive way in a city regressing to the *Leave It to Beaver* era. Our sense of accomplishment in the Panic Manor experiment is unshadowed by guilt. As my crusty partner likes to point out, my vision of what's been lost at Panic Manor is absurdly hyperbolic. We have not lived through *War and Peace* or *Götterdämmerung* or a domestic version of 9/11. Napoleon's armies have not invaded London, Ontario. Panic Manor has not been destroyed by Wagnerian fire and flood. A jet plane has not slammed into my house. We've simply changed, as all families do, over time. And in the long run—Manfred suggests, wagging his tail—perhaps not for the worse.

NOTES

1. Screwball comedy doesn't get much screwier than the unapologetically escapist gay antics in Joe Keenan's *Blue Heaven* (New York: Penguin, 1988), where a chosen family cheekily beats an upper-crust WASP family at its own marriage game. Novels of this gossamer type provide a blessed relief for readers weighed down with a surfeit of heavily elegiac AIDS fiction.

2. For a moving vision of the reconciliation of a chosen family and a birth family around the deathbed of a gay PWA (person with AIDS), see the 1986 New Zealand film *A Death in the Family*, written by Peter Wells, directed by Stewart Main and Peter Wells, and produced by James H. Wally.

3. On the impact of Bryant's Save Our Children campaign on the gay and lesbian movement, see Lillian Faderman, *Odd Girls and Twilight Lovers: A History of Lesbian Life in Twentieth-Century America* (New York: Penguin, 1991), pp. 199–200. For a stirring blast of paranoid familialism, see Bryant's own inimitable manifesto: *The Anita Bryant Story: The Survival of Our Nation's Families and the Threat of Militant Homosexuality* (Old Tappan, NJ: Fleming H. Revell, 1977).

4. The first clause of Section 28 of the *Local Government (Amendment) Act*, which became law in the United Kingdom on March 24, 1988, reads: "A local government shall not (a) intentionally promote homosexuality or publish material with the intent of promoting homosexuality; (b) promote the teaching in any maintained school of the acceptability of homosexuality as a pretended family relationship." For a discussion of the political background and pedagogical consequences of this clause, see Simon Watney, "School's Out," in *Inside/Out: Lesbian Theories, Gay Theories*, edited by Diana Fuss (New York and London: Routledge, 1991), pp. 387–401.

5. Robert L. Barret and Bryan E. Robinson, *Gay Fathers* (Lexington, MA: D.C. Heath, 1990).

6. For an exposé of media compliance with the London police department's scandalously McCarthyite "Project Guardian," see Gerald Hannon's feature article "The Kiddie-Porn Ring That Wasn't" in *The Globe and Mail* (11 March 1995): D1, D5.

KEY TERMS

Chosen family: A network of friends, lovers, and ex-lovers to whom a gay man or lesbian turns for support as a compensatory alternative to his or her family of origin.

Closet: A symbolic image of imprisonment, secrecy, and (false) security signifying the culturally demanded and subsequently self-imposed silence a gay man or lesbian endures before disclosing his or her sexual identity.

Coming out: The more or less public act of declaring oneself a gay man or lesbian (as in "I've come out of the closet"); a continuous psychological, social, political, and religious process of affirming and celebrating one's pride as a gay man or lesbian in a world that regards such identities as shameful.

Discourse: (1) In common parlance: the way we talk about our social world, and the way it becomes known to us through our use of language; (2) in contemporary cultural theory: a system of prejudicial terms, distinctions, definitions, and imperatives by which a provisional world view is institutionally constructed, articulated, defended, and promoted as inevitable or "natural."

Dyke: (1) Still in common parlance: a slang term of abuse denoting (in general) a lesbian, but connoting (in particular) the gender treachery of female toughness or mannishness as in the expression "bull dyke"; (2) more recently, in gay and lesbian liberation discourse: a term of pride signifying a woman-loving woman who defies the conventionally shameful implications of the term.

Fag: (1) Still in common parlance: a slang term of abuse denoting (in general) a gay man, but connoting (in particular) the gender treachery of male wimpiness or effeminacy, like its synonym "fairy"; (2) more recently, in gay and lesbian liberation discourse: a term of pride signifying a man-loving man who defies the conventionally shameful implications of the term.

Familialism: A rigidly conservative view that the only real family is a traditional 1950s-style white, middle-class household with a faithfully married dad and mom whose sex life is strictly yet blissfully procreative, and whose high moral standards are passed on like old china to their perfectly heterosexual children.

Gay: (1) Still in common parlance: a synonym for "homosexual" (in general) but especially for "male homosexual"; (2) in gay community discourse: a term of pride denoting not simply a sexual identity at odds with conventional gender expectations (and hence opposed to "straight") but also a social and political identity forged in opposition to familialism, heterosexism, and conservatism.

Gaytriarchy: An anarcho-democratic parody of patriarchy in which the traditional centralizing of authority in straight males is deliberately counteracted by the loosening up of power structures through camp subversion of family hierarchies and gender roles.

Heterosexism: The prejudicial privileging of heterosexuality as a dominant cultural institution over minority sexualities, which are in turn "inferiorized" and even "demonized" by comparison with the heterosexual ideal.

Heterosexuality: (1) In common parlance (derived from late 19th-century medical and sexological discourse): a sexual identity narrowly defined by preference for partners of the "opposite" sex; (2) in contemporary cultural theory: a religiously sanctioned and politically promoted institution in which membership is implicitly compulsory for all men and women who want their sexual relations and family arrangements to be celebrated publicly, supported financially, and recognized legally without opposition from the Powers That Be.

Homophobia: An as-yet poorly explained (though culturally pervasive) fear of homosexuality, which expresses itself as a trivializing contempt or a crusading hatred for homosexuals.

Homosexism: The counter-privileging of homosexuality as a spiritually or aesthetically superior institution to heterosexuality; usually in reaction to heterosexism.

Homosexuality: (1) In common parlance (derived from late 19th-century medical and sexological discourse): a sexual identity narrowly defined by preference for partners of the "same" sex; (2) in contemporary cultural theory: a seemingly objective but deeply exclusionary term denoting the ideologically charged opposite of all that heterosexuality as a dominant institution values, promotes, and defines itself by (including "The Family" in a familialist sense).

Out (adjective): (1) Privately and/or publicly identified as gay or lesbian, usually qualified with respect to family, friends, colleagues, and so on: as in "I'm out to Joe and Sally, but not out to my parents," and "Svend Robinson is still the only out member of Parliament"; (2) markedly unconventional in showing a positive celebratory attitude toward gays and lesbians, and in supporting the antidiscrimination agenda of gay liberation: as in "Aunt Marion's straight, but she's really out about her membership in Parents and Friends of Lesbians and Gays."

Out (verb): (1) To bring someone out of the closet by public disclosure, usually against his or her conscious wishes, and sometimes for punitive political purposes, as in "Roy Cohn was outed by his political enemies"; (2) to compel a person or a group of persons (regardless of their sexuality) to deal with the presence, the problems, and the pride of out gays and lesbians, as in "Now that Mummy's out as a radicalesbian, our whole family feels outed by her public campaign for same-sex spousal benefits."

Post-nuclear: See *post-nuclear extended family*.

Post-nuclear extended family: Any close-knit supportive combination of parents, children, friends, relatives, lovers, and ex-lovers that forms after the meltdown of a nuclear family through divorce; in particular, the synthesis of a chosen family with (or around) an out family.

Queer: (1) Still in common parlance, a homophobic label applied to anyone (male or female) who is perceived to be sexually "different" from the heterosexual norm; (2) in contemporary outspeak, a term of pride denoting a gay man, lesbian, bisexual, or transsexual who is allied with the radical end of post-Stonewall politics, as in "We joined Queer Nation last week to protest gay-bashing on Church Street."

Semiotics: The structuralist study of sign systems, especially nonverbal "signs" such as ritual actions or images that are "read" as if they were elements in a language.

Stonewall: The name of a Greenwich Village, New York, bar where a riot broke out in June 1969 between the bar's mainly gay clientele and the police; hence, the mythical origin of the gay liberation movement, as in "After Stonewall, gays and lesbians marched in the streets to proclaim their self-empowerment."

Uncloseted: See *closet.*

DISCUSSION QUESTIONS

1. What, according to the author of this essay, are the characteristics of an out family? In what contexts does he define its values? How is the out family to be distinguished from the chosen family, and against what background is this distinction made?

2. What is the most immediate effect of the author's uncloseted gayness on his children? What other reasons does he give for outing his family?

3. List the ideological foes of out and chosen families.

4. Sketch the social context of the Panic Manor out family. Outline how the author, his ex-wife, his partner, and the children each experience outness.

5. What strategies are suggested for combatting the homophobic backlash directed against out families?

6. How can "Out Family Values" be defined as an "anti–case study"? Why does Miller so strongly resist the genre of the case study even as his essay seems to conform to, and indeed is explicitly classified under, this category? What does the elaborate diagram of the relationships in the Panic Manor out family reveal when compared with the configurations in conventional social science case studies?

6

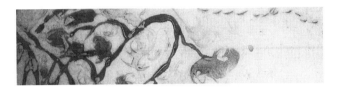

Families and Parents with Disabilities

Karen A. Blackford
Neita K. Israelite
Faculty of Education, York University

Karen Blackford died on January 13, 2000, in Winnipeg, Manitoba. The original essay, which she wrote for inclusion in the first edition of this text, has been revised by Neita Israelite. This essay is dedicated to the memory of Karen Blackford as a recognition of her work in the area of disability.

Objectives

- To consider the variety of experiences and choices that family members can encounter in the context of family life and parents with disabilities.[1]

- To uncover the barriers associated with disability that come from how society is organized.

- To show that strengths such as flexibility and acceptance of difference can be associated with families with a parent with a disability.

INTRODUCTION

Imagine you are a new mother who is deaf or hard of hearing. Your infant, like many other infants, cries a lot, especially at night. Your landlady views the crying as a sign that you are an unfit mother, and phones the Children's Aid Society (CAS). Shortly thereafter, while you and your newborn son are visiting with some friends, a team of CAS workers and police officers descends upon you and apprehends your baby.

Although people might think that an incident like this could not possibly happen in the 21st century in an enlightened country such as Canada, it recently did happen to a single mother in Toronto. "There was no sign language interpreter. We had no idea what they were talking about. I didn't know why and where they were taking my baby." All the mother was left with was a business card (Keung 2002).

The belief that people with disabilities are incapable of adequately parenting their children is not uncommon. Results of the first national survey of parents with disabilities in the United States indicate that 42 percent of the parents studied reported facing serious attitudinal barriers to parenting, especially in the form of discrimination (Barker and Marilani 1997). This issue was also the focus of *I Am Sam*, a 2001 American movie that chronicled the experiences of a single father with a developmental disability attempting to raise a daughter on his own.

In Canada, approximately 4.2 million Canadians (15.5 percent of the population) of all ages reported some degree of disability in 1991.[2] Of this group, 3.8 million were aged 15 and over, representing 17.8 percent of the total Canadian adult population. The incidence of disability increases with age; in 1991, for example, 7 percent of children under 15 experienced some degree of disability as compared to 13 percent of individuals aged 15 to 64 and 50 percent of individuals aged 65 and over (Human Resources Development Canada 1998). Although many people with a disability are beyond childbearing years, accidents and chronic illnesses such as multiple sclerosis (MS) and lupus more frequently affect adults during this period. We can presume, therefore, that there are a substantial number of Canadians with disabilities who are parents.

As Dr. Blackford noted in the original version of this chapter, there are relatively few studies that take up the issue of a parent with a disability and fewer yet that look at the topic from a non-pathological perspective. Now, as then, the dynamics of family life in relation to parents with disabilities remains a challenge for sociologists. Researchers are only beginning to uncover the patterns of family life associated with a parent with a disability and to illuminate the barriers and strengths found in these families.

This chapter begins with a discussion of the theoretical positions that frame perceptions of nondisabled people toward parents with disabilities, then it reviews the literature on family life and parents with disabilities. Finally, the chapter presents an intimate view of family life from the perspective of children and adults in families in which a parent has MS, based on Dr. Blackford's (1995) doctoral dissertation. Throughout the chapter, we shall see how family members play an active part in working out relationships in the face of obstacles associated with disability. It is a testament to Dr. Blackford that my part in this endeavour has been little more than providing an update to an already comprehensive and moving discussion of the barriers that families in which a parent has a disability face and how they work out relationships in spite of these barriers.

THE STUDY OF PARENTS WITH DISABILITIES AND THEIR FAMILIES

Theoretical Foundations

Two major theoretical positions inform attitudes and beliefs about disability and their implications for families: the traditional **medical model** and the **social model**. The medical model assumes that differences in physical, sensory, or mental capabilities necessarily produce a defective member of society who must be cured or fixed. This model holds that any difficulties people with disabilities experience are due to problems located within the individual, and not due to environmental, societal, physical, or attitudinal barriers within the larger society. For instance, people with physical disabilities have housing problems because they cannot climb stairs; people with visual impairments have transportation problems because they cannot read bus timetables. People who are deaf have parenting problems because they cannot hear their children.

A critical dimension of the medical model is the notion of power. Identifying disability as a defect within the individual gives permission to those who are not disabled to take charge. This gives rise to paternalism and a patriarchal-like set of dynamics in which the power is held by and transferred through nondisabled people. The medical model is the foundation for legislation, education, and rehabilitation aimed at people with disabilities, and patriarchal values have long been a dominant force in these areas. The continual application of this view has institutionalized discrimination against people with disabilities in all aspects of their everyday lives.

In contrast to the medical model, the social model views disability as a social identity. It holds that the "problem" of disability is inherent not to the individual, but rather to the social structure. The cause of disability is society's failure to provide appropriate services and to adequately ensure that the needs of people with disabilities are fully taken into account. Disability, from this perspective, is constructed as all the things that impose restrictions on people with disabilities: individual prejudice, institutional discrimination, inequitable legislation, inaccessible buildings, unusable public transit, segregated educational environments, and exclusionary work arrangements. These types of problems are institutionalized in our society and they affect not only the individual, but also people with disabilities as a group.

Related to the medical and social models are the taken-for-granted or commonly held beliefs that people without disabilities hold about those with disabilities. As Krogh (1998: 4) explains, "People in society are frequently unconscious of beliefs that are socially hidden but that strongly condition social behaviour." One such belief is that, because of their deficits, people with disabilities have a **stigma**; that is, a mark or sign of shame, disgrace, or disapproval, or, in the words of Erving Goffman, an "attribute that is deeply discrediting" (1963, 3). According to Goffman, people who are stigmatized (e.g., people with disabilities) are frequently seen as "not quite human." The effects of this perception as well as the attitudes and behaviours that stem from it are damaging not only to people with disabilities, but also to their family, friends, and the community at large. Stigma also plays a role in the perpetuation of **ableism,** a pervasive system of discrimination and exclusion that operates on the individual, institutional, and societal levels to oppress people with disabilities. Ableism reflects the commonly held view that people with disabilities are inadequate in meeting normative expectations for economic roles as well as social roles such as parenting. The prevalence of stigma and ableism in our society play a large part in the assumptions of dysfunction that emerge when families with a parent with a disability are identified.

Given the inequitable power differentials that characterize relations between people with and without disabilities, it is important to focus on fostering social change through raising awareness. One way of doing so is to attempt to increase the general public's sense of social responsibility by giving voice to the personal stories of people with disabilities (Krogh 1998). This chapter seeks to make known the experiences of families in which a parent has a disability through firsthand accounts of their experiences as they attempt to construct productive lives for themselves and their families.

Research Knowledge

There are few studies on parents with disabilities and their nondisabled children in the research literature. Much of this work is based on the medical model, dealing to a large extent with ways that professionals can best involve people with disabilities in instructional and/or remedial programs to improve their parenting skills. Studies of family life when a parent has a disability generally tend to take a pathological perspective. Families have been labelled as **dysfunctional** (Sullivan 1980) and pathologically close in terms of family interactions (Rice 1986; Kikuchi 1985; Kikuchi and Molzahn 1989). Those children whose parents have chronic disabling conditions such as kidney disease, lupus, and MS are presented as antisocial, depressed, angry (Arnaud 1957), and precociously mature (Arnaud 1957; Friedlander and Viederman 1982). More recently, there has been debate and discussion regarding the role of children of parents with disabilities (see, for example, Keith and Morris 1996; Olsen and Parker 1997). Of concern to this critique is the term used to describe these children; that is, "young carers," with its implicit assumption that parents with disabilities indeed are in need of care. As well, young carers have been described as having lost their childhoods due to the overwhelming responsibility that having a parent with a disability engenders.

Although some studies have identified barriers to social relations in families with a parent with a disability, exploration of the sources of that oppression is lacking. Instead, as per the medical model, these studies leave the impression that it is the parent with the disability who is the problem. Disability activists and theorists supporting the social model (e.g., Abberley 1987; Oliver 1990) insist, however, that it is necessary to look beyond the problem of the individual's adaptation to disability. The disability of a parent must be understood not merely as a problem for the family that must be "fixed" through a medicalized therapeutic approach. Instead, it is important to acknowledge problems that rest outside the individual and to question the extent to which barriers to successful parenting are societally imposed.

As we have explained, disability is socially created through everyday practices. A narrow view of families with a parent with a disability that focuses only on what happens inside the family fails to sufficiently take into account stigma and ableism in the larger society. Such a view results in what has been called "blaming the victim" (Ryan 1972). Society frequently views parents with disabilities, especially mothers, as totally dependent individuals who have somehow committed an immoral act by becoming parents (Fine and Asch 1988; Finger 1991). Mothers with disabilities, in particular, "shoulder the burden of society's perception of them as incompetents who have irresponsibly become mothers who will, along with their offspring, unquestionably become a burden on society" (Baskin and Riggs 1988, 240). When problems exist for family members, mothers are commonly blamed (Caplan 1989). And when mothers are women with disabilities, society's sexist views compounded by its ableist views make them easy targets for criticism.

Cogswell (1976), for example, reports that family stress is associated with changes in traditional gender roles when rigid sex-role boundaries existed prior to the onset of a disabling condition. Merchant (1969) found that children of disabled mothers are oppressed by excessive helping responsibilities when able-bodied fathers do not alter previous gendered expectations. Mothers with disabilities have also reported abusive husbands and a slightly higher rate of abuse than other disabled women (Ridington 1989). In fact, the rate of abuse among women with disabilities is greater than in the general population. If the father is the disabled parent, his manliness is called into question by society, perhaps by family members and by himself. Stigma is simply assumed to be acceptable and "natural." That the pressures of stigma from outside the family may intrude on social relations within the family is rarely considered.

Poverty is another major factor that must be addressed when considering families and parental disability. Adults with disabilities generally have lower incomes than other Canadians. They tend to have less formal education and to be less often in waged employment. For example, in the 1991 census, 43.7 percent of people with disabilities were not in the workforce, in contrast to 37.8 percent of people without disabilities (Fawcett 1996).

Women with disabilities are more likely to live in poverty than male counterparts, most likely due, at least in part, to the influence of childbearing, childrearing, marital status, and domestic responsibilities. In 1991, women with disabilities who were mothers of preschool-aged children were less likely to be in the labour force than women with no dependants and/or women with school-aged children. Those mothers of preschool-aged children who were employed indicate a need for job redesign in order to continue to work. Fawcett (1996) posits that this need for a change in job structure was due to factors related not only to their disability but also to domestic responsibilities, and those mothers who made changes to the nature of their work experienced greater poverty levels than male counterparts who also made changes.

Incomes of even middle-class families with disabled parents are substantially reduced by expenses associated with the purchase of accessibility devices or with necessary adaptations to housing and transportation. When any family member is disabled, that family must absorb extraordinary costs associated with physical access at home, transportation, accessibility devices, and either attendant care or housekeeping assistance such as wheelchairs. When it is the parent who is disabled, parental employment income is often reduced or lost entirely. These factors work together to push families with a parent with a disability into poverty.

Results of the 1991 census indicate that women with disabilities tend to be more likely to be lone parents of dependent children than women without disabilities. This finding is illustrative of a trend toward increased separation and divorce associated with a parent with a disability, particularly when the disabled spouse is a woman, in Canada (Fawcett 1996; Ridington 1989) as well as the United States (Litman 1974; Hoover, MacElveen, and Alexander 1975) and England (University of Southampton 1989). Typically, it is able-bodied women who stay and provide care, and able-bodied men who leave the family. However, as Dr. Blackford points out, we cannot always assume that the spouse with the disability is being abandoned. In her research, some parents with MS saw the period in which they were adjusting to their initial diagnosis as an opportunity to reconsider their lives and end their unhappy marriages. Nevertheless, there were also instances in which spouses with disabilities did feel abandoned. They described their partners who left the marriage as "not able to take" the disability. Such stories must be considered in the context of contemporary society with its ableist attitudes and deeply entrenched biases against people with disabilities. That external societal forces such as these have an important impact on life in families with a parent with a disability cannot be denied.

New Perspectives on Family Life with Parents with Disabilities

Traditional research with parents with disabilities has failed to acknowledge the creative ways in which families have come to deal with their situations. Consideration has not often been given to the potential for alternative definitions of family life that might emerge when a parent has a disability. In the 1930s, pioneering sociologist George Herbert Mead (1964) advocated seeking the person's own definition of her or his situation. However, few researchers have adopted this perspective when studying families with a parent with a disability.

One such researcher is Heather Beanlands (1987), who used open-ended interviews with children of parents with kidney disease. Beanlands found that children described a hardy appreciation for life in the present, a strong sense of hope, and an understanding that the course of their lives is linked with the course of their parents' lives, including the course of their parents' chronic illness.

More recently, following in-depth interviews with parents with learning disabilities, Booth and Booth (1993) conclude that the competence of parents with disabilities must be assessed within the context of their lives and upbringing. Subsequent research by these authors (1994) demonstrates the value of in-depth interviewing for giving voice to the issues and concerns of individuals with learning disabilities. In another study conducted from a non-pathological perspective, Llewellyn (1995) explored views on relationships and social support for parenting with couples with mental retardation or intellectual disability. Participants did not always see professional support as beneficial, preferring to access assistance from their partners and/or family members before seeking professional help.

There have been several studies of families involved in self-help groups for persons with disabilities. Results of one project suggest that some children in families with chronically ill parents demonstrate increased achievement and responsibility in the school situation (Rhode Island Chapter of the MS Society 1989). Other researchers have shown that, although responses to parents with disabilities are mixed, some children with a parent with a disability show high levels of confidence and self-sufficiency (University of Southampton 1989). Dr. Blackford's (1990) findings in a study conducted in conjunction with Persons United for Self Help in northeastern Ontario show children and their parents with various disabilities creating flexible family systems that are not always bound by traditional expectations of the division of labour with regard to age, gender, and physical condition. Many family members were more accepting of "difference" in their relationships outside the family. Children and parents lived in and for the moment, rather than constantly anticipating the future. These results suggest that consideration of families with parents with disabilities can enlarge our view of what family life could or should be.

Dr. Blackford argues that most researchers studying the subject of parents with disabilities have failed to take into account both structure and agency. The term *structure* describes the broad social system that constrains all of us. We are affected by our economic circumstances, by government policies and programs, and by others who see us in particular ways and who have the power to exclude us from relationships. At the same time as the world is affecting us, we interact with that world in a way that demonstrates human agency. **Agency** can be seen in the social action we take, through our communications, and in the way we see the world or imagine a world that could be. Through our own agency we create our own history (Abrams 1982). An understanding of the ways in which we create the world we live in, even while we are responding to that world, is missing from previous literature on families with disabled parents.

To illustrate how both constraint and individual agency are important to the everyday life experience of families with disabled parents, Dr. Blackford shares, in the following pages, some of what she learned through interviews with families in which parents have MS. MS affects women more often than men through the destruction of myelin, a substance that protects nerve tissue, so that nerve transmission to and from the brain and spinal cord becomes disrupted. Mild to severely disabling outcomes are possible (Wakesman, Reingold, and Reynolds 1987). Between 1990 and 1992, as part of her doctoral work, Dr.

Blackford visited 18 families with a parent who had MS. Individual in-depth interviews with each family member at home permitted her a glimpse of family life when a parent has a disability. To give you a flavour of these interviews, and to demonstrate how structure and agency are played out in everyday family relations with a disabled parent, we now introduce the Taylors,[3] one of the 18 families Dr. Blackford studied.

Brian Taylor and His Family

Sixteen-year-old Brian Taylor is the eldest of three children. His siblings are Sandra, aged 14, and 9-year-old Brent. Their mother, Joanne Taylor, was diagnosed with MS after the birth of her youngest son, when Brian was 7 years old. The family lives in a low-income high-rise two-bedroom apartment in a large southern Ontario city. Mr. Taylor, a police officer, left his wife shortly after her illness was diagnosed. He now lives with his second wife. The children usually visit him on alternate weekends.

Brian is a strongly built, thoughtful young man whose main focus appears to be his family's well-being, in particular that of his mother. Other interests include school work, his friends at school, and the school swim team. For Sandra, friendships appear to be the highest priority. Sandra also seems determined to prepare herself for college or university. Brent responds cheerfully and briefly to direct questions, but he does not initiate or elaborate discussion. His conversation is focused mostly on his sports activities.

Mrs. Taylor uses a scooter (instead of a wheelchair) almost constantly. At times, she needs assistance to get on and off. Prior to her marriage she did factory work and her husband worked on the docks. She expected that he would continue at his work while she stayed at home with the children. She explained that around the time her husband joined the police force, he took on a new lifestyle. He became involved in socializing late at night and in abusing alcohol more often. It was at this point in their relationship that Brent was conceived. Her MS began shortly after Brent's birth, and the marriage ended about this time. Mrs. Taylor says, "I'm not saying he left because of the MS," although her presentation of events implies that she believed MS to be an important motivator to the divorce.

Structural Constraints: A Family Marginalized

Housing and Transportation

With three children, a dog, and Joanne Taylor's scooter, the Taylor home is crowded. Mrs. Taylor shares a bedroom with her 14-year-old daughter Sandra. Brian and Brent share the other bedroom. Because of their low-income housing, Mrs. Taylor worries a great deal about where Brent goes to play and with whom. This creates stress as well as an additional chore for Brian and Sandra, since they have the responsibility of finding their brother for meals and keeping track of him.

The high-rise apartment has an elevator, but one with doors that close very quickly. According to Brian, Mrs. Taylor is virtually a prisoner during the day when her children are at school.

Trying to back into an elevator takes time, and the elevator would close on you. There was one main-floor accessible apartment going to be built downstairs but they did not bother. But that would have been good for her. She could have went to the store.

Brian recounts an incident when his mother fell in the bathroom, and she couldn't get up until a concerned neighbour investigated her unanswered telephone.

One time, Mom was on the ground. She couldn't stand up. Like the heat makes you lose energy with your MS. So she was all tired and couldn't get on her scooter. She hurt her wrist. Eventually the lady upstairs came down.

Since Sandra shares a bedroom with her mother, her day begins with helping out if necessary. Sandra points out her bed in the bedroom where the interview took place.

Right here. So if anything happens in the morning, she calls me. The dog's crying, she calls me. If she has to go to the washroom, she calls me. She can't get out of bed, she calls me. But it's OK—sometimes. Sometimes she doesn't call me, though.

The Taylor children all want their own rooms, so Mrs. Taylor tries to keep the peace.

Brian wants his own bedroom, so I said to Sandra, "We will bring Brent's bed in and put it over here." "Oh, yeah, Brian's got his own bedroom. What about me?" I say, "Well, Brian's older," "Well, I want my own bedroom, too!" The bickering!

Because of their crowded housing, Mrs. Taylor worries that her children may someday choose to move in with her ex-husband. When he first left, she was aware that he was abusing alcohol. She has had concerns that the children have been exposed to his drinking on their visits to his new home. Joanne Taylor has strong views about the importance of collective responsibility and of keeping the family together. Therefore, this concern about inadequate housing gives her a good deal of stress.

I know that MS is not a killer, but [our housing problem] is on my mind constantly … What I am scared of is that I am not going to be able to raise the three children till they are of age—that they will end up going with their father. That is my biggest fear. I don't like to look into the future because I don't know what's in store. The future scares me … I am willing to go into a nursing home. In fact, I am looking forward to it. But I want to raise the kids first. I wear diapers now because I can't get to the bathroom on time.

Personal-Care Services

Until recently, home care provided the Taylor family with services three times weekly. These services included a nurse, a homemaker to assist with laundry and housecleaning, and a physiotherapist to ensure that Mrs. Taylor could maintain as much muscle strength as possible. Joanne Taylor explained that recently these services have been reduced.

A nurse used to come, and a physiotherapist. But then the physio showed Brian and Sandra how to exercise my legs. Not that they do it, but she showed them. They know to do it if I ask them; [otherwise] I don't exercise at all. But if I ask them to come do the exercises they might fuss, but they come. They are really great kids!

Joanne Taylor takes great interest and pride in her children's development. She encourages them to get their homework done and worries if they do not have time to spend with friends. Brian Taylor corroborates his mother's description of reduced services:

> She got a call from some social worker and they cut her down to one day a week. They said we [the children] can do a lot of it. But they don't get it. Do they expect us only to clean? Like, homework, going out with friends—like, do they expect us only to clean all the time? I don't really think they take if it's fair into consideration! Like, school's finished at 3:05 and you are going to be home all this time. They don't care whether you go out or do this or that. That's it. They don't care. That's what I think.

When the home-care services were reduced, the expectation of home-care staff was that Brian and Sandra would help with their mother's exercises. The expectation that family life can and should revolve around a medical regime reflects the medicalized view of disability. Such a view forces parents with disabilities into the dependent role of patient and makes the demands of medical science a priority in family life.

Mrs. Taylor does not feel that she can also ask Brian and Sandra for their help for her exercise program, since this would further reduce their opportunities for homework and peer socializing. Therefore, her muscles become progressively weaker. From one perspective, Mrs. Taylor is depriving herself of an opportunity of sustained muscle strength. As her legs weaken she will have to rely on others increasingly for physical assistance. From an alternative perspective, Joanne Taylor can be seen as resisting medical dogma by insisting that her role is mother within a child-centred family. She is the family leader and decision-maker, and refuses to give up that role for a more dependent one. This ironic situation is one that many families with a parent with a disability face. The dilemma is a product of three interacting structural forces: the medicalization of disability; societal expectations that family labour will be divided along gender and age lines; and insufficient publicly funded home-care services.

Extended-Family Relations

Out of the 18 families Dr. Blackford interviewed, 4 shared accommodation with extended-family members for all or part of the week. It is no coincidence that 3 of these 4 families were single-parent families.

Once every weekend, Joanne Taylor and her children go to her parents' home. Since Joanne does not have a car, her father and brother do the family's weekly grocery shopping. As Brian Taylor explains:

> They shop around different stores for different prices. They do that because [I don't] drive. So I don't really do the grocery shopping. They buy it at my grandmother's on the weekend and we take it Sunday night when we come home.

As Mrs. Taylor explains, accessible housing is an issue for the Taylor family in her parents' home, as well as in their own residence.

> [At my mother's on the weekend,] Brian helps me through the door onto the scooter and then he helps me off the scooter back up the stairs. He lifts my legs up.

Brian Taylor provides his perspective on access at his grandparents' home:

When she gets off her scooter at my grandparents' and she is going up the stairs and she is having a whole lot of trouble, then I can tell that she is in a good mood, but she is exhausted with her leg. Like, it doesn't seem to want to work today. It is a disease that affects the leg. My Mom's legs tighten.

Within extended-family relations, Mrs. Taylor is placed in a special category so that her position as a family leader—as a parent—is sometimes jeopardized. Well-meaning extended-family members are reminded of Joanne's disability when she struggles up the stairs in her parents' home. Joanne says that once she is there, "My mother waits on me hand and foot. I can't do anything for myself there. If my kids don't jump to get me a cup of coffee, she's on their back!"

Brian provides his own impression of his grandparents:

They help a lot. They do a lot for her, so that helps out a lot. My grandmother, she sort of gets into different moods. She usually gets grouchy on Sandra. But that gets my mom in a bad mood.

Other sole-support mothers in the study raised the issue of lack of respect from extended family with regard to their judgment as parents. Although grandparents were not interviewed, accounts of other family members indicate that grandparents are anxious about their adult children's disability and feel an increased sense of responsibility for their grandchildren. This was most evident when the disabled parent was a woman and a single parent. Yet there also appeared to be *cohort* (or generational) differences in parenting style and expectations of children between mothers and fathers and their older parents. For example, one woman with MS was caught between following through on agreements she had made with her children and the expectations of her parents on whom she was continually dependent for transportation, housing, and financial assistance. In this household, the teenagers' bedtime was a source of contention, since the grandparents lived upstairs. When physical disability increases the need for help, relations with extended family are rarely recognized as reciprocal. In the case of Joanne Taylor, the interest she takes in her nephews and the emotional support she provides for her mother are overlooked. She is seen only as disabled and dependent.

Community Relations

As Sandra and Brian Taylor describe their school experiences, making provisions for parents with disabilities appears to be outside the school's mandate. In fact, as Brian indicated, these children learned at school that MS is "not something to talk about."

They must have figured that something was wrong. Some of them knew what it was. Some didn't. All the teachers I had never mentioned it, you know. I figured that's as it should be.

Sandra's teachers know that Joanne Taylor is disabled. They also know that she is a single parent, since she regularly attends parent–teacher evenings.

We had this school where my mom couldn't get in the front doors where the office was. She had to go all the way 'round the school through the janitor doors. It was the only place in the whole school that she could get in. My classrooms were usually upstairs. My mom couldn't climb the stairs. She said, "Get your teacher to meet me in the office." I had to explain to them and they said, "OK, sure." So then they would go down to the office. One time when I was in Grade 7 my mom went to one parent–teacher interview, and then there was another one, and then my father went, so he could walk up the stairs. I was in my class-room listening to all that she [the teacher] said. Then she said, "Now it's time for me to talk to your father. Out!"

Teachers presume that Sandra is there to look after her mother in some way. She is therefore allowed to be present when her mother attends parent–teacher interviews, as though she and her mother have equal status. In contrast, when her father is there he is privileged with a private interview. This school situation demonstrates to Sandra that there is more respect for a nondisabled, employed male than for a full-time mother with MS. When her father arrives, she is ordered out. Thus, it is quite clear to Mrs. Taylor's children that their mother receives exceptional treatment as a parent in the school setting.

Volunteer organizations that raise money for research by presenting parents with dis-abilities as tragic victims or heroes also contribute to their stigma and to the stigma of other family members. In addition, this type of representation of disability influences a disabled parent's view of herself and a child's view of that parent. For example, in its early years, the MS Society of Canada depicted women with MS as "sufferers," as a strategy for playing on public sympathy in order to raise funds for cure-directed biomedical research (Blackford 1993). Over time, the image presented changed to one of "fighters" against MS. The notion of persons with disabilities as either victims or heroes has since been criticized by sociolo-gists (Abberley 1987; Oliver 1990) as a way to maintain social distance between people with disabilities and other people. Confined as they are by these limiting definitions, parents with disabilities face a more difficult task as they work to define themselves as family leaders. One boy in the study described his mother with MS as a "hero, like Terry Fox," a represen-tation that made his mother extremely uncomfortable. As she expressed it, such an expec-tation is "a lot to live up to."

Mrs. Taylor expresses concern that the MS Society, which is eager to have members raise money for medical research, does not meet her own needs for a support group. She also sees that her children have need of "someone to talk to" about their feelings and questions about her MS. Brian Taylor explains: "I haven't really read a book on it. I don't know if reading about it will do much, you know."

Abberley (1987) has argued that the oppression associated with disability is socially cre-ated. This discussion demonstrates how this is true for families with disabled parents. As we have seen, **disability oppression** presents itself in reduced financial resources because of reduced parental employment and increased expenses for supports and services. Thus, middle-class families are strained and working-class families are impoverished. But disability oppression is much broader than economic oppression alone. It presents itself in the form of increased incidence of intrafamily abuse and divorce, increased family workload, insufficient family support services, inadequate housing and essential services, and disability stigma.

142

INDIVIDUAL AND COLLECTIVE AGENCY: FAMILIES TAKING ACTION, CONSTRUCTING IDENTITIES, AND MAKING CHOICES

Dr. Blackford's findings suggest that children growing up with a parent with a disability might be among those who Philip Abrams (1982) describes as "most actively in the market" for new meanings of disability, childhood, and family. They might be most likely to seize "opportunities for constructing new versions" of these concepts. But how do they become active and embark on such constructions? Abrams explains that, in spite of the external coercive way in which individuals experience society, they are still "busy making and re-making it through their own imagination, communication and social action" (1982, 2). The participants in Dr. Blackford's study clearly described their own agency as part of a family with a parent with a disability in these three areas.

Social Action: Modifying Work and Recreation

Children and their parents with disabilities demonstrate many ways in which they insist on directing their own lives and carrying out family goals. In our ageist, sexist, and ableist society, families are expected to be child-centred if children are present and patient-centred if a person with disabilities is present. Caring inside the family is expected to be the responsibility of adult females. Some families with a parent with a disability resist these outsiders' definitions. Family members acknowledge the parent's position as family leader, disabled or not. They support each other in getting on with the business of sharing tasks and participating in recreational activities. Sandra Taylor provides a picture of how work is done in her home.

> Usually it's my brother who cooks [after school]. My little brother usually plays outside. Then he comes in yelling at us. "You should have called me!" Meanwhile, we were trying to find him all over the building. But we can't do anything 'cause we don't want to start a fight and get Mom all upset. So we just keep our mouths shut.

We see in this example that Brian and his sister work with their mother to maintain family functioning. These teenagers do what they can to assist with childcare, meals, and keeping peace in the family. Brian also helps by accompanying his mother to medical clinic visits. This can include lifting his mother at times.

> One time I was with her and we went to see her neurologist. She got a note to get an X-ray. I was trying to figure out what they [were] taking an X-ray of. It was pretty tough. She had to lie down on the X-ray table and it was hard getting her up there.

Recreational arrangements are modified, along with work arrangements. Brian Taylor chooses to take part in swimming, which allows him to practise in the early hours of the day. This way he can be available after school to make supper, but can still maintain peer connections, enjoy a sport he loves, and keep fit.

> Swimming hasn't actually started yet. Actually, next Tuesday we get to practise for a month. Then the season starts. It's always good if you haven't swum in a while. You get to swim com-

petitively, so you get to swim. You swim 10 laps and then 20. You work yourself up. We go to [the nearby] university for water polo finals. It's a sort of soccer with the hands in the water. We go there to play.

Sandra enjoys her paid part-time baby-sitting job after school, so she simply brings her younger brother along. She integrates social relations with friends into school and family life by having a friend come over to be with her at her grandmother's house on weekends.

Ten of us come together at lunch. We sit on this spot. I have a best friend, too. We get together and tell each other what happened in classes. My best friend lives just down the street. She usually comes to my grandmother's on the weekend. We walk to school together and walk home together—everything.

Adaptations in work and recreation are not automatic; choices are involved. By determining that they will not be limited to choices in the division of labour as they are commonly regulated according to gender, age, and disability, children in the families described here are creating a more flexible set of expectations of parents, of children, and of disability.

Communication

In their communication with people outside the family, these family members assert particular meanings for disability, parenting, and family life. Sandra Taylor has found that she can be quite comfortable sharing aspects of family life with a parent with a disability. Through shared confidences with friends, she has discovered that things at home are not so different than in other families.

My friend says that happens a lot in her family. They start fighting. Then her brother comes in and they start arguing. I told her what our family is like and she goes, "Oh, it's no different. My family does that all the time."

Communication includes sharing and building social support networks with peers. Most children in the study described close friendships. Friendship is an important element in children's lives for a number of reasons. Intimacy and mutuality in friendships have been seen as indicators of emotional maturity (Bigelow and LaGaipa 1980) and have been found to contribute to the development of a child's self-concept (Mead 1964; Youniss 1980). Furthermore, a friendship network provides social support in times of worry (Caplan 1974).

Gender and age influence friendship relations. Girls have been found to demonstrate intimate peer relations more often than boys, and older children more than younger ones (Bigelow and LaGaipa 1980). Therefore, it is not surprising that Sandra Taylor, a 14-year-old girl, was one of the most vocal in the study about the nature and value of her friendship.

I usually phone my best friend and ask her if she can go to my grandma's house on the weekend. I talk to her. Or I talk to her in the morning [before school]. We tell each other everything! Every little secret in our life. She knows about me and I know about her. Not once has she told my secret, and neither have I unless she said you can tell anybody this. But if she says don't tell anybody, I don't. She was in my class from Grade 5. We didn't really become friends until Grade 7. Now we are in Grade 9 and we are really good friends.

Another friend [who moved away], I don't really see her—only on Saturdays, when we go bowling together. We still try and phone each other. My friends want me to join the drama club, but I don't know. If not, I'll join the basketball team. I am really shy with new people. That's one of the reasons why I joined drama as one of my classes. My friend is really excited. She tried to get me to open up for the past three years: "Finally you're opening up!"

Not all children in the study were as open in discussing home life with their friends. This was particularly true of the boys. Sandra's brother Brian is a good example of someone more inclined to keep family life private.

The only time we sit down and talk is at lunch. There [are] not many places to go. We only have an hour. So we just play cards. But we don't talk about parents. It never comes up, for some reason. There's so many people there at once you don't usually talk about specific things. There is a whole bunch of other people talking. They would interrupt you.

We can consider Brian's reticence with peers in the light of the reticence often associated with males. He may experience group pressure to conform to stereotypical images of manliness. If so, helping his mother onto the X-ray table would probably not be a story he could share in that setting. The teen peer group has been described as a place in which adolescents can create a social world separate from their parents (Youniss and Smollar 1985). Thus, parents would not enter into the conversation. Nevertheless, many children in the study described close friendships that entailed trusting, reciprocal relations with peers. Applying social skills to engage peers in friendship relations is a demonstration of children's agency.

Imagination

According to C. Wright Mills (1959), history and biography intersect in the lives of ordinary people. Mills coined the term *sociological imagination* to describe the responsibility and skill sociologists have in understanding and describing this intersection. The term *imagination* is used here to describe how family members interpret their world and how they see themselves in relation to that world. If we consider imagination from this perspective, we can identify three characteristics of family members that emerged from interview data: a sense of personal competence, hopefulness, and spirituality.

Dr. Blackford found striking examples of a sense of personal competence in members of the Chapman family, including Penny, aged 11, Tom, aged 8, and their parents. The father, Brad Chapman, was diagnosed with multiple sclerosis six years before the interview; the mother, Carol Chapman, recently returned to full-time employment following her husband's early retirement owing to disability.

Penny Chapman is "going on [her] eighth year in figure skating." She takes lessons five days a week and enters competitions very seriously because she hopes to coach or to skate professionally some day. Her father is an avid fan but can no longer attend many events in distant or inaccessible arenas. Nevertheless, the family has devised ways of keeping him involved, as Penny explains:

We usually get someone to tape my figure skating and bring it home to watch.... But sometimes, we're able to get him in, like if the arena's not wheelchair accessible, but we find a way to get him in, like if I'm skating just here or (locally) and he comes and watches me.

Finding a way "to get him in" in spite of obstacles shows persistence, ingenuity, determination, and a sense of personal competence. These traits were also evident in the Chapmans' efforts to establish an accessible transit service for their northern Ontario town. They worked with disability rights self-help groups such as Persons United for Self Help and organized a large lobby group. The children took an active part in demonstrations, and the effort was a success. In sum, all family members acted out of a sense of personal competence.

Family members in Dr. Blackford's study expressed hopeful yet realistic attitudes about their own future and the future of family members, including their disabled parent. Penny Chapman, for example, said:

I'm not asking for a miracle that he'll walk someday. But getting better, where he'll maybe be able to use his walker and walk with the walker around, stuff like that, or have enough strength. Like, when we go on vacation, we can't take his electric wheelchair because of the acid batteries, so we'll take his push wheelchair. Maybe just enough strength to push that.

Some family members in the study referred overtly to religious faith by praying for their parent's improved health and praying for a better world. The Chapman children, for instance, first made their community aware of their father's MS when they asked teachers to pray in school for their father's improved health. Members of other families in the study also talked about praying at school for the health of a parent with a disability.

Children in the study also shared ideas for improving the general health of the population at large. Some hoped research would find a cure for MS and for AIDS. Others considered how to alter disability stigma. Their feelings of hope extended beyond the personal to a more global notion of shared responsibility and spirituality.

Developmental psychologist Susan Harter (1982) said that children define feelings of self-efficacy or personal competence in terms of qualities they perceive themselves as having. Harter's scale measures perceived self-competence in various domains, and as a single global measure. The notion of internal locus of control has been used (Crandall 1967) to explain why some people see that their behaviour can have an influence on their world. An *external locus of control* is said to reflect a sense that fate or a force outside oneself controls one's life. Its opposite, *internal locus of control,* and a sense of competence (Harter 1982) have been found to be correlated with self-esteem. Experiences of success, or achievements that are visible or measurable and have the approval and recognition of others, are said to enhance a person's self-image (Cooley 1902), self-esteem, or self-concept (Harter 1982).

Hopefulness has been related to a sense of personal competence. Success in the present or the past can create an expectancy of success in the future. Hopefulness is said to reflect the experience of seeing the wished-for outcome of one's own behaviour.

Spirituality, a sense of being connected with a positive force or being greater than oneself, is associated with positive expectations for the future. Spirituality has been linked to positive coping behaviours in stressful situations, searching for clues that confirm one's hope, and appreciating even the smallest experiences (Miller 1983). Existential hope, as Miller defines it, has the "never ending possibility of improving" one's own being and of living life fully. One is realistic without losing the capacity to dream.

How can we explain evidence of such personal strength in families with parents with disabilities? It may be that family members develop an intimate understanding of MS acquired through proximity, disclosure, and inclusion in the caring process. They can learn to identify indicators of incremental change in their parents' conditions even when that change is minimal. For example, Penny Chapman justified her hopeful attitude about her father's physical condition based on his extended time tolerating a wheelchair.

> He's been better in the last few years. Like, being able to do more things. He can stay in the wheelchair a lot longer. He used to be able to stay in it for about two hours. Then he started getting really tired and sore. [Recently] when we were watching the baseball game, he stayed in his wheelchair four and a half hours.

These observed changes in a disabled parent's condition serve as indicators of the family member's own efficacy and successful helping interventions. They form the basis on which hope and faith emerge, along with a belief that the agent is part of a larger, beneficent world in which better things are possible. Caring that makes even a small positive difference, especially one that is recognized, appreciated, and visible, assures children that they can do something right and that they can make a difference in the world.

CONCLUSION

The research presented here provides insights into the workings of families with parents with disabilities that are certainly worthy of further investigation. Sociologists must recognize that families may be disabled not by medical conditions, but rather by exclusionary thinking, unimaginative public policy, inadequate financial support, insufficient support services, and inaccessible transportation, housing, and employment. All these are part and parcel of an ableist society with laws, institutions, values, attitudes, and beliefs contributing to disability oppression.

Not all families in Dr. Blackford's study were able to overcome the barriers they faced. And at the time the study was conducted, there were few, if any, options for support. However, beginning in 1997 the Centre for Independent Living in Toronto initiated the Parenting with a Disability Network (PDN), which provides a comprehensive range of resources through networking, peer support, information-sharing, and education for parents and prospective parents with disabilities. As well, PDN maintains a Web site (www.cilt.ca/Parenting/PDN.htm) with a comprehensive list of program information, publications, and links to online resources. One example of PDN programs is Nurturing Assistance, a consumer-directed service for parents with disabilities who require physical assistance to care for their young children. All work is done by paid employees under the direction of the parent. Nurturing Assistance is an example of a program that stems from the social, rather than medical, model. As of summer 2002, 264 individuals were members of PDN, including 252 Canadians. Of the Canadian members, 161 were parents and/or prospective parents with a disability. Parenting Service Providers accounted for 91; however, some Parenting Service Providers were parents with disabilities themselves (K. McKennitt, personal communication, July 10, 2002).[4]

The families that acknowledge parental disability and accept it as part of their everyday world tend to negotiate home-care tasks based on necessity rather than traditional social roles. Children contribute to the family labour pool; sons and husbands share responsibilities for home-care tasks along with mothers and daughters. When a parent has a disability, there may be more work and fewer hands to do it. Thus, the collective concerns of keeping the family as a whole running smoothly takes precedence over individual desires. These families provide a setting in which children could learn healthy ways of understanding disability. Through helping to care for their parents, they have the potential of seeing the positive results of their efforts and of receiving approval and appreciation.

Some members of families with a parent with a disability model flexible ways of living family life. They resist the assumption that labour must be divided according to gender, age, or physical condition. They reject the notion that the only purpose of family life is to bring happiness to individuals; instead they adopt a feeling of collective responsibility. In putting aside outmoded ideas of the idealized normal body and the idealized normal family, these families are creating social space for the concept of the parent with a disability. They are actively demonstrating that considerable family strengths can emerge out of choices made to support the family as a whole when a parent has a disability.

NOTES

1. This chapter uses "person-first terminology" to refer to people with disabilities. This terminology is generally preferred by people with disabilities because it acknowledges that disability is only one aspect of an individual.

2. More current data based on post-censal survey on disability-related issues in conjunction with the May 2001 Census of Canada will be available from Statistics Canada in 2003.

3. Pseudonyms have been used for all participants to ensure confidentiality.

4. Interested readers should also explore Through the Looking Glass (www.looking glass.org), a disability community–based organization in Berkeley, California whose mission is to "create, demonstrate and encourage non-pathological and empowering" resources and services for families with disabilities (Through the Looking Glass, 2002, 1).

KEY TERMS

Ableism: A pervasive system of discrimination and exclusion that operates on the individual, institutional, and societal levels to oppress people with disabilities. Ableism reflects the commonly held view that people with disabilities are inadequate in meeting normative expectations for social and economic roles.

Agency: Constant and more or less purposeful action whereby individuals make history and society. Individuals in this chapter are shown to demonstrate agency through the ways in which they take social action, communicate with others, and choose to interpret their world.

Disability oppression: A term coined by Michael Oliver (1990) to describe the various constraints associated with living with disability including economic hardship, inadequate government intervention, and negative social attitudes.

Dysfunctional: Poorly adapted to society or the environment; functioning abnormally.

Medical model: Assumes that differences in physical, sensory, or mental capabilities necessarily produce a defective member of society who must be cured or fixed.

Social model: Defines disability as a social identity. It holds that the "problem" of disability is inherent not to the individual, but rather to the social structure.

Stigma: A term originally used by the Greeks to refer to bodily signs designed to expose something unusual and bad about the moral status of the person referred to. Erving Goffman (1963) defined *stigma* for sociologists as any attribute or characteristic that is discrediting.

DISCUSSION QUESTIONS

1. The principal of your former high school asks your advice about how to enhance the school experience of students whose parents have a disability. What advice would you offer? As you respond to this question, think about structural constraints revolving around physical access, economic concerns, attitudes toward disability, human rights, and everyday rules and practices.

2. There is some evidence that MS has a genetic component. However, people with MS have only a slightly greater chance than other people of having a child with MS. Imagine that your spouse is diagnosed with MS after one year of marriage. How would this diagnosis affect your decision to have children? Refer to the description of family in this essay to explain your choice.

3. This essay makes reference to collective values and contrasts them with the individualistic values that family members might hold. Considering your own family of origin, would you say that family social relationships were based on collective or individual ideals? Provide two examples of relationships in your family that justify your answer.

4. The author claims that living in a family with a disabled parent can encourage flexibility in social arrangements and can promote an accepting attitude toward differences

in general. Compare family life described in this essay to family life described in an essay of your choice in Part II or Part III of this text. Describe how family life in the culture or ethnicity you have chosen may promote or discourage family members' flexibility and accepting attitudes toward difference.

5.   Think about the taken-for-granted assumptions you may have had about families with parents with disabilities prior to reading this chapter. Did your assumptions reflect the medical model, the social model, or both? Were they ableist? Identify the sources of these assumptions. Discuss ways in which they can be dispelled.

REFERENCES

Abberley, P. 1987. "The Concept of Oppression and the Development of a Social Theory of Disability." *Disability, Handicap and Society* 2(1): 5–19.

Abrams, P. 1982. *Historical Sociology*. West Compton House, Somerset: Open Books.

Arnaud, S. 1957. "Children of M.S. Parents: Their Psychological Characteristics." *Dissertation Abstracts 17*: 1809.

Barker, L.T., and V. Marilani. 1997. *Challenges and Strategies of Disabled Parents: Findings from a National Survey of Parents with Disabilities*. Berkeley, CA: Through the Looking Glass.

Baskin, B.H., and E.P. Riggs. 1988. "Mothers Who Are Disabled." In B. Birns and D.F. Hay, *Different Faces of Motherhood*. New York: Plenum Press.

Beanlands, H. 1987. "The Experience of Being a Child in a Family Where One Parent Is on Home Dialysis." Master's thesis, University of Toronto.

Bigelow, B.J., and J.J. LaGaipa. 1980. "The Development of Friendship Values and Choice." In H.C. Foot, A.J. Chapman, and J.R. Smith, eds., *Friendship and Social Relations in Children*. New York: Wiley.

Blackford, K.A. 1990. "A Different Parent." *Health Sharing* (Summer): 20–25.

Blackford, K.A. 1993. "Feminizing the MS Society of Canada." *Canadian Woman Studies* 13 (4): 124–28.

Blackford, K.A. 1995. "Growing Up With a Parent Who Has Multiple Sclerosis: A Micro-Historical Sociological Perspective. Doctoral dissertation, York University.

Booth, W., and T. Booth. 1993. "Accentuate the Positive: A Personal Profile of a Parent with Learning Difficulties." *Disability, Handicap and Society*, 8: 377–392.

Booth, T., and W. Booth. 1994. "The Use of Indepth Interviewing with Vulnerable Subjects: Lessons from a Research Study of Parents with Learning Difficulties." *Social Science and Medicine 39*: 415–424.

Caplan, G. 1974. *Support Systems and Community Mental Health*. New York: Behavioral Publications.

Caplan, P. 1989. *Don't Blame Mother*. New York: Harper & Row.

Cogswell, B.E. 1976. "Conceptual Model of Family as a Group: Family Responses to Disability." In G.L. Albrecht, ed., *The Sociology of Physical Disability*. Pittsburgh: University of Pittsburgh Press.

Cooley, C.H. 1902. *Human Nature and the Social Order*. New York: Scribner's.

Crandall, V.C. 1967. "Achievement Behavior in Young Children." In *The Young Child: Reviews of Research*. Washington, DC: National Association for the Education of Young Children.

Fawcett, G. 1996. *Living with Disability in Canada: An Economic Portrait*. Ottawa: Canadian Council on Social Development.

Fine, M. and A. Asch, eds. 1988. *Women with Disabilities: Essays in Psychology, Culture and Politics*. Philadelphia: Temple University Press.

Finger, A. 1991. *Past Due: A Story of Disability, Pregnancy and Birth*. London: The Woman's Press.

Friedlander, R.J., and M. Vierderman. 1982. "Children of Dialysis Parents." *American Journal of Psychiatry 139*: 100–103.

Goffman, E. 1963. *Stigma: Notes on the Management of Spoiled Identity*. Englewood Cliffs, NJ: Prentice-Hall.

Harter, S. 1982. "The Perceived Competence Scale for Children." *Child Development 53*: 87–97.

Hoover, P., P. MacElveen, and A. Alexander. 1975. "Adjustment of Children with Parents on Haemodialysis." *Nursing Times 71*: 1374–76.

Human Resources Development Canada. 1998. *Canadians with disabilities: Backgrounder #98-21*. Retrieved June 30, 2002 from <http://www.hrdc-drhc.gc.ca/>.

Keith, L. and J. Morris. 1996. "Easy Targets: A Disability Rights Perspective on the 'Children as Carers' Debate." In *Encounters with Strangers*, ed. Jenny Morris. London: The Woman's Press.

Keung, N. 2002. "Deaf Woman's Newborn Taken By CAS." *Toronto Star*. March 2.

Kikuchi, J. 1985. *Children and Adolescents of Parents with MS: Their Reported Quality of Life*. Edmonton: University of Alberta.

Kikuchi, J. and A.E. Molzahn. 1989. *Children and Adolescents of Parents with Renal Failure on Dialysis: Their Reported Quality of Life*. Edmonton: University of Alberta.

Krogh, K. 1998. "Conceptual Framework of Community Partnerships: Perspectives of People with Disabilities on Power, Beliefs, and Values." *Canadian Journal of Rehabilitation 12*: 123–134.

Litman, T.J. 1974. "Family as a Basic Unit in Health and Medical Care." *Social Science and Medicine 8*: 495–519.

Llewellyn, G. 1995. "Relationships and Social Support: Views of Parents with Mental Retardation/Intellectual Disability." *Mental Retardation 33*: 349–363.

Mead, G.H. 1964. *On Social Psychology*, edited with an introduction by Anselm Strauss. Chicago: University of Chicago Press.

Merchant, M. 1969. "Homemaking Time Use of Homemakers Confined to Wheelchairs." Unpublished master's thesis. University of Nebraska.

Miller, J.F. 1983. *Coping with Chronic Illness*. Philadelphia: F.A. Davis.

Mills, C.W. 1959. *The Sociological Imagination*. New York: Oxford University Press.

Oliver, M. 1990. *The Politics of Disablement*. London: Macmillan.

Rhode Island Chapter of the MS Society. 1989. *Kids Talk MS—The Video*.

Olsen, R., and G. Parker. 1997. "Denial of Young Carers: The Dangers of Zero-Sum Arguments." *Critical Social Policy 17*: 50–53.

Rice, J.S. 1986. "The Effect of Having a Chronically Ill Mother on the Adolescent." Master's thesis in Social Welfare, University of California, Los Angeles.

Ridington, J. 1989. *The Only Parent in the Neighbourhood: Mothering and Women with Disabilities*. Vancouver: Women with Disabilities' Network.

Ryan, W. 1972. *Blaming the Victim*. New York: Vintage Books.

Sullivan, J.A. 1980. "Family Members' Perceived Level of Family Adjustment and Symptomalogy in Other Members in Families with a Chronically Ill Patient." Doctoral dissertation, New York University, 1974. Ann Arbor, MI: University Microfilms International. No. 75-8566.

University of Southampton. 1989. *Rehabilitation Unit and Department of Sociology and Social Policy. MS in the Southampton District*. Southampton, U.K.: MS Society of Great Britain, February.

Wakesman, B.H., S.C. Reingold, and W.E. Reynolds. 1987. *Research on MS*, 3rd ed. New York: Demos Publications.

Youniss, J. 1980. *Parents and Peers in Social Development*. Chicago: University of Chicago Press.

Youniss, J., and J. Smollar. 1985. *Adolescent Relations with Mothers, Fathers, and Friends*. Chicago: University of Chicago Press.

7

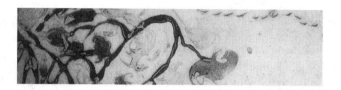

Family/Work Challenges among Mid-Life and Older Canadians

Susan A. McDaniel

Department of Sociology
University of Alberta

Objectives

- To share new research about work and family challenges in mid- and older life.

- To dispel some prevailing myths about family and work in the past and at present.

- To reconsider how the realities of family/work challenges affect thinking about families and about work.

- To rethink what we can do to address family/work challenges.

INTRODUCTION

Families in mid- and older life have not been given much explicit attention. This may be because families are not typically categorized and analyzed by life-course stage or age. There is, however, growing attention to older families these days, so the time may be ripe to focus more directly on families as they age and the challenges they face in balancing family with work. Families in the middle of their lives, whose members often have generations both older and younger than themselves, enable glimpses of families in process. Families in the middle open opportunities to see family/work challenges in different ways. A dynamic perspective on families over time and life change becomes possible.

In studies of the challenges of balancing work and family, young families with children have largely captured the interest of both research and policy. The presumption seems to be that families in mid-life face fewer challenges as children grow up and leave home. This focus on young families (although important, particularly when daycare remains such a vital issue in Canada, where work and family life increasingly co-exist) has made invisible many of the challenges faced by families in mid-life. Since most Canadian families involve children we give more attention here to families with children, but childless families are also discussed, as are the diversity of family situations that exist among mid-life and older Canadians today.

The focus here is on the particular challenges mid-life Canadian families face in balancing work and family. We begin with brief attention to the emergence of interest in mid-life families and work, and to work and families in Canada's past, then move to how family and work are theorized, caregiving and elder-care issues, and workplace and policy challenges. The focus throughout is on contemporary Canadian families and recent research.

THE EMERGENCE OF INTEREST IN MID-LIFE FAMILIES AND WORK

Several converging trends have brought growing attention to mid-life families and their family/work challenges. First, there is the massive growth in lifelong work among women in Canada over the past two decades. In 2000, for example, the majority of women worked in the paid labour force—56 percent, according to Statistics Canada (2001, 4). This is in contrast to 42 percent in 1976. Women account for 46 percent of employed workers in Canada currently. Among women aged 45 to 54, 72 percent were in the paid labour force, whereas in 1976, 46 percent of women between 45 and 54 were employed, as shown in Table 7.1. If more women in mid-life are working, and most have families as well, family/work challenges exist in more than young families with small children.

Second, increases in life expectancy have meant that older relatives live longer and have longer contacts with their adult children. It has been estimated, for example, that in 1910 only 16 percent of those aged 50 would have had a surviving parent, while in 1991, 60

Table 7.1 Percentage Employed by Age, 1976–2000

| | People Aged | | | | | | | |
| | 15–24 | | 25–44 | | 45–54 | | 55–64 | |
	Women	Men	Women	Men	Women	Men	Women	Men
1976	51.6	60.0	49.9	90.9	45.6	88.9	30.4	72.8
1980	56.0	63.0	57.8	90.1	49.7	88.2	31.0	71.3
1985	56.0	58.4	63.5	85.5	56.2	84.6	30.6	63.1
1990	59.9	62.3	71.4	86.6	63.9	85.8	33.0	60.3
1995	53.5	54.2	70.5	83.1	66.8	83.1	33.4	53.7
2000	55.8	56.7	75.2	86.5	71.5	84.4	39.3	57.7

Source: Adapted from Statistics Canada, "Women in Canada: Work Chapter Updates," Catalogue 89F0133XPE, p. 11.

percent of 50-year-olds had a surviving parent (Gee 1990). Now it is quite common for parents and children to share 50 years of life together and for grandparents to see their grandchildren reach adulthood (Martin-Matthews 2000). Many in mid-life, of course, may have more than one surviving parent, and may even have surviving grandparents. A noticeable increase in the likelihood of living alone with age is clear, as is the increased proportion of those over 80 years of age who return to living with their children, as apparent in Figure 7.1. Of elders who live with their children, Schmertman et al. (2000) find that younger elders are more likely to co-reside with sons, while older elders are more likely to live with daughters. This points to a trend where, as the need for care increases, so does the incidence of living with one's daughter.

Third, those in mid-life have come to be seen as increasingly vital to the economy and to social policy. It is the labour force in the middle that keeps the economy going and it is those in the middle who are responsible, through public taxes and various other policy supports, for the pensions of those no longer in the labour force. They also support the young who are dependent, many for increasing lengths of time as they stay in school or are in and out of work. Further, it is the middle generation that takes on direct caring for elders, for children, and for youth. It is not surprising, therefore, that more attention is being given to how exactly people live in mid-life and older families and how they manage their multiple responsibilities.

Mid-life is often defined in family life-course terms: it is said to begin when the kids grow up and leave home. Sometimes mid-life is seen to begin when Mom returns to work. The diversity of family lives for those in mid-life, and the changed workforce participation over the life course among women, however, make these definitions contentious. Some may be just beginning to have children in their late 30s or 40s, particularly those who are remarried after a divorce or raising a new spouse's children. Others may be grandparents, some with major responsibility for their grandchildren, as the children's parents work and face inadequate childcare options. Still others may never have had children, so cannot be

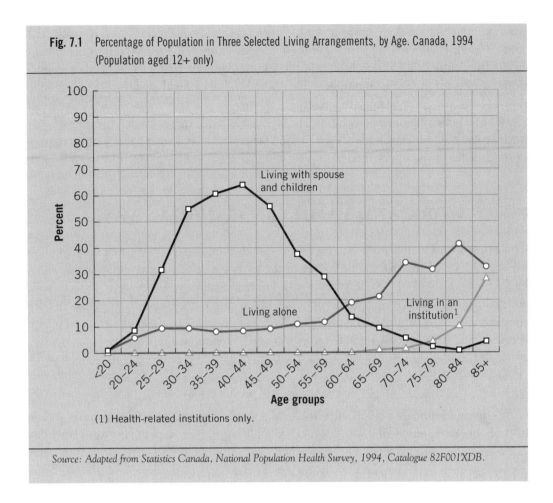

Fig. 7.1 Percentage of Population in Three Selected Living Arrangements, by Age. Canada, 1994 (Population aged 12+ only)

(1) Health-related institutions only.

Source: Adapted from Statistics Canada, National Population Health Survey, 1994, Catalogue 82F001XDB.

defined as mid-life only when the children leave home. Approximately one million mid-life Canadians live alone now, double what the number was a decade earlier (Crompton 1994, 30). Among those who have children, the children may stay in the parental home longer with fewer employment opportunities for youth, or while they are in college or university (Boyd and Pryor 1989; Mitchell 2000). Today approximately 50 percent of young adults aged 20 to 34 live with their parents, a proportion that has been steadily increasing since the 1970s (Mitchell 2000). It may well be that diversity of family peaks in mid-life.

When mid-life begins for individuals is also far from clear. As part of the research I did on mid-life working Canadians in large and small companies in the public and private sectors, I sought estimates from managers, executives, or human resources officers of the numbers of employees in their companies between the ages of 45 and 64. The first estimates provided were almost always substantially under the actual numbers. Those in the best positions to know often underestimated by one-half the number of employees in their company who were in the mid-life age group. Mid-life looks younger than it is, apparently!

Companies may also be concerned about having a youthful image and thus overestimate the youth of their employees as a symbol of their company's vibrance and vitality.

In the course of my research on mid-life families, age was found to be highly sensitive in the workplace. Mid-life employees were justifiably fearful for their jobs, with economic restructuring and corporate downsizing that sometimes targets them specifically (McDaniel 1994b; McDaniel, Lalu, and Krahn 1993). Because of this, the research downplayed age, focusing instead on balancing work and family generally but posing questions only to those in the specific age groups of interest.

WORK AND FAMILY IN CANADA'S PAST

Challenges in balancing work and family are sometimes thought to be new in Canadian experience, something that did not occur in the misty past when women were presumed to be almost exclusively involved in family and out of the public world of work. In fact, work and family have always gone together. Throughout all but a small period of Canada's history (largely the 1950s), work and family have been inseparable. Family lives were tied to the economy, and the economy to family lives. As one historian puts it:

> For the vast majority throughout history, familial relations have been intermeshed with the structures of work. Feelings may have been more rather than less tender or intense because relations are "economic" and critical to mutual survival. (Thompson 1977, 501)

Certainly throughout much of history there was, as Silverman (1984) suggests in her book about prairie pioneering women, no choice but for women to work and work hard, "to just keep going." She shows a photo of a plough with ten women hooked up to pull it! The image of women as leisured and lovely in Canada's past may be more wishful than real. On farms and homesteads, on ranches and in fishing villages, women's work on the land, in the home, in the homes of others, on boats, and in shops was essential to feed, clothe, and house their families.

The invention of work and family as separate spheres took a long time to catch on (McDaniel 1994b). At the time of industrialization in Canada in the 19th century, women who could be spared from the main work of farming were among the first factory workers. As soon as children were old enough, they worked too (and old enough was often eight years old!). Children too young to work often went along with mother to work, not to workplace daycare but to grimy, dingy, polluted early factories where their young lives were spent being quiet under Mom's worktable or sink. It was only about 130 years ago in Canada that concerns about children were sufficient that compulsory education was brought in to become the dominant experience of childhood. However, lest anyone conclude that the motivation for educating all children was interest in the children's well-being, this was *not* the case. The idea was, as Gaffield (1990) has shown, to maintain social control by keeping children off the streets while their parents worked. At the same time as compulsory education was instituted, so was the "cult of true womanhood," the redefining of women's roles as primarily familial and domestic.

So, if work and families have always gone together, what is the big concern at present about family/work balances and challenges? The simple answer is that the artificial and historically short-lived separation of work and family no longer works. Families are no longer storage and maintenance facilities for people when they are not at work—where they are cleaned up, fed, and housed, and the hurts of the public world mended. Families often have no one at home whose job it is to do all the unpaid work for the economy because women, who traditionally did the work, are now out working as well in the paid labour market. This poses a particular challenge for mid-life families (as we shall see), where women are caring for both younger and older generations at the same time as they are also working in the paid labour market.

The intensity of family/work challenges has increased in recent times. In Canada's past a significant portion of the population remain unmarried for life. As many as one-quarter of the adult female population at the turn of the 20th century never married (Jeffreys 1985). By comparison, 95 percent of women today marry at some point in their lives. Unmarried daughters were most often designated as those on whom their aging parents and other aging relatives could rely (Synge 1980). This essentially freed their married sisters and their brothers from the responsibilities of elder care. For the "spinsters," freedom arrived on the deaths of their parents. Spinsters, who were seen as not family-oriented, were often the ones with the heaviest family connections and responsibilities. Today, mid-life daughters are still called upon to care for aging relatives, but in addition they often have their own families and paid jobs at the same time (Aronson 1986; Info-Age 1995; Kaden and McDaniel 1990; McDaniel 1988b; McDaniel and Gee 1993; McDaniel and McKinnon 1993; Poirier 1998; Rosenthal 1985). These demands can have serious negative consequences for the women called upon to do the caregiving, including stresses (Evans 1991), role conflict (Rahman 1999), widely noted time crunches (Glossop 1994, 3; Vanier Institute of the Family 1994, 108), employment disruption including absenteeism, lower opportunities to advance, and loss of benefits (Martin-Matthews 2001; Poirier 1998), and poverty that cycles from mid-life into old age (*Globe and Mail* 14 November 1994, A6; Perkins 1993).

THEORIZING FAMILY AND WORK IN MID- AND LATER LIFE

Family/work has become an intense concern of family researchers and policymakers in this new century. This may not be surprising since most people have families and also work in the paid labour force. Currently two-thirds of caregivers work outside the home (Poirier 1998). Yet family/work issues have not been given much theoretical attention until recently. Not long ago, work and family were theorized to be *role conflicts* for women—a woman could be a family member or a worker but not both without feeling internal conflicts in her self-definition. This concept has now been replaced with attempts to conceptualize work and family together to permit understanding of, and insights into, the challenges that exist for both men and women and the changes that occur over the life course (Kruger and Levy, 2001). Family/work challenges was the theme chosen by the Canada Committee for the International Year of the Family in 1994, and has been a vital source of policy consideration and a focal point of change since.

Why has there been increased theoretical attention to family and work? First, growing concern about family security and insecurity (Glossop 1994; Maxwell 1993; McDaniel 1992a, 1992b, 1993b) has led to worries. "A family with two incomes, a home, two cars and a large mortgage can be shaken to the core by the loss of one of those incomes" (Maxwell 1993, 32). Insecurities tie generations together.

> I think the majority of Canadian families feel economically insecure today. Canadians are worried about their own economic security in the short and long term, and also about the economic prospects of their children. (Glossop 1994, 3)

Second, there is growing recognition that the one-breadwinner family is a thing of the past. Today's families rely on at least two, and very often more than two, earners (Baker 1994; Duffy, Mandell, and Pupo 1989; Marshall 1994). Although still resisted, the evidence is convincing (Conference Board of Canada 1994). Dual-earner families made up only 36 percent of two-parent families in 1976, but they make up 62 percent of two-parent families today (Johnson, Lero, Rooney 2001). Third, there is the recognition that both family and work matter, and that appropriate attention to the challenges of doing both is necessary. The *Globe and Mail* (19 May 1994: A20) noted the challenges in an editorial: "Employers need to understand more about the juggling act of parents ... Companies who are leaders in family-friendly policies—firms with a high proportion of female employees—cite positive returns." It concludes that "an investment in children begins at home, but it is also an investment that is everyone's business—and to everyone's benefit." Theorizing family and work intersections is an idea whose time has come.

A life-course look at families and work focuses on particular age groups. Age and aging have social significance and touch delicate nerves in our society, as we have seen already. Families in mid-life may be very different from one another. But a life-course look is perplexing for another reason as well. Those aged 45 to 64 in 2002, for example, may not be at all like those who will be these ages in 2021. Generations are shaped by pivotal social events that colour their expectations and worldviews throughout their lives. Those aged 45 to 48 in 1993, for example, are *baby boomers*, a generation that transformed every social institution it touched including schools, universities, politics, law, government, music—and certainly work and families. Those aged 60 to 64 in 1993, however, were born during the Depression, so their generation is very much smaller than generations of younger mid-lifers, and their life views are shaped by their parents' experiences of the Depression. Relations with elder relatives are also affected by shared history, so that Depression-era parents, as they age, may have very different expectations of life and of their adult children than parents born earlier or later. These generations have also had very different experiences in how work and family fit together, particularly for women. It is crucial, then, not to generalize from the experiences of one **cohort** or age group in mid-life to others who will be at the same ages in the future. The challenge is to sort out what is age-related from what is cohort-related (or related to the common life experiences of age groups or generations). A profound shift has also occurred in the way families and life course are seen and analyzed. As discussed in other chapters, the recent quantum leap in theorizing about families, about power within families, about how social structures such as the economy have impacts on and in turn are affected by families, and about how families change over life courses is due in major part to the theoretical work of feminist sociologists. Previously, theories were largely silent on issues of inequalities in the home, either between men and women or among generations. The multiple ways in which families are linked to and shaped by wider social forces were largely overlooked as well. Families were studied, in the past, almost as if they were separate from the wider society. Silences in theories, of course, can speak more loudly than their claims.

Much of what families do, including the vital work they do, is "hidden in the household"—little-examined and not well understood. One example is the informal economy of the household, which comprises not only what is done for pay and not reported as income, but entire aspects of our domestic lives. For the first time ever, the 1996 census of Canada collected data on unpaid work. Caring work is but one example. Evans (1991) shows how **gendered expectations** about caring shape women's identities and lives in profound and fundamental ways. For adolescent girls, for example, learning how to be caring is learning how to be adult women, as is shown starkly in research by Reitsma-Street (1991). Learning to be a "good woman," according to one adolescent girl, is learning to care for others, putting one's own needs second: "I am learning to stop being selfish, and to think of others and to like myself. I am learning to be passive and also to get out of my shell. I am learning that if I stay home and be good, all will be O.K." (Reitsma-Street 1991, 116). This continues throughout women's lives. In interviews by Paoletti (1998), mid-life women describe caring as their responsibility and ineluctable destiny.

Termed **compulsory altruism** by Orloff (1993), the compulsion to care compels us all—but perhaps differentially women in mid-life—to take on more and more of the "bits and pieces" of the stresses the economy and the government create or can no longer face. Older relatives forced out of health-care institutions early as a result of cutbacks "come home" to mid-life families, largely mid-life women, for care. Youth who face difficult job markets or rocky family starts return to the mid-life family for care and shelter. People of all ages (spouses, siblings, friends, and so on) who face the stresses of economic restructuring rely on mid-life women for emotional support (McDaniel 1993b; 1994a). It is women, most often mid-life women, who are called upon disproportionately to do the caring for older relatives, regardless of the costs to themselves and the disruptions to their own lives and employment prospects (Keating et al. 1999; Kaden and McDaniel, 1990; McDaniel and McKinnon, 1993). These disruptions and potential disruptions are considerable: a study by the author of a representative sample of Alberta women aged 45 and over who have ever had a child (including an adopted child) shows that 60 percent of mid-life women have considered quitting their jobs because of family responsibilities. This shows the extent of the compulsion to care for others over all else. Research by Dautzenberg et al. (2000) finds that women anticipate the need to caregive such that they self-select and adapt so as to minimize the potential conflict between work and family. The percentages are very high as well for considering turning down a promotion, for declining a job, and for declining retraining because of family responsibilities (Singleton 1997; Watson and Mears 1996). The impact of unpaid work can clearly be seen as a factor in the large amount of time it requires, as shown in Table 7.2. Women between the ages of 45 and 64 who work full-time, are unmarried, and have no children under their care spend 3.5 hours per day on unpaid work. In comparison, men of the same age without children spend 2.2 hours per day. At this age women are spending almost one hour more per day on unpaid work than unmarried women without childcare responsibilities between the ages of 25 and 44. The time spent on caregiving continues to grow with retirement, as women over 65 spend on average 4.8 hours per day on unpaid work.

It has been argued that caregiving might be in crisis (Myles 1991). My own research (McDaniel, 1993a) certainly supports this, as does other research (Aronson 1986; Hooyman 1992; Keating et al. 1999; Osterbusch et al. 1987; Walker 1983). The crisis, according to Myles, results not from increases in the demand for care (although demand is increasing) but more from "the dramatic decline in the amount of unpaid working time available to women who have traditionally performed these tasks" (1991, 82). This, of course, presumes that women do the bulk of the caregiving. According to Statistics Canada's 1998 General Social Survey, 21 percent of Canadian women over age 15 felt time-stressed, an increase from 16 percent six years earlier. Twenty-two percent of women aged 45 to 54 reported that they felt time-stressed (Statistics Canada, The Daily 1999c). Women's caring works in two ways, both largely invisible to society and to policymakers (McDaniel,1993a). Women work extra hard at home in caring when times get tough in the work world, but women, largely women in mid-life, also work harder during tough economic times in the workplace to support their families and to prevent growth in family poverty (Statistics Canada 1994). Orloff (1993) and Folbre (1988) point out that the gendered family aspects of caring and work in society are only beginning to be theorized.

Mid-life families do not necessarily prefer to provide care to older relatives. When close examination is made of how family care is selected, or who in families becomes the designated caregiver, it is found that there is often little alternative (Aronson 1986, Daatland 1990; Dautzenberg et al. 2000; Gee and McDaniel 1992). People in mid-life do not see family care as the preferred option should they become old and frail. Instead, respondents strongly prefer professional home care or institutional care (Phillipson 1997). As the baby boom generation becomes old and frail, this generation—grown accustomed to buying the services it needs, from daycare when and where it is available to financial advice—may well prefer professional care to family care. To sum up their sentiments, when they are old they don't want amateurs mucking around with their health care just because they happen to be relatives!

Table 7.2 Average Time Spent on Selected Activities by the Population Aged 15 and Over by Sex and Role Group, Canada, 1998

| | Work | | | | Personal Care | | |
	Total	Paid Work	Unpaid Work	Education	Total	Sleep	Free time
	(Hours per day averaged over a 7-day week)						
Males							
Age 18–24, unmarried student	7.6	1.5	1.3	4.8	10.1	8.5	6.3
Age 25–44, employed full-time, married parent	10.3	6.9	3.3	N/A	9.7	7.5	4.2
Age 25–44, employed full-time, unmarried non-parent	8.7	6.7	2.0	N/A	9.6	7.7	5.6
Age 45–64, employed full-time, married parent	9.9	6.9	3.0	N/A	9.6	7.4	4.5
Age 45–64, employed full-time, unmarried non-parent	8.8	6.5	2.2	N/A	9.5	7.5	5.7
Age 65+, not employed or a student, married non-parent	4.2	N/A	4.0	N/A	11.5	8.2	8.3
Females							
Age 18–24, unmarried student	9.0	1.1	1.6	6.2	10.0	7.9	5.1
Age 25–44, employed full-time, married parent	10.5	5.5	4.9	N/A	9.9	7.8	3.6
Age 25–44, employed full-time, unmarried non-parent	8.7	5.8	2.7	N/A	9.8	7.9	5.5
Age 45–64, employed full-time, married parent	10.4	6.4	4.1	N/A	9.7	7.5	3.9
Age 45–64, employed full-time, unmarried non-parent	9.5	5.9	3.5	N/A	10.0	7.6	4.5
Age 65+, not employed or a student, married non-parent	5.0	N/A	4.8	N/A	11.7	8.4	7.4

Parent: those with never married children aged less than 19, who live at home.

Non-parent: those without never married children aged less than 19 living at home.

N/A: insufficient figures.

Source: Adapted from Statistics Canada. *Overview of the Time Use of Canadians in 1998,* Catalogue 12F0080XIE, p.14.

Families are undeniably shaped by economic pressures, but people in families cannot easily refuse family responsibilities. Within families, power to make choices is not equally distributed (Keith, Wacker, and Schafer 1992), as seen above in compulsory altruism among mid-life women. And, of course, families are not driven completely by individual self-interest in deciding resource allocation and maximization—where to invest their time, effort, and money most efficiently. If, for example, each member of a family made decisions based on self-interest, competition could arise and families would fall apart. Mid-life families might simply rebel on the argument that too many demands on them are not in their self-interest. Sharing among family members is a basic aspect of family living. Clearly, systems of health care and social welfare, whether they acknowledge it or not, are very much dependent on the unpaid and largely unrecognized work of mid-life families, and centrally women in mid-life families (Cote et al. 1998; Gee and McDaniel 1992; Neysmith 1989).

CAREGIVING AND ELDER CARE IN MID-LIFE AND OLDER FAMILIES

A broad definition of work is needed when contemplating work and mid-life and older families. The most concentrated focus thus far when considering mid-life and older families has been on caregiving, largely unpaid caregiving. The "**sandwich generation**," women caught in the middle of the demands of both younger and older generations, was highlighted, for example (McDaniel 1988b). The extent of the demands placed on women in mid-life by older and younger relatives is well known (Abu-Laban and McDaniel 2000; Dautzenberg et al. 1998; Kaden and McDaniel 1990; Keating et al. 1999). Women in mid-life remain the primary people on whom family members rely for support and care (see Figure 7.2).

Women also tend to be relied upon for emotional support to older, younger, and same-age relatives to a much greater degree than men (McDaniel 1993b; 1994a). While women diversify those on whom they would rely if in emotional need, men are found to rely most heavily on their spouses. When asked, for example, to whom they would turn first for help if depressed, women mention spouses, daughters, sons, siblings, friends, extended family, neighbours, professional helpers, and even God. Men, on the other hand, to an overwhelming degree quickly say that they would call on their spouses. Both men and women tend to turn to women for emotional support.

Women, not surprisingly, tend to be more emotionally connected to family than men are. Respondents in a Canada-wide survey were asked to whom they would turn if they were upset with their spouse. Men much more often stated that they would have no one to whom to turn. Women, on the other hand, except for the very old, mentioned numerous possible people (McDaniel 1993b; 1994a). This lack of support was particularly salient for older men with few or no children. If they did have daughters, they frequently become the preferred contact (Martel and Legare 2000). For example, 75 percent of widows over 65 live in their own homes, but report not being isolated from social supports, as is commonly believed. Many have lived in their homes for a long time, enabling them to build up strong relations with neighbours, and have close relations with friends and their adult children (Statistics Canada, The Daily 1999a). This is caregiving of a more overarching kind than is typically

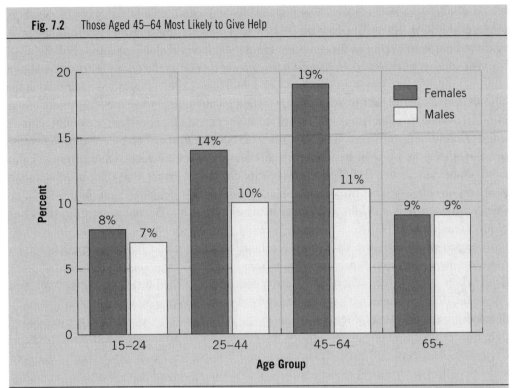

Fig. 7.2 Those Aged 45–64 Most Likely to Give Help

Source: *Statistics Canada* The Daily. *"Who Cares? Caregiving in the 1990s,"* Catalogue 11-001-XPE. *August 19, 1997,* p. 5.

considered. It involves women, often mid-life women, in widespread and largely invisible caring and listening networks.

As providers of informal welfare and social services, families and the mid-life women who most often do the caregiving and support work in families are generally ignored or taken for granted (Baker 1994; Singleton 2000). In providing these services, "private" (family) providers face dilemmas and tensions that are not visible in economic indicators or social policies. For example, female caregivers have significantly lower household incomes than male caregivers (Fredriksen 1996; Keating et al. 1999). Women also face more competing demands on their time than men who do similar caregiving (Stone, Cafferata, and Sangl 1987). This can be seen in Table 7.2 when the time spent on unpaid labour by men is compared to that of women in any category of age and role. This, of course, makes women worry about their paid work as well as their family work, and can create health challenges (Hawranik and Strain 2000; Paoletti 1998; Stone and Short 1990). Brubaker and Brubaker (1992), as well as Perkins (1993), Poirier (1998), and Richardson (1999), show how informal caregiving can affect women's retirement prospects, incomes, and benefits. Women in mid-life are also more likely than any other group to use sick time to take care of family members (Martin-Matthews 2001). They are more likely to relocate to improve caregiving, despite the perceived negative impact of this on other family relations (Hallman and Joseph 1999).

The scripts of family lives in Canada are changing, with implications for caregiving and older families. Most women who marry can reasonably expect to outlive their husbands. The sharply different patterns of life expectancy for men and women begin to emerge in mid-life, as more women than men are left without spouses. By age 65, approximately three times as many women than men have lost their spouses to death. This means that men most often live out their last years in an intact marriage with a wife as caregiver, or potential care-giver. Women much less often have that security. Since women also have less access to good pensions, due largely to the impacts of caregiving and family obligations on their work lives, they more often rely on adult children or institutions to provide care to them in their last years (Richardson 1999).

Women who experience disruptions in their lives during mid-life may experience even more strains, which can result in greater needs for care. For example, women who are divorced in mid-life are much more often left impoverished in later life (Hayes and Anderson 1993). Women with multiple family responsibilities may struggle with the many demands placed on them to help others, perhaps at the very time when they are in need of help themselves. Women struggling with the challenges of mothering while their job security might be in peril will experience serious mid-life stresses. In my research on employed and unemployed working people aged 45 to 64, the overwhelming majority of women described their lives as very or somewhat stressful.

Gendered division of housework tends to peak in mid-life (Keith, Wacker, and Schafer 1992). Women in mid-life take most of the responsibility for organizing day-to-day family life, as well as cleaning, cooking, and shopping for essentials (Keating et al. 1999). Women in mid-life are also the *kinkeepers* (Rosenthal 1985), the ones who most often keep in touch with the distant relatives (McDaniel 1994a). It is this contact that places women in the position to notice problems that occur with relatives and to be compelled to attend to them.

Elder care is being given attention by policymakers and employers in Canada (Keating et al. 1999; Conference Board of Canada 1994). This is largely due to increasing awareness of an aging population and to increasing workplace absenteeism due to responsibilities to older relatives. Employers are thinking more now of developing elder-care benefits packages as their workers age and have more and more demands placed on their time by aging relatives (Liebig 1993). McKinnon (1992) found in a random sample of Albertans that one-third provide some kind of assistance to an elderly relative. About 14 percent report having taken time from paid employment to provide assistance to an elderly relative. Medjuk, Keefe, and Fancey (1998) report that although there has been an acknowledgment of the importance of childcare, current workplace policies do not take into consideration the complex needs and diverse situations of women caring for elderly relatives. This is despite reports that elder care is often more stressful than childcare (Singleton 1998). That it is up to private corporations to deal with these caregiving issues underlines the inadequacy of existing arrangements for caring for elders. Even if corporations all instituted paid care-giving leaves for employees, the problem of providing care to family members would be far from solved, since fewer and fewer Canadians are employed in large corporations. Having a supportive supervisor, however, is one factor that is shown by McBride-King (1999) to have positive consequences. This survey of Canadian employees finds that employees with super-visors sensitive to personal needs are more satisfied with their jobs and miss half as many workdays as employees with non-supportive supervisors.

Current attention to caregiving and elder-care issues is challenging social policy as never before. That this is occurring at a time of severe economic constraint may be prob-lematic, but there is no turning away from the problem.

WORKPLACE AND POLICY CHALLENGES FOR MID-LIFE AND OLDER FAMILIES

The Challenge

Work as the essential means of family security looms large as a concern to all families, per-haps even more so for mid-life and older families. This is so for three interrelated reasons. First, there is widespread insecurity about work in Canada at present—finding work, keeping work, whether work will continue, and whether it will provide an income on which people can live. These concerns are well justified in light of the massive economic restruc-turing that has taken and is taking place in Canada in the 1990s and now in the 2000s. A significant portion (one-half to two-thirds) of the three-quarters of a million workers dis-placed from their jobs in recent years are, in fact, in mid-life (between the ages of 45 and 64) (Statistics Canada 2001a). Corporations and governments often soften this aspect of lost employment by terming it "early retirement" or "attrition." Whatever it is called, the effects on families in mid-life have been the same: they are left without work, and often without pensions or real opportunities in the future for full-time work with benefits. Most of those in my research sample of unemployed mid-life people received no severance pack-ages on layoff. Mid-life workers find it much more difficult than younger workers to land new jobs quickly, and tend to remain unemployed for longer periods (Statistics Canada 2001a). Statistics Canada (2001a) finds that age is strongly linked to the duration of job-lessness: males over 55 have a 66 percent lower chance of finding a job than males between 16 and 24. For females over 55 their chance is 77 percent lower. There is a volatility in labour-market participation of displaced mid-life and older family members as they boomerang into and out of part-time and full-time paid, but often temporary or insecure, employment. The dynamism of transitions into and out of the labour force by mid-life workers is only now beginning to be examined (McDaniel, Lalu, and Krahn 1993).

Second, there is often multiple jeopardy within mid-life families as various members of the family lose work or cannot find work. In 1994, for example, at least one family member in 32 percent of families experienced unemployment (Vanier Institute 1997). In my research on unemployed mid-life middle managers, I found that unemployed youth were often in the same families as unemployed mid-life people. This is a family perspective on economic security that looks very different than thinking of youth or older worker employment pools, as is often done. In one situation, the entire family was living on the earnings of the adolescent son, who worked at a fast-food restaurant. Both parents had lost their jobs as a result of government downsizing and had not been able to find new jobs. What seems to be occurring in these situations is a reassertion of family commitment, but not necessarily out of choice. There is simply little alternative but to huddle together to help each other out. The strains on everyone in the family can be immense.

Third, there is a shift in family/work roles within families as the so-called old economy is replaced by the new service-based economy. Men have disproportionately lost jobs in the old economy, while women and youth have been the first to join the new economy. This means, however, that although women may have work, they are much more likely than men to be involuntarily employed part time (Statistics Canada 1994) or in temporary or short-term jobs. Even if part-time work is a voluntary option, as a means to enable women to combine family and work, its consequence can be to reduce women's status in *both* work and family (Duffy and Pupo 1992; Orloff 1993). Within families, it may be more often the case that women's incomes provide the essential family income, but that income is at a much lower level than previously. Those working full-time (over age 25) earn on average $16 per hour, while those involuntarily working part-time earn on average $12 per hour (Marshall 2000). Non-permanent and part-time workers are also much less likely to receive employee-sponsored pensions, health, or dental benefits (Akyeampong 1997), which have important, long-term impacts. This has led Maxwell (1993), among others, to express deep concern about the erosion of family incomes in Canada, and Glossop (1994) to worry that the enduring expectation that each generation will do better than the last may need adjustment. For those born between 1969 and 1974, for example, their total income was 20 percent lower than those born 20 years earlier (Government of Quebec 1999). Shifts in family/work roles may leave individuals feeling vulnerable and threatened, with possible implications for family violence or family breakdown.

It is significant to note that it is often when families are under the most intense family demands that they face the greatest work and economic insecurity. The already intense demands on women for emotional as well as other kinds of support become even more intense under threat of job loss, or loss of their spouse's job, and realignment of family roles. Those who have done everything according to social expectations—going to school, obtaining job skills, raising families, and staying with their jobs—may be hardest hit by economic restructuring. Self-blame can result. One female unemployed senior manager in mid-life in the health-care field told me that she blamed herself for feeling "too content" in her previous job, which she said she had just loved. The implication may be that caring in one's work is not prudent in insecure times.

The conjunction of these forces in mid-life families has a number of implications. If women are thought to be more equal to men than ever before and society acts as if this is true, while in fact economic and workplace changes tend to make women less equal both in families and in the wider society, women will distrust their experiences or will experience a kind of disjuncture from reality. Orloff (1993), Osterbusch et al. (1987), and Skocpol and Ritter (1991) look more closely at some possible outcomes. Women in mid-life may become caught between social perceptions and economic realities; in other words, they pick up as individuals the bits and pieces not covered by the paid labour market, as women do in families as well.

For men in mid-life, the challenges are no less severe. They may lose their sense of being providers for their families along with their incomes and their future plans. Men in mid-life may feel lost in a new world they do not understand, with implications for familial relations yet to be known or understood. In addition, a clear need emerges for much greater attention to the relations of family and work in mid-life and later life, an area that, as pointed out above, has received scant attention. Growth in the demand for family support and care (largely as a function of cutbacks in public sectors), combined with an increase in the number and proportion of women who work outside the home, places mid-life families, and particularly women, in a crunch of expectations (Singleton 2000). Some who recognize the problem define it as a "women's issue," requiring better adaptation *by women* to the new realities. Mid-life women, in the absence of realistic workplace policies, are bearing increased family responsibilities as well as increased work responsibilities (Armstrong and Armstrong 2002). Workplace and community-care policies presume traditional concepts of family, of femininity, and of limited (and decreasing) government involvement in matters that are defined as familial. In contrast to this, what is needed to deal with the asymmetry between work and family, and between men and women, are new, more open and flexible institutional arrangements (Han and Moen 1999).

The Policy Debate

In Canada today, policies are of growing importance to family/work challenges in mid- and later life. First, social policies, now being reviewed and reduced on grounds of affordability, can both modify the impact of the economy on families and individuals and at the same time allow economic forces to play out within the benefits of government supports (Maxwell 2001; McDaniel and Gee 1993). Second, family is becoming more central to political and policy agendas on both sides of the 49th parallel. A recurrent theme is the need for stronger families and more private self-reliance, family care as best for both young and old, family as a stabilizing influence in society, and so on. Third, the growth in women's labour-force participation and in the women's movement has led to the generalized acceptance of the idea that work in the home matters to society generally, not only to the individuals who benefit directly. Paradoxically, the "family values" campaign pushing private responsibility for caring rests on this very insight. It is thought that children brought up in families (most are, of course, whether or not Mom also works for pay) are best adjusted and suited to becoming solid, contributing citizens. The focus in these arguments is almost exclusively on the care recipient (the child) rather than the care provider, who typically is held accountable for not doing enough regardless of all she actually does with limited supports and resources.

Three examples of policy debates and discussions in Canada are offered here as illustrations of some of the contradictions and challenges that lie ahead. First, the Canadian health-care system, designed for acute medical intervention, is ill-suited to chronic health problems whether they occur in young or old. Cutbacks to health care mean that hospital stays are shortened and patients are sent home while still in need of ongoing care. The very real possibility exists that medicare will be abandoned or substantially altered in the near future, as federal transfer payments to the provinces dwindle and as power to control health care falls more and more to the impatient provinces. Provincial governments claim that health care costs are using up too much of their budgets and without new money they will be forced to alter services. In Alberta, for example, the Premier's Advisory Council on Health is recommending the introduction of user fees and the de-listing of some insured services (Wilson 2001). This also will mean ever more pressure on mid-life families, as their older relatives need health care just at the time that alternative options to family care become more limited.

Second, *respite care* (the provision of temporary help to give the caregiver a much-needed break from routine care, so she can go to the hairdresser or on a holiday, or even walk the dog) is the most universally demanded of public programs to help caregivers to elders. Respite care, because of various federal–provincial "deals," is not available to all who need it in Canada. This puts added stress on mid-life women who disproportionately have responsibility for caregiving, with or without supports.

Third, social policies developed for caregiving in Canada have focused almost completely on the person in need of care, with almost no attention paid to the caregiver. Concerns about the dollar costs of care have become so large that it is forgotten that caregiving is costly in human terms to all who do it, regardless of income level. Caregiver "burnout" is a very real phenomenon in demanding, 24-hour-a-day situations. The costs to families in stress and family breakdown can also loom large. An extreme example of the impact of caregiving stress was seen in the murder-suicide of the Baulne family in British Columbia. The Baulnes, the aging parents of a severely handicapped son, had repeatedly pressed the government for help at home, had lost all of their income sources, and were in poor health. Their only option, according to their suicide note, was to take the life of their son and themselves (Matas 2002).

Caregiving and other family-related policies in Canada are not only contradictory, but also under serious attack (Armstrong and Armstrong 2002; McDaniel and Gee 1993). In part, this stems from the widely recognized turn to the right in social policy, which sees individuals and strong families as the substitute for shrinking government responsibility. There is a revival of the ideals of the family as self-sufficient, as weakened by government interventions, and as a better place than any other (and less costly, which is crucial to the espousing of these ideals) to care for people (Maxwell 2001). These tendencies parallel the surge in public thinking that situates troubles in the private rather than the public realm and therefore holds that inadequacies of families cause societal problems rather than any weaknesses in the collective will. Women and women's issues come front and centre in this tendency to **privatize**, so that it is women's "selfish" desire to work that is seen to result in family troubles. Women's "abandonment" of family is seen as the problem with elder care. That little of this has any shred of evidence to support the claims is lost quickly in the rhetoric. Indeed, these conservative attitudes may have significant negative consequences (Rosenthal 1997).

Behind this new political approach lie models of family that are simply outmoded. Social policy is being made on the basis of families that simply do not exist, in the hope that they might perhaps come to exist with policy pressures. Outdated models of family are poor models indeed on which to build policy (Baker 1994; Duffy, Mandell, and Pupo 1989; Gee and McDaniel 1992; McDaniel 1993a; Neysmith 1989). For example, assumptions that women in families are either men's dependants, as in the case of eligibility for many pensions, or completely equal to men in terms of labour market competitiveness, are simply not borne out by evidence. Instead, policy must take into account the interactions and connections between work and family if parity is to exist (Richardson 1999).

Social policies tend to work in such a way as to reward traditional male breadwinner families and reproduce the familial model of women's dependency (McDaniel 1993a; O'Rand and Henretta 1999). Thus, women more often make claims on social policy based on their family status (mothers with dependent children, widows, and so forth) than on their labour-market status. This, in effect, substitutes the state (governments) and the significantly termed *caring professions* for the head of the family. Women on social assistance are often treated as irresponsible semi-adults in need of constant monitoring who must justify what they do with their money. At times, the monitoring has a high moral tone as well, so that a woman on social assistance is expected to be "faithful" to the state and not have men in her life. Should there be evidence of a man in her life—the infamous search for the men's shoes under the bed by social workers—then that man is expected to support her and her children. The substitution of an individual man's support for state support becomes direct: the gender structures of familial and patriarchal dependency are further reinforced, and gender inequalities rendered normative (that is, defined as standard and morally proper).

As Orloff (1993) and others (Gee and McDaniel 1992; McDaniel 1992a, 1993a; Neysmith 1989; Rosenthal 1997) have pointed out, threats to universality in public programs such as family allowances, pensions, and now even health care differentially disadvantage women and the elderly. This is so because women have not had and continue to not have equal access to opportunities in the labour market and continue to be disadvantaged by their family status and gender (O'Rand and Henretta 1999; Young 2000). This disadvantage peaks in mid-life for women. Thus, women's claims on public programs as workers tend to be much more tenuous than those of men, for multiple reasons including women's more discontinuous career paths (interrupting careers and forgoing promotions to raise children, care for family, and move with husbands' jobs); lesser access to workplace benefits programs; and lower incomes. Women's claims on programs as family members—for example, as single mothers with dependent children, displaced homemakers, and divorced pensioners—also become tenuous as the affordability of these **entitlements** is publicly questioned (McDaniel 1988a, 1993a; Orloff 1993, 308). The presumption is that women and men are equal in today's society, a presumption that is simply not borne out by the facts.

Gendered differences in policy entitlements are accentuated in mid-life. Men's cumulative advantages in both work and family sharply contrast with women's accumulated disadvantages. And this does not take into account that gendered patterns of care and support place extra burdens on women in mid-life. The inequities that stem from gender continue on into one's later years. Women, because they spend more time on unpaid labour throughout their working years, have less time for paid labour, which has negative impacts on their retirement incomes (Farkas and O'Rand 1998; Marshall 2000). The impact of this can be seen in the high levels of women over 65 with low income. Although the overall numbers of those over 65 with low incomes has decreased dramatically, from 34 percent being low income in 1980 to 19 percent in 1994, the number of unattached senior women with low incomes has remained relatively high at 53 percent (Statistics Canada 1999b). These gender inequities remain largely obscure to policymakers who want to believe that gender inequality is something of the past.

CONCLUSION

It is clear from this brief overview of family and work in mid-life and older families, and the challenges they face in balancing family and work in the context of caregiving, the workplace, and policy change, that more attention can usefully be devoted to family/work challenges in this life stage. It is also clear that families of all types—single-parent families, stepfamilies, those living common-law, and so on—experience, to varying degrees, many of the challenges discussed here. Almost nothing is known about how they manage and what supports they might need. The relationships between **state policy** and families and between employers and families are conditioned by the power these forces have over definitions, for example, of "need" and of "standard" family roles and by their presumption to shape individual expectations and performance within families. It is certain that we must learn more about families in mid-life and their family/work challenges, since it is mid-life families who are at the centre in providing support to both the young and old, as they juggle work at the same time. Enhanced understanding could make for better (more productive) workers, less-stressed family members, and happier and healthier old age.

KEY TERMS

Cohort: A term used by demographers to designate a group with some common characteristic for the purpose of analysis (usually an age group, or people whose births fall on a specific date or between two specific dates).

Compulsory altruism: A term used by Orloff (1993) to refer to the compulsion women feel to care for others that derives from their social conditioning and society's expectations.

Entitlement: Claims to services or benefits based on citizenship rather than need or other criteria.

Family: Defined inclusively by bonds of affection and relationships in which people understand that they are taken care of and that they have obligations to take care of others. (The definition of family used by the Canada Committee for International Year of the Family was based on what families do, rather than what form they take.)

Gendered expectations: A set of expectations for individuals based on their gender and on society's notion of what is appropriate for people of that gender.

Mid-life: Defined arbitrarily as between the ages of 45 and 64; as shown, this is a difficult term to define precisely.

Privatize: A term given currency in the work of C. Wright Mills, referring to society's tendency to identify public (social) problems as private (individual) ones and thus to blame these problems on the individuals who suffer from them.

"Sandwich generation": The generation now in mid-life caught in the middle of the demands of both younger and older generations for caregiving and support; applies in particular to the women of this mid-life generation.

State policy: Public policy made by any level of government.

DISCUSSION QUESTIONS

1. What accounts for the growing interest in mid-life families in Canada? Why are mid-life families of policy interest?
2. What do myths about families and work in the past do to our thinking about what families are and what they do today?
3. What are the implications for mid-life women and mid-life families of current changes in the nature of work? Of current changes in what families are and what they do? Of current or proposed changes in social policy?
4. What are the implications of separate spheres of family and work for mid-life men and women? How has this situation changed over time?
5. How does the concept of *compulsory altruism* contribute to our understanding of the particular pressures on mid-life women?

REFERENCES

Abu-Laban, Sharon, and Susan A. McDaniel. 1994. "Aging Women and the Standards of Beauty." In Nancy Mandell, ed., *Feminist Issues: Race, Class and Sexuality.* Toronto: Prentice Hall.

Akyeampong, Ernest. 1997. "Work Arrangements: 1995 Overview." *Perspectives on Labour and Income* 9(1): 48–52.

Armstrong, Pat, and Hugh Armstrong. 2002. *Thinking It Through: Women, Work and Caring in the New Millennium.* Halifax: Nova Scotia Advisory Council on the Status of Women.

Aronson, Jane. 1986. "Care of the Frail Elderly: Whose Crisis? Whose Responsibility?" *Canadian Social Work Review*: 45–59.

Baker, Maureen. 1994. "Thinking about Families: Trends and Policies." In Maureen Baker, ed., *Canada's Changing Families: Challenges to Public Policy.* Ottawa: Vanier Institute of the Family.

Boyd, Monica, and Edward T. Pryor. 1989. "The Cluttered Nest: The Living Arrangements of Young Adult Canadians." *Canadian Journal of Sociology* 14(4): 461–77.

Brubaker, Ellie, and Timothy H. Brubaker. 1992. "The Context of Retired Women as Caregivers." In Maximiliane Szinovacz, David J. Ekerdt, and Barbara H. Vinick, eds., *Families and Retirement.* Newbury Park, CA: Sage.

Conference Board of Canada. 1994. *The Work and Family Challenge: Issues and Options.* Ottawa: Conference Board of Canada.

Cote, Denyse, Eric Gagnon, Claude Gilber, Nancy Guberman, Francine Saillant, Nicole Thivierge, and Marielle Trembley. 1998. "Who Will Be Responsible for Providing Care?" Ottawa: Status of Women in Canada. <www.swc-cfc.gc.ca/publish/research/qwcare-e.html>.

Crompton, Susan. 1994. "Adults Living Solo." *Perspectives on Labour and Income* 6(4): 30–36.

Daatland, Svein Olav. 1990. "'What Are Families For?' On Family Solidarity and Preferences for Help." *Aging and Society* 10: 1–15.

Dautzenberg, Maaike, Jos Diederiks, Hans Philipsen, and Fred Stevens. 1998. "Women of a Middle Generation and Parent Care." *International Journal of Aging and Human Development* 47(4): 241–262.

Dautzenberg, Maaike, Jos Diedriks, Hans Philipsen, Fred Stevens, Frans Tan, and Myrra Vernooij-Dassen. 2000. "The Competing Demands of Paid Work and Parent Care: Middle-Aged Daughters Providing Assistance to Elderly Parents." *Research on Aging* 22(2): 165–187.

Duffy, Ann, Nancy Mandell, and Norene Pupo. 1989. *Few Choices: Women, Work and Family.* Toronto: Garamond.

Duffy, Ann, and Norene Pupo. 1992. *Part-Time Paradox: Connecting Gender, Work and Family.* Toronto: McClelland & Stewart.

Evans, Patricia. 1991. "The Sexual Division of Poverty: The Consequences of Gendered Caring." In Carol Baines, Patricia Evans, and Sheila Neysmith, eds., *Women's Caring: Feminist Perspectives on Social Welfare.* Toronto: McClelland & Stewart.

Farkas, Janice, and Angela O'Rand. 1998. "The Pension Mix for Women in Middle and Late Life: The Changing Employment Relationship." *Social Forces* 76(3): 1007–1032.

Folbre, Nancy. 1988. "The Black Four of Hearts: Towards a New Paradigm of Household Economics." In D. Dwyer and J. Bruce, eds., *A Home Divided: Women, Income and the Third World.* Stanford, CA: Stanford University Press.

Fredriksen, Karen. 1996. "Gender Differences in Employment and the Informal Care of Adults." *Journal of Women & Aging* 8(2): 35–53.

Gaffield, Chad. 1990. "Social and Economic Origins of Contemporary Modern Families." In Maureen Baker ed., *The Family: Changing Trends in Canada*, 2nd ed. Toronto: McGraw-Hill Ryerson.

Gee, Ellen M. 1990. "Demographic Change and Intergenerational Relations in Canadian Families and Social Policy Implications." *Canadian Public Policy* 26(2): 191–99.

Gee, Ellen M., and Susan A. McDaniel. 1992. "Social Policy for an Aging Canada." *Journal of Canadian Studies* 27(3): 139–52.

Glossop, Robert. 1994. "On the Canadian Family." *Canadian Social Trends* 35 (Winter): 2–10.

Government of Quebec. 1999. "From One Generation to the Next: Evolution of Living Conditions." <www.stat/gouv.qc.ca/bul/demograp/envvie1-2_an.html>.

Hallman, Bonnie, and Alun Joseph. 1999. "Getting There: Mapping the Gendered Geography of Caregiving to Elderly Relatives." *Canadian Journal on Aging* 18(4): 387–414.

Han, Shin-Kap, and Phyllis Moen. 1999. "Work and Family Over Time: A Life Course Approach." *Annals of the American Academy of Political and Social Science* 562: 98–110.

Hawranik, Pamela, and Laurel Strain. 2000. "Health of informal Caregivers: Effects of Gender, Employment and Use of Home Care Services." Prairie Women's Health Centre of Excellence. <www.pwhce.ca/pdf/informal_report.pdf>.

Hayes, Christopher L., and Deborah Anderson. 1993. "Psychological and Economic Adjustment of Mid-Life Women after Divorce." *Journal of Women and Aging* 4(4): 83–99.

Hooyman, Nancy R. 1992. "Social Policy and Gender Equities in Caregiving." In Jeffry W. Dwyer and Raymond T. Coward, eds., *Gender, Families and Eldercare*. Newbury Park, CA: Sage.

Info-Age. 1995. "Men's and Women's Caring Work." National Advisory Council on Aging. <www.nc-sc.gc.ca/seniors-aines/pubs/info-age/iaIZ_e.htm>.

Jeffrys, Sheila. 1985. *The Spinster and Her Enemies: Feminism and Sexuality, 1880–1950*. London: Routledge & Kegan Paul.

Johnson, Karen, Donna Lero, and Jennifer Rooney. 2001. *Work-Life Compendium 2001: 150 Canadian Statistics on Work, Family and Well-Being*. Centre for Families, Work, and Well-Being, University of Guelph.

Kaden, Joan, and Susan A. McDaniel. 1990. "Caregiving and Care-receiving: A Double Bind for Women in Canada's Aging Society." *Journal of Women and Aging* 2(3): 3–26.

Keating, Norah, Janet Fast, Judith Frederick, Kelly Cranswick, and Cathryn Perrier. 1999. *Elder Care in Canada: Context, Content and Consequences*. Ottawa: Statistics Canada, Catalogue number 89-570-XPE.

Keith, Pat M., Robbyn R. Wacker, and Robert B. Schafer. 1992. "Equity in Older Families." In Maximiliane Szinovacz, David J. Ekerdt, and Barbara H. Vinick, eds., *Families and Retirement*. Newbury Park, CA: Sage.

Kruger, Helga, and Rene Levy. 2001. "Linking Life Courses, Work and the Family: Theorizing a Not So Visible Nexus between Women and Men." *Canadian Journal of Sociology* 26(2): 145–166.

Liebig, Phoebe S. 1993. "Factors Affecting the Development of Employer-Sponsored Eldercare Programs: Implications for Employed Caregivers." *Journal of Women and Aging* 5(1): 59–78.

Marshall, Katherine. 1994. "Balancing Work and Family Responsibilities." *Perspectives on Labour and Income* (Spring): 26–30. Ottawa: Statistics Canada.

Marshall, Katherine. 2000. "Part Time by Choice." *Perspectives on Labour and Income* 1(2): 5–12. Ottawa: Statistics Canada. Catalogue no. 75-001-XIE.

Martel, Laurent, and Jacques Legare. 2000. "The Orientation and Content of the Reciprocal Relationships of Seniors." *Canadian Journal on Aging* 19(1): 80–105.

Martin-Matthews, Anne. 2000. "Change and Diversity in Aging Families and Intergenerational Relations." In N. Mandell and A. Duffy (eds). *Canadian Families: Diversity, Conflict and Change* (2nd Edition). Toronto: Harcourt, Brace & Company. 323–360.

Martin-Matthews, Anne. 2001. "The Ties That Bind Aging Families." Vanier Institute of the Family. <www.vifamily.ca/pubs/pubs.htm>.

Matas, Robert. 2002. "Couple Kill Disabled Son, Themselves." *Globe and Mail*. January 4, 2002. A1.

Maxwell, Judith. 1993. "Globalization and Family Security." In *Family Security in Insecure Times.* Ottawa: National Forum on Family Security.

Maxwell, Judith. 2001. "Rethinking Institutions for Work in the New Economy." Canadian Policy Research Networks.

McBride-King, Judith. 1999. "Managers, Employee Satisfaction and Work-Life Balance." Ottawa: Conference Board of Canada.

McDaniel, Susan A. 1988a. "Getting Older and Better: Women and Gender Assumptions in Canada's Aging Society." *Feminist Perspectives 11,* Canadian Research Institute for the Advancement of Women.

McDaniel, Susan A. 1988b. "An Aging Canada: Sandwich and Caregiver Dilemmas." *Perspectives: Journal of the Gerontological Nursing Association* 12(2): 15–18.

McDaniel, Susan A. 1992a. "Caring and Sharing: Demographic Aging, Family and the State." In Jon Hendricks and Carolyn Rosenthal, eds., *The Remainder of their Days: Impact of Public Policy on Older Families.* New York: Garland.

McDaniel, Susan A. 1992b. Life Rhythms and Caring: Aging, Family and the State. 23rd Annual Sorokin Lecture. Saskatoon: University of Saskatchewan Sorokin Series.

McDaniel, Susan A. 1993a. "Where the Contradictions Meet: Women and Family Security in Canada in the 1990's." National Forum on Family Security. Ottawa: Canadian Council on Social Development.

McDaniel, Susan A. 1993b. "Emotional Support and Family Contacts of Older Canadians." *Canadian Social Trends* 28 (Spring): 30–33.

McDaniel, Susan A. 1994a. *Family and Friends 1990 General Social Survey Analysis Series.* Ottawa: Statistics Canada. Catalogue no. 11-612E, no. 9.

McDaniel, Susan A. 1994b. "Families and the Economy: New Partnerships, New Strategies." Keynote address, Ontario Women's Directorate Conference, Toronto, 29 May.

McDaniel, Susan A., and Ellen M. Gee. 1993. "Social Policies Regarding Caregiving to Elders: Canadian Contradictions." *Journal of Aging and Social Policy* 5(1, 2): 57–72.

McDaniel, Susan A., N.M. Lalu, and Harvey Krahn. 1993. "Labour Force Transitions of Older Canadian Women: A Multistate Life Table Approach." Paper presented at the Population Association of America meetings, Cinncinati, OH, April.

McDaniel, Susan A., and Allison McKinnon. 1993. "Gender Differences in Informal Support and Coping among Elders: Findings from Canada's 1985 and 1990 General Social Surveys." *Journal of Women and Aging* 5(2): 79–98.

McKinnon, Allison. 1992. *Eldercare and Labour Market Activity in Alberta: Results of the 1992 Alberta Survey.* Report prepared for the Seniors Advisory Council for Alberta. Edmonton: Population Research Laboratory, University of Alberta.

Medjuck, Sheva, Janice Keefe, and Pamela Fancey. 1998. "Available but Not Accessible: An Examination of the Use of Workplace Policies for Caregivers of Elderly Kin." *Journal of Family Issues* 19(3): 274–299.

Mitchell, Barbara. 2000. "The Refilled 'Nest': Debunking the Myth of Families in Crises." In E.M. Gee and G.M. Gutman (eds.) *The Overselling of Population Aging: Apocalyptic Demography, Intergenerational Challenges, and Social Policy.* Don Mills: Oxford University Press. 80–99.

Myles, John. 1991. "Editorial: Women, the Welfare State and Caregiving." *Canadian Journal on Aging* 10(2): 82–85.

Neysmith, Sheila. 1989. "Closing the Gap between Health Care Policy and the Home-Care Needs of Tomorrow's Elderly." *Canadian Journal of Community Mental Health* 8(2): 141–50.

O'Rand, Angela, and John Henretta. 1999. "Asynchronous Lives: The Normal Life Course and Its Variations." In *Age and Inequality: Diverse Pathways Throughout Later Life,* ed., Angela O'Rand and John Henretta. Boulder CO: Westview. 71–98.

Orloff, Ann Shola. 1993. "Gender and the Social Rights of Citizenship: The Comparative Analysis of Gender Relations and Welfare States." *American Sociological Review* 58(3): 303–28.

Osterbusch, S., et al. 1987. "Community Care Policies and Gender Justice." *International Journal of Health Services* 17: 217–32.

Paoletti, Isabella. 1998. "The Gendered Construction of the Moral Order: Interviews with Women Caregivers." International Sociological Association.

Perkins, Kathleen. 1993. "Recycling Poverty: From the Workplace into Retirement." *Journal of Women and Aging* 5(1): 5–24.

Phillipson, Chris. 1997. "Family Care in Great Britain: Sociological Perspectives." *Aging International* 24(1): 63–80.

Poirier, Lesley. 1998. "Spare 28 Hours a Week? Caregiving Still in Women's Job Description." *The Canadian Women's Health Network* 1(3).

Rahman, Naila. 1999. "Understanding Conflict: Perception of Female Caregivers." *Australasian Journal on Ageing* 18(3): 140–144.

Reitsma-Street, Marge. 1991. "Girls Learn to Care; Girls Policed to Care." In Carol Baines, Patricia Evans, and Sheila Neysmith, eds., *Women's Caring: Feminist Perspectives on Social Welfare.* Toronto: McClelland & Stewart.

Richardson, Virginia. 1999. "Women and Retirement." *Journal of Women and Aging* 11(2–3): 49–66.

Rosenthal, Carolyn. 1985. "Kinkeeping in the Familial Division of Labor." *Journal of Marriage and the Family* 47: 965–74.

Rosenthal, Carolyn. 1997. "The Changing Contexts of Family Care in Canada." *Aging International* 24(1): 13–31.

Schmertman, Carl, Monica Boyd, William Serow, and Douglas White. 2000. "Elder-Child Coresidence in the United States: Evidence from the 1990 Census." *Research on Aging* 22(1): 23–42.

Singleton, Judy. 1997. "The Impact of Family Caregiving to the Elderly on the American Workplace: Who Is Affected and What Is Being Done?" American Sociological Association.

Singleton, Judy. 1998. "The Impact of Family Caregiving to the Elderly on the American Workplace: Who Is Affected and What Is Being Done?" In *Challenges for Work and Family in the Twenty-First Century*, ed., Dana Vannoy and Paula Dubeck. New York: Aldine de Gruyter. 201–214.

Singleton, Judy. 2000. "Women Caring for Elderly Family Members: Shaping Non-Traditional Work and Family Initiatives." *Journal of Comparative Family Studies* 31(3): 367–375.

Silverman, Elaine. 1984. *The Last Best West: Women on the Alberta Frontier, 1880–1930.* Montreal: Eden Press.

Skocpol, Theda, and Gretchen Ritter. 1991. "Gender and the Origins of Modern Social Policies in Britain and the United States." *Studies in American Political Development* 5(Spring): 36–93.

Statistics Canada. 1994. Women in the Labour Force. Ottawa: Statistics Canada. Catalogue number 75-507-XPE.

Statistics Canada, General Social Survey. 1998. "Overview of the Time Use of Canadians in 1998." Ottawa: Statistics Canada. Catalogue number 12F0080XIE.

Statistics Canada. 1999a. "Selected Highlights." *A Portrait of Seniors in Canada.* Ottawa: Statistics Canada. Catalogue number 89-519-XPE.

Statistics Canada. The Daily. 1999b. "Widows Who Live Alone." Ottawa: Statistics Canada. June 8, 1999. Catalogue number 11-008-XPE.

Statistics Canada. The Daily. 1999c. "General Social Survey: Time Use." Ottawa: Statistics Canada. November 9, 1999. Catalogue number 12F0080XIE.

Statistics Canada. The Daily. 2001. "After the Layoff." Ottawa: Statistics Canada. October 25, 2001. Catalogue number 75-001-XIE.

Statistics Canada. 2001. *Women in Canada: Work Chapter Updates.* Ottawa: Statistics Canada. Catalogue number 89F0133XPE.

Stone, R., G.L. Cafferata, and J. Sangl. 1987. "Caregivers to the Frail Elderly: A National Profile." *The Gerontologist* 27: 616–26.

Stone, R., and P.F. Short. 1990. "The Competing Demands of Employment and Informal Caregiving to Disabled Elders." *Medical Care* 28: 513–26.

Synge, Jane. 1980. "Work and Family Support Patterns of the Aged in the Early Twentieth Century." In Victor W. Marshall, ed., *Aging in Canada: Social Perspectives*. Don Mills, ON: Fitzhenry & Whiteside.

Thompson, E.F. 1977. "Happy Families." *New Society* (8 September): 501.

Vanier Institute of the Family. 1994. *Profiling Canada's Families*. Ottawa: Vanier Institute of the Family.

Vanier Institute of the Family. 1997. *From the Kitchen Table to the Boardroom Table: The Canadian Family and the Work Place*. Ottawa: Vanier Institute of the Family.

Walker, A.J. 1983. "Care for Elderly People: A Conflict between Women and the State." In J. Finch and D. Groves, eds., *A Labour of Love: Women, Work and Caring*. London: Routledge & Kegan Paul.

Watson, Elizabeth, and Jane Mears. 1996. "Stretched Lives: Working in Paid Employment and Caring for Elderly Relatives." *Family Matters* 45: 5–9.

Wilson, Dawn. 2001. "Alberta Ads Tout Changes to Medicare." *Globe and Mail*. December 29, 2001. A5.

Young, Claire. 2000. "Women, Tax and Social Programs: The Gendered Impact of Funding Social Programs Through the Tax System." Ottawa: Status of Women Canada.

Acknowledgments: I thank Marion Lynn for inviting me to revise this chapter for this second edition; Joanna Cotton of Nelson Thomson Learning for her organized summary of suggestions for updating and changing the chapter; Rachel Campbell for her always cheerful and generous editing and suggestions; Naomi Castle, Sociology Information Centre, University of Alberta, for her help tracking elusive page numbers; and the instructors and students who provided useful suggestions for revising this chapter for the second edition.

Ethnocultural Issues

The five essays in Part II examine families shaped by their membership in communities that are socially defined in Canada by race, ethnicity, immigrant experiences, and local economy. Members of some of these communities may not always choose to have race or ethnicity as a primary identity, but they live with the consequences of their identity as it is socially constructed. The central question that is asked is how being located within a racially or ethnically identified category shapes family forms and relationships. The families in these communities, like all families, are also influenced by the other factors discussed in this text: class, region, and local culture; political and economic forces, past and present; and the division of paid and domestic work. They may be single-parent families and stepfamilies, gay and lesbian households; they are affected by aging and by disability.

These five essays can be seen as case studies: they do not purport to be representative of all family arrangements shaped by race, ethnicity, immigration, and local economy within the diverse and complex mosaic of Canada. The section begins with a look back to Part I. The first essay is a study of a First Nation whose experience since initial contact with Europeans has been largely determined by its distinctive family structures and relationships based on the matrilineal kinship group.

As the original people of pre-colonial North America, native Canadians have had a unique experience in trying to maintain family systems in the face of colonization and European imperialism. The essay on native families is co-written by Rose Johnny, a member of the Lake Babine First Nation of central British Columbia, and Jo-Anne Fiske, a Canadian anthropologist of European background (Chapter 8). Although placed within the history of European suppression of First Nations cultural and legal traditions, this essay sets out to explore the effects of this history on families of only this one native community.

The authors recognize the differing impact and consequences of European domination on native North Americans depending on region, class, and provincial as well as federal policies. Johnny and Fiske pay particular attention to the interference by the Roman

Catholic Church in native spirituality and family practices, the impact of residential schools, the loss of rights through *status designation* (government registration of band members to determine who could live on the band's lands and have treaty rights), and adoption of native children by non-aboriginal families. They pay particular attention to the suppression of the complex matrilineal kinship system of the Lake Babine people. (In a matrilineal kinship system, descent and inheritance are traced from the mother's side, and the mother's kin typically have authority over the children.) Johnny and Fiske reveal the centrality of this family system to Lake Babine society. In examining the implications to this people of matrilineal kinship and its suppression, the authors integrate the study of the family into the broader social and cultural framework. (In a very different context, Catherine Krull makes the same kinds of social, cultural, and institutional connections in her discussion of the family in Quebec in Chapter 13.)

Historical narrative and personal reminiscence combine to give this essay a dramatic structure. The voice of Rose Johnny brings alive the experiences of one family in attempting to maintain and pass on a way of life and a set of values at the same time as they must adapt to current social and economic realities.

Agnes Calliste, an African-Canadian sociologist, analyzes the intersection of race, class, and gender as these variables operate on black families in Canada (Chapter 9). Immigration policies and practices, segregated educational systems, and restricted access to wage labour shape family structures and roles in particular ways among African-Canadians. These social forces influence the gendered division of paid labour and domestic labour, and of private and public spheres of family life.

At one time it was common to study disadvantaged groups from a deficit perspective that looks at them as problematic and unhealthy or pathological. Calliste takes a political economy perspective that uses large-scale economic and political structures to explain social data. She discusses the history of black settlement in Nova Scotia, where free black Loyalists and slaves owned by Loyalists arrived after the American Revolution. Limited economic opportunities—especially for the men—inspired social adaptations, including women's entry into the public sphere of paid labour while men often cared for children and worked in or around the private sphere of the home. As with the better known case of Chinese immigrants, black immigrant railway workers were barred from bringing in their wives; recently, women domestics from the Caribbean have faced restrictions on the entry of their fiancés.

Calliste reports on qualitative data on contemporary African-Canadian family dynamics based on in-depth interviews she conducted. She ties the complexity of gendered roles and of sexism within families to a lack of economic power. This essay contains an extended argument based on quantitative data taken from the 1991 Canadian census and presented in a series of tables. Calliste provides a comparison of African Nova Scotians with other Canadian blacks and other ethnic groups to explain different family and marriage patterns. This analysis points out the significance of class-related variables—income, education, and employment—on families, regardless of race and ethnicity. This line of argument implicitly opposes interpretations based on the "essence" or "character" of the people studied. Where Calliste finds that race intersects with class in determining a particular family structure, such as single motherhood, she outlines the specific circumstances in the black population that can contribute to an explanation.

Chinese Canadians, like those of African/Caribbean descent, have been shaped partially by discriminatory immigration policies and practices. In a study of recently immigrated middle-class families from Hong Kong, Guida Man points out the need to examine the experiences of immigrant families' class position in their country of origin as well as in Canada (Chapter 10). One of her aims is to disprove the notion that Chinese immigrants are a homogeneous group; it is noteworthy that she accomplishes this by presenting interviews with a small group of women who come from the same city and the same social class, showing their different means of coping with their new situation.

Earlier Chinese immigrants to Canada experienced unique forms of discrimination, including the imposition of a head tax (a fee that each person was made to pay) and the almost complete exclusion of Chinese women immigrants. These policies and practices laid the foundation in the 19th century and early 20th century of male-only communities and of families in which a wife and children in Asia saw their husband and father only every 10 or 20 years. The current immigration laws that encourage the arrival of well-off, educated Chinese, especially investors, make it appear that even today, the Canadian government views Chinese immigrants as an economic resource.

Man criticizes earlier studies for neglecting the complex interaction between social structures and individual lives. She looks at how large-scale structural forces (which she calls macrostructural) are experienced by her 30 interviewees in employment opportunities, the gendered division of household work, relationships with husbands and children, and other categories. The technique she uses is the *experiential study*, a series of open-ended interviews in which subjects are encouraged to talk freely about their personal experiences; the organization of these very concrete discussions of mundane, day-to-day topics (shopping, housework, employment) into large social-structural categories makes for a powerful analysis.

Catherine Krull's analysis of changes in Québécois families since the beginnings of New France represents a study of demographic developments in Quebec (Chapter 11). She examines general changes in marriage and families with a particular emphasis on the position of women. This study of Québécois families is organized around three stages of Quebec history: New France; the early 20th century; and the period since the Quiet Revolution of the 1960s.

Krull shows how demographic conditions influence people's behaviour and can affect an entire society. For example, the shortage of women in early New France led to the custom of marrying at an unusually young age (12 or 13 for girls)—a result of the competition for wives. This, in turn, contributed to the high birth rate. Krull's account of Quebec society and especially its evolution through time demonstrates how social, legal, institutional, political, and economic facts are interrelated and how they can be woven into the study of the family. For example, the Civil Code legal system in effect in Quebec decreed women's loss of legal rights upon marriage.

In accounting for the breakdown of the traditional model of the Québécois family, Krull points out the significance of rising political consciousness, the reduction in the power of the church, and the impact of women's participation in the paid labour force as well as their involvement in the women's movement. The explanatory framework in which Krull places these facts—the concept that helps her make sense of these changes—is her definition of the Quiet Revolution as a complex structural and ideological process.

These changes in Quebec are in contrast to the continuity of cultural patterns that emerge in Pauline Gardiner Barber's study of gender, family, and working-class culture in industrial Cape Breton, on the East Coast of Canada (Chapter 12). Barber's essay comes out of fieldwork she did in *ethnography*—the study of cultures. The culture that Barber uncovers in Cape Breton is not an ethnic heritage, however, but a way of life based on social class and economic circumstances. "The culture of making do" is the response of Cape Breton working-class families to the precarious economic opportunities of their region.

Barber places these families within the social context of their work. She uses the structure and agency approach that Karen Blackford employs in her research on families with a disabled parent. Barber, however, analyzes the social class and economic structures of the specific region—a political economy analysis—and emphasizes agency as the collective responses of an entire community. She outlines the adjustments both men and women make to their circumstances. The women in Cape Breton families preserve the family and the community by making do with what they have, exchanging goods and services outside the cash economy, and helping their kin and neighbours. Thus, Barber notes, economic strategies are central to women's social dealings in this community. This point, in turn, contributes to the feminist argument repeated by Barber that gender and family relations penetrate all areas of daily life.

8

The Lake Babine First Nation Family:
Yesterday and Today

Jo-Anne Fiske

First Nations and Women's Studies
University of Northern British Columbia

Rose Johnny

Lake Babine Nation

Objectives

- To present a historical overview of government policies and practices that have directly and indirectly shaped First Nations family structures and relations and have particularly affected First Nations women.

- To explain the impact of government policies and practices on First Nations families within a combined feminist/political economy theoretical framework.

- To illustrate through personal experience how imposed cultural changes eroded the unity and respect of traditional family relations.

- To link the personal experiences of Rose Johnny, a member of the Lake Babine First Nation in central British Columbia, to the history and experiences of First Nations women across Canada.

- To promote understanding of the ties between Canadian families in all of their diversity and the power of the Canadian state to intervene in kin relations, and in so doing to redefine family structures and personal identity.

INTRODUCTION

What happened to this "one big family" that the village once was? Our ancestors used to help each other and share with each other. My dad speaks of gatherings when he was young. Everyone shared the moose or the thousands of fish caught.

Family and kinship relations lie at the heart of community organization and personal identity in First Nations communities. It is often said that a First Nations community is "one big family." This not only signifies an assertion of communal purpose and shared responsibility, but also indicates the intricate kinship ties that exist as a result of frequent village **endogamy.** The *extended family*, therefore, is often seen to be the basic unit of social identity, economic support, and psychological nurture. The importance of family and kin relations takes precedence over all other emotional and social ties in most, if not all, First Nations communities. Family organization marks a significant cultural distinction from other sociocultural groups in Canada, most dramatically from the Euro-Canadian majority who stress an autonomous *nuclear family* organization and for whom other social relations may be equally if not more significant than family ties.

To understand cultural differences in family and kinship relations, we must always be critically aware of the way they are represented. Scholarship on family and kinship is grounded in the language and norms of the dominant society. For example, "extended family" is a term used to describe family organizations that embrace three or more generations and ties to other relatives. However, the notion of "extension" makes sense only if a smaller unit, the nuclear family, is taken as the norm. The assumption of a normative unit, the patriarchal nuclear family, has shaped colonial relations in Canada for centuries. Fur traders and Christian missionaries were the first Europeans to impose foreign forms of family organization on the original peoples of North America. Many did so because they disapproved of any marriage or family relations that differed from their own; specifically, they opposed **polyandry** and **polygyny**, and scorned maternal leadership (Leacock 1980; Anderson 1991). Christian missionaries insisted that marriage was a holy sacrament and refused holy rites to men or women with more than one spouse. Children who were born "out of wedlock" were labelled *illegitimate*, a European category unknown in Aboriginal North America.

The power of European settlers and later of the Canadian government and dominant society to impose foreign family structures and values on the original peoples of North America has its roots in the ethos and practices of colonialism. Central to colonial relations between First Nations and the Europeans was a perception of cultural and moral superiority. When France and Britain entered what is now Canada they wanted more than the natural resources and land, they wanted to change forever the people of these lands by assimilating them into the Euro-Canadian society. To do so meant changing family values and structures and gender relations to mirror those of the dominant society (Bilharz 1995; Byrne and Fouillard 2000; Stevenson 1999). The colonial governments of New France and the British colonies were supported in their efforts to change First Nations families by Christian missionaries; with the Canadian confederation of British colonies in 1867, the Canadian government assumed unto itself these rights and powers and continued to deploy Christian missionaries to this end.

This power continues today and is understood as *internal colonialism*; that is, power relations between First Nations and the dominant society remain ones of subordination marked both by ideological and political subordination (Frideres 1988). Historically, colonialism is characterized by deliberate deployment of ideological, political, and economic strategies to exploit and expropriate the resources held by the colonized population and to undermine, if not eradicate, their world views, family and kinship organization, cultural practices, and religion.

Colonialism, however, is not just a historical practice of early settlement; it is a persistent power relation that shifts its facade and ideology with changing social dynamics and moral values. Internal colonialism refers to the power relations that emerged in the 20th century, and most particularly in the last 60 years. In this era, colonial relations endure within a rhetoric of equality and social justice. In fact, as Frideres makes clear, equality is more a myth than a lived experience. The myth of equality provides the rationalization to continue what the early colonizers began: eradication of social and cultural uniqueness and denial of inherent rights of the First Nations (267).

The overall outcome of European settlement has been an overpowering of all aboriginal peoples. They have steadily lost the political autonomy they knew before colonization, suffered economic constraints through loss of land and resources, and endured massive cultural change not of their choosing. From the time of early European settlement to the present, the dominant Canadian society and government have intruded on First Nations family relations in myriad ways, some subtle and some overtly oppressive, some intended and others not. By means of the *Indian Act, 1876* (which has been amended several times), the federal government assumed control over First Nations and their lands. The *Indian Act* also divided communities into "status" (registered Indians who receive government benefits) and "non-status" Indians, and denied First Nations peoples rights enjoyed by other Canadian citizens. It enforced changes in family relations ranging from marriage practices, adoptions, and residence rights to an inability to bequeath property according to established custom.

Provincial governments interfered more recently. Social welfare and child protection policies and practices directly and indirectly affected the daily lives of all First Nations peoples. For instance, family ties were severed when social workers apprehended infants for adoption into non-aboriginal families.[1] Exportation of infants to the United States signified to the bereft mothers and their kin incomprehension of, if not outright contempt for, aboriginal family practices. Less obvious, but none the less damaging, were a profusion of economic and political encroachments that altered the daily and seasonal economic activities of communities. As we shall see, capitalist expansion, changes in resource management laws, and educational policies have all had a radical impact on First Nations families.

Although broad similarities of changing family relations and structures exist for all First Nations families, clear differences prevail as a result of specific First Nations cultural and legal traditions, particular adaptations to Euro-Canadian influences, and distinct effects of provincial policies. In this account, we offer a glimpse into the contemporary Lake Babine Nation family. We weave reminiscences of Rose Johnny and the history of the Lake Babine Nation into the context of Canadian colonial history, highlighting major historical crises that have shaped family and community. We place Rose's recollections and perspectives within the concept of a changing **political economy** in which the Canadian government foisted paternal practices upon the Lake Babine Nation, usurped their traditional lands and resources; rendered them dependent upon government funds; and subjected them to debilitating policies and practices. We examine colonial strategies of family disruption: *Indian Act* definitions of "Indian"; removal of children to residential schools, imposed patriarchal family relations, and apprehension of children and infants.

THE LAKE BABINE FIRST NATION FAMILY

The Lake Babine First Nation (also known as the Nedu'ten) is one of several nations known to us as the Yinkadinee or Carrier, who are related by language (an Athapaskan dialect), political and legal structures, and cultural traditions.[2] The First Nations of central British Columbia were among the last in Canada to encounter the full effects of the process of **colonization**. Europeans did not settle in Lake Babine First Nation territories on the shores of Lake Babine in large numbers until the middle of the 20th century. Because the Lake Babine First Nation was more isolated than many First Nations, their family structures have retained culturally distinct features that have supported the people through periods of acute social disruption and personal stress.

Europeans first arrived permanently in Lake Babine First Nation territory in 1822, when the Hudson's Bay Company established its first trading post on Lake Babine. The men of the trading post had an immediate effect on Lake Babine First Nation family relations. Traders and the subordinate "company men" entered into "country marriages" with Lake Babine First Nation women, who were often left behind when their men were transferred to another post or were retired from the company. Few records remain of these European–Lake Babine First Nation marriages but, judging from other studies of "country marriages," it is safe to assume that considerable hardship emerged for many of the women and their children (Brown 1980; Van Kirk 1980). Frontier marriage relationships were marked by ambiguity and contradictions. First Nations women were condemned for sexual behaviours alleged to be promiscuous and adulterous, even while European men were exonerated for parallel conduct. The newcomers interpreted *polygyny* (the practice of having several wives) and mourning practices— which included painful rituals at the time of the deceased spouse's cremation and long periods of mourning marked by *affinal servitude* (services performed for relatives by marriage)—as signs of women's subjugation.[3] They also understood onerous work and trading that took women from their home communities to indicate a miserable existence for women. At the same time, the traders' own practices devalued women's autonomy and defined arduous domestic labour as the natural lot of women. Interracial marriages on the trading frontier often forced wives, even if temporarily, into dependence upon their foreign husbands and alienated them from their own kin and thus from the economic and personal autonomy they would have known as participating members in their extended families.

Although the Lake Babine First Nation was and remains a **matrilineal** people—that is, one that traces descent, membership, inheritance rights, and so on from the mother's side—the Lake Babine First Nation family soon became influenced by European patrilineal practices and **patriarchy**, and by principles of European marriage as a legally binding monogamous lifetime relationship. The Oblates of Mary Immaculate, a Catholic order from France, were regular visitors to the Lake Babine First Nation. The priests reviled Lake Babine First Nation practices of divorce and attempted to prevent marriage between Catholic converts and adherents of traditional sacred practices. They boldly separated couples united by custom and forced marriage arrangements against the will of principals and family, instilling fear of eternal damnation and denying the sacraments to those who resisted. As Betty Patrick, a band member and researcher for the Lake Babine First Nation, commented upon reading a missionary's account of his own interventions and the people's staunch resistance, "No wonder the people were so confused and had such a hard time!"

Conversion to Catholicism brought an entire new social order to the Lake Babine people, one marked by new notions of authority and punishment for social and sacred transgressions. Missionary priests introduced new forms of all-male village councils, which they authorized to administer corporal punishment, commonly whipping, to adults who broke church laws; to enforce a curfew for adults and children alike; and to intervene in family conflicts and interpersonal tensions. The priests discredited the traditional matrilineal family, in which authority over children was assumed by the mother's kin in harmony with complementary obligations and authority resting in the father's family, in favour of patriarchal authority of the husband over wife and children.

Conversion also required baptism and Christian naming, a practice that ended the use of traditional names and introduced the use of the *patronymic* (the family name inherited from one's father). Prior to this practice, family names did not exist. Rather, matrilineal ties were indicated by membership in the House, a matrilineal kin group who shared common resources and who displayed clan and House crests to symbolize social identity and personal entitlements. The Lake Babine people are divided into four matrilineal clans, which are further divided into the Houses. Individual identity is derived from clan and House membership, not from the father's line. Nonetheless, the father's House did, and continues to, perform important functions throughout a person's lifetime, most particularly in times of personal conflicts and economic stress, and at death.

Missionaries' hostility toward Lake Babine First Nation marital practices was rooted in concepts of morality. The priests firmly believed that matrilineal societies existed because of rampant promiscuity and female immorality. They also abhorred principles of matrilineal clan organization because Lake Babine people valued cooperative labour and communal ownership over private ownership. In the priests' eyes, communal principles constituted a derogatory state and an impediment to "civilization," which was presumed to rest upon private ownership and accumulation of wealth. Compounding their antipathy toward the Lake Babine First Nation and the other Yinkadinee nations was their attitude toward the *bah'lats* or "potlatch," which was the cornerstone of social organization and cultural identity.

The seat of government and legal order, the *bah'lats* was a ceremonial feast of public witnessing. All important community and intercommunity affairs were decided at a gathering of community members, all of whose interests were represented through the hereditary clan and House chiefs. Witnesses assumed an important role; they could be called upon to validate any decision or transaction, and for this they received presentations of gifts and food corresponding to their social rank and responsibilities. The potlatch or feast, an institution shared in various forms with other First Nations of the Pacific region, could not be eradicated or even altered without disruption of every social relationship. At the heart of society, *bah'lats* regulated membership in matrilineal clans and Houses, relations between maternal and paternal kin, succession to seats of honour and leadership, hereditary chieftainship, and virtually every aspect of resource access, management, and distribution. In the inseparable world of the sacred and the profane, the *bah'lats* was, and remains, sacred; all social relations and obligations of the *bah'lats* have spiritual significance, and all teachings of elders and hereditary chiefs are steeped in esoteric knowledge and wisdom.

In a matrilineal society, a balance of rituals and services is needed to reinforce paternal ties. The *bah'lats/clan complex* protects these relationships. At all rites of passage, from birth to death, an individual's father's House (now generally called the "sponsoring clan") performs necessary services and rituals. **Exogamy**, marriage between clans, was and remains the rule; matrilineal succession to seats of honour and resource territories the law. In the past, ethnographers tell us, a man succeeded his mother's brother to important positions in the potlatch and with them gained specific rights to resource territories (Jenness 1943; Morice 1889). Today, other maternal relationships grant similar rights; a woman will follow her maternal aunt or grandmother, for instance, or a man will succeed a brother. Each individual has membership in her or his mother's House, which was the primary productive unit and which remains the primary social unit.

For myriad reasons colonizing powers, representing the government and corporate enterprises as well as the church, reviled the *bah'lats*, and in 1884 the practice was criminalized by means of amendments to the *Indian Act* that became known as the "potlatch law." Although criminalization did not eradicate the *bah'lats* as was intended, Lake Babine First Nation families endured considerable stress as they sought to retain the social and legal customs upon which family life depended.

The 20th century wrought further radical changes. Colonial education was introduced by the Catholic missionaries. Initially children attended day schools in their home community. In 1922, the Lejac Residential School opened. Now children were taken more than 150 kilometres from home for 10 months a year. As in the other residential schools across North America, students were forbidden to speak their language, interact with children of the opposite sex, or maintain cultural traditions (Deiter 1999; Knockwood 1993; Milloy

1999). For a few hours each day, the children studied the Bible and learned the rudiments of literacy and arithmetic. The main thrust of the school, however, was toward agricultural training and the school's own economic self-sufficiency. Boys toiled in the fields and raised livestock, while girls worked at domestic chores in preparation for a life as dependent wives. The intent was to eradicate traditional gender roles and to instill in the girls a sense of bodily shame and a Christian view of the sinful nature of sexuality. For some girls, this meant remaining in school until they were of marriageable age (15 to 16), when under the auspices of the "church chief"—an appointee of the priest—and kin they entered into arranged marriages.

Although relatively few Lake Babine children attended Lejac for any length of time compared to children in other Yinkadinee communities, the consequences were devastating for the entire community. Parents had no influence over the curriculum or even the staff, who were members of foreign missionary congregations. Few could spare the several days needed to travel to the school for visits with their children. Moreover, when day schools on the reserves did operate, they offered a similar curriculum and also excluded parents and community leaders from the administration and routine practices. As has been well documented elsewhere, residential school life was harsh, frequently abusive, and dangerous (Fiske 1991; Knockwood 1993; English-Currie 1990). Contagious diseases took lives and left survivors weak and vulnerable.

Not only were families torn by death and absence, intergenerational alienation emerged with cultural loss. Traditions surrounding puberty and the special preparation of young girls for motherhood and adult female responsibilities were seriously disrupted. Traditions of lengthy menstrual seclusion, with accompanying sacred and practical instruction from female kin and uninterrupted periods of intense craft work, were condemned by missionaries. School residence, of course, made such practices impossible, and so valued teachings were lost or at least diminished for many Lake Babine First Nation women and girls. By the 1970s, rituals honouring the onset of womanhood had been altered. Some families no longer passed on the ancient teachings or did so only in a truncated manner.

> "Oh my God! I'm bleeding!" As I sat there fearful, thinking I was going to die, I kept asking myself, "Why me?" All of a sudden Mother grabbed me and dragged me into the room. She immediately put covers over the window and a blanket all around my bed. I sat there stunned and shocked, but was too scared to speak. The only ones that were allowed into this small, dark room were Mom and my sisters. I was forbidden to look at Dad and my brothers, let alone speak to them. "What have I done?" I kept wondering. Mom brought me my meals, and she gave me a small pail to urinate in. This went on for a whole week. I was going nuts. On my last day Mom double-checked to see if I was still bleeding. Thank God I wasn't! I never thought I'd be so happy to see school again.

> Mom later explained to me what was going on. I was becoming a woman. Our tradition was that when a female bleeds for the first time, she is to have no contact at all with any of the males in the family or the village. This was considered bad luck for the male hunters. I freaked out. "Would I have to do this every month?" I asked. Thank God, that was only

during a female's first period. I don't think I could have lasted if I had to do this ritual once a month.

Unfortunately, I was the second oldest. By the time my younger sister became a woman this ritual was no longer practised.

Not only did residential schools teach girls to be ashamed of their bodies, they taught all the children to be ashamed of their language and culture. When the children left the colonial institution, many found it difficult to speak their language, others were ashamed to do so. Recognizing the need for English to get jobs in the dominant society, some parents discouraged their children from learning their own language. Communication became difficult between children and parents, as was the case for Rose and her relatives.

My parents were raised when the residential schools were in. I think they were totally brainwashed; therefore, they were not able to teach us the language. It did not help [that] when they did speak the language, they did it in two different dialects. Yet I do understand most of the language.

Harsh schooling practices have left a bitter legacy for First Nations families. Residential schooling has had an intergenerational impact. Anxious to have a better life for their children, parents encourage academic success, yet cannot do so with confidence. Their own painful experiences, coupled with the racism their children still experience, sabotage the determination of many. Others, whatever the odds, refuse to diminish their aspirations. For nonstatus parents, the challenges are aggravated by lack of the community and financial support enjoyed by their status kin. Notwithstanding the hardships they endured, Rose's parents enabled her to finish her schooling even as she resisted.

Another thing that my parents taught me about was *style*. I had no use for it. While my friends had the latest trends, I was wearing hand-me-downs. I'd only receive new clothes for Christmas or for my birthday. Wanting to be like the others or wanting the same clothes was not going to get me anywhere in life. The only thing important to my parents was that we had food on the table and a home to live in.

Except for education. I had to have that in order to get ahead. I remember one day I decided I wasn't going to go to school any more. Being the brave girl I thought I was, I told my parents. Talk about explosive! My dad hit the ceiling, mumbling at the same time. He grabbed me and made me pack my clothes. In between smacking me, he yelled, "Go ahead! Let's see how far you go without an education!"

I pleaded through my tears and was terrified. Where was I going to go? Finally I told him I would continue my schooling. Believe me, after that I did my homework every night right up until I graduated. I did not realize it then, but I should've been honoured that I was the only Indian to graduate in my class.

Colonial schooling did more than hasten cultural disruption; it also separated generations of children and parents. A primary motivation for developing schools away from the children's community was to limit contact between children and parents in the hopes that children would internalize the moral and religious values of Europeans and structure their adult lives so as to fit into the capitalist political economy either as wage labourers or as small-scale agriculturists (Miller 1996; Milloy 1999) As a consequence, girls and boys who remained in the system for long periods reached adulthood with little knowledge of how to be effective parents and how to form and sustain close emotional relationships. School discipline was harsh, often seemingly capricious, and was premised on alien codes of ethics and morals that failed to respect the children's parents or their spiritual values. Whereas in the past Lake Babine parents and grandparents had shared child rearing and fostered feelings of affection while leaving children free to learn by experience and subtle teaching, a new parenting style emerged that was patterned after the harsh routines and physical punishments introduced by missionaries and was forged to meet crippling social and economic constraints. As Rose explains, respect for parents remained strong even as the younger generations struggled for more autonomy and pursued new ways to adjust to their changing world.

> One month after I graduated I began working. My parents were still strict with me. I felt as though I never really grew up. Here I was, 21 years old, sitting in the bar and my dad would come in after me. I would quickly run out the other door. This went on until I was 23. My friends would tease me, and it did not help that they were younger, much younger than I. My parents had this power over me. I was brought up never to speak back or to disobey them. Then my mother died of cancer. I waited a couple of years before I moved out on my own.

Economic transformation also affected family structure and kin relations. In the 1920s the provincial government required First Nations peoples to "register" trap lines, essentially huge tracts of land possessed and used by the matrilineal kin groups for trapping, hunting, fishing, gathering, and other purposes. In keeping with state paternalism, rules for registering the traplines were rigid and left little opportunity for community or personal discretion in management of ancestral lands and resources. This new form of legal resource regulation brought with it the government's expectations of patrilineal, nuclear family relations. Applying sexist practices, the government did not countenance female possession or inheritance, except in the case of widows who could hold land for sons until they reached adulthood. Earlier on, the federal government, through the Department of Indian Affairs, had assumed control over "Indians and the lands reserved for them." Among other intrusions, this meant government interference with personal estates, and, accordingly, matrilineal inheritance of traplines (for example, from brother to sister's son or from sister to brother) and collective ownership by a clan or House were denounced and often denied in favour of father-to-son inheritance. The once undisputed role of the matrilineal kin group comprising the House as the owner/manager of a bounded resource territory was undercut and came to compete with patrilineal membership within a trapline "company." In this way, the government was able to coerce families into accepting a new family order, a process that further undermined the collectivity of the extended family and the authority and dignity of the House.

Colonial undermining of the traditional family relationships continued into the mid-20th century as the federal government persisted in its efforts to assimilate First Nations into mainstream society. In particular, the department of Indian Affairs sought ways of moving former trappers and hunters into wage labour. For the Lake Babine people, this meant working in the rapidly expanding forestry industry at manual jobs. In the 1950s many Lake Babine families were removed from their traditional village of Old Fort, an isolated community that could be reached only by boat, to Pendleton Bay on the opposite shore of Lake Babine, where the men were employed in small sawmills. A temporary village emerged, one without the services and facilities that could ease the burden of homemaking. Adolescent girls were routinely responsible for helping with heavy housework. They carried water from the lake for washing and emptied chamber pails each morning. Women boiled water for laundry and housecleaning and cooked meals on the wood-burning range. Hard physical work at the mills and in the home strained parents' patience and this, coupled with the growing acceptance of physical punishment learned from the missionaries, often led to family tensions and conflicts as parents struggled to teach the values of hard work, self-discipline, and respect. Even an unfortunate accident or the mischievous behaviour of children could provoke unanticipated and misunderstood punishment, as Rose discovered the day her brother tripped her as she went to empty the family's chamber pail.

> I get shivers just thinking about it today. Anyways, I went tumbling down. I smelt so bad that a skunk would run away from me. I sat there on the ground, crying. Then Mom came along. Boy, was she ever angry. I thought to myself, "Good for you George, now you're going to get it." Then to my surprise she came charging at me. I'm telling you, I got the spanking of my life. What was going on? She ordered me into the house to change. "I just finished doing laundry, you little...." You see, we had to wash our clothes in a tub with a washboard. As I was sobbing, I looked up. I could see my brother George just killing himself laughing.

> "After you change, I want you to clean up this mess," she yelled. I was so angry at my mother. What she had just done did not make any sense to me.

The transformation from a trapping economy to mill work created new family stresses. Economic hardship pressed upon parents and children alike; food could not be wasted. Since time immemorial salmon, which appears in Lake Babine each summer, has been the traditional staple of the Lake Babine First Nation diet. Families at Pendleton Bay netted salmon and then dried and canned it in amounts large enough to last all winter. Dry staples, purchased at the Hudson's Bay Company stores in the traditional villages or from a small store at Pendleton Bay, supplemented the traditional bush foods. For most families these goods were relatively expensive, and for parents as concerned about their children as Rose's parents were, waste was a major concern.

> I learned very quickly how to cook. There was an incident when I burnt the rice. I remember how angry my dad was. "Do you know how much food costs?" Let's just say that against my will I have acquired the taste for burnt rice. Yes, I had to eat the whole thing. My parents did not believe in wasting food.

It was difficult for children to understand the tensions felt by their parents. Rose's experiences were by no means unusual, for nearly everyone in the community faced the same constraints and had been influenced by Euro-Canadian notions of punishment and self-discipline. Children and adolescents were attracted to popular culture, which created further tensions between themselves and their parents and grandparents.

> We weren't allowed to watch too much television. Our bedtime was at 8:00 p.m. But on the weekends, and some weeknights, we were able to stay awake later than that. I remember my sisters and I used to get up on the table and pretend we were go-go dancers, especially when the *Ed Sullivan Show* was on. We used to say that we would be stars one day. We would name off the stars that we wanted to be like.

Rose, like her peers, felt a range of mixed emotions toward her parents. They delighted, as all children do, in the freedom of playing together when their parents left them alone.

> I used to love it whenever they went out to socialize. They used to take us along and leave us in the car. Our treat was pop and chips. We used to play tag and hide-and-seek in the streets.

Rose did not attend the residential school, but a Catholic school in the village of Burns Lake. Her school experience granted greater opportunities than the schooling of her parents' generation. By the time she was a teenager, Rose was busy with her peer group, independently contributing to her family and her community through volunteer work and social events.

> I enjoyed my teen life. For that is when a group of us got together and started a youth group. When the Immaculata School was in existence, the white people used to hold balls for every occasion. We would dress up as waitresses and serve drinks and food. We also used to hold concessions at the bingo every Friday. Bingo was only held once a week. With the money we raised, we would go on trips. We also had fun with bake sales, car washes, garage sales. We used to sing as a group in choir every Sunday. We were too exhausted from all of that hard work to run around at night. Not that we were allowed to, anyways.

With maturity, misunderstanding and resentment disappeared and ambivalent feelings deepened into understanding and respect. Rose understood the values of hard work and appreciated the care and training that underlay the strict discipline.

> I really hated my parents and tried to figure out why they treated me so badly. I finally realized why Mom and Dad were so hard on me. I feel that I would not be here if it wasn't for them.

The community at Pendleton Bay did not remain for long; by the mid-1960s centralization of the logging industry and new harvesting technology forced many small mills to close. The Department of Indian Affairs, aware that Pendleton Bay mills would soon disappear, planned a second move for the Lake Babine First Nation, this time to Burns Lake, a small village lying outside Lake Babine First Nation traditional lands. The move, the government officials thought, would bring new prosperity to the people—jobs for the men, improved schooling for the children. Reluctantly, the people left the forests and lakes that had nurtured their ancestors. But the promises proved to be false; today unemployment remains high, social integration difficult, and educational achievement, while steadily improving, remains minimal.

The residential and reserve schools did not prepare parents for active involvement in their children's education. Nor has the contemporary integrated school met the community's vision of an appropriate education. Like the residential schools of the past, the curriculum of today is directed to non-aboriginal Canadians, while the schools themselves remain under non-aboriginal authority. Few opportunities to speak and study the language are offered in these schools; little is taught about traditions, and even less is experienced. Cultural differences in learning styles have not been transcended. Migration to Burns Lake has exacerbated intergenerational misunderstanding; grandparents pine for their traditional homelands, while young adults and their children settle into a village lifestyle removed from traditional economic rounds and opportunities to enjoy the lakes and forests. This has led to sadness and tensions in families and the elders' fear that the young generations have lost both respect for and understanding of time-honoured practices that made the Lake Babine family and community strong. Central to the traditions of the past were ceremonies that celebrated womanhood and taught adolescent girls their maternal, social, and spiritual duties, all of which had been ridiculed by the missionaries as superstition or primitive. The consequences for Rose were disturbing.

> Today, a girl's first menstruation and other traditions are not fully practised by any family, which perhaps explains the radical change within today's generation. Children are having children today. The schools are teaching the young ones about sex. If we ever thought about a boy it was confession on Sunday. The same with swearing. I remember [I was made to eat] soap and wanting to vomit. After that, I didn't even want to think about that swear word.

> Today's children are the lost generation. White society has taken over and manipulated us. There is no curfew for the children. It has been tried, but they rebel. The children today stay up late. Many are in trouble with the law, and started to do drugs and alcohol. We even have teenagers getting pregnant at a very early age now. Where did things go wrong?

> I remember attending the potlatch when I was young and before my mother died. We had to sit there for hours and hours. All of the children sat quietly listening to what was going on. Today that is not so. The children are tearing about the place.

Integration into the economic and social institutions of the dominant society also brings changes in cultural practices. Rose laments recent changes in the mourning traditions and rituals she knew as an adolescent 20 years ago, practices that later sustained her during the loss of her mother. Today, funeral and mourning rituals blend Lake Babine traditions of the *bah'lats* with Catholic practices. At death, the deceased is brought home to rest in the chapel on the reserve. The father's clan performs all the necessary rituals for caring for and watching over the body, the burial, and other necessary routine tasks. Following the funeral, the deceased's maternal clan hosts a *bah'lats*; the father's clan is repaid for its services as all the seated guests of the remaining clans witness the transactions. Traditionally, the entire community mourned; parties, bingos, and other entertainments were suspended. As communities have grown and developed economic institutions integrated into the regional political economy, cultural practices are adapted to a new sense of time and social obligations.

When a member of the family passed on, we had to wear black all year round. We did not have the TV or radio playing. There were a few times that I had to stay up late with my parents. I got a big smack across the back of my head if I was ever caught sleeping. My parents embedded into my head that I do not cry at another family's funeral, especially if they were not related to me. This was pretty hard for me, seeing that I am very emotional. I guess you could say that I was being constantly corrected.

Now a few of the families do not mourn for the whole year. Today it is all right to simply wear a tiny black ribbon on the arm. A female or a male used to be shunned for playing bingo before the year was up. But that does not stop them now.

The shift to a cash economy has accentuated individualism, which in turn introduces new perceptions of generous distribution of gifts and money at the *bah'lats*. Communal production of food and other items from the traditional lands has dramatically declined, altering the tenor of extended-family relations. Reciprocal exchange of goods and services is no longer as obvious, nor is communal pooling of staple foods that elders recall from their youth. Significant obligations performed by the father's clan were traditionally honoured at the *bah'lats* by payments of articles harvested from the clan's land; more recently payment has been made in cash and goods. These goods, given generously, symbolized respect for the hereditary chiefs and appreciation for the mutual exchange of services and goods that unite the four clans into a strong community.

Today, however, other services are also paid for as clans and Houses take on new obligations for one another. Participation in the reciprocal exchange of services and goods can become expensive. In consequence, tensions within and between families rise as they juggle multiple obligations. The people can no longer rely on resources of their ancestral lands to carry out their mutual obligations. Resolution of these tensions is not easy. The demand for cash and consumer goods is, after all, the driving force of a capitalist society that coerces us all to be consumers. As Rose explains, consumerism and the personal accumulation of commodities violate the principles of family cooperation she learned from her parents.

> Money has taken over the lives of the Indians. Everybody wants to get paid for something. We must get out of that trap. If your sister wants you to baby-sit or asks you to take her somewhere, you should not charge her. If your cousin or any relative needs a lift into town to purchase food you should not ask them for any money. If you catch a lot of fish, you should not sell it to your in-laws or your nephews.

Lake Babine First Nation resistance to the economic intrusions of colonialism reaches beyond idealistic statements about past practices. Their resistance to colonial impositions has been steadfast and is perhaps best symbolized by their responses to the *Indian Act*, which affected virtually all aspects of family relations. Sexist determinations of who constitutes a "status" or state-recognized Indian have been the most damaging.[4] Prior to 1985, Indian status and band membership rules (that is, registration in an Indian band as defined by the state) were sexually discriminating. Women, but not men, lost status when they married a spouse without status, whether their husbands were non-aboriginal or aboriginal. Patrilineal rules prevailed, so that these women could not transfer Indian status to their children. Status could pass only from the father to the children. Therefore, nonstatus women and women of any other racial origin gained status when they married a status man, and so did all the children of that marriage. Loss of status meant banishment from the First Nation community; when they lost status women were compelled to leave their home community and to give up any personal property on the reserve. They were denied access to family resources and refused the right of burial with their kin for themselves and their children.

The hardship thrust upon First Nations families by the sexist provisions of the *Indian Act* cannot be overstated. With the forced removal of some of their sisters, siblings found themselves alienated from one another and from nieces and nephews. The economic relations of extended families were weakened when Canadian law denied resource rights to the women stripped of their Indian status. The Lake Babine First Nation, for example, is one of many nations that rely on salmon as their staple food. Women of the matrilineal group commonly share the work of netting and preserving a year's supply; where the government enforced its ruling, smaller groups found it difficult to preserve adequate salmon, and, of course, the nonstatus sisters could not contribute through their own labour. Men were also enfranchised—that is, were stripped of Indian status and granted Canadian citizenship— either because they so chose or because of several rules of the *Indian Act* regulating their place of residence and rights to education and professional careers.

Children who grew up away from their kin were deprived of their language and culture as well as the companionship and support offered by the extended family. Often they were rejected by white Canadians and unwelcome in their home communities.

> Life was not any better at school. You see, I was considered nonstatus. According to the government I was not an Indian. Talk about confusion. The white kids called me down and laughed at me for being Indian. Then the Indian [status] kids would taunt me and accuse me of acting white. Most of my school years were spent going home crying. I tried to seek comfort from my father. He finally explained that the government was very smart. They made up this rule that if any one Indian was off the reserve for more than one year, he/she was automatically off the band list. This happened to my father. He was so angry. You see, there were no jobs on the reservations then. The men had to work off-reserve in another town. So, when Mom married Dad, she lost her status. Nobody had any answers as to why they were following the white man's rules.

First Nations women across Canada protested the sexist provisions of the *Indian Act* that divided families and robbed women of their identity. Eventually, two women in eastern Canada took their complaints to the courts, which ruled against them. In 1980 Sandra Lovelace of Tobique, New Brunswick, turned to the international courts for justice. Realizing that it could not win, the Canadian government instigated changes to eradicate the offensive measures. Its first gesture, in 1981, was to issue a Governor General's proclamation allowing First Nations the right to opt out of the discriminatory provisions. The Lake Babine First Nation was the first to do so.

In 1985, the *Indian Act* was amended;[5] women who had lost status through marriage became eligible for reinstatement of status and band membership, and their children for status and band membership contingent upon their mother's band agreeing to recognize them. For the Lake Babine First Nation this meant a long-awaited reunification of many of their families. But it also meant greater demands upon their dwindling resources. State promises for adequate support proved illusory as the federal government retreated from social programs in fear of the burgeoning public debt and as popular sentiment shifted to a neo-liberal ideology that rejects "special rights." Like all other First Nations, Lake Babine First Nation also faces the dilemma of not being able to freely define its own membership. Revisions to the *Indian Act* in 1985 did not eliminate the state's power to refuse the transmission of Indian status but merely redefined the conditions. Today, under a rule known as the "second-generation cutoff," children of mixed status–nonstatus parentage are unable to transfer status to their own children, which creates new tensions for the community. Families continue to be divided as resource-strained community governments face the dilemma of accepting residents for whom they cannot offer social and cultural services.

The struggle now is one of gaining self-government grounded in the traditional laws of the Nation, which place extended family relationships at the heart of Lake Babine society. The nation stands at a new threshold in family relations as the colonial legacy of patriarchy and paternalism is being confronted and resisted in new ways. An impressive housing program in the 1990s allowed many families to return to their home villages. Social and administrative services were expanded shortly afterward: social assistance, child welfare, and health programs are now under the Nation's own administration. The courts have recognized the jurisdiction of customary family law, which provides greater power to the Nation in determining how and when to intervene in individual families' lives. When the B.C. Court of Appeal affirmed legal plurality in 1993, customary adoption laws were affirmed thereby re-establishing the legal and moral strength of traditional family relationships. Clearly some steps toward decolonization have been successful.

Nonetheless, the journey of Lake Babine families toward decolonization is not without its pitfalls. In 2002 the British Columbia government held a "treaty referendum," ostensibly to gather public direction regarding treaty negotiations. This controversial exercise posed eight questions as to what British Columbians as a whole would be willing to negotiate regarding self-government, treaty rights, resource rights, and so on. Although only a little more than one-third of the voters returned their ballots, the Liberal government took the results as a strong endorsement to curtail the powers of self-governance to "municipal powers." Should the provincial government succeed in this goal, Lake Babine Nation— along with all other First Nations in B.C. with the exception of the Nisga'a, which signed a treaty prior to the Liberal victory in 2001—will face continuing status as internal colonies in their own lands. The impact of political setbacks is exacerbated by the current decline of the region's resource-based economy. Unemployment, inflation, and withdrawal of provincial services are having a negative impact on the people as once again families look elsewhere for work and social opportunities.

CONCLUSION

C. Wright Mills argued in *The Sociological Imagination* that a historical perspective is indispensable when analyzing structural relations of power. Feminists assert that in order to conjoin "personal troubles" and "public issues," as Mills urges us to do, historical narratives must move beyond the history of the nation to the personal histories of the people of the nation. In this paper we have sought to do both. By linking the national history of the racist and sexist colonial regime to the stories of Rose Johnny, we have attempted to explicate the colonial legacy that burdens First Nations people, in particular the women.

Rose's life experiences illuminate the intergenerational impact of colonial policies and practices that intrude into the very core of family relations. Personal narratives reveal the pain of colonial exploitation and the degradation of aboriginal families and thereby illustrate the *connections* between the political and the personal. Analysis of the specific colonial mechanisms that intruded upon the lives of Rose and her family—loss of traditional lands, removal from the homeland, residential schools, and the *Indian Act*—not only demonstrates the racist, sexist ideology that underlies assimilationist practices, but also portrays the strength of families coping with and resisting new intrusion into their way of life.

NOTES

1. For a personal account of life as a foster child see Leanne Green, "Foster Care and After," *Canadian Woman Studies/Les cahiers de la femme* 10 (2, 3); for a comprehensive survey of the consequences of welfare policies see Patrick Johnston, *Native Children and the Child Welfare System* (Toronto: Canadian Council on Social Development, in association with James Lorimer, 1983).

2. The family life of the Saik'uz whut'enne, a Yinkadinee nation to the east of the Lake Babine First Nation, has been described in several publications. See, for example, Bridget Moran, *Stoney Creek Woman: The Story of Mary John* (Vancouver: Tillacum Library, 1988); Bridget Moran, *Judgement at Stoney Creek* (Vancouver: Tillacum Library, 1990); Jo-Anne Fiske, "Carrier Women and the Politics of Mothering," in Gillian Creese and Veronica Strong-Boag, eds., *British Columbia Reconsidered: Essays on Women* (Vancouver: Press Gang, 1992).

3. Several European observers described the mourning rituals of widows and their condemnation of these rituals, but apart from Father Adrian Morice failed to mention the restrictions placed upon widowers at the time of the wife's death and for a period of at least a year thereafter.

4. Several studies have been made of the impact of these provisions upon First Nations women and families. See, for example, Kathleen Jamieson, *Indian Women and the Law in Canada: Citizens Minus* (Ottawa: Advisory Council on the Status of Women/Indian Rights for Indian Women, 1978); Janet Silman et al., *Enough Is Enough: Aboriginal*

Women Speak Out (Toronto: The Women's Press, 1987); Shirley Bear et al., "Submission for the Standing Committee on Indian Affairs and Northern Development. Bill C-31: A Comment on the Elimination of Sex-Based Discrimination in the Indian Act by the Women of Tobique Reserve" (unpublished manuscript, 1985); Lilianne Ernestine Krosenbrink-Gelissen, *Sexual Equality as an Aboriginal Right: The Native Women's Association of Canada and the Constitutional Process on Aboriginal Matters, 1982–1987* (Saarbrucken, Germany: Breitenbach Verlag, 1991).

5. The amendments are popularly known as Bill C-31. Far from resolving the discriminatory issues, new ones were created for most First Nations, not the least of which has been the emerging practice of calling reinstated women "Bill-C31s," an expression that denigrates and implies a lack of legitimacy to their claims for full First Nations citizenship.

KEY TERMS

Colonization: Establishment of power over an indigenous group by foreign conquest or settlement so that the indigenous group is dominated by external authorities, impoverished by loss of rights to and control over vital resources, and subjected to an ideological regime that redefines social identity, laws, and moral principles.

Endogamy: Customs that mandate marriages within a clearly defined group; for example, village endogamy demands marriages be restricted to members of the same village.

Exogamy: Customs that prohibit marriages within a clearly defined group; for example, the prohibition of marriages between members of the same matrilineal clans whether they are united by kinship relations or not.

Matrilineal: The practice of defining social identify and kinship ties by descent in the mother's line.

Patriarchy: A practice that allocates male power over women, built upon perceptions of the natural power of a husband/father in a family group. Patriarchal power may either be "private" (e.g., within a family group) or "social" (e.g., the power of the state to relegate women's reproductive decisions, sexual relations, and so on to benefit men of a defined social group).

Political economy: Links between political powers and economic practices. Analysis of the political economy generally focuses on the ways in which state powers uphold allocation of economic and social resources to the advantage of some groups at the expense of others.

Polyandry: Marriage of a woman to two or more husbands.

Polygyny: Marriage of a man to two or more wives.

DISCUSSION QUESTIONS

1. What external forces led to the disintegration of the matrilineal extended family?
2. What are the possible implications of the "second-generation cutoff rule" of the 1985 amendments to the *Indian Act*?

3. How has loss of Indian status affected individuals and family organization?
4. How does the Lake Babine First Nation retain a harmonious relationship between a person and her or his paternal relatives?
5. Why is it important to study political economy in order to understand fully the family experiences of Lake Babine First Nation women?

REFERENCES

Anderson, Karen. 1991. *Chain Her by One Foot: The Subjugation of Native Women in Seventeenth Century New France.* New York, London: Routledge.

Brown, Jennifer, S.H. 1980. *Strangers in Blood: Fur Trade Company Families in Indian Country.* Vancouver: University of British Columbia Press. Toronto:

Byrne, Nympha, and Camille Fouillard, eds. 2000. *It's Like the Legend: Innu Women's Voices.* Toronto: Gynergy Books.

Bilharz, Joy. 1995. "First Among Equals? The Changing Status of Seneca Women." In Laura F. Klein and Lillian A. Ackerman, eds., *Women and Power in Native North America.* Norman, OK: University of Oklahoma Press.

Deiter, Constance. 1999. *From Our Mother's Arms: The Intergenerational Impact of Residential Schools in Saskatchewan.* Toronto: United Church of Canada.

English-Currie, Vicki. 1990. "The Need for Re-evaluation in Native Education." In Jeanne Perreault and Sylvia Vance, eds., *Writing the Circle: Native Women of Western Canada.* Edmonton: NeWest.

Fiske, Jo-Anne. 1991. "Gender and the Paradox of Residential Education in Carrier Society." In Jane Gaskell and Arlene McLaren, eds., *Women and Education,* 2nd ed. Calgary: Detselig.

Frideres, James S. 1988. *Native Peoples in Canada: Contemporary Conflicts.* Scarborough: Prentice Hall.

Jenness, Diamond. 1943. *The Carrier Indians of the Bulkley River: Their Social and Religious Life.* Washington DC: Smithsonian Institution, Bureau of American Ethnology; Anthropological Papers No. 25.

Knockwood, Isabelle. 1992. *Out of the Depths: The Experiences of Mi'kmaw Children at the Indian Residential School at Shubenacadie, Nova Scotia.* Lockeport, NS: Roseway Publishing.

Leacock, Eleanor Burke. 1980. "Montagnais Women and the Jesuit Program for Colonization." In Eleanor Leacock and Mona Etienne, eds., *Women and Colonization: Anthropological Perspectives.* New York: Praeger.

Miller, J.R. 1996. *Shingwauk's Vision: A History of Native Residential Schools.* Toronto: University of Toronto Press.

Milloy, John S. 1999. *A National Crime: The Canadian Government and the Residential School System 1879 to 1986.* Winnipeg: University of Manitoba Press.

Mills, C. Wright. *The Sociological Imagination.* Oxford, 1959.

Morice, Adrien G. 1889. "The Western Dénés, Their Manners And Customs." Proceedings of the Canadian Institute, 3rd Series, Vol. VII, No. 1.

Stevenson, Winona. 1999. "Colonialism and First Nations Women in Canada." In Enakshi Dua and Angela Robertson, eds., *Scratching the Surface: Canadian Anti-racist Feminist Thought.* Toronto: Women's Press.

Van Kirk, Sylvia. 1980. *"Many Tender Ties": Women in Fur Trade Society, 1670–1870.* Winnipeg: Watson & Dwyer Publishing Ltd.

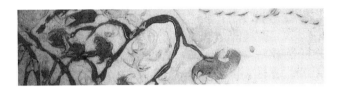

9

Black Families in Canada: Exploring the Interconnections of Race, Class, and Gender

Agnes Calliste

Department of Sociology and Anthropology
St. Francis Xavier University

Objectives

- To discuss the effects of social inequality on black families in Canada and examine some of their survival strategies as they cope with unequal power relations.

- To provide a historical background to understanding contemporary **African Nova Scotian** and **Caribbean** families.

- To analyze black family structures from the 1991 census and discuss the similarities and differences between black family structures and those of the general Canadian population.

- To explore some preliminary findings on racial and gender socialization and gender division of labour in black families.

INTRODUCTION

Blacks have been in Canada for more than 300 years. However, the study of black families, their most basic institution, has been largely ignored in social science research. The few studies (Calliste 1995; Christensen and Weinfeld 1993; Henry 1994) that exist are preliminary and exploratory. Moreover, Chambers (1977) and Tyszko (1959) focus on common-law relationships, family instability, and out-of-wedlock births among working-class blacks from a deficit perspective (Moynihan 1967), while ignoring middle-class families and stable poor black families. This focus on the deviation of black families from white middle-class norms gives the impression that black families are pathological. However, some researchers (Barrow 1996; Brewer 1988; Blackwell 1991; Calliste 1995; Collins 2000; Dill 1994) suggest that some black family lifestyles in the Caribbean and North America are adaptive responses to the social structure—the complex interaction of racial, class, and gender oppression in their lives.

This essay discusses the effects of the intersection of race, gender, and class on black families in Canada, focusing on black families in Nova Scotia and Caribbean families in Toronto. It also examines the role of culture and cultural retention in black families' adaptations as they cope with unequal power relations. The research methods used in this study include analysis of the 1991 census, 30 in-depth interviews of black families conducted in 1993–95 in Nova Scotia and Toronto, archival research, and review of the literature. All names of interviewees have been changed to maintain confidentiality.

Blacks in Canada have always occupied a subordinate position in economic, political, and ideological relations. This has had a distinct impact on black families. They were allowed into Canada as slaves, refugees, and cheap labour to do mostly hazardous and dead-end jobs in racial- and gender-segmented labour markets. Black men worked as railway porters and in the blast furnaces of steel plants, while most black women worked as domestics performing reproductive labour in white households (Calliste 1987, 1991, 1993/94; Winks 1971). Harold Potter (1949, 29) estimates that in 1941 80 percent of black women in Montreal's labour force worked as domestics. Blacks provided a reserve army of labour and were employed in the split labour market (Bonacich 1972, 1976) where they were paid less than white workers for doing the same or comparable work. For example, in the early 1960s Caribbean domestics earned about $150 a month less than white domestics, though employers reported favourably on their performance (*New Nation*, 31 May 1964). Racially specific gender and classist ideologies have been used to justify the racial division of labour and the exploitation and the devaluation of black, especially women's, labour. Stereotypes of black women (such as the asexual, nurturing, and subservient mammy; the "bad black woman"; and the "superstrong Amazon woman") have played an important role in relegating them to specific occupations, in barring them from entry into others, and in influencing managerial strategies of control (Calliste 1991, 1993/94, 1996; Collins 2000; Davis 1981; Thornhill 1991). Blacks, particularly in Nova Scotia, are still disproportionately concentrated in heavy, low-wage, part-time, and seasonal employment (e.g., wood-work, nurses' aides, orderlies, and domestic service) (Shadd 1987). Research indicates that because of racial and gender segmentation of the Canadian labour force, blacks, particularly women, experience more employment and income inequality than other minority groups despite above-average education (Reitz, Calzavara, and Dasko 1981; Li 1988; Ornstein 2000; Richmond 1989).

The educational system produced and reproduced racial, gender, and class inequality through segregated schools in Nova Scotia and Ontario,[1] a Eurocentric, sexist, and class-biased curriculum that bred low academic achievement, and high dropout rates in high school (BLAC [Black Learners Advisory Committee] 1994; Dei, Mazzuca, McIsaac, and Zine 1997). For example, the 1991 census indicates that among African Nova Scotians aged 20 to 24, less than 30 percent have graduated from Grade 12 (BLAC 1994, 60). The completion rate is much lower for the older age groups (BLAC, 64). Racism and sexism in education and employment lead to high rates of unemployment and poverty. In 1994, the estimated unemployment rate among black adults in Nova Scotia aged 20 to 29 exceeded 40 percent. For those aged 30 to 45, who are in the prime of their working careers, unemployment averaged 25 percent[2] (BLAC, 85). Similarly, unemployment rates for blacks in Toronto in 1996 (32 percent for young people aged 15 to 24, and 17 percent for adults) were almost twice the rates for the Toronto average (Ornstein 2000, 53). Such economic conditions are highly correlated with family structure and family instability (Canadian Mental Health Association 1983; Hill 1981).

Canada's racialized, gendered, and class-oriented immigration regulations and policy reinforced the subordinate status of black workers and hindered the proper formation and reunification of black families. Before the late 1960s, working-class black men and women were imported to Canada solely for their labour power, not as future citizens. Canadian immigration officials and some white Canadians stigmatized black people, especially those from the lower class, as inferior and a potential economic and social problem (such as crime and dependence on the state's resources). Immigration officials sought to avoid the problem by restricting the entry of black settlers and their families and by controlling their reproductive lives. For instance, a 1972 agreement between Canada and Jamaica for the recruitment of Jamaican women domestics stipulated that the domestic worker be "single, widowed, or divorced, without minor children or the encumbrance of common law relationships and the issue thereof, and between 18 and 40 years old" (Canada, Department of Manpower and Immigration 1972). In this way, Canada could extract labour from the domestic workers without incurring the economic and social costs of family reunification and maintenance. Some Jamaican women who immigrated under the scheme did not declare that they had children. During the economic recession in 1975–78 many of these women were deported for falsifying their immigration applications. However, a few of the women publicly challenged the deportation orders and they were allowed to return to Canada. This immigration policy and practice demonstrated the devaluation of black women and men as parents and a denial of black women's reproductive freedom. Caribbean blacks, particularly those in the lower class, were stereotyped as promiscuous, prone to indiscriminate procreation, and likely to become single and "unfit" parents. The dominant ideology of parenthood (making and caring for children within the context of the "ideal" nuclear and patriarchal family) constructed some locations within social relations of race, class, and citizenship that were more appropriate for parenthood than others. That is, some racial groups or classes were defined as less appropriate parents. These stereotypes of black women and men as less deserving of parenthood further rationalized and reinforced their subordination in Canada. Images of the undesirability of black women as immigrants and unfit mothers are still current (see Barnes 2002; Galt 1999).

THE IMMIGRATION AND HISTORY OF BLACK FAMILIES IN NOVA SCOTIA

The history of black families in Canada began with slavery, which was given its legal foundation in New France between 1689 and 1709 to help solve the chronic shortage of unskilled labour. By 1759, of the 3,604 slaves in New France, 1,132 were black (Winks 1971, 9). A small number of slaves and free blacks also were brought to Nova Scotia between 1686 and 1750 by British families from New England. By the 1770s, there were several hundred slaves living in Nova Scotia (Olivier 1968; Walker 1976).

Slavery undermined the family as the most fundamental unit of the social order blacks had known in West Africa, even though it never completely destroyed marriage and the family as important social institutions. Slaves had no marital or parental rights. They were allowed to marry with their owner's consent (Winks 1971); however, the children born of slaves became the property of the mother's owner, irrespective of the status of the father. Thus female slaves were commercially valuable to their masters not only for their labour, but also for their capacity to produce more slaves. Controlling black women's reproduction and denying blacks parental rights were essential to the creation and perpetuation of capitalist class relations. They were also manifestations of a systematic and institutionalized devaluation of black women and men as parents. Working-class black families have been stigmatized as *deviant* (for example, the "bad" promiscuous mother and ineffectual father). Slavery distorted black gender relations and shaped black gender roles, since black women generally performed the same work as men.

During slavery many family units were destroyed by the practice of selling fathers, mothers, and children separately. Even free black families were not safe from slave owners who sold them illegally. For example, Ellen Wilson (1976) reports that William Castels pretended to send Randon, a black Loyalist, from Birchtown to Barrington, but actually sent him to the Caribbean and sold him—leaving his wife, Mary Randon, aged 20, destitute. However, black parents struggled to regain and protect their families. Free black parents sued those who enslaved their children or sold them without holding the properly authorized documents of indenture. In 1791, Mary Postell sued Jesse Gray of Argyle for taking away her children (Shelburne Records 1791).

The majority of indigenous African Nova Scotian families are descendants of black Loyalists and refugees of the War of 1812. In 1783–84, more than 3,500 free black Loyalists (10 percent of all Loyalists) and 1,200 slaves owned by white Loyalists arrived in Nova Scotia (Walker 1976; Winks 1971). Unlike white Loyalists, few black Loyalists received land,[3] and even when they did their farms were too small to maintain their families and were usually located in the most isolated and infertile regions of the province, such as Preston and Lincolnville. Thus, the state marginalized black families and helped to reinforce and maintain their subordination. The unequal distribution of land and the exploitation of black labour (for example, through the split labour market) contributed to poverty and oppression of generations of Nova Scotian blacks. Some impoverished black Loyalists, unable to sustain their families, unwillingly indentured or apprenticed themselves and their children (Wilson 1976). Moreover, some black communities (such as Upper Big Tracadie in Guysborough County and Rear Monastery in Antigonish County) are still located on dirt roads on the fringes of white communities.

Black Loyalist families, dissatisfied with broken promises, denial of their democratic rights, and visions of a bleak future for their children, petitioned the British government for redress of their grievances. As a result, 1,196 black Loyalists migrated to Sierra Leone in 1792 (Fergusson 1971; Walker 1976; Winks 1971).

During the War of 1812, approximately 2,000 black refugees were brought to Nova Scotia (Grant 1990). Initially, they were welcome as a source of cheap labour. However, with the postwar depression and the arrival of 40,000 Scots labourers who tended to drive blacks out of the labouring and semi-skilled jobs upon which they had come to rely, the black workers became dependent on the state (Walker 1976, 101–2). In 1815, since blacks no longer had a valid economic role, white Nova Scotians began to oppose further black immigration.

Many black families did not fit the model of separate private and public spheres (Kerber 1988; Morton 1993) developed from the experiences of white middle-class nuclear families. Such families are characterized by a male breadwinner (active in the public sphere) and a financially dependent full-time housewife (confined to the private sphere). Given that many black men could not earn family wages, black women often had to work outside the home to maintain the financial survival of their families. Similarly, women, men, and the extended family shared in child rearing to ensure the family's survival. Thus, there has been a fluid public/private sphere in black families, offering opportunities for egalitarian relationships. For example, given the lack of employment opportunities for African Nova Scotian men in the early 1800s, many families practised gender interdependence and reversals of traditional gender roles in the division of labour. Some women worked in the paid labour force as domestics, laundresses, and seamstresses, or became market vendors, while their husbands took care of the children, made brooms, or gathered items such as berries and bouquets of fern, which the women sold in the Halifax market. As Seth Coleman (1815) reported to the Legislative Assembly about African Nova Scotian families:

> I found a disposition in them to labour, and to help themselves but the fact is they have nothing to do, I found but four men that had families that had employment, others were

making brooms or taking care of the family, while the mother was out to seek a day's work at washing or sewing; on their scanty pittance depended the subsistence of perhaps themselves and 4 or 5 children.

African Nova Scotian women's active economic role in their families' subsistence, their relative sexual autonomy, and the importance of the extended family in black communities partly reflect a West African cultural tradition (Sudarkasa 1981) as well as survival strategies. Given the pressures of the Canadian political economy (for example, poverty, and children orphaned by sale or death of their parents), taking on childcare responsibilities for each other's children served a critical function in the black community.

The survival of black families against extreme oppression and hardship reflects their strength and resilience. One of their strengths was their strong kinship bonds. They took relatives and fictive or symbolic kin (often, older people who were treated as "uncles," "aunts," and "grandparents") into their households more frequently than did white families, partly because it was a West African tradition and partly because their survival depended on their ability to help one another (Hill 1971; Stack 1974; Sudarkasa 1981). Research on African-American history (Foster 1983) reveals that the earliest forms of family organization recreated in America by enslaved blacks represented both a *syncretization* (a fusion or combination) of African patterns and an adaptation of certain universal features of the realities and demands of slave life. Among the African patterns that were transplanted and transformed by African-American slaves were kin networks, husband–wife relations, sibling bonds, socialization practices, relationships between alternate generations (grandparents and grandchildren), and the extension of kinship terminology to elders throughout the community.

With specific reference to black families in Nova Scotia, James Walker (1976, 85) reports that a Halifax official in the 1790s commented on blacks' strong attachment to their families, which impelled them "always to act together." Similarly, John Clarkson (Fergusson 1971; Walker 1976) noted in 1791 that black Loyalist families went beyond the British definition of family to include godchildren, orphans, widows, neighbours, people from the same church, or simply people in the same black community. Moreover, African Nova Scotian parents brought up other people's children as if they were their own, without distinction between biological and adopted children. The extended-family system and the practice of sharing childcare reflect a survival strategy as well as a West African cultural tradition that is found in many black communities, including the Caribbean (Bryan, Dodzie, and Scafe 1985; Collins 2000).

Commenting on black Loyalist family structure, Walker (1976, 85) points to the common stereotype that there was "a casual attitude towards sexual relationships, or at least towards the sacrament of marriage." He argues that common-law relationships and "illegitimacy" were frequent even among professed Christians. However, Herbert Gutman (1977) argues that slaves had their own ideas of morality. Though prenuptial intercourse was common among slaves in Virginia and Carolina (from which many black Loyalists and refugees migrated), there was hardly any indiscriminate mating. Prenuptial intercourse was viewed as a prelude to settled marriage, and marriage followed most prenuptial slave pregnancies. This practice was not peculiar to slave populations. It was also found in diverse "premodern" populations. Moreover, giving birth to a child at a relatively early age diminished the probability of the physical separation of its mother from her family of origin and made the future of a new slave family much more secure, since slave owners were less likely to sell a fecund than a "barren" woman. The relative frequency of common-law relationships and "illegitimacy" among some black Loyalists in Nova Scotia may be attributed partly to the lack of legal recognition given to marriages performed by black preachers and to slaves' marriage rituals, such as jumping over a broomstick.

Though the baptismal records of the Anglican Church in Shelburne (1783–1869) indicate that some black children came from single-parent families, marriage records for the same period show that many black Loyalists were married in that church. In the period 1785–90 there were 23 weddings of black Loyalists. The baptismal records of the Anglican Christ Church in Guysborough (1785–1879) indicate that 24 out of 25 black children who were baptized in the years 1785 and 1786 had parents who were married.

The 1871 and 1881 censuses for Halifax County indicate that though there were some common-law relationships among African Nova Scotians, most households included a married male and female. For example, the 1871 census for Halifax County lists 48 female-headed households and 208 households with a married couple with children under 12. What seems to be most distinct about African Nova Scotians' family structure in the late 19th century was the number of extended families, including households with children with surnames different from the household head, and/or the number of households in which third-generation children were residing. This probably also included neighbours' children. For example, the 1871 census lists 45 extended families for Halifax and 32 for Guysborough. The evidence suggests, however, that the role of the extended family and black community in socializing and disciplining children weakened considerably after the Second World War with the emergence of the state's social programs, migration of African Nova Scotians to cities such as Toronto and Montreal, industrialization, and societal emphasis on competition and individualism (D. Brown, personal communication, 18 August 1993; S. Jones, HERO tapes, 24 June 1971;[4] Jones 1993). Some programs, such as social development and welfare, weakened black families and communities by assuming roles and responsibilities traditionally held by parents, neighbours, and church leaders. Thus, the communities began to rely on the state for solutions to their problems such as economic survival and family conflict.

African Nova Scotian family structure varied by location according to adaptive responses to the social structure. In 1970, Clairmont and Magill (1970, 50–51) found that while rural nonfarm African Nova Scotian households had a tendency to include "other" (non–nuclear family) relatives and boarders as an adaptive response to racism and poverty, they tended, along with urban fringe families, to have fewer female lone-parent households. Blacks in Halifax mid-city had 28 percent female-headed households compared to 11 percent in the urban fringe and 12 percent in rural nonfarm communities. For Halifax as a whole, 10 percent of the families had female heads in 1961. Thus, the urban fringe and rural nonfarm black families were similar to the general Halifax population, while blacks in Halifax appeared "to have a family structure similar to that found in Black ghettoes in the

United States" (52). Literature on ethnicity and single parenting in the United States supports Clairmont and Magill's finding. Laosa (1988, 27) found that there is a dramatic increase in the incidence of single parenting as one moves away from rural areas and into urbanized settings. In addition to the impact of more intense racism and poverty in rural areas of Nova Scotia such as Guysborough and Preston, the low proportion of female-headed households could be attributed to the role of the church and pressure from the community to conform to societal norms. Oldtimers in Guysborough recall that families tended to exert pressure on pregnant single women and their partners to marry before the child's birth (D. Brown, personal communication, 18 August 1993; D. Smith, personal communication, 2 August 1993). In Halifax one could live in comparative anonymity, and the church and community had less social control. Recently, however, black family structures in rural communities have changed dramatically from mostly married families to some common-law relationships and female lone-parent households. In many of the latter families, the fathers moved out as a family survival strategy for the mothers to be eligible for social programs such as the family allowance and welfare (I. James, personal communication, 29 July 1994).

BLACK FAMILY STRUCTURES IN CANADA AND NOVA SCOTIA

The 1991 census indicates that nearly three-fifths (58.2 percent) of black families, compared to four-fifths (78.0 percent) of Canadian families of all ethnic groups, involve a married couple (Table 9.1). However, there is a slight tendency for proportionately more Canadian families than black families (except African Nova Scotians) to live in common-law relationships (9.9 percent versus 7.2 percent versus 12.2 percent, respectively). The rates of common-law families have probably increased for all three groups given the rise in such relationships in Canada from 6 percent in 1981 to 12 percent in 1996 (Statistics Canada 1996). African Nova Scotian families are even less likely to be married than blacks in Metropolitan Toronto and Canada in general (48.4 percent versus 55.6 percent versus 58.2 percent, respectively). This lower proportion of married families among blacks is mostly a result of socioeconomic forces—high unemployment rates and low wages.

These factors place added strains on marriages or keep them from forming in the first place. A significantly larger percentage of black than nonblack households are headed by a woman. While 10 percent of nonblack families have a female head, 31 percent of black families in Canada and 36 percent of African Nova Scotian families are headed by a woman. Black family structure reflects the interaction of race, gender, and class inequalities. Blacks, particularly in Nova Scotia, are more likely to be concentrated in the lowest paying and lowest status jobs (BLAC 1994; Ornstein 2000).

Table 9.2 presents data indicating that family structure varies by income. Controlling for geographical location and race, married families earn the highest income, followed by those in common-law relationships. Female-headed single-parent, especially

Table 9.1 Comparison of Family Structure of Blacks and Canadians of All Ethnic Groups, 1991

| | Blacks | | | All Ethnic Groups |
	Nova Scotia	Metro Toronto	Canada	Canada
Family Structure:				
Married	48.4%	55.6%	58.2%	78.0%
Common-law	12.2	6.0	7.2	9.9
Male lone parent	3.8	3.7	3.6	2.1
Female lone parent	35.6	34.7	31.0	10.0
Total	100.0	100.0	100.0	100.0
	(3,515)	(37,545)	(77,825)	(7,146,825)

Source: *Calculated from the Statistics Canada Nation Series, 1991 Census of Population. Based on a 20-percent sample.*

black (lone-parent), households earn the lowest income—about half the income of married families. Male lone-parent households, on the other hand, earn about three-fourths the income of married families. These great differences in income reflect the **feminization and racialization of poverty**—female gender, black race, and single parenthood influence the likelihood of poverty (Brewer 1988). Table 9.2 also shows that black families, particularly in Nova Scotia, earned lower average incomes in 1990 than the Canadian population. Blacks in Nova Scotia earned the lowest income partly because they reside in a poor region and partly because of more intense racism due to the "greater competition for jobs, particularly in the high wage, monopoly sector of the economy" (Shadd 1987, 109). As levels of education and income rise, so does the number of male-headed households. Marriage is as much the result of economic security, well-being, and upward mobility as it is the cause of economic well-being among families.

Black household heads with post-secondary education are more likely than those with less education to be married (Table 9.3). For example, about 78 percent of those with a uni-

Table 9.2 Comparison of Family Structure of Blacks and Canadians of All Ethnic Groups by 1990 Average Income for Selected Geographic Locations

| | Nova Scotia | | Metro Toronto | | Canada | |
	Blacks	All Ethnic Groups	Blacks	All Ethnic Groups	Blacks	All Ethnic Groups
Family Structure:						
Married	$44,823	$49,322	$58,698	$72,967	$54,177	$57,410
Common-law	34,428	39,538	48,013	65,036	44,736	48,287
Male lone parent	30,985	38,650	43,159	57,630	40,360	46,400
Female lone parent	20,143	24,201	29,192	38,006	26,170	28,972

Source: *Calculated from the Statistics Canada Nation Series, 1991 Census of Population. Based on a 20-percent sample.*

Table 9.3 Canadian Black Family Structure by Education

	Less than Grade 9	Grades 9–13	Trades Certificate or Diploma	Other Non-University	Some University	University Degree or Higher
Family Structure:						
Married	53.2%	53.0%	67.6%	54.7%	61.9%	78.5%
Common-law	5.8	7.7	6.0	7.4	8.4	5.5
Male lone parent	5.1	3.6	3.9	3.3	3.6	3.5
Female lone parent	35.9	35.7	22.5	34.6	26.1	12.5
Total	100.0	100.0	100.0	100.0	100.0	100.0
	(6,495)	(24,150)	(26,350)	(8,235)	(3,320)	(9,285)

Source: Calculated from the Statistics Canada Nation Series, 1991 Census of Population. Based on a 20-percent sample.

versity degree or higher compared with about 53 percent of those with a high-school certificate or lower are married. Conversely, about 12 percent of household heads with a university degree or higher compared to about 35 percent with a high-school certificate or lower are female single parents. At the highest level of education, the percentage of black families that are married is comparable to that for the Canadian population.

The percentages of African Nova Scotian married families whose household heads obtained either less than a Grade 9 education or a university degree or higher are comparable to those for other blacks in Canada with similar levels of education. However, at other levels of education, the effect of education on family structure is weaker for blacks in Nova Scotia than for other blacks. This is due largely to the greater economic marginalization of African Nova Scotians. Table 9.4 indicates, for example, that about 54 percent of African Nova Scotian household heads with a trades certificate or diploma are married. The percentage for all Canadian blacks at that education level is about 67 percent (Table 9.3).

Table 9.4 African Nova Scotian Family Structure by Education

	Less than Grade 9	Grades 9–13	Trades Certificate or Diploma	Other Non-University	Some University	University Degree or Higher
Family Structure:						
Married	55.8%	39.6%	54.1%	39.1%	47.6%	77.8%
Common-law	7.9	14.4	5.4	14.9	19.0	11.1
Male lone parent	6.3	4.5	5.4	2.5	4.8	3.7
Female lone parent	30.0	41.5	35.1	43.5	28.6	7.4
Total	100.0	100.0	100.0	100.0	100.0	100.0
	(950)	(1,110)	(185)	(805)	(210)	(270)

Source: Calculated from the Statistics Canada Nation Series, 1991 Census of Population. Based on a 20-percent sample.

Family structure fluctuates by education; however, given employment and income inequities, occupation and income might be better predictors of family structure among African Nova Scotians. The interaction of age and income also has an effect on family structure. A plausible assumption is that the relatively high proportion of married families among those with less than Grade 9 education is attributable to age and income. Older people are more likely to be married and less likely to be single parents. Controlling for education and occupation, older people earn more than younger people. Generally, older people also tend to have more resources than younger people.

Table 9.5 allows us to discount the effect of education. Controlling for education, the higher the income of African Nova Scotian families the more likely they are to be married. For example, among those with some secondary education, almost nine out of ten families

Table 9.5 African Nova Scotian Family Structures by Income, Controlling for Education

Less than Grade 9

Family Structure:	<$20,000	$20,000–$34,999	$35,000–$49,999	$50,000 and Over
Married	47.1%	66.0%	63.6%	64.7%
Common-law	6.9	6.0	15.1	0.0
Male lone parent	3.5	8.0	6.1	11.8
Female lone parent	42.5	20.0	15.1	23.5
Total	100.0	100.0	100.0	100.0
	(435)	(250)	(165)	(85)

Grades 9–13

Family Structure:	<$20,000	$20,000–$34,999	$35,000–$49,999	$50,000 and Over
Married	14.5%	39.1%	78.4%	87.5%
Common-law	12.0	20.3	8.1	0.0
Male lone parent	3.6	6.2	0.0	0.0
Female lone parent	69.9	34.4	13.5	12.5
Total	100.0	100.0	100.0	100.0
	(415)	(320)	(185)	(80)

Post-Secondary

Family Structure:	<$20,000	$20,000–$34,999	$35,000–$49,999	$50,000 and Over
Married	7.5%	34.6%	62.0%	81.7%
Common-law	5.7	19.2	22.0	12.7
Male lone parent	0.0	3.9	4.0	2.8
Female lone parent	86.8	42.3	12.0	2.8
Total	100.0	100.0	100.0	100.0
	(530)	(260)	(250)	(355)

Source: Calculated from the Statistics Canada Nation Series, 1991 Census of Population. Based on a 20-percent sample.

(87.5 percent) who earn $50,000 and over are married, compared to four out of ten (39.1 percent) of those who earn $20,000 to $34,999. Conversely, also controlling for education, the lower the income the more likely a family is to be headed by a female lone parent. For example, among families whose household head has some post-secondary education, female lone-parent families make up 87 percent of those who earn less than $20,000, compared to 12 percent of female lone-parent families who earn $35,000 to $49,999. The relatively high proportion of female lone-parent families among household heads with some post-secondary education in the lowest income group might be attributable to occupation/employment status and age.

Other factors that account for racial differences in family structure are the shortage of black men of marriageable age,[5] the tendency for more black men than women to be involved in interracial marriages, and a cultural tradition that is partly a legacy of colonialism and slavery. Though marriage is the most common form of family structure in the Caribbean, less emphasis is placed on marriage as a context for child bearing, particularly among the lower class (Smith 1988). The higher rate of single-parent families among blacks also is related to high separation and divorce rates (Christensen and Weinfeld 1993; Henry 1994; Richmond 1989), which result partly from the economic and social stress experienced by blacks across all social lines. Some black women have reacted to the black male shortage by parenting outside marriage. Another factor that has contributed to the growth of black single-parent homes is the high ratio of out-of-wedlock births. Many of these children are born to teenagers and young adults.

Table 9.6 indicates that more than half (56.3 percent) of black families in the 15 to 24 age group are headed by female lone parents. The corresponding proportion for African Nova Scotians is about 66 percent, compared to about 20 percent in the general Canadian population (Tables 9.7 and 9.8). Moreover, the 1991 census indicates that 85 percent of these young black female lone parents in Canada and 91 percent in Nova Scotia earned less than $20,000 in 1990. These statistics reflect the multiple jeopardy of race, class, gender, and age. Though being a single parent causes poverty, the widespread poverty among young blacks and their slim prospects for future economic stability are important causes of the for-

Table 9.6 Canadian Black Family Structure by Age

	15–24	25–34	35–44	45–54	55–64	65+
Family Structure:						
Married	23.5%	53.1%	58.8%	63.4%	69.6%	71.9%
Common-law	18.8	11.3	5.7	5.2	2.5	1.8
Male lone parent	1.4	2.4	3.9	4.9	3.6	5.2
Female lone parent	56.3	33.2	31.6	26.5	24.3	21.1
Total	100.0	100.0	100.0	100.0	100.0	100.0
	(3,895)	(19,670)	(25,720)	(18,170)	(6,965)	(3,380)

Source: Calculated from the Statistics Canada Nation Series, 1991 Census of Population. Based on a 20-percent sample.

mation of single-parent households among blacks. The feminization and racialization of poverty have serious consequences for young black families. This suggests the need for programs in education and employment equity and sex education, and the need for better communication between parents and children. Many parents, particularly blacks, do not talk frankly about human sexuality with their children, especially their daughters, or they give them contradictory messages (J. Brown, personal communication, 29 June 1993; G. Williams, personal communication, 22 July 1994). For instance, in the Caribbean, adolescent pregnancies have been linked to a social context in which taboos against sexual behaviour in girls paradoxically co-exist with tacit approval of early child bearing (Hardee 1997). Thus, many teenagers rely on their peers for sex education that is sometimes inaccurate.

Table 9.7 shows that in addition to high percentages of female lone-parent families among the youngest age groups (15 to 34), African Nova Scotian families aged 15 to 24 are four times more likely to live in common-law relationships than to be married (27.3 percent versus 6.0 percent). The corresponding percentages for other blacks in the same age group are about 19 percent common-law and about 23 percent married (Table 9.6). The low proportion of marriages in the youngest age groups (15 to 34) suggests that African Nova Scotians marry at a later age than other blacks and the general Canadian population.

About one-third (34.7 percent) of young heads of households in the 15 to 24 age group in the Canadian population are married (Table 9.8). Conversely, a single woman heads one in five families in this same age group (20.4 percent). Surprisingly, four out of ten Canadian families in this age group live in common-law relationships (44.4 percent). While this reflects economic instability, it also indicates the increasing tendency of young people to live in a trial marital arrangement. Common-law relationships are becoming acceptable in Canada, especially with the high separation and divorce rates.

Racial differences in births to single women could be attributed to differences in the frequent and effective use of contraceptives and abortion, as well as differences in *legitimation* (or "shotgun") weddings (Cutright and Smith 1988). Less-educated and poorer people are less likely to use contraceptives. Also, abortion has never been as popular in the black community as in the white community; moreover, many black youths cannot afford abortions.

Table 9.7 African Nova Scotian Family Structure by Age

	15–24	25–34	35–44	45–54	55–64	65+
Family Structure:						
Married	6.0%	31.7%	50.0%	62.0%	69.4%	62.1%
Common-law	27.3	19.4	12.8	8.8	3.2	2.1
Male lone parent	0.0	2.1	2.8	5.3	4.8	8.4
Female lone parent	66.7	46.8	34.4	23.9	22.6	27.4
Total	100.0.	100.0	100.0	100.0	100.0	100.0
	(165)	(930)	(1,060)	(565)	(310)	(475)

Source: Calculated from the Statistics Canada Nation Series, 1991 Census of Population. Based on a 20-percent sample.

Table 9.8   Family Structure by Age for Canadians of All Ethnic Groups

	15–24	25–34	35–44	45–54	55–64	65+
Family Structure:						
Married	34.7%	69.6%	77.1%	81.6%	87.3%	89.2%
Common-law	44.4	18.3	8.9	6.0	3.5	1.8
Male lone parent	0.5	1.1	2.5	3.1	2.1	1.9
Female lone parent	20.4	11.0	11.5	9.3	7.1	7.1
Total	100.0	100.0	100.0	100.0	100.0	100.0
	(229,280)	(1,606,725)	(1,942,470)	(1,359,260)	(1,014,165)	(994 920)

Source: Calculated from the Statistics Canada Nation Series, 1991 Census of Population. Based on a 20-percent sample.

Thus, race intersects with class. Blacks are also less likely than whites to put their children up for adoption, which affects the relative proportions of single-mother households. Historically, black women were substantially more inclined to incorporate the child of an unwed mother into the basic family structure or the extended family, occasionally explaining the newborn as the child of its grandmother or as a relative's child. Thus, children resulting from "unplanned" pregnancies were not referred to as "unwanted" (Clarke 1975).

GENDER-ROLE IDENTITIES, GENDER DIVISION OF LABOUR, AND GENDER RELATIONS

Black women have needed to be strong in order for the family to survive, and since most black women have been forced to work outside the home they tend to be relatively independent. However, black women often have not had the resources to impose their authority on black men in this society. Given patriarchy and gender ideologies, there is a *gendered division of labour* in black households. Generally, women perform the domestic labour *inside* the house while men tend to do the tasks *outside* (such as barn and yard work). In farm families in rural Nova Scotia both men and women work on the farm during planting and harvesting time (D. Jones, personal communication, 24 August 1993; M. Payne, personal communication, 27 July 1993; P. Sam, personal communication, 22 July 1993). In some families, men and women share in the making of family decisions as well as the housework and childcare, but it is still assumed that women are primarily responsible for domestic labour and that men are "helping" their wives. In exceptional cases, there are exchanges or role reversals, which sometimes are structured by the social situation and sometimes take place when family members prefer to perform a favourite task. For example, in one Caribbean family interviewed, the wife's job requires a great deal of travel, therefore the husband does most of the domestic labour except cooking, because he is not a good cook. The wife also performs some tasks outside (such as painting and gardening) because she prefers to do them (J. Brown, personal communication, 29 June 1993). The woman described her relationship with her husband as egalitarian. The literature on families (Blackwell 1991; Collins 2000; Eichler 1983) suggests that role exchanges or fully developed role sharing are characteristic of egalitarian families.

Black women, like other women (Luxton 1983), have developed a variety of strategies and tactics with which to get the men to take on more work. These range from appeals to fairness to militant demands for greater or equal participation (P. Sam, personal communication, 22 July 1993; Group interviews, personal communication, 26 June 1993). However, some men perceive these attempts as a challenge to their power and their traditional notions of masculinity and femininity. Thus, they resist their wives' attempts to be assertive and to change some gender roles. This sometimes results in power struggles and marital problems, including separation and divorce (Mendoza 1990).

Despite black men's resistance to changing gender roles, some are adapting and learning to accept women as "equals" partly as a survival strategy (P. Sam, personal communication, 22 July 1993; Focused Group, personal communication, 26 June 1993). As one Caribbean woman points out:

> A number of them have changed. They have to change. I think it's a change of survival, and not of understanding, understanding that women are people too. Because it's a superficial change in a sense, our children are coming up in homes where they are not seeing black men respecting black women and vice versa and teaching our sons that black women are to be respected and got a lot going for them. It's an accommodation by black men, not a change. There's no illumination on their parts. No genuine awakening. I don't see too many black men walking with their children. (Mendoza 1990: 329)

Some women who still internalize traditional notions of masculinity and femininity also resist men's efforts to change gender roles and patterns of domestic labour. A Caribbean man explained that his attempt to perform childcare functions and some of the domestic labour was interpreted as feminine and resulted in family conflict and separation. In his words:

> My wife was in nursing school. So I decided to stick by her and support her. I took care of the children, made her breakfast and lunch. After she left for school, I took the children to the day care before I went job hunting ... She told me that I was acting like a woman and that her mother said I looked like the type of man who would stay at home and let the woman work. (P. Peters, personal communication, 26 June 1993)

His behaviour challenged the two women's notions of gender roles. In the Caribbean, men generally did not participate in childcare and domestic labour (Barrow 1996; Smith 1988). The two women also perceived him as not performing his role as provider.

Though many black women acknowledge that black families simultaneously oppress them and act as a site for shelter and resistance against racism, most black men tend to deny or downplay sexism. They argue that racism and class exploitation are the major problems affecting black families and communities. They also claim that black men's oppression of their families is largely a result of the frustrations and powerlessness they experience in society and its major institutions ("Sexism in Our Community" 1987; "A

Woman Is Killed" 1987). For example, at the Black Family Strategy conference in Halifax in 1993, some women pointed out the need to discuss gender relations in black families and for black men to accept financial and social responsibility as fathers. Some black men responded that discussing sexism would be divisive and that they experienced more difficulties in the labour force than black women since they present a threat to the white male dominant group. In other words, they maintained that racial subordination of black men negates their advantages as males. An effective strategy, however, requires that both women and men address sexism in black families and communities in order to foster egalitarian relationships.

Most black families are very reluctant to speak about domestic violence. They fear that such disclosure will reinforce stereotypes of the violence of black men and increase the criminalization of the black community. This conspiracy of silence is also encouraged by the church, community leaders, and the police. For example, one woman's pastor blamed her for leaving her husband after five years of physical, mental, and emotional abuse because, as he said, marriage is intended to be for good and bad (Douglas 1986; "A Woman is Killed" 1987). This supports Aldridge's (1991) argument that the ideology of sexism and the Judaeo-Christian ethic have an interactive effect on black male–female relations since these ideologies support the inequalities that exist in these relations. As Wells (1986, 7) points out:

> Given the racism and sexism in Toronto, when Black women are battered it is treated lightly by the police and general community ... There are countless cases of Black women being battered and the police treat our complaints with mocking disrespect.

The failure of the police to charge Lesline Senior's husband despite repeated beatings and the Toronto black community's silence after he murdered her illustrate Wells's point. The evidence suggests that, as in other communities, "woman abuse is common behaviour in the Black community" ("A Woman Is Killed" 1987).

SOCIALIZATION IN BLACK FAMILIES

Black parents face an extraordinary challenge in raising children who will be able to survive in a racist, sexist, and capitalist society. They have to socialize children to develop a high self-concept and positive racial identity in a society in which being black has negative connotations. Black children must learn to achieve in a school system in which the curriculum negates their lived experiences and the contributions of people of African descent. They also must learn to cope with deterrents and roadblocks that inhibit their access to mainstream Canadian life. Simply put, black children must be socialized to deal with the racism that they will encounter daily. Black girls and women must be encouraged to be independent because many of them will carry family and economic responsibilities alone.

Peters (1985, 161) defines **racial socialization** as "raising physically and emotionally healthy" black children in a society with anti-black racism. Many black families in Canada develop racial socialization strategies to develop positive self-concepts and racial identity to prepare their children to deal with racism. In addition to teaching Black Heritage, some parents emphasize to their children that they are as good as other people: beautiful, intelligent, and so forth. Given the importance of education for upward social mobility, parents emphasize the value of education. Some parents also instill in their children that, given racism, they have to be "twice as good" as whites to compete, and black women have to be "ten times better" because of gendered racism and racialized sexism. However, some parents argue that this strategy puts too much pressure on children. Thus, they simply encourage them to do their best (Focused Group, personal communication, 4 August 1993).

Another racial socialization technique that some black parents use in preparing children to deal with racism is the teaching of folklore and telling of anecdotes about their experiences with racism and how they resisted. Thus some children learn about oppression and resistance very early. Black families and churches have also taught blacks to be strong and to stand up for their rights by emphasizing spiritual values such as equality and justice (D. Barnes, personal communication, 31 August 1993).

Some black parents claim that they are socializing their daughters and sons to be non-sexist. For example, some parents assign domestic chores by casting lots or ensuring that their sons learn to cook and clean (S. Paul, personal communication, 11 August 1993; Focused Group, personal communication, 4 August 1993). This does not guarantee that black males treat women as equals, particularly given other socialization agents such as the media and peers, and role modelling by some parents. Black youths regard their mother as the mainstay of the family. They claim that though their father may provide financial support, it is usually their mother who supervises their homework and encourages them to pursue higher education (C. James, personal communication, 16 January 1994).

Ironically, some feminists are socializing their sons for traditional male roles such as not sharing most domestic labour. One feminist has stated that she would socialize her children in traditional parenting patterns as she was socialized. For example, she would be more protective of her daughter than her son and teach her to do domestic labour. She says that feminism is an ideology that we strive for, but it is not reality (L. Bain, personal communication, 24 June 1994). Research is needed on the interaction effects of race/ethnicity and class on gender socialization.

Some first-generation Caribbean parents tend to be strict disciplinarians. They believe that they should not "spare the rod and spoil the child." Since they have not been trained to make the transition from the traditional parenting in the Caribbean to the Canadian pattern, they tend to socialize their children in traditional parenting patterns. They emphasize values such as respecting older people (for example, not calling them by their first names) and obeying parents (Mendoza 1990; L. Bain, personal communication, 24 June 1993). They argue that the Canadian tradition of parenting gives children too much freedom and that they do not want their young daughters or sons to act "womanish" or "mannish." For example, an eight-year-old girl was scolded for being womanish because she wanted a particular hairstyle and decided what outfit she should wear. Her parents felt that it was her mother's right to decide, not hers. Some parents regret that they cannot scold their children as they would like to, since children are knowledgeable about Canadian abuse laws. This difference in Caribbean and Canadian parenting patterns accounts for some allegations of child abuse. However, some parents have incorporated elements of their traditional Caribbean socialization patterns into the more liberal Canadian patterns. This syncretization has assisted them in providing their children with a more rounded upbringing.

Some first-generation Caribbean parents tend to direct their children and are protective of them for much longer than are Canadian parents (L. Bain, personal communication, 24 June 1993; James 1981; Mendoza 1990). For example, Caribbean parents do not approve of their children leaving home in their late teens. This extended protection tends to delay the maturation process and results in intergenerational conflict.

Another source of conflict in some Caribbean families is the effect of their migration patterns. Parents, particularly single mothers and those from low-income groups, tend to leave their small children in the care of relatives when they emigrate. Sometimes it takes several years before the parents have the money to sponsor their children's entry into Canada. Years of separation tend to strain parent–child relations. Some children see their stepfather and siblings for the first time when they arrive. They are expected to simultaneously fulfill their parents' aspirations and expectations, adjust to their stepfather, siblings, and an unfamiliar child role, and adapt to the new society.

Undoubtedly, the circumstances under which some Caribbean families "reunite" and the drastic social changes that the children experience result in psychological problems and intense family conflict. DaCosta (1976, 63–69) found that over 75 percent of Caribbean students seen in therapy were depressed and that their depression stemmed largely from the migration pattern of their families. Most of the children in his study had been separated from the parent or parents and had rejoined them up to 12 years later; in many cases they came into new family constellations. Some of the problems involved the children's distorted perception of their place among their siblings and in the family; fear of stepparents, particularly stepfathers; and parental shame when their newly arrived children failed to establish an immediate and harmonious relationship with them. In addition to the negative effect of migration patterns on parent–child relationships, there may also be stresses on the marriage.

CONCLUSION

This study of the interconnected effects of race, class, and gender on black families in Canada supports the view that blacks' subordinate position in economic, political, and ideological relations has an impact on black families. Though working-class blacks are less likely to be married than their Canadian counterparts, middle-class black family structure is similar to that of the Canadian population. Similarly, while there are proportionately more black female lone-parent families than in the general Canadian population, contrary to the popular stereotype blacks are less likely to live in common-law relationships than other young Canadians. The high rate of teenage pregnancy and the feminization and racialization of poverty among blacks, particularly in Nova Scotia, deserve serious attention by the state and the black community, including programs in education and employment equity, sex education, and parenting. The black community must also address sexism and male–female relationships, strengthen black families, and continue to struggle for justice and equity.

ACKNOWLEDGMENTS

The author would like to thank the men and women whom she interviewed and five anonymous reviewers for their helpful comments. Funding from the Centre for Regional Studies and the University Council for Research, St. Francis Xavier University, is gratefully acknowledged.

NOTES

1. Schools were officially desegregated in 1954. However, in Nova Scotia segregated schools continued to exist in isolated black communities.

2. The comparable unemployment rates for all Nova Scotians from Statistics Canada's Labour Force Survey ranged from a high of 27 percent for those aged 20–24 to a low of 10.7 percent for those aged 45–54 (BLAC 1994, 85).

3. During the American War of Independence, the British offered freedom, security, and self-sufficiency through land acquisitions and provisions to rebel-owned slaves who joined the British army (Walker 1976; Winks 1971).

4. The transcript for S. Jones's (1971) interview is in Black Historical and Educational Research Organization collection, Black Educators Association, Halifax.

5. Research (Calliste 1991; Christensen and Weinfeld 1993; Simmons and Turner 1991) indicates that black women in Canada experience a sex-ratio imbalance largely as a result of Canada's immigration policy of recruiting domestic workers and nurses from the Caribbean.

KEY TERMS

African Nova Scotians: Black people living in Nova Scotia.
Caribbeans: In this paper, black people from the English-speaking Caribbean.
Feminization and racialization of poverty: The prevalence of poverty in black female-headed households.
Racial socialization: Raising emotionally and physically healthy black children in a society in which being black has negative connotations.

DISCUSSION QUESTIONS

1. In what ways do black families experience social inequality?

2. How did black Loyalist and refugee families in Nova Scotia cope with social inequality?

3. What are the similarities and differences between African Nova Scotian and other black families in Canada as discussed by the author?

4. Discuss the similarities and differences between black family structures and those of the general Canadian population.

5. What role do black families play in racial and gender socialization of children?

6. Based on the other readings in this textbook, in what ways is the gender division of labour in black families similar to or different from that found among other groups? What does this say about patriarchy and, in particular, its ideological underpinnings?

REFERENCES

"A Woman Is Killed, Community Silent." 1987. Editorial. *Our Lives* (July/September), 2.

Aldridge, D. 1991. *Focusing: Black Male-Female Relationships*. Chicago: Third World Press.

Anglican Christ Church, Guysborough. 1785–1879. Records. Guysborough Museum, Guysborough, NS.

Barnes, A. 2002. "Dangerous Duality." In W. Chan and K. Mirchandani, eds., *Crimes of Colour*. Peterborough: Broadview Press: 191–203.

Barrow, C. 1996. *Family in the Caribbean*. Kingston, Jamaica: Ian Randle Publishers.

BLAC. 1994. *BLAC Report on Education*, vol. 3. Halifax: BLAC.

Blackwell, J. 1991. *The Black Community*. New York: HarperCollins.

Bonacich, E. 1972. "A Theory of Ethnic Antagonism." *American Sociological Review 37*: 547–59.

Bonacich, E. 1976. "Advanced Capitalism and Black/White Relations in the United States." *American Sociological Review 41*: 34–51.

Brewer, R. 1988. "Black Women in Poverty." *Signs* 13(2): 331–39.

Bryan, B., S. Dodzie, and S. Scafe. 1985. *The Heart of The Race*. London: Virago Press.

Calliste, A. 1987. "Sleeping Car Porters in Canada." *Canadian Ethnic Studies* 20(2): 1–20.

Calliste, A. 1991. "Canada's Immigration Policy and Domestics from the Caribbean." *Socialist Studies* 5: 136–68.

Calliste, A. 1993/94. "Race, Gender and Canadian Immigration Policy." *Journal of Canadian Studies* 28(4): 131–48.

Calliste, A. 1995. "Black Families in Canada." M. Lynn, ed., *Voices*. Scarborough, Ontario: Nelson Canada, 243–69.

Calliste, A. 1996. "Antiracist Organizing and Resistance in Nursing." *Canadian Review of Sociology and Anthropology* 33(3): 361–90.

Calliste, A. 2000. "Nurses and Porters." In A. Calliste and G. Dei, eds., *Anti-Racist Feminism*. Halifax: Fernwood, 143–64.

Calliste, A. 2001. "Immigration of Caribbean Nurses and Domestic Workers to Canada, 1955–1967." In B. Hesketh and C. Hackett, eds., *Canada: Confederation to Present*. CD-ROM. Edmonton: Chinook Multimedia.

Canada, Department of Manpower and Immigration. 1972. "Manpower Circular: Elements of Arrangement for Recruiting Jamaican Domestics Reached between the Jamaican Ministry of Labour and Employment and the Department of Manpower and Immigration": 1–2.

Canadian Mental Health Association. 1983. *Unemployment: Its Impact on Body and Soul.* Toronto: Canadian Mental Health Association.

Chambers, G. 1977. An Analysis of the Lower-Class West Indian Family Pattern in Toronto. Master's thesis, University of Windsor.

Christensen, C., and M. Weinfeld. 1993. *The Black Family in Canada.* Canadian Ethnic Studies 24(3): 26–44.

Clairmont, D., and D. Magill. 1970. *Nova Scotian Blacks.* Halifax: Institute of Public Affairs, Dalhousie University.

Clarke, A. 1975. *The Bigger Light.* Boston: Little, Brown.

Coleman, Seth. 1815. Assembly Papers, vol. 22 (March). Public Archives of Nova Scotia.

Collins, P. 2000. *Black Feminist Thought,* 2nd ed. New York: Routledge.

Cutright, P., and H. Smith. 1988. "Intermediate Determinants of Racial Differences in 1980 U.S. Nonmarital Fertility Rates." *Family Planning Perspectives 20*(2): 119–23.

DaCosta, G. 1976. "Counselling and the Black Child." In V. D'Oyley, ed., *Black Students in Urban Canada.* Toronto: Citizenship Branch, Ministry of Culture and Recreation.

Davis, A. 1981. *Women, Race and Class.* London: Women's Press.

Dei, G., J. Mazzuca, E. McIsaac, and J. Zine. 1997. *Reconstructing "Drop Out."* Toronto: University of Toronto Press.

Dill, B. 1994. "Fictive Kin, Paper Sons, and Compadrazgo." In M. Zinn and B. Dill, eds., *Women of Color in U.S. Society.* Philadelphia: Temple University Press, 149–69.

"Domestics Should Get Better Deal." 1964. *New Nation,* 31 May.

Douglas, D. 1986. "Danger at Home: One Woman's Voice." *Our Lives.* (May/June): 3.

Eichler, M. 1983. *Families in Canada.* Toronto: Gage.

Fergusson, C. 1971. *Clarkson's Mission to America, 1791–1792.* Halifax: Public Archives of Nova Scotia.

Foster, H. 1983. "African Patterns in the Afro-American Family." *Journal of Black Studies 14* (December): 201–32.

Galt, V. 1999. "Excellent Mom Faces New Fight to Stay Here." *Globe and Mail* (10 July): A3.

Grant, J. 1990. *The Immigration and Settlement of the Black Refugees of the War of 1812 in Nova Scotia and New Brunswick.* Halifax: The Black Cultural Centre.

Gutman, H. 1977. *The Black Family in Slavery and Freedom, 1750–1925.* New York: Vintage.

Hardee, K. 1997. "Reproductive Knowledge, Attitudes and Behavior Among Young Adolescents in Jamaica." *Social and Economic Studies* 46(1): 95–109.

Henry, F. 1994. *The Caribbean Diaspora in Toronto.* Toronto: University of Toronto Press.

Hill, R. 1971. *The Strengths of Black Families.* New York: Emerson Hall Publishers.

Hill, R. 1981. *Economic Policies and Black Progress.* Washington, DC: National Urban League Research Department.

James, C. 1981. *Working with Immigrant Adolescents. The Family: Interventive Strategies in a Multicultural Context.* Toronto: The Multicultural Workers Network.

Jones, R. 1993. The Conspiracy to Destroy the Black Community. Address delivered at the Black Family Conference, Halifax, August 28.

Kerber, L. 1988. "Separate Spheres, Female Worlds, Woman's Place." *Journal of American History* 75(1): 26.

Laosa, L. 1988. "Ethnicity and Single Parenting in the United States." In M. Hetherington and J. Arasteh, eds., *Impact of Divorce, Single Parenting and Stepparenting on Children.* Hillsdale, NJ: Erlbaum.

Li, P. 1988. *Ethnic Inequality in a Class Society.* Toronto: Wall and Thompson.

Luxton, M. 1983. "Two Hands for the Clock." *Studies in Political Economy, 12:* 27–44.

Mendoza, A. 1990. An Exploratory Study on the Socioeconomic, Cultural and Sociopsychological Experiences of Caribbean-Born Women in Ontario, Canada. Ph.D. thesis, York University.

Moynihan, D. 1967. "The Negro Family: The Case for National Action." In L. Rainwater and W. Yancey, ed., *The Moynihan Report and the Politics of Controversy*. Cambridge, MA: MIT Press, 39–124.

Morton, S. 1993. "Separate Spheres in a Separate World." *Acadiensis* 22(2): 61–83.

Oliver, W.P. 1968. *The Negro in Nova Scotia, 1668 to 1967*. Public Archives of Nova Scotia, vol. 42, document 111.

Ornstein, M. 2000. *Ethno-Racial Inequality in the City of Toronto*. City of Toronto.

Peters, M. 1985. "Racial Socialization of Young Black Children." In H. McAdoo and J. McAdoo, eds., *Black Children*. Beverly Hills, CA: Sage.

Potter, H. 1949. The Occupational Adjustment of Montreal Negroes, 1941–48. Master's thesis, McGill University.

Reitz, J., L. Calzavara, and D. Dasko. 1981. *Ethnic Inequality and Segregation in Jobs*. Toronto: Centre for Urban Community Studies, University of Toronto.

Richmond, A. 1989. *Caribbean Immigrants*. Ottawa: Statistics Canada.

"Sexism in Our Community." 1987. Editorial. *Our Lives*. (March/April): 2.

Shadd, A. 1987. "Dual Labour Markets in Core and Periphery Regions of Canada." *Canada Ethnic Studies* 19(2): 91–109.

Shelburne Records. 1791. General Sessions. Public Archives of Nova Scotia.

Simmons, A., and J. Turner. 1991. *Caribbean Immigration to Canada, 1967–1987*. York University.

Smith, R.T. 1988. *Kinship and Class in the West Indies*. Cambridge: Cambridge University Press.

Stack, C. 1974. *All Our Kin: Strategies for Survival in a Black Community*. New York: Harper & Row.

Statistics Canada. 1996. *Census Handbook*. Catalogue No. 92-352-XPE. Ottawa: Statistics Canada.

Sudarkasa, N. 1981. "Female Employment and Family Organization in West Africa." In F. Steady, ed., *The Black Woman Cross-Culturally*. Cambridge, MA: Schenkman.

Thornhill, E. 1991. "Focus on Black Women!" *Socialist Studies* 5: 27–38.

Tyszko, L. 1959. Family Life and Family Stability of Negroes in Halifax. Diploma in Social Work thesis, Dalhousie University.

Walker, J. 1976. *The Black Loyalists*. New York: Africana Publishing.

Wells, J. 1986. "Shelter Whitewash." *Our Lives* (November/December): 7.

Wilson, E. 1976. *The Loyal Blacks*. New York: Capricorn Books.

Winks, R. 1971. *Blacks in Canada*. Montreal: McGill–Queen's University Press.

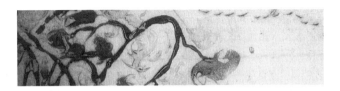

10

The Experience of Middle-Class Women in Recent Hong Kong Chinese Immigrant Families in Canada

Guida Man
York University

Objectives

- To elucidate the experience of middle-class Chinese immigrant women from Hong Kong, which cannot be discoverable through statistical data.

- To demonstrate the importance of institutional processes in the form of immigration policies and practices on family formation of the Chinese in Canada.

- To illuminate how the experience of Chinese immigrant women has been transformed due to the difference in the social organization of Canadian and Hong Kong societies.

- To deconstruct the notion of the homogeneity of all Chinese immigrant families, and to show the importance of class and gender as well as race/ethnicity in shaping the experiences of family members.

INTRODUCTION

A plethora of studies have been written on the Chinese in Canada. Many of them examined the history of Chinese immigration (see, for example, Roy 1989; Chan 1983; Wickberg 1982), or addressed racial discourse and racism toward the Chinese (see, for example, Creese and Peterson 1996; Anderson 1991; Baureiss 1987). Others focused on Chinese professionals and business immigrants, particularly on their labour market participation and their business development (see, for example, Basran and Zong 1998; Wong and Ng 1998; Li 1993). Many of the studies on the Chinese in Canada, however, have adopted a perspective that either does not include women or treats women the same as men. Moreover, as is common in the treatment of ethnic groups by many social scientists, "the Chinese" are routinely conceptualized as a homogeneous group. In fact, the Chinese come from diverse geographical areas (Taiwan, China, and Hong Kong, to name a few), have varied cultural backgrounds and dialects, and occupy different class, gender, age, and sexual locations. Rather than homogenizing them into one group, my goal is to re-evaluate the situation of the Chinese in Canada and to articulate their experiences from their different locations. In this chapter, I focus on a specific group of Chinese immigrants; that is, the experience of women in middle-class Hong Kong Chinese immigrant families that have recently immigrated to Canada.

THE BACKGROUND: CHINESE IMMIGRATION TO CANADA

The Canadian government has historically adopted an approach to immigration characterized by pragmatism and economic self-interest. Its immigration policies toward the Chinese have in the past been characterized by racism, sexism, and class discriminatory measures, and continue to be partial to people from middle- and upper-class backgrounds. Hence, the entry of Chinese women and consequently the formation of Chinese families in Canada have been hampered by these restrictions.

The Canadian government's expansionist economic strategy as applied to immigration and the way in which the social relations of **race, gender, and class** intersect determine at any historical moment whether the Chinese are allowed into Canada and what category of Chinese are permitted. During the early periods of Chinese immigration, many racially discriminatory measures such as the *head tax* and the *Chinese Exclusionary Act* were imposed on the Chinese but not on Western European immigrants (see Li 1998; Taylor 1991; Hawkins 1988; Baureiss 1987; Abella and Troper 1982). And although some Chinese labourers were admitted into Canada to work on the railways and the mines, the Canadian government prohibited Chinese women from entering Canada to prevent the proliferation of the Chinese population. This measure effectively reduced the reproductive activities of the Chinese and hence the formation of Chinese families. But while the head tax was imposed from 1885 to 1923 to prohibit Chinese labourers and their wives from entering Canada, affluent Chinese merchants and their wives seeking entry were exempt from the head tax during the period 1911 to 1923 (Sedgewick 1973, 129; Wickberg 1982: 94). These wealthy merchants were useful in procuring trade for Canada, and therefore were accorded preferential treatment vis-à-vis their poor counterparts. Even during the exclusionary period between 1923 and 1947, when no Chinese were officially admitted, special privileges were granted to an elite class of Chinese who would otherwise have been prevented from entering Canada due to their race. But the number of women who belonged to the elite class was minuscule; hence, the population of Chinese women in Canada remained very small. Consequently, the number of Chinese families was low even as late as 1951.

The pivotal shift occurred in 1967, when the Canadian government adopted a universal point system of selecting immigrants, thus allowing the Chinese to be admitted under the same conditions as other groups (Hawkins 1988). The new initiative supposedly eliminated racial and gender discrimination from the *Immigration Act,* but the class discriminatory measures remained intact. The 1967 point system and its subsequent revisions in 1978, 1985, and 1993 inevitably privileges people from middle- and upper-class backgrounds who have the opportunity to acquire the "appropriate" educational, vocational, and language skills required by the Canadian government (see Table 10.1), or who came in as business-class immigrants such as entrepreneurs, investors, and the self-employed (see Table 10.2).

TABLE 10.1 Immigration Selection Factors for Independent Applicants: 1967, 1978, 1985, and 1993

	Maximum Score			
Factor	1967	1978	1985	1993
Education	20	12	12	16
Specific vocational preparation	15	15	10	18
Experience	N/A	8	8	8
Occupational demand	15	15	10	10
Arranged employment or designated occupation	10	10	10	10
Location	5	5	N/A	N/A
Age	10	10	10	10
Knowledge of official language(s)	10	10	15	15
Personal suitability	10	10	10	10
Relative in Canada	5	5	N/A	5
Levels control	N/A	N/A	10	N/A
Demographic factor	N/A	N/A	N/A	8
Bonus for self-employed immigrants	N/A	N/A	N/A	30
Potential maximum	100	100	100	140
Minimum required	50	50	70	70*

Source: Compiled from Employment and Immigration Canada, The Revised Selection Criteria for Independent Immigrants, 1985, p. 18, and Government of Canada, Canada's Immigration Law, 1993, p. 13. Adapted with permission of the Minister of Public Works and Government Services Canada, 2002.

*See Table 10.2.

TABLE 10.2   1993 Selection Criteria for Business Immigrants, Assisted Relatives and Other Independent Immigrants*

Minimum Selection Units Required per Category	
Entrepreneur	25
Investor	25
Self–employed	70 (includes 30 bonus points)
Skilled worker	70
Assisted relative	70 (includes 5 bonus points for assisted relative)

Source: Compiled from Government of Canada, Canada's Immigration Law, 1993, p. 13. Adapted with permission of the Minister of Public Works and Government Services Canada, 2002.

*The Quebec selection has some differences in the factors and units of assessment, but the intent and results are similar.

Accordingly, many Chinese (and other immigrants) who were admitted into Canada in recent years belong to such privileged groups (see Salaff and Wong 1995).

The 1967 revision of Canadian immigration policy coincided with riots in Hong Kong, resonating the Cultural Revolution in China. Although Hong Kong was under British colonial rule, many feared political and economic upheaval and sought refuge in a stable country. This resulted in a large exodus of Hong Kong Chinese immigrants to Canada in the late sixties and seventies. Those admitted were middle-class professionals such as physicians and engineers. They were highly educated, cosmopolitan, possessed professional or technical skills, and were proficient in English. Many of the Chinese women who came into Canada at the time were sponsored by their husbands and relatives. But the selection policy also attracted some Chinese women professionals who had the educational and occupational skills to come in as independent applicants. Consequently, the gender ratio of the Chinese became more equalized. By 1971, 83 percent of the Chinese in Canada were recorded as belonging to a census family household according to the Canada census.

With the approach of 1997 and the impending change of government in Hong Kong from British to Chinese sovereignty, the 1980s and 1990s witnessed a second wave of the exodus of Chinese immigrants from Hong Kong to Canada. Many of the Chinese immigrants were worried about the possibility of social, political, and economic instability under Chinese rule. The Canadian media responded to the influx of new immigrants by focusing on the wealthiest of the business immigrants. They were dubbed "Gucci Chinese" (Cannon 1989) or "yacht people" (*Calgary Herald* 14 February 1988, D3), as opposed to their poor Vietnamese cousins, the "boat people." Hence, a particular image of the immigrants was created: that of affluent businessmen, driving Mercedes-Benzes and living in monster homes (*Halifax Chronicle-Herald* 25 January 1988: 15; *Vancouver Sun* 26 May 1989: B4; *Maclean's* 7 February 1994, 30). In fact, this image typifies only a small minority and is far from the actual "lived experiences" of most of the Chinese immigrants, particularly the Chinese immigrant women.

Table 10.3* Level of Schooling for Foreign-Born and Canadian-Born Chinese-Canadians and Other Canadians by Sex, 15 Years of Age and Over, 1996

| | Chinese-Canadians | | | | Other Canadians | |
| Level of Schooling | Foreign-born % | | Canadian-born % | | % | |
	F	M	F	M	F	M
Some high school or less	38.5	33.7	28.7	27.9	34.6	43.3
Completed high school	14.1	11.7	8.7	9.5	15.8	13.0
Trade certificate or diploma	1.5	1.6	0.4	1.2	2.6	5.0
Non-university without certificate	5.4	4.8	5.0	6.3	6.9	6.1
Non-university with trade or other certificate	12.5	11.2	13.8	10.3	18.0	17.9
Some university	10.7	11.8	19.1	20.2	9.9	9.2
University with degree	17.5	25.2	24.3	24.6	12.2	14.0
Total	100.0	100.0	100.0	100.0	100.0	100.0
Total sample number	8,787	8,001	1,121	1,198	312,745	295,323

Source: Compiled from Statistics Canada, Individuals File, Public Use Microdata Files: 1996 Census of Population. These data are based on a sample of 792,448 cases, including those under age 15.

*Table created with the assistance of Dr. Monica Boyd.

Table 10.4* Occupations of Foreign-Born and Canadian-Born Chinese-Canadians and Other Canadians by Sex, 15 Years of Age and Over, 1996

| | Chinese Canadians | | | | Other Canadians | |
| Occupations | Foreign-born % | | Canadian-born % | | % | |
	F	M	F	M	F	M
Senior managerial, middle/other managerial	3.7	9.8	4.4	7.3	3.8	8.3
Professional	8.5	12.9	13.8	16.4	9.8	9.3
Semi-professional/technician	1.9	4.4	4.4	5.8	3.5	4.4
Supervisory, including crafts/trades	0.8	1.6	1.6	1.3	1.7	5.0
Administrative/senior clerical	4.6	1.3	6.5	1.4	6.2	1.1
Skilled sales, intermediate sales, other sales/services	17.2	19.0	22.9	22.6	21.8	15.6
Skilled crafts/trade	0.7	4.2	0.4	2.9	0.5	10.0
Clerical	9.7	4.2	15.4	7.7	10.5	4.4
Semi-skilled manual and other manual work	8.4	8.4	1.3	7.0	4.5	17.5
Not applicable	44.5	34.1	29.3	27.5	37.7	24.1
Total	100.0	100.0	100.0	100.0	100.0	100.0
Total sample	8,787	8,001	1,121	1,198	312,745	295,323

Source: Compiled from Statistics Canada, Individuals File, Public Use Microdata Files: 1996 Census of Population. These data are based on a sample of 792,448 cases, including those under age 15.

"Not applicable" includes persons who were never in the labour force and those who were only in the labour force before 1995.

*Table created with the assistance of Dr. Monica Boyd.

Although the media image of the Hong Kong Chinese immigrants does not include women, since 1988 the number of Chinese immigrant women from Hong Kong has exceeded that of their male counterparts. For example, in 1988, 9,592 females versus 8,763 males immigrated to Canada from Hong Kong, and in 1996 the numbers for females and males were 12,790 and 11,339, respectively (EIC 1988–92, CIC 1992–96). Despite their numbers and their contributions, Chinese women's experiences have remained invisible. This is congruous with the fact that the study of women was not legitimized as a topic of discourse and that women's perspective was largely ignored in academic research until fairly recently (Smith 1990; Eichler 1985). Moreover, women's labour has almost always been incorporated into the family or into their husbands' work (Luxton and Reiter 1997; Kynaston 1996; Kanter 1993; Finch 1983; Luxton 1980). Consequently, their experience is seen to be either subsumed under that of men or tied to that of their male counterparts, and therefore they are perceived as not having a separate reality.

THEORETICAL FRAMEWORK AND METHODOLOGY

Since the 1980s we have seen the emergence of studies on immigrant women in general (see, for example, Mojab 1999; Lee 1999; Das Gupta 1996; Boyd 1990; Estable 1986; Ng 1981) and on Chinese immigrant women in particular (see, for example, Man 2002, 1997; Preston and Man 1999; Chinese Canadian National Council 1992; Yee 1987; Adilman 1984; Nipp 1983). This has ruptured the silence of women's experience. Nipp (1983) and Adilman's (1984) studies shed light on the historical accounts of Chinese immigrant women in Canada, while Man (2002, 1997), Preston and Man (1999), Yee (1987) and the Chinese Canadian National Council's (1992) book project illuminated Chinese women's lives by making space for Chinese women to voice their stories from their own perspectives. These studies have found Chinese women to be actors who toiled and laboured alongside their male counterparts and who were involved actively in political and community organizing.

Many social science research studies on immigrants derived their theoretical perspectives from a body of work centred on the concepts of adaptation and adjustment. Such analyses put the onus on the individual immigrant to adjust. The immigrant's failure to assimilate is seen to be her or his own fault. Studies based on these theoretical perspectives often focus only on **microstructural processes**—that is, on the individual and the immediate family. They seldom go beyond the individual to investigate the interaction between her or him and the **macrostructure** and to look at how socially constructed opportunities and limitations rooted in **institutional** and **organizational processes** shape individual immigrants' lives. In my analysis of the research data, I have used a methodology that addresses the intersections of gender, race, class, and other discourses of inequality, and that places women as subjects of the study (see Ng 1993; Hill-Collins 1990; hooks 1984). The analysis takes into account both structural processes and individual negotiations. This methodology has enabled me to investigate how individual Chinese immigrant women as subjects account for their situations, and how their subjective experiences are shaped by objective structures (in the form of organizational and institutional processes). Organizational and institutional processes are interconnected; I distinguish them in order to obtain clarity in my exploration.

As mentioned previously, the Chinese come from diverse backgrounds and locations. Here, I will focus on exploring the experiences of middle-class women in recent Chinese immigrant families from Hong Kong, and I will attempt to explain how their experiences in Canada have been transformed as a result of institutional processes and the difference in the social organization of the two societies. I have artificially categorized their experiences into topics: employment opportunities, housework and childcare, relationships with husbands and children, and social life. In actuality, people's everyday lives are not neatly delineated into categories. Human experiences and interactions with others occur in complex dialectical rather than simple linear relations. Events and feelings diverge and converge. Similarly, these categories overlap and transgress into one another.

THE SAMPLE

The data for this study were generated through in-depth interviews with 30 middle-class Chinese immigrant women from Hong Kong. The women were all married with at least one child. They had immigrated to Canada between 1986 and 1990. A snowball sampling method was used to locate the interviewees. Interviews lasted from one-and-one-half hours to three hours; an interview schedule was used as a guideline. All questions were open ended. Interviewees were encouraged to talk freely about their experiences in Canada and in Hong Kong.

INSTITUTIONAL PROCESSES

Institutional processes here refer to those processes and practices that are embedded in government, law, education, and professional systems. Such processes can engender and perpetuate social injustice in our society. I have already described how the institutionalized discriminatory process and practice of Canadian immigration policies regulated the entry of Chinese women into Canada. In this section, I will show how the employment opportunities of Chinese immigrant women have been impeded as a result of institutionalized processes.

Employment Opportunities

Most of the women in this study came to Canada as dependents of their husbands, who were the principal applicants under the "Independent Class"[1] as "business" or "other independent"[2] (professionals such as engineers, accountants, and so on) immigrants. These women therefore need not have had high education levels to score entry points. But owing to their middle-class background, on the whole their education level is quite high. The majority have university degrees or post-secondary education (21 out of 30). Despite the fact that these women were classified as "dependants" by the immigration policy and were therefore supposedly not destined for the labour market, in fact many of these women had worked as professionals in Hong Kong. Although not all of these women actively sought employment when they first arrived, those who did were either underemployed or unemployed. Institutionalized practices in the form of the requirement of "Canadian experience" and the lack of an accreditation system to calibrate their qualifications have made it difficult for them to obtain employment commensurate with their qualifications. Consequently, some women found themselves dependent on their husbands economically for the first time in their lives. Often, immigrant men are subjected to the same institutionalized discrimination.

Their experiences are not different from the experiences of other Chinese immigrant women. Although the 1996 census gives a very positive picture of Chinese immigrant women's educational level (Table 10.3) and participation in the labour market (Table 10.4), both in comparison with their male counterparts and with other Canadians, on closer examination the data reveal that a higher percentage (17.5 percent) of Chinese immigrant women ("foreign-born") have obtained a bachelor's degree or higher as compared to "other Canadians," both female and male (12.2 percent and 14 percent, respectively). However, fewer Chinese immigrant women have been able to enter the highly coveted managerial and professional occupations (3.7 percent and 8.5 percent, respectively) as compared to "other Canadian" women (3.8 percent and 9.8 percent, respectively) and "other Canadian" men (8.3 percent and 9.3 percent, respectively).

Similarly, a study conducted in 1991 found that of 512 Hong Kong immigrants between the ages of 30 and 39 who entered Canada after 1980, 23 percent reported no change in income, 46 percent recorded a drop, and 31 percent reported a rise in income. The majority (62 percent) experienced a drop in occupational status, 25 percent had experienced no change, and only 13 percent had acquired a higher status (*Canada and Hong Kong Update* 1992, 7).

Another survey conducted in 1989 that focused specifically on Chinese immigrant women's needs in Richmond, British Columbia (S.U.C.C.E.S.S., 1991) found that whereas 70 percent of the women surveyed had worked prior to immigrating to Canada, fewer than 50 percent were employed when surveyed. Of those who were employed, there was a significant degree of frustration and loss of self-esteem as a result of underemployment, low salaries, and limited opportunities for advancement. Nearly one-quarter of the respondents stated that their foreign education was not recognized in Canada. More than 46 percent of these women had completed secondary education and 41.2 percent had post-secondary education, including college/university or professional training.

At the same time, Chinese-Canadians are concerned about the upsurge in racism. They feel that they are disadvantaged when it comes to getting jobs and being promoted—a "glass ceiling" keeps them from advancing to management ranks. In a survey conducted for the

Chinese Canadian National Council, 63 percent of survey respondents from Chinese-Canadian organizations and 59 percent from non–Chinese-Canadian social service organizations reported their belief that Chinese-Canadians are being discriminated against (*Globe and Mail* 26 April 1991, A7).

These findings concur with my interview data. One of the women I interviewed, who has a post-graduate degree and has worked as a translator and teacher in Hong Kong, became so exasperated with her job search that she gave up the idea of entering the labour force altogether. She lamented:

> It's a Catch-22. I cannot get a job because I don't have Canadian experience, and yet I don't see how I can possibly get Canadian experience without being hired in the first place!

Her frustration is echoed by other Chinese immigrant women.

A common strategy adopted by many immigrant women I interviewed is what Warren (1986) describes as a "positive and pragmatic bridge" toward their new positions. As one woman who worked in Hong Kong as a chief executive officer supervising more than 300 employees rationalized:

> In terms of my employment here, when I first arrived I couldn't work as a manager as I didn't have Canadian experience. I couldn't work as a secretary because I was told I was overqualified. I was lucky to get a job with this company. They wanted to do business with Hong Kong ... That's why they hired me. They wanted someone to start the HK market. I was hired as an assistant ... They paid the B.comm. graduates $1,200 a month. They paid me $1,500 a month. So they really respected me ... Either you don't work for someone, but if you work for them, you have to do your best, [it] doesn't matter what the pay is. I kept telling myself that they were paying me to learn. I was in a new country. I didn't have a choice. I was paving my way for the future.

These women were cognizant of the futility of hoping for changes in processes that are institutionalized and embedded in the social system. Since they could not transform the macrostructure, they therefore resolved to change their own attitude toward their situations. Others went through retraining and re-certification to qualify for professional status in Canada, so as to gain a sense of security. Some immigrant women dealt with their disillusionment with the Canadian bureaucratic system by establishing their own businesses utilizing their expertise in a particular profession; ingenuity, drive, and industriousness were key to their success.

For many Chinese immigrant women, their underemployment and unemployment in the new country has undermined their sense of stability and well-being. Their class privilege, however, does allow them the option of withdrawing from the paid labour force altogether. Nonetheless, the transition from being an active participant in the labour force, with a fair amount of responsibilities and status, to being a stay-at-home housewife has been a challenging adjustment for many women. In response to underemployment and unemployment in Canada, in recent years many immigrants have resorted to return to their businesses or professional jobs in Hong Kong after they have obtained citizenship in Canada. This is a strategy to ensure family members will continue to enjoy middle-class social and economic status and privilege. Other immigrants (typically the husbands, and increasingly the wives as well) chose to return to Hong Kong alone, conducting transnational relationships with family members in Canada. This family arrangement is known amongst the Chinese immigrants as the "astronaut family."[3] The phenomenon is also prevalent among immigrants who are either unable to complete the transfer of their businesses from Hong Kong to Canada in time for their departure or who are afraid of relinquishing all their business contacts in Hong Kong. They opt to spend half of the year in Hong Kong and commute to Canada to visit with their family members periodically.

ORGANIZATIONAL PROCESSES

Organizational processes are the actual material changes that the Chinese immigrant women experience as a result of immigrating to Canada. Often, immigrants are judged by their ability to "adjust." What are neglected, however, are the differences in social organization of the society from which the immigrant has emigrated and the immigrant's new society. By uncovering how individual women's experiences are shaped and determined by the larger socioeconomic structure, we can begin to understand the problems that seemingly dwell only on the "micro" level. The organizational differences of diverse forms of societies determine the different ways a person gets her or his work done, conducts her or his life, and relates to other people. In this section, I demonstrate how the Chinese immigrant women's everyday lives have been transformed as a result of the different organizational processes in Hong Kong and Canadian societies.

Relationships with Husbands and Children

Being in a new country may change the relationships these women have with family members. Their transformed relationships with husbands and family members have divergent results for different women depending on their labour-market participation and that of their husbands. Apart from the institutional processes that hamper immigrants' opportunity to enter the Canadian labour market, the differences between the social and organizational structures of Hong Kong and Canadian societies also contribute to new immigrants' unemployment and underemployment.

Under British colonial rule, Hong Kong adopted what economists consider a pure capitalist system. With an industrious workforce, this system has on the one hand created a very low unemployment rate (3 to 4 percent prior to 1998); on the other hand, it engenders a wide disparity between professionals and low-level blue-collar workers and between the rich and the poor. As well, unions have a relatively low profile, and workers enjoy few benefits. Despite the robust economy prior to 1998, the absence of a guaranteed minimum wage and the lack of an adequate social safety net (Cheng and Kwong 1992) make life extremely difficult for the poor and the unemployed. But for middle-class citizens the situation appears to be promising. The low unemployment rate, coupled with the brain drain due to emigration, allows professionals, whether men or women, to enjoy good salaries and excellent benefits.

In Canada, the situation is quite different. The relative strength of the union benefits many workers, whether white- or blue-collar. Compared to Hong Kong, the wage gap between blue-collar workers and mid-level professionals is relatively narrow. The average low-level worker fares better in Canada than in Hong Kong. Those workers who participate in full-time employment generally enjoy fairly good employee benefits and wages and there is a guaranteed minimum wage. However, since the 1980s, the Canadian neoliberal state's endorsement of globalization and its strategies for economic restructuring has drastically eroded the welfare state, with dire consequences (Shields and Evans 1998; Evans and Werkele 1997; Bakka 1996; Brodie 1995). Citizens can no longer depend on a social safety net. Furthermore, the unemployment rate has remained high, exacerbated by the continuing economic recession. Consequently, the number of poor people is on the rise, particularly women and children (Tarasuk et al. 1998). Since competition for jobs is keen, employers can be discriminatory in their hiring practices. This does not provide for an ideal situation for a new immigrant looking for work (Man 2002; Mojab 1999).

Some middle-class immigrant women professionals, unemployed or underemployed since their arrival, have found themselves economically dependent on their husbands for the first time in their lives. Such dependency has put some Chinese women in a relatively powerless position vis-à-vis their husbands. Other women, however, have more positive experiences. They have found that their relationship with their husband has improved because of their husband's diminished career demands in Canada, which allows them to spend more time with their spouse. Their husbands either have become underemployed or have reduced their business activities because of the lack of business connections and opportunities in a country with a less favourable economic environment. These women reported an escalated intimacy with their husbands. The spouses were drawn closer in their common struggle to overcome obstacles in the new country and to comfort each other when they were overwhelmed by feelings of isolation and alienation. One woman whose husband used to be a part owner of a manufacturing business in Hong Kong told me:

> My relationship with my husband has improved since we've emigrated. We are now much closer to each other ... In Hong Kong, my husband needed to entertain his clients, so he was out in the evenings a lot. He also used to travel back and forth to China quite often. So, even though we were living together, we led separate lives. Here, we only have a small business. He doesn't need to entertain any clients. Also he doesn't know that many business contacts, so he's home every evening. And because we are still struggling with the new business, I now help out in the store quite a bit, so we are together a lot. I'm really enjoying this togetherness. It's brought a new dimension to our marriage. We've discovered a renewed intimacy in our relationship. Now that we are together a lot, he really appreciates my help. He consults everything he does with me, something which he [never did] when we were in Hong Kong. He used to consult with his mother, but not with me. They have a very close relationship, you see.

There were others, however, who found that the isolation of being new immigrants and the stress of unemployment heightened their incompatibility and lack of communication, leading to marriage breakdown. One of the women I interviewed complained about her situation:

> My husband has been unemployed for over a year now. He had a very good position as an administrator with lots of benefits when he was in Hong Kong. The first year we were here, he found a job as a clerk. He was getting less than half of what he was making before ... But then the company went bankrupt, and he was unemployed. He's so depressed now that he is making me down too. He also kept blaming me for making him come here. We've had a lot of fights, and I'm not sure what will happen next. We talked about separating. I'm just living day to day at the moment.

For the "astronaut families," the long-distance arrangement has varying consequences for the wives, who were typically left alone in Canada to care for children. One astronaut's wife lamented the burden and the loneliness of maintaining the household on her own. She confided, "I can't wait for the time when my husband can stop travelling back and forth. I'm tired of being here alone with the kids." Her dissatisfaction concurs with that of women in the same situation in another study who expressed considerable worries stemming from their husbands' absence (S.U.C.C.E.S.S. 1991).

In contrast, another astronaut's wife in my study marvelled at her newfound independence, and attributed her heightened communication with her husband to his frequent absences. Interestingly, her positive reaction was similar to the findings of studies on dual-career commuting couples[4] in which some couples' relationships improved because of their time apart (Gerstel 1984; Man 1991). Here is what she told me:

> The first year when [my husband] was still spending a lot of time in Hong Kong, he used to call me long distance all the time. We also wrote love letters to each other regularly. We were missing each other very much. We hadn't been that close together since we were married. And every time he came back to visit, it was like reliving our honeymoon again. It was really the sweetest year we have had for a long time.

One woman reported that she had been having problems with her two teenage children since they immigrated to Canada. What appear at first to be this family's adjustment problems due to immigration in fact have a concrete, material base. As this woman confided to me:

> Mothering is of course a lot easier in Hong Kong than here. There, the kids can be a lot more independent. My kids usually just hop on a cab right after school and go to their respective tennis or music lessons. Afterwards, they just hop on a cab to go home. By the way, cabs are really cheap in Hong Kong. Also, Hong Kong is such a small place, you can go to any place within half an hour. I never had to worry about my children's transportation. The situation here is very different. It is too expensive for my kids to take cabs every day, and the public transportation in my area is not very good. I have to dovetail my work schedule with that of my children.

This woman now works late every night, so she can go straight after work to pick up her teenage son from his extracurricular activities. By the time she gets home, finishes making dinner, and cleans up, she is usually so exhausted that she just goes straight to bed. But her relationship with her children has become strained. Her son resents his loss of independence because he now has to wait for his mother to pick him up; her daughter is annoyed that her mother cannot spend quality time with her. It is clear that what seem to be this woman's private, personal problems with her children in fact originate in external factors. The differences in social organization in Canada and the home country, seen in the size of the city, the transportation system, and the high cost of living, have tremendous impact on the individual woman, affecting her everyday life and the relationships of family members.

Housework and Childcare

In highly industrialized capitalist societies such as Canada and Hong Kong, housework and childcare are privatized. Rather than acknowledging childcare as a public issue and allocating funding for establishing childcare facilities accordingly, these governments have shifted the responsibility onto private households—that is, onto women (Luxton and Reiter 1997). The relegation of household work to the private sphere and the lack of social support for that work has made life seem insurmountable for many women, and has driven them to depression (Coontz 1992). Despite the fact that economic demands have pushed many married women into the labour market, housework and childcare have remained primarily women's responsibilities. Cultural ideology and structural support reinforces the social construction of womanhood that defines a woman by her child-rearing and domestic abilities. The image of the "loving mother" and "ideal wife" is so powerful that women, regardless of race and class, are unable to deconstruct that image.

Many upper-class women, and increasingly some middle-class women, try to "resolve" the demands and pressures of juggling paid work, housework, and childcare by employing domestic labour. Such a solution, however, inevitably creates a division among women along class lines and threatens to undermine the collectivism within the feminist movement. In Canada and Hong Kong, this solution is endorsed by the governments, possibly as a way of shifting the burden of household work from being a public issue to being a private responsibility, and as a strategy to avoid implementing structural changes.

Although the gendered division of household labour is in some ways similar in patriarchal societies such as Hong Kong and Canada, the differences in family structures and the social organization in these societies transform the situation of the Chinese immigrant women, making their day-to-day living vastly different for them in Canada than when they were in Hong Kong.

While the nuclear family structure is prevalent in Hong Kong, many Chinese families (whether in Hong Kong, in Canada, or elsewhere) retain vestiges of the extended-family form (this is also true of many Canadian families from other backgrounds). In such cases, three generations typically reside in the same residence. In cases when families adopt the nuclear family structure, the small geographical area of the colony enables relatives to live in close proximity, a situation amenable to developing a close-knit support network. But categorizing families in such a fashion (as nuclear or extended families, and so on) is problematic (Eichler 1997; Fox and Luxton 2001). Chinese households (as with other households in Canada) appear in diverse forms and structures. It is therefore more meaningful to talk about personal support networks (Fox and Luxton 2001) and familial interactions (Eichler 1997). I am therefore using the terms *nuclear* and *extended families* here for descriptive purposes rather than as analytical categories.

One woman described her situation in Hong Kong:

> When we were in Hong Kong, my mother-in-law used to live with us. She did the cooking and the cleaning. She also picked up my oldest son after school so I didn't have to rush home right after work. My mother, on the other hand, lived close to my youngest son's school, so she used to pick him up after school and looked after him until I got to her place to pick him up after work. That's why my oldest son is very close to his *maj-maj* [paternal grandmother], and my youngest one is attached to his *paw-paw* [maternal grandmother]! You see, I had a lot of support in Hong Kong. Here, I have to do everything myself.

Beyond assistance in housework and childcare from members of the extended family, the class privilege of these middle-class Chinese women permitted some of them the luxury of hired help when they were in Hong Kong. This support system enabled the women to pursue their career interests and allowed them the free time for recreational or creative activities. Many of these women have taken this support system for granted.

Transplanted to Toronto, these women experience, first, a loss of support from the extended family (many older parents are reluctant or unable to emigrate); and second, a decrease of their earning power due to the women's unemployment or underemployment, thus making it no longer economically feasible for them to have hired help. The extra burden of domestic labour is almost always assumed by the woman as her sole responsibility. The women who tried to cope with a dual workload of housework and paid work often felt exhausted at the end of the day. Their predicaments are echoed by Chinese immigrant women in another study who described problems in child care, household maintenance, and transportation (S.U.C.C.E.S.S. 1991).

A few women managed to recreate in Canada the support system they had in Hong Kong. Unlike other women, these women did not experience a drastic change in household duties and were therefore able to maintain the balance of work and family responsibilities. Lily,[5] whose parents had immigrated to Canada a few years prior, described how she maintained this mutually supportive network with her parents:

> When I came here in 1987, I told my parents that I've brought money with me to buy a house. But I promised them that we'll live close by ... So we bought a house very close to theirs, so close that my younger daughter could go there after school. And we now eat dinner at my parents' place every night ... It's not only because of the fact that I don't know how to cook, but my mother felt that since my husband and I had to work, it would be better that we eat at their place. Also, because my younger daughter's school is very close to my parents' house, it's very convenient for my daughter as well ... So this is how my parents help us out. My mother cooks for us Monday to Friday, and on the weekends I take them out for dinners. This way, my mother gets to have the weekends off. So, we take care of each other ... Also, it gives my mother something to look forward to every night when we go over there.

While in Hong Kong, many of these middle-class women did not actually engage in the physical labour of doing housework (cooking and cleaning), but rather the management of it. But since they clearly identified the management and control of the household as domestic labour, and as such an important task, they were therefore proud to define themselves as capable housewives, concurrent with being successful career women. For these women, power lies very much in the management and control of every aspect of family life. Nor is this image contradictory to their commitment to participation in the labour market in Hong Kong. These women were able to juggle the dual or triple workload of housework, paid work, and childcare owing to the household support system they had when they were in Hong Kong. There, many Chinese husbands took for granted that their wives would share the breadwinner role as well as being the sole manager of the household. Domestic harmony was maintained even though the wives went out to work, because the husbands were cared for and fed. Dinner still appeared on the table on time (although not prepared by the wife); shirts and pants were washed and ironed, ready to be worn the next morning (compliments of the mother or the hired help); and household maintenance chores were taken care of (services rendered by the hired workmen). All this, however, did require skillful management by the wives. The husbands were relieved of virtually all these tasks when they were in Hong Kong.

When asked whether her husband shared the housework in Canada, one of my interviewees laughed:

> No way! He had never lifted a finger all his life. Before we got married he used to live at home, and his mother did everything for him. I would never dream of asking him to help me with housework. Besides, Chinese women don't do that. To ask your husband to help you with housework is to admit that you are incapable of being a good wife! It is a loss of face on the woman's part!

Since many of the husbands had never done housework before, they therefore did not offer to help their wives after they immigrated to Canada, nor did these women seek their help. As one woman explained:

> I feel that if I can manage it myself, I wouldn't ask. Furthermore, if my husband really wants to do it, he can offer to help. But he hasn't! As for my children, I would rather they spend their time studying or having fun. I don't really want them to waste their time on housework.

Some women, however, did get help from other family members, particularly in cleaning and grocery shopping:

> There's a lot of work. Fortunately, my husband and sons do help me with vacuuming. They also do the yard work and cut the grass. Grocery shopping is very convenient here. There are also many Chinese supermarkets close to where we live. My husband loves to go grocery shopping. Usually, we just pick up some groceries on our way home from work. We shop several times a week because it's so convenient.

For some women, galvanizing the help of family members with lots of planning and organization was the key to "getting things done" in Canada:

First of all, domestically, I have a lot of help. But I also have to be organized. My daughters are now older, so it's not like they would dirty up the walls, etc. Also, being daughters, they are much tidier than boys. I plan my schedule carefully. We only do laundry once a week. Every Friday night, we do the laundry. We also take turns ironing, me and my daughters usually. Sometimes my husband would offer to help ... Actually, there aren't too many things we buy that need ironing. I do everything the easy way; for example, in terms of flowers, I buy pots of cactus. I change them only once every one or two months ... Also, there's not much dust here, so we only dust once a month. Once in a blue moon, we'll do a spring cleaning. Vacuum cleaning is my husband's responsibility. So is changing light bulbs, fixing the water faucet, gardening. He really enjoys gardening. We call him "the gardener."

While the cheaper housing cost allowed the families to have bigger residences in Canada, it had the concomitant effect of increasing the amount of housework for the women. Here is a comment from an interviewee:

There seems to be more housework here. One reason could be that our house here is more than twice as big as our apartment in Hong Kong, so there's a lot more space to clean. As well, in Hong Kong, people usually have parquet floors or tiled floors. Here, we have carpeting, which needs vacuuming more often.

In regard to doing other, more "male-oriented" types of housework, Mabel revealed her and her husband's ignorance in this kind of work:

Oh, he had never even used a hammer ... and I'm definitely not handy myself, either. I don't know how to fix a lock, or even to put up a nail. Most Canadians know how to do these things, but I never had to do it, so I didn't know how to do it at all. In the winter, I didn't know that I had to put caulking on my window. All these are little things, but they all add up ... In Hong Kong, services are so easily available people never think of doing anything themselves. You call up a handyman even just to put up a picture, or screw in a light bulb. It sounds ridiculous, but that's the reality there.

Both Mabel and her husband are highly educated professionals. They are capable and motivated people. However, they felt inadequate when they first came to Canada because they were not able to do small household maintenance chores like "other Canadians." This is due to the fact that the labour market is organized in Hong Kong quite differently from Canada. Until 1980, because of a constant flow of legal and illegal immigrants from China (Wong 1992), there had been a stable supply of cheap labour in Hong Kong and services were relatively inexpensive. This alleviated the burden of maintenance chores in middle-class households where both spouses participated full time in the paid labour force. In Canada, because of the high cost of services, people learn to do many household maintenance chores out of necessity.

Chinese immigrant wives carry a triple burden of paid work, housework, and childcare in cases when the children are young, or when they participate in extracurricular activities, which requires the wife to chauffeur them back and forth. The way in which a society organizes its childcare facilities can have a tremendous impact on women who work full time for pay. Kathy, a social worker, voiced her criticism of the inadequacy of daycare in Canada:

I have a five-year-old and a two-year-old. I'm finding that daycare is a serious problem. Daycare is not flexible enough to accommodate working parents. Their hours of operation don't fill our gaps. We have to choose between quality or service. Sure, there are a few day-care centres now which run from 7:00 a.m. to 6:00 p.m. They are all privately run. They offer the service, but not necessarily the quality. So sometimes you don't want to put your child at risk. I have to choose very carefully. I have now found a very good quality daycare, and I can trust them very much ... They have a lot of educational activities, lots of good materials which enable my children to learn a lot. On the other hand, they don't provide the service—that is, their hours of operation are limited. So I have to juggle with my time to put my kids there. I am always dashing about like a mad woman ... I have no social life at all.

Most of the women I interviewed chose to live in close proximity to friends and relatives, in neighbourhoods with easy access to Chinese grocery stores. However, the actual location of the houses is almost always determined by their children's schools and husband's workplace. Their own work location was not a determining factor in their initial decision. This can be attributed to the fact that children are considered the wives' responsibility. In order not to cause the women any more time loss in chauffeuring the children to and from school, it makes perfectly good sense to have the homes located close to schools.

Social Life

The immigrant women I interviewed have frequent interactions with other Hong Kong immigrants. Socializing with people who have common backgrounds and experiences creates for them a sense of continuity and is a stabilizing force in their new country (Warren 1986). Agnes, a secretary turned housewife, commented:

I feel we have more in common with each other. We often get together and reminisce about our lives in Hong Kong. We also laugh about our ignorance of Canadian culture and the little faux pas that we get ourselves into. Other times, we exchange information about schools, dentists, and other practical knowledge. Or we marvel at the high price we now pay for little things such as cooking wares and stockings. I have a feeling of solidarity when I talk to these people. They understand where I'm coming from.

Some women, however, also have friends from different ethnic groups. Usually these friends are neighbours or parents of their children's friends, and occasionally friends they have met at work. This is in contrast to their lives in Hong Kong, where most working women customarily socialize with their colleagues. As well, social life in Hong Kong is more spontaneous. As one woman succinctly puts it, "We usually just get together after work for movies and dinners; it's never planned."

While it is common and economically feasible for most of those people to organize frequent dinner parties at restaurants in Hong Kong, the high cost of dinner parties at restaurants in Canada forces many to have small dinner parties at home, and only occasionally. This kind of change is seen by some as having positive effects. One woman expressed it this way:

Life is comparatively quieter here. On the other hand, I now feel closer to my few friends. Our conversation is more personal and more meaningful, whereas before, I was always with a big crowd, and the conversation was usually superficial.

Typically, women who have to juggle paid work, housework, and childcare are too exhausted at the end of the day to have much social life (Duffy, Mandell, and Pupo 1989; Bernardo, Shehan, and Leslie 1987). A mother of two who has a demanding career explained:

I don't have any time for social life at all. Even if someone invites me for dinner on the weekend, I find it tiring to go. I don't know how everybody else does it here. There's no time for social life here at all. I have a lot of friends here, but I never have time to see them.

In Hong Kong, her situation was quite different:

I was a member of a pottery club, calligraphy club, and an alumni choir. Here, I don't have any extracurricular activities. I simply don't have the time or energy. It seems foolhardy to drive an hour to go to a class when I don't even have enough time to manage my household chores. On the other hand, I really need this kind of outlet. But I don't have the kind of time and energy.

It is clear that the differences in social organization between Hong Kong and Canadian societies in terms of the household support system and the size and spread of the city transform this woman's everyday experience.

CONCLUSION

Many previous migration studies have assumed that migration involves moving from a less developed to a more developed country, and from a rural to an urban area. It is further assumed that the entry of female migrants into the host labour market will lead to a rejection of their traditional roles and subjugated positions. These studies argue that the economic independence migrant women acquire through their engagement in waged work will ensure them a higher status and a more equitable position in the family. Hence, migration has the positive effect of engendering equality of the sexes, as well as generating beneficial changes in domestic relations (Schwartz-Seller 1981; Morokvasic 1981).

These migration theories become more nuanced when applied to middle-class Chinese immigrant women. Many of these highly educated, urbanized women do not necessarily enjoy a "liberating" or "less oppressive" experience when they settle in Canada. Owing to the differences in social organization of Canadian society, some of these middle-class women have lost the support system they had in Hong Kong. The lack of household help provided by members of an extended family (mother, mother-in-law) or hired help has exacerbated the workload of these middle-class working women, making their struggle to negotiate the conflicting demands of family and career even more difficult. Consequently, some of them experience an escalation of traditional gender-role differences, unequal distribution of household labour, and gender and sexual oppression in the home. This, compounded with institutionalized discrimination in the form of the requirement of "Canadian experience" rendering their previous work experience obsolete, and the absence of an adequate accreditation system, has caused some of them to become unemployed or underemployed. This in turn has forced them to become economically dependent on their husbands, who are themselves subjected to the same discrimination.

While some of the women interviewed experienced improved relations with their husbands after immigration, there were others who suffered communication problems and marriage breakdowns. For some women, their power and status inside and outside the home actually deteriorated after they immigrated to Canada. Moreover, those who had professional careers in their home country have experienced a loss of economic power through unemployment or underemployment, although some of their husbands also experience such losses. They also experience diminished buying power and a general lack of opportunity.

Regardless of whether the woman has paid work outside of the home, her paid work is always subsumed under her care for her husband and children. Her everyday, routine activities are organized around the schedules of her husband and her children. Thus, her labour is incorporated into the family. But while her domestic labour is essential for the perpetuation of capitalism, it is not valued.

Feminist scholars have previously addressed the induction of the wife's labour in terms of structural and economic relations (Kanter 1993; Finch 1983). The dynamics of familial power relations of the women in this study (in terms of decision-making and autonomy) do change in accordance with their education and their earning power, among other factors. For example, Mabel, a professional woman, perceives herself as having relatively more power in the home than Marion, a part-time secretary, and Joan, a housewife. However, for these women, such power is not necessarily transferred to a more equitable distribution of the household responsibilities and a fairer division of labour, as was found by previous studies (Maret and Finlay 1984; Sekaran 1986). This can be attributed to the fact that power, as seen by some of these women, lies very much in the management and control of every aspect of family life. To relinquish control is synonymous with relinquishing power. However, without the support system that they had taken for granted in their home country, they are now burdened with double and triple workloads, resulting in constant exhaustion and leaving them with little time for social life or recreation.

The employment of live-in domestic labour has long been presented to middle- and upper-class women in Hong Kong and Canada as a viable solution to solving the housework and childcare dilemma. This "solution" has been endorsed by both the Hong Kong and Canadian governments, who adopt active roles in the importation of foreign domestic workers into their countries (Bakan and Stasiulis 1997; Cheng and Kwong 1992; Giles and Arat-Koc 1994; Arat-Koc 1990). It is a strategy by these governments to divert attention from the debates on domestic labour as being a public issue—with its solutions rooted in the equality between men and women in both the home and the workforce, in the transformation of the organization of work, and in the provision of socialized services for families—to that of a private responsibility to be resolved within individual private households. This solution polarizes and divides women along class and racial dimensions. As Tong (1994) has warned, while widely available educational opportunities have elevated the position of many Hong Kong women, economic prosperity has desensitized middle-class or professional women to the plight of the less privileged, notably the foreign domestic workers (385–386). While it has been argued that the middle-class identity and frame of reference were not conducive to collective struggles for the improvement of working conditions (Pessar 1984), there may be positive effects to the middle-class Chinese immigrant women's migration process. The intensification of gender and racial subordination as a result of migration may produce a liberating potential over time (Parmar 1986). Their relegated position in the home and at work, and the actual performance of housekeeping duties, may empower them to develop a collective consciousness so that they may join, transcending race and class boundaries, with working-class women in their struggle against gender and racial inequality.

This study is an exploratory pilot project. It does not purport to be conclusive; rather, it intends to demonstrate that there are multiple realities for Chinese immigrants. Further research is recommended for the in-depth exploration of Chinese immigrants of different age, gender, class, and sexual locations. A comparative study of older, established immigrant women with recent women immigrants will provide us with insights into the perpetuation of job discrimination and into family relationships. Future research will, it is hoped, further enhance our knowledge of the long-term effects of immigration on Chinese women in Canada.

Author's Note

I would like to thank the anonymous reviewers and the editors for their constructive comments. I deeply appreciate Monica Boyd's generous assistance in creating the census data tables.

NOTES

1. "Independent Class" immigrants under the Immigration Act are selected on the basis of criteria that are tied to Canada's economic needs. They include skilled workers, also known as "other independents," and "business immigrants," who include entrepreneurs, investors, and the self-employed (see Margaret Young, Canada's Immigration Program, Library of Parliament, Research Branch, July 1992).

2. This is a subcategory under the "Independent Class" immigrant category. The immigrants who come in under this category are primarily workers who can contribute to the Canadian economy through their possession of skills and training in occupations for which there is a demand: computer scientists, accountants, and similar occupations.

3. Some immigrants took advantage of an immigration clause (Canada 1985) that allowed a permanent resident to be outside of Canada for 183 days in any one 12-month period without losing their permanent residency status, by continuing to conduct business

between Hong Kong and Toronto. In fact, one husband I interviewed started his first year of immigration by conducting his business this way, and another husband was still commuting between Hong Kong and Toronto at the time of the interview. For an in-depth study of the astronaut phenomenon, see Guida Man (1995).

4. Dual-career commuting couples are dual-career couples who live apart in different geographical locations and commute to see each other periodically. The paramount element in the marriges of commuter couples and astronaut couples is the long periods of time the partners in these relationships spend away from each other.

5. The names mentioned here are pseudonyms, since the interviewees were assured anonymity. Most Chinese (especially the baby-boomers and post–baby-boomers generation) who were brought up in the British educational system in colonized Hong Kong find themselves adopting English names in addition to their Chinese names. Many Chinese in Hong Kong use their English names at school, work, and for everyday use, but keep their Chinese names for official documents. In Canada, most Chinese maintain the same practice.

KEY TERMS

Institutional processes: Processes and practices that are embedded in government, law, education, and professional systems, and that can engender and perpetuate social injustice.

Microstructural versus **macrostructural processes:** Processes that focus on the personal and psychological (*micro-*) as opposed to processes that focus on the larger social structure (*macro-*).

Organizational processes: The actual material processes in the organization of a society that have an impact on how an individual does his or her work, conducts his or her life, and relates to other people.

Race, gender, and class: Real and concrete relations that have to do with how people define themselves and how they participate in social life. They converge, diverge, and change over time as people's relations to productive and reproductive activities change within a given society.

DISCUSSION QUESTIONS

1. What impact have Canadian immigration policies had on the formation of Chinese families in Canada?
2. Man asserts that Canadian immigration policies have historically been discriminatory in terms of race, gender, and class, and continue to be partial to people from middle- and upper-class backgrounds. Find evidence in her essay to support her assertion.
3. Why does the media-constructed image of Chinese immigrants exclude Chinese women? Why has there been so little research on Chinese women?

4. How are the daily experiences of Chinese immigrant women in Canada different from their lives in Hong Kong? Discuss.

5. What are institutional and organizational processes? Cite examples from the experiences of the Chinese immigrant women to illustrate your answer.

REFERENCES

Abella, Irving, and Harold Troper. 1982. *None Is Too Many: Canada and The Jews of Europe*. Toronto: Lester & Orpen Dennys Ltd.

Adilman, Tamara. 1984. Chinese Women and Work in British Columbia. B.A. thesis, University of Victoria.

Anderson, Kay J. 1991. *Vancouver's Chinatown: Racial Discourse in Canada, 1875–1980*. Montreal & Kingston: McGill–Queen's University Press.

Arat-Koc, Sedef. 1990. "Importing Housewives: Non-Citizen Domestic Workers and the Crisis of the Domestic Sphere in Canada." In Meg Luxton, Harriet Rosenberg, and Sedef Arat-Koc, eds., *Through the Kitchen Window: The Politics of Home and Family*. Toronto: Garamond Press.

Bakan, Abigail B. and Daiva Stasiulis, eds. 1997. *Not One of the Family: Foreign Domestic Workers in Canada*. Toronto: University of Toronto Press.

Bakka, Isabella, ed. 1996. *Rethinking, Restructuring: Gender and Change in Canada*. Toronto: University of Toronto Press.

Basran, Gurcharn S., and Li Zong. 1998. "Devaluation of Foreign Credentials as Perceived by Visible Minority Professional Immigrants." *Canadian Ethnic Studies* 30(3): 6–23.

Baureiss, Gunter. 1987. "Chinese Immigration, Chinese Stereotypes, and Chinese Labour." *Canadian Ethnic Studies* 14(3): 15–34.

Bernardo, Donna H., Constance L. Shehan, and Gerald R. Leslie. 1987. "A Resident of Tradition: Jobs, Careers and Spouses' Time in Housework." *Journal of Marriage and the Family* 49: 381–90.

Boyd, Monica. 1990. "Immigrant Women: Language, Socioeconomic Inequalities and Policy Issues." In S. Halli, F. Trovata, and L. Driedger, eds., *Ethnic Demography: Canadian Immigrant Racial and Cultural Variations*. Ottawa: Carleton University Press.

Brodie, Janine. 1995. *Politics on the Margins: Restructuring and the Canadian Women's Movement*. Halifax: Fernwood Publishing.

Canada and Hong Kong Update. 1992. *7* (Summer).

Cannon, Margaret. 1989. *China Tide*. Toronto: HarperCollins.

Chan, Anthony. 1983. *Gold Mountain: The Chinese in the New World*. Vancouver: Newstar Press.

Cheng, Joseph Y.S., and Paul C.K. Kwong, eds. 1992. *The Other Hong Kong Report 1992*. Hong Kong: Chinese University Press.

Chinese Canadian National Council. 1992. The Women's Book Committee. Jin Guo: *Voices of Chinese Canadian Women*. Toronto: The Women's Press.

Citizenship and Immigration Canada (CIC). 1994–99. Citizenship and Immigration Statistics 1992–1996. Ottawa: Public Works and Government Services Canada.

Coontz, Stephanie. 1992. *The Way We Never Were: American Families and the Nostalgia Trap*. New York: Basic Books.

Creese, Gillian, and Laurie Peterson. 1996. "Making the News, Racializing Chinese Canadians." *Studies in Political Economy* 51 (Fall): 117–145.

Das Gupta, Tania. 1996. *Racism and Paid Work*. Toronto: Garamond Press.

Duffy, Ann, Nancy Mandell, and Norene Pupo. 1989. *Few Choices: Women, Work and Family*. Toronto: Garamond Press.

Eichler, Margrit. 1985. *On the Treatment of the Sexes in Research*. Ottawa: Social Sciences and Humanities Research Council of Canada.

———. 1997. *Family Shifts: Families, Policies, and Gender Equality*. Toronto: Oxford University Press.

Employment and Immigration Canada (EIC). 1988–92. Immigration Statistics 1986–91. Ottawa: Minister of Supply and Services Canada..

Employment and Immigration Commissions (EIC). 1985. *Immigration Act*.

Estable, Alma. 1986. *Immigrant Women in Canada: Current Issues*. Ottawa: Canadian Advisory Council on the Status of Women, March.

Evans, Patricia M. and Gerda R. Werkele. 1997. *Women and the Canadian Welfare State*. Toronto: University of Toronto Press.

Finch, Janet. 1983. *Married to the Job: Wives' Incorporation in Men's Work*. London: Allen & Unwin.

Fox, Bonnie J., and Meg Luxton. 2001. "Conceptualizing 'Family.'" In Bonnie J. Fox, ed., *Family Patterns, Gender Relations*, 2nd ed. Toronto: Oxford University Press.

Gerstel, Naomi. 1984. "Commuter Marriage." Unpublished thesis, Columbia University.

Giles, Wenona and Sedef Arat-Koc, eds. 1994. *Maids in the Market: Women's Paid Domestic Labour*. Halifax: Fernwood.

Hawkins, Freda. 1988. *Canada and Immigration: Public Policy and Public Concern*, 2nd ed. Kingston and Montreal: McGill–Queen's University Press.

Hill-Collins, Patricia. 1990. *Black Feminist Thought*. Toronto: HarperCollins.

hooks, bell. 1984. *Feminist Theory: From Margin to Centre*. Boston: South End Press.

Kanter, Rosabeth Moss. 1993. *Men and Women of the Corporation*, 2nd ed. New York: Basic Books.

Kynaston, Chris. 1996. "The Everyday Exploitation of Women: Housework and the Patriarchal Mode of Production." *Women's Studies International Forum* 19, (3): 221–37.

Lee, Jo-Ann. 1999. "Immigrant Women Workers in the Immigrant Settlement Sector." *Canadian Woman Studies/les cahier de la femme* 19, (3): 97–103.

Li, Peter S. 1993. "Chinese Investment and Business in Canada: Ethnic Entrepreneurship Reconsidered." *Pacific Affairs* 66(2): 219–243.

———. 1998. *The Chinese in Canada*, 2nd ed. Toronto: Oxford University Press.

Luxton, Meg. 1980. *More Than a Labour of Love: Three Generations of Women's Work in the Home*. Toronto: Women's Educational Press.

Luxton, Meg, and Ester Reiter. 1997. "Double, Double, Toil and Trouble …Women's Experience of Work and Family in Canada 1980–1995." In Patricia M. Evans and Gerda R. Werkele, ed., *Women and the Canadian Welfare State*. Toronto: University of Toronto Press.

Man, Guida. 1991. "Commuter Families in Canada: A Research Report." Report presented to the Demographic Review Secretariat, Health and Welfare Canada, September. Unpublished.

———. 1995. "The Astronaut Phenomenon: Examining Consequences of the Diaspora of the Hong Kong Chinese." *Managing Change in Southeast Asia: Local Identities, Global Connections*. Calgary: University of Calgary: 269–281.

———. 1997. "Women's Work Is Never Done: Social Organization of Work and the Experience of Women in Middle-Class Hong Kong Chinese Immigrant Families in Canada." In *Advances in Gender Research*, Vol. 2: 183–226. Greenwich: JAI Press Inc.

———. 2002. "Globalization and the Erosion of the Welfare State: Effects on Immigrant Women from China and Hong Kong." *Canadian Woman Studies/les cahier de la femme* 21/22 (1), July.

Maret, Elizabeth, and Babbura Findley, eds. 1984. "The Distribution of Household Labour among Women in Dual-Earner Families." *Journal of Marriage and the Family* 46 (May): 357–64.

Mojab, Shahrzad. 1999. "De-skilling Immigrant Women." In *Canadian Woman Studies/les cahier de la femme* 19, (3): 110–114.

Morokvasic, M. 1981. "The Invisible Ones: A Double Role of Women in the Current European Migrations." In L. Eitinger and D. Schwarz, eds., *Strangers in the World*. Bern, Stuggart, Vienna: Hans Huber.

Ng, Roxana. 1981. "Constituting Ethnic Phenomenon: An Account from the Perspective of Immigrant Women." *Canadian Ethnic Studies 13*.

———. 1993. "Racism, Sexism, and Nation Building in Canada." In Cameron McCarthy and Warren Crichlow, eds. *Race, Identity and Representation in Education*. New York: Routledge.

Nipp, Dora. 1983. "Canada Bound: An Exploratory Study of Pioneer Chinese Women in Western Canada." Unpublished M.A. thesis, University of Toronto, Department of East Asian Studies.

Parmar, Pratibha. 1986. "Gender, Race, and Class: Asian Women in Resistance." In Centre for Contemporary Cultural Studies, ed., *The Empire Strikes Back: Race and Racism in 70s Britain*: 236–75. London: Hutchinson.

Pessar, Patricia R. 1984. "The Linkage between the Household and Workplace of Dominican Women in the U.S." In *International Migration Review* 18(4), Winter: 1188–1211.

Preston, Valerie, and Guida Man. 1999. "Employment Experiences of Chinese Immigrant Women: An Exploration of Diversity." In *Canadian Woman Studies/les cahier de la femme* 19 (3): 115–122.

Roy, Patricia E. 1989. *A White Man's Province: British Columbia Politicians and Chinese and Japanese Immigrants, 1858–1914*. Vancouver: UBC Press.

Salaff, Janet and Wong Siu-lun. 1995. "Exiting Hong Kong: Social Class Experiences and the Adjustment to 1997." In *Emigration from Hong Kong*, edited by Ronald Skeldon. Hong Kong: The Chinese University Press.

Schwartz-Seller, M. 1981. *Immigrant Women*. Philadelphia: Temple University Press.

Sedgewick, Charles P. 1973. "The Context of Economic Change: Continuity in an Urban Overseas Chinese Community." Unpublished thesis, University of Victoria.

Sekaran, Uma. 1986. *Dual-Career Families*. San Francisco: Jossey-Bass.

Shields, John, and B. Mitchell Evans. 1998. *Shrinking the State: Globalization and Public Administration "Reform."* Halifax: Fernwood Publishing.

Smith, Dorothy. 1990. *The Conceptual Practice of Power: A Feminist Sociology of Knowledge*. Toronto: University of Toronto Press.

Statistics Canda. 1996. Census of Population, Public Use Micro-File of Individuals.

S.U.C.C.E.S.S. Women's Committee Research Group. 1991. *Chinese Immigrant Women's Needs Survey in Richmond*. Vancouver: S.U.C.C.E.S.S.

Tarasuk, Valerie, Jennifer Geduld, and Shelly Hilditch. 1998. "Struggling to Survive: Women in Families Using Food Banks." In Luciana Ricciutelli et al. *Confronting the Cuts: A Sourcebook for Women in Ontario*. Toronto: Inanna Publications.

Taylor, K.W. 1991. "Racism in Canadian Immigration Policy." *Canadian Ethnic Studies* 23 (1): 1–20.

Tong, Irene. 1994. "Women." In Donald H. McMillen and Man Si-Wai, eds. *The Other Hong Kong Report 1994*. Hong Kong: The Chinese University Press.

Warren, Catharine E. 1986. *Vignettes of Life*. Calgary: Detselig.

Wickberg, Edgar, ed. 1982. *From China to Canada: A History of the Chinese Communities in Canada*. Toronto: McClelland & Stewart.

Wong, Lloyd, and Michelle Ng. 1998. "Chinese Immigrant Entrepreneurs in Vancouver: A Case Study of Ethnic Business Development." In *Canadian Ethnic Studies*, 30 (1): 64–85.

Wong, Siu Lun. 1992. "Emigration and Stability in Hong Kong." *Asian Survey* 32(10).

Yee, May. 1987. "Out of the Silence: Voices of Chinese Canadian Women." *Resources for Feminist Research* 16 (1).

11

Pronatalism, Feminism, and Family Policy in Quebec

Catherine D. Krull

Department of Sociology
Queen's University

Objectives

- To explain why the relationship between family size and the vitality of Québécois culture is and continues to be a highly contentious political issue in Quebec.

- To understand the relationship between the rise of Quebec feminism and its historical link with nationalism/pronatalism.

- To outline demographic trends pertaining to marriage and family and to understand how Quebec's trends differ from those for the rest of Canada.

- To understand the impact of the Quiet Revolution on family structures and the status of women.

- To outline Quebec's pronatal policies from 1988 to 1997 and discuss reactions to these policies.

- To discuss Quebec's current family policies, which are now the most innovative in Canada.

INTRODUCTION

Over the past four decades, Quebec society has witnessed historic changes to family life and to the status of women. These changes include dramatic increases in **cohabitation**, voluntary childlessness, divorce, and births to unmarried women, as well as a substantial decline in religiosity (Langlois et al. 1992). Moreover, as shown in Figure 11.1, this society has gone from having unusually high and sustained reproductive levels—lasting over three centuries—to one in which the fertility of its people reached historic lows (Krull 2000). As Romaniuc pointed out as far back as 1984, both the speed and the magnitude of Quebec's fertility decline has been astounding (16). This decline has coincided with the socioeconomic transformation of Quebec into a modern, predominantly French-speaking society, a process that occurred gradually over time but intensified during and after the **Quiet Revolution**. Nationalism, **pronatalism**, and feminism are powerful elements in understanding these historical developments and their relevance to contemporary families in Quebec.

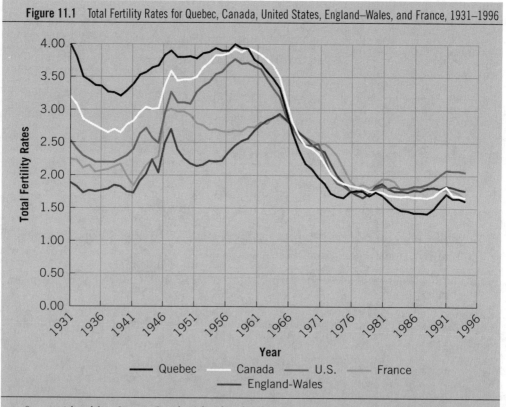

Figure 11.1 Total Fertility Rates for Quebec, Canada, United States, England–Wales, and France, 1931–1996

Sources: Adapted from Statistics Canada "Selected Birth and Fertility Statistics," Canada, 1921–1990 (Cat. No. 82-553) March 15, 1993. "Births and Deaths," (Cat. No. 84-210) 1995 and 1997; and "Report on the Demographic Situation in Canada," (Cat. No. 91–209), 2001.

EARLY FRENCH-CANADIAN SOCIETY (1608–1759)

From the time of the first permanent French settlement in what is now Quebec, population size has been viewed as central to the survival of first French and then French-Canadian Québécois culture (Caldwell and Fournier 1987). Although long settled by Aboriginal peoples, the lower valley of the St. Lawrence River was "discovered" by a French expedition led by Jacques Cartier in 1535. Cartier's purpose was to find a western route to China and the East to exploit its wealth. He failed. But he did claim the lower St. Lawrence in the name of the French king. For a variety of reasons, however, this region emerged as an overseas colony of France only in 1608, when Samuel de Champlain with 30 others established the colony of New France at what is now Quebec City. De Champlain's effort was then followed by a number of small waves of settlers from France. By 1663, the population of New France increased to just over 3,000 people. A century later, by the beginning of the English regime in 1760, there were around 70,000 French-speaking people in North America, of whom approximately 60,000 lived in the St. Lawrence Valley (that is, Quebec) (Beaujot and McQuillan 1982; Henripin and Péron 1972). This phenomenal population growth has been attributed to a very high rate of child bearing. Indeed, very few societies "have ever exhibited such prolific childbearing for so long a period of time" (Beaujot and McQuillan 1982, 4).

This population descended from immigrants from France, numbering about 10,000 over a period of 150 years. Hence, the evolution of francophone Quebec society is very different from that of most classical European nations, whose origins in the Old World go back to ancient times. Quebec began with only a handful of colonists. These fur traders and settlers gradually built a new society in the face of many adversities, including extreme cold, conflict with the indigenous peoples, and war with the English, who ultimately gained control of New France in 1760 (Henripin and Peron 1972; Wade 1968; Bergeron 1975). The uncharted territory, the severe climate, and the uncertainty of the frontier environment dictated from the very beginnings of this society that its members married early and produced large families.

Immigrating to New France liberated French women from the confining traditional roles expected of them in their homeland and, at the same time, gave them the opportunity to play a vital role in establishing the colony. Because survival was dependent on the labour of each colonist, women founded religious institutions and became merchants, soldiers, administrators, and missionaries. Hundreds of women, "as capable of work as any man," cleared land and helped to populate the colony (Clio Collective 1987, 49). Although women enjoyed a certain degree of autonomy while the colony was being established, the culmination of four major events relegated women once more to traditional female roles. The first entailed the collapse of the fur trade and the simultaneous rise in agriculture. A traditional family structure, often impossible to maintain when the fur trade flourished, became essential to life on agricultural **seigneuries**. Success in farming depended on having large families. In fact, the number of land concessions for a family often depended on how many sons a couple had. Over a short period of time, marriage and family life became viewed as a means of stability for the colony.

The second event concerned governmental efforts to strengthen the colony against the close-at-hand British colonies. Increasing the number of colonists became essential. Unwilling to do so by adopting Britain's strategy of promoting massive immigration to its North American colony, the French Crown relied instead on promoting high fertility as a means of increasing the population. To stimulate the number of births, France sent almost 800 young women to the colony between 1663 and 1673 to become the wives of unattached settlers. These women, known as *filles du roi* (the King's Daughters) because the monarch provided them their transport and **dowry**, had an enormous impact on the **marriage rates** of New France. As the number of marriages increased and family life became the norm, unmarried women in nontraditional roles were increasingly seen as an anomaly. Within a short period of time, women's options for economic security were limited either to getting married or entering the convent. Ironically, "survival of the colony" initially depended on women's work in the public domain, but later it depended on their work in the private domain—namely, that of making babies. Thus, well before the Battle of the Plains of Abraham, the link in Quebec was established among survival of the nation, pronatalism, and women's roles.

The third event that affected women involved the growing authority of the Roman Catholic Church in New France. As new farming communities emerged, the number of parishes increased. Although the Church wielded enormous power and influence over individuals, women were particularly affected. Through its control of education, the Church was able to entrench women further in the private domain. Curriculum was gender-specific: girls were taught to be faithful servants to the Church, good wives, and mothers; boys were instructed in the ways of the world. Women who did not comply were ostracized. As the Clio Collective (1987, 93) points out, the image of the evil witch became one of the strongest stereotypes applied to non-conforming women. The Church, then, played a significant role in reinforcing the Crown's pronatal agenda. Finally, the end of the Iroquois wars in 1701 rendered women unnecessary in terms of defending the increasingly agrarian "habitant" colony. This was, so to speak, the last nail to be put in the coffin of women's independence. Women, who had played a vital role in establishing the colony and who had worked alongside men, were now under the authority of their husbands or fathers (the "*seigneurs*") and the Catholic Church. Women were prized for their obedience and their ability to fulfill their "natural" role—the bearing of children. Accordingly, fertility was high, with **crude birth rates** ranging from 50 to 65 births per 1,000 population.[1]

Henripin (1994) estimates that women in the colony, who married at 15 years of age and who lived until the end of their reproductive years, had between 12 and 13 children (27). However, this figure may be somewhat inflated since not all women married at 15. Moreover, the maternal mortality rate was higher in New France than in most European countries, which means that many women died before the end of their reproductive years. Taking these factors into account, Henripin and Péron (1972) estimate that for the period

1711 to 1865 married women had an average of 7.1 children, a rate much higher than that found in contemporary European countries.

Several factors account for the high birth rate under the French Regime. First, the average age of the population was 20.6 years. Thus, the majority of women were in the early part of their fertile years. Flowing from this fact, couples in New France tended to marry at a much younger age than they did elsewhere (Beaujot and McQuillan 1982, 7). This tendency to marry early was reinforced by government policies, a part of which were monetary rewards offered to females who married under the age of 16 and males who married under the age of 20. Indeed, it was not uncommon for girls to marry as early as 12 or 13 years of age. The French government, providing an annual monetary reward to couples who had at least ten legitimate children, also reinforced pronatalist attitudes. Finally, marriage was viewed as a natural state, one that everyone would eventually enter and in which they would remain until their death. To strengthen this ideology, in 1659 the government passed a law forbidding celibacy (Peters 1990, 169). Because family solidarity was thought to be far more important than marital happiness, there was a tendency for husbands and wives to stay together.

As elsewhere, a monolithic family did not exist in New France (although the literature is replete with such descriptions). However, we can say that many early families in French Canada shared several characteristics such as **sex-segregated** roles, pronatalist attitudes, a **neolocal** nuclear household, self-selection in mating (but with parental approval), and kin interaction (Nett 1993, 102). Government officials and the Catholic Church played crucial roles in preserving this patriarchal family system until the middle of the 20th century.

PRE-QUIET REVOLUTION QUEBEC

After the British conquest in 1759–60, Quebec received a number of rights as a colony within the British Empire that allowed it to retain its distinct linguistic and cultural complexion. The most important of these were that the use of the French language was not proscribed, that established French law governed civil cases, and that the Roman Catholic Church was allowed to continue its work, a major concession from the leading Protestant Power in Europe. And as constitutional and political changes to the British colony of Canada evolved afterward—for instance, the establishment of local government after 1792 and the acquisition of provincial status with provincial rights in an independent Canada after 1867—Québécois also gained public office. Accordingly, within Quebec after 1760, government officials and the Catholic Church continued to promote the ideology of "strength in numbers," often referred to as *"la revanche des berceaux"* (the revenge of the cradles). Lasting until the early 1960s, this pronatal strategy was a means of overcoming Québécois subordination to English Canada. For the most part, the strategy succeeded. Between 1760 and 1960, world population increased four times, Europe's population increased five times, but French Canada's population increased 80 times, despite losing approximately 800,000 people to emigration (Henripin and Peron 1972).

Until the early 1960s, Québécois **total fertility rates** (TFR) were much higher than Canadian ones—or, importantly, those of Ontario, Quebec's chief anglophone neighbour. In 1921, for example, women in Quebec had an average of 5.3 children, and more than half of the women living in rural areas had at least 7 children (Beaujot and McQuillan 1982, 68). These rates are very high in comparison to Ontario and Canada, where the TFRs were 3.2 and 3.5, respectively. As Hamilton (1995) notes, Canadians outside of Quebec construed Quebec's higher fertility levels as a threat:

> ...if the French continued to reproduce at the current rate, they would eventually overrun the country. The victory on the Plains of Abraham would turn out to be hollow. For having won the battle, the English would lose the war that was being waged, not on the battlefields, but in bedrooms throughout Quebec. (137)

Prior to the 1960s, a number of factors contributed not only to the maintenance of high fertility in the province but also to keeping Quebec an essentially rural/traditional society. First, the socioeconomic modernization of Quebec evolved slowly compared to Ontario (Behiels 1986; Guindon 1988; Laczko 1995; Latouche 1988). While Ontario had by the late 1800s embarked on its "Industrial Revolution," Quebec remained largely rural-agrarian well into the 1930s.[2] For instance, Pestieau (1976) suggests that in contrast to the rest of the industrializing world, "Quebec was almost completely cut off from important nineteenth-century currents, particularly those of industrialization and female emancipation" (in Wilson 1986, 147).

To a large extent, delayed economic modernization can be attributed to the reluctance of Quebec's government to abandon the Church's ideology and vision of Quebec as a rural religious community. The Catholic Church had great influence over the lives of individuals, the education system, and government affairs. The Church reinforced traditional gender roles by encouraging early marriage and large families, while at the same time discouraging individual socioeconomic advancement. Although a few changes in family structure had occurred by the beginning of this century—such as a shift in some authority of the habitant father to the civil government and a slight increase in the number of married women who worked outside the home—distinctive features persisted. The family remained structured around the father, who had complete authority over family members, including his wife. An extended-family structure continued to characterize the rural areas. Although **nuclear families** were the norm in the urban areas, kinship membership remained important. Urban families lived in close proximity to one another and kinship obligations remained crucial. As Garigue (1956) states, the "characteristics of urban French Canadian kinship are no new development, but seem to have been in existence since the period of New France" (135). Thus, in many ways, the extended-family structure network was perpetuated in the city (Clio Collective 1987, 208).

Women's status had also changed little from that in the 18th century. For the most part, proper roles for women remained that of wife/mother or nun, although it was acknowledged that some women were unfortunate enough to have to work outside of the home. As Moreux (1971) contends, the belief system during the 1930s—and one that was reinforced by the Church—"was that the male adult is the 'real finished product' of the traditional French Canadian culture, capable of mature judgment and integrity in private, religious, and civic life, by contrast 'immature youth' and 'weak womanhood' are incapable in these crucial respects" (157–58). Overall, women's subordination was especially notable in three areas: access to an education, access to employment opportunities, and the loss of civic rights upon marriage.

Unlike anglophone girls in Quebec, who were entitled to a high school education, francophone girls were allowed only primary schooling, although they could enrol in private secondary schools if their families could afford it. These schools were run by nuns and specialized in the **domestic sciences** to better prepare their students for married life and motherhood. French-Canadian women were encouraged to marry early and to value family life above all else, while being discouraged from pursuing individual advancement in the form of careers. Moreover, once married, women lost all legal rights to an education (Clio Collective 1987).

Although it was common for single women to be employed during this era, most women gave up their jobs after they married. Of the 25.2 percent of women who were employed in 1921, more than half were under the age of 25 and only 1.8 percent were married. The percentage of married women in the workforce increased to 3.3 percent in 1941 and to 17 percent in 1951. During this period, women earned approximately 58 percent of men's average incomes and were employed primarily in three gender-specific occupational sectors: in factories, in the service industry, and as office clerks. Because women's paid employment was viewed as temporary, gender equity in the workplace was not a priority.

Women's status decreased significantly once they married, which was justified by the Catholic Church and legalized by the Quebec Civil Code. Although single women shared the same legal rights as most men in Quebec, they lost virtually all rights when they married. Wives were legally defined in terms of general incapacity (akin to minors, prisoners, and mentally challenged persons) and were legally required to submit to their husbands (Clio Collective 1987, 254–55). According to the Civil Code, married women were incapable of signing a legal contract, offering a defence, or suing before the courts. A husband was free to seek a separation on grounds of adultery, but a wife could do so only if her husband kept his mistress in their home. Wives could not engage in commerce without their husband's consent and only husbands could legally administer property. Interestingly, wives were responsible for their husbands' debts but husbands were not responsible for debts incurred by their wives. Moreover, a wife could not legally dispose of her own earnings nor discipline her children but she could, by legal definition, supervise her children or make a will (254–55).

The lack of legal rights for married women maintained the "natural" distinction between the sexes. In his defence of the gender differential in the allocation of legal rights, a jurist at the beginning of the 20th century argued that:

> it is based on the common interest of the husband and the wife, and the former would be jeopardized if the fate of their partnership were left to the lack of foresight and thoughtless-

ness of the member of the association who is the least competent to be in charge and whose very nature impels her to be subordinate. (in Clio Collective 1987: 252)

It is important to note that women in Quebec were by no means unaware of or passive about these inequalities. As Dumont (1995) notes, women of the French-Canadian elite "spoke of the *'féminisme chrétien'* in their magazine *Le coin du feu* (1893–6); they joined the Montreal chapter of the National Council of Women in 1893 (Pinard 1983); and finally, in 1907, they formed their own feminist association, *La Fédération nationale Saint-Jean-Baptiste* (Lavigne et al. 1983), and published their own feminist journal *La Bonne parole*" (153–54).

By 1929, Quebec feminists were actively lobbying for changes to the Civil Code, arguing that the restrictions imposed on married women had not changed in almost 300 years. Opposition came from nationalist elites and from the church, who argued that the Civil Code and the traditional family reflected French-Canadian identity and that any change in either could destroy French-Canadian society. Despite these objections, in 1929 Premier Taschereau created the Dorion Commission, composed of four male jurists, to make recommendations on reforming women's civil rights. Their report consisted of three volumes, but as impressive as this may sound the commission recommended very little change. Most of the report consisted of justifications for women's subordinate status:

> …When a woman marries, … her identity, without disappearing, is defined by the father of her children, and this complies with the inescapable law of nature and our Christian morals, our laws take into account this fact that governs the situation of women, who are naturally dependent … And this is why a woman who marries sacrifices, quite simply, her freedom, her name and her identity, and at the same time and as a consequence, sacrifices a part, not as they say, of her legal rights but of the exercise of these rights. (*Premier rapport de la Commission des droits civils de la femme*, 1929–30, 234–35, in Clio Collective 1987)

> …A woman's activity has taken on new forms, she is exploring new areas of education, her attitudes which seem new, only show that although some things have changed in the milieux where she is evolving, women themselves have not really evolved. Created to be the companion of a man, a woman is still, above all, a wife and a mother. (*Deuxième rapport de la Commission des droits civils de la femme* 1929–30, 365–66, in Clio Collective 1987)

In terms of the double standard in the Civil Code regarding separation on the grounds of adultery, the commission had this to say:

> Whatever we say, everyone knows that in fact, the wound to the heart of the wife is not usually as severe as the wound to the husband who has been deceived by his wife … [In] a woman's heart, forgiveness is naturally easier; also, in her mind, the wound to her self-esteem is not as cruel. (*Premier rapport de la Commission des droits civils de la femme* 1929–30, 234–35, in Clio Collective 1987)

Married women were finally granted certain rights: exclusive access to the money they earned, the right to administer and dispose of any assets they bought with that money, witnessing wills before a notary, and preventing their husbands from giving away joint property (Clio Collective 1987). However, these gains provided little satisfaction to those who had fought for change. There remained a huge gap between the rights of women in Quebec and those in the rest of Canada—who, between 1916 and 1922, had won the right to vote in provincial and federal elections and to run for public office. Women in Quebec, however, had to wait another 20 years before they could vote in provincial elections,[3] obtain higher education, and work in certain professions. Even having achieved these rights in 1940, political participation by women in Quebec was minimal. Between 1940 and 1962, only 35 women ran as candidates in provincial and federal elections; none of them were elected (Drouilly 1980, 9). Without political power, women in Quebec continued to be defined in terms of their "natural" role.

Another major obstacle in their fight for equity was the view—held especially by government officials and the clergy—of feminists as anti-nationalists. It was thought that if women had equal status with men they would abandon their role as mothers, the birth rate would plummet, and the survival of French Canada would be in peril. As evidence of this, the clergy needed only point to the disparity that existed between urban and rural birth rates—an average of three to four children in urban areas compared with seven to eight children in rural areas[4] (Henripin 1972; Hamilton 1995; Trofimenkoff 1983). As Hamilton (1995) notes,

> Given the link between nationalism and a high birth rate, feminism was a particularly acute threat to Quebec intellectuals during the early decades of this century. For men like Henri Bourassa, influential writer and editor of *Le Devoir*, feminism was yet another insidious foreign doctrine intent on sabotaging French Survival. While men everywhere, and many women too, believed that a woman in a ballot box was an unseemly sight that would lead only to neglected and even abused children, as well as to general social decay, French nationalists in Quebec—clerical and lay—harboured, expressed, and organized around their own special dilemma. For national survival itself, it seemed, depended upon women's devoting themselves to motherhood—sublimely undistracted by activities best left to men. (138)

Consequently, first-wave feminists in Quebec focused on ways to increase women's rights without appearing anti-nation, anti-Church, and anti-family. Despite their platform that gender equity would enhance women's role as mothers, they had little support. Hamilton (1995) concludes that "their public enemies remained unconvinced, and many women indifferent, if not actively hostile, even to the most muted feminist pressure" (139).

IMPACT OF THE QUIET REVOLUTION

By the late 1950s significant changes were already under way, and the "traditional nationalist ideology of surviving as a Catholic, French-speaking, predominantly rural people no longer corresponded to the needs of an urban, industrial population" (Laczko 1995, 19). The intellectual elite of Quebec advocated a new vision for the society, no longer based on the authority of the Catholic Church but on the philosophy of liberalism and **secularization**. In the early 1960s, the Quebec government led by Liberal Jean Lesage instituted a massive plan to bring Quebec society in line with the rest of Canada politically and economically.

Government policies were implemented to promote industrial development and urban growth (Behiels 1986). This initiative was viewed as a necessity if French Canada was to extricate itself from Anglo domination on one hand, and the overreaching authority of the Roman Catholic Church on the other.

This "new" Quebec nationalism is commonly referred to as the "Quiet Revolution" because it transformed Québécois society (Thomson 1984; Dumont 1995).[5] Moreover, the pursuit of the Lesage government's strategy, while involving a planned process as much as an ideological shift in the vision of society, occurred with relatively little conflict and political rancour in the population. In fact, there were only 174 incidents of political violence between 1963 and the October Crisis in 1970, which is insignificant when compared with other revolutions (Latouche 1979). Generating liberal values and advancing education for both sexes, the Quiet Revolution provided an environment conducive to feminist reform. As Dumont (1995) notes, the Quiet Revolution "presented itself as a champion of equality for women" (154). During the early 1960s, women demanded the removal of restrictions on their right to participate in political and social life; they also demanded equal wages for equal work, access to contraception, and civic rights for married women. By the late 1960s, Quebec feminists had become more organized and the second wave of feminism was well under way in the province. Women's groups were growing at unprecedented rates. Most notable was the founding of the **Fédération des femmes du Québec (FFQ)**, an umbrella association consisting of individual members and representatives from many women's groups (Dumont 1995).

> The *Fédération des femmes du Québec* was soon represented regularly on parliamentary committees [...]. Its agenda was clearly reformist and feminist: revision of the Civil Code, legalization of divorce, equality in the workplace, protection of part-time workers, minimum work standards, maternity leave, day-care centres, educational opportunities and orientation for girls, information about family planning, and protection of women in the reform of pension plans. [...] Most important, during every election campaign, it published information about each party's policies on women's issues, pointing out that one voter in two is a woman. The FFQ was a leader in offering specialized courses for women in political education, political action, and political process. (155)

Despite political affiliation or mandate differences among the various women's groups, feminism in Quebec, unlike in the other provinces, was incessantly linked with nationalism. This relationship between nationalism and feminism would at times be amicable (during the early years of the Parti Québécois' first term, 1976–85) but more often than not, quite contentious (during the second term of the PQ, 1994–present). A major reason for the conflict between the two rests in the pronatal attitudes of the nationalists, which repudiated feminist reform. As Hamilton (1995) maintains: "Ambivalence towards feminism and women's participation in the public sphere was masked in a discourse strikingly reminiscent of that of the 1920s nationalists: the nation was in jeopardy because couples had reduced the size of their families in order to pursue pleasure and possessions" (144). An example of such controversy occurred during the late 1970s over daycare legislation. Although both feminists and nationalists lobbied for a government-sponsored daycare program, they did so for different reasons. Whereas feminists saw daycare as a means of advancing women's equity in the public sphere, nationalists viewed it as a means of promoting births. Nevertheless, feminism and nationalism remained contiguous, and despite the numerous obstacles feminist voices became more and more prominent in Quebec. Indeed, by 1985 there were more than 300 feminist groups involved in political action (Dumont 1995, 158). Based on a solidarity that was stronger than ever, feminists moved to bring about change, especially in the areas of education, employment, marriage, and family.

A well-educated population was crucial to the transition of Quebec into a modern industrial society. Accordingly, the transformation of Québécois society involved the removal of education from the Church; schools, thus, were placed under the secular regulation of the government. Concurrently, the educational system was extensively expanded and modernized. For the first time in Quebec's history, females were entitled to the same education as males—especially post-secondary education. The Ministry of Education, created in 1964, gave females and males the right to a free education in co-educational schools. Changes to the educational system included a decrease in the number of private schools, the appearance of composite secondary schools, the abolition of domestic-science schools, the creation of the *Collége d'enseignement général et professionnel*, the founding of the multicampus *Université du Québec*, and the integration of teacher training into the university system. Educational reform provided women with a variety of options. For the first time in Quebec's history, women could pursue individual advancement beyond that of joining a convent. Interestingly, between 1968 and 1978, approximately ten nuns left the convent every week (Clio Collective 1987, 326–27).

The most exceptional change involved the increase in the proportion of women who received post-secondary education. In 1961, 3.6 percent of women between the ages of 15 and 44 had received a university education (Statistics Canada 1961). By 1991, this proportion increased to 8.9 percent. Women between the ages of 20 and 24 experienced the sharpest increase in university education, from 4.7 percent in 1961 to 27 percent in 1991 (Statistics Canada 1991). It is important to note that although educational opportunities opened up for women, they were concentrated in traditional fields, such as education and the health sciences. Where individuals were once discouraged from pursuing individual advancement, they were now encouraged to engage actively in productive labour for a capitalist economic system (Laczko 1995; Rousseau 1992). This had an enormous impact on married women, who entered the labour force in droves. By the early 1980s, there were more married women in the labour force than there were women who lived alone. The number of married women who were employed and still in their childbearing years rose from 15 percent in 1961 to 74 percent in 1991 (Langlois 1992, 123). More than 50 percent of mothers whose children were under the age of 2 were employed by the mid-1980s, and in 1996: 70.3 percent of mothers with children under the age of 16 worked outside the home (*Ministère de la Famille et de l'enfance* 1999, 1). By 1996, both parents worked outside the home in almost two out of three two-parent families (64 percent) and 56.6 percent of women heading single-parent households were in the labour force (*Ministère de la Famille et de l'enfance* 1999: 1). Although women's representation in the labour force increased remarkably, the types of jobs they held changed very little, as the majority of women continued to be employed in the clerical, health, teaching, and service sectors.

Along with the changes that occurred for women in education and in the labour force, the legal rights of married women were considerably extended. On July 1, 1964, the Quebec Assembly passed Bill 16, giving married women equal rights with their husbands and equal responsibility for their children. The recognition of women's identities as being autonomous from their husbands was a major victory for women in Quebec. In fact, some have even argued that gender equality in Quebec surpassed that in the rest of Canada (Eichler 1988), a remarkable achievement considering how much longer women in Quebec had to wait for even the right to vote!

An equally profound effect of the Quiet Revolution is found in the area of values. The conscious policies of the Lesage Liberals promoted strong values of **individualism** within Québécois society, accompanied by the erosion of two basic and traditional institutions: marriage and religion (*Bureau de la Statistique du Quebec* 1998; Krull and Trovato 1994; Krull 2000; Wu 2000). "Young women especially became harsh critics of their male-dominated society, in particular the Church, the institution they now held responsible more than any other for the successful defense of patriarchal relations" (Hamilton 1995, 142). It is not surprising, therefore, that Quebecers now have lower church attendance rates than they did before 1960; indeed, their attendance rates are lower even than Roman Catholics elsewhere in Canada (Guindon 1988; Lazcko 1995). Marriage rates in Quebec have also followed an accelerated pattern of decline since the early 1970s, dropping from 8.2 per 1,000 population in 1971 to only 3.3 in 1995, well below the national average of 5.4 (Statistics Canada 1976, 1995). The percentage of never-married individuals at age 50 is almost twice as high in Quebec compared to the other provinces, and the average age of marriage is about one year higher than for the other provinces (Dumas and Belanger 1994, 36). Moreover, by 1991, Quebec had the lowest proportion of married-couple families in all of Canada (69 percent compared to 80 percent in the other provinces). In fact, almost one out of every two children in Quebec is born outside of marriage (Statistics Canada 1997).

As well, **divorce rates** and common-law unions have been on the rise (Langlois et al. 1992; Wu 2000). According to Turcotte and Bélanger (1997), common-law unions are not only more frequent in Quebec but they also occur at an earlier age than anywhere else in Canada (4–5). In 1995, Quebec accounted for almost half of all common-law unions in Canada; throughout the 1990s, 80 percent of first unions in Quebec were common-law (2–3). Couples have been choosing to restrict their fertility or opt to remain childless (Langlois et al. 1992). By 1982, more than 42 percent of Quebec men and women still in their reproductive ages had undergone some form of sterilization, and by the late 1980s more than half of couples with two children had undergone a sterilization operation (Dandurand et al. 1989). The abortion ratio increased from 17.9 per 100 live births in 1978 to 41.8 in 1998 (Statistics Canada 2002). This is considerably higher than the 1998 ratios for Canada

(32.2) or Ontario (32.0) (Statistics Canada 2002); according to one report, Quebec's abortion rates are among the highest in the western world (CBC 2000). By 1987, Quebec's TFR had dropped to 1.37 children per woman compared to the national rate of 1.59 (Statistics Canada 2001). Since this time, there has been a slight upsurge in the TFR (to 1.47 in 1998), but it remains below replacement level (that is, a TFR of 2.1).

QUEBEC'S PRONATAL POLICIES

Not surprisingly, pronatal nationalists reacted strongly to the fertility collapse, claiming that the cultural, social, and political well-being of Quebec was in peril. Indeed, the link between the survival of Québécois society and women's reproductive behaviour became most salient as far back as 1971. For example, according to the Council on French Life: "If births continue to decline in Quebec, neither independence, nor wealth, nor immigration can assure the survival of the French Canadian people" (1971, 6). Demographers Caldwell and Fournier (1987) voiced similar concerns when they stated that Quebec, "in achieving the much-sought-after modernism, has effectively liquidated the essential spring of its survival as a society, its demographic dynamism" (118). Similarly, Houle (1987) posits that "although traditional Quebec could and knew how to resist change in order to assure its survival after the conquest [...], today's Quebec has, so to speak, taken its revenge in the form of an impulse toward economic and political independence in which the family, once so dear to traditional Quebec, has borne all the cost" (5). In a speech just prior to the sovereignty referendum in 1995, Lucien Bouchard, then the Bloc Québécois leader, emphatically asked: "Do you think it makes sense that we have so few children in Quebec? We are one of the white races that has the least children; that doesn't make sense. It means something, it means that we haven't resolved family problems" (Thanh Ha 1995).

In a population-engineering effort unprecedented in North America, the Quebec government in 1988 implemented three programs to boost fertility: allowances for newborns that, after amendments, paid women $500 for a first birth, $1,000 for a second, and $8,000 for a third and each subsequent birth; a family allowance for all children under 18 years; and an additional allowance for children under age 6 (Baril et al. 2000, 6). These programs were based on three principles: they were universal (applied to all children); they increased according to the rank of the child; and more money was offered to young children (7). The three allowance programs cost the government approximately $580 million annually (6).

Families were also offered a $7,000 interest-free loan to help purchase a first home on the condition that they had at least two or more children under the age of 18 and that the home cost no more than $95,000. Moreover, parents were given 34 weeks of unpaid parental leave upon the birth of their first or second child, and 27 weeks of paid leave for the birth of their third or subsequent child. This was in addition to 15 weeks of federal maternity benefits. Overall, Quebec families received nearly $4 billion annually in direct and income-tax assistance from the provincial and federal governments. Interestingly, when Liberal Premier

Robert Bourassa announced the policies, he argued that raising the birthrate "is the most important challenge of the decade for Québec … because our future is imperiled. [These new policies will] ensure the future of French in North America and the place of Québec within Confederation" (in Baker 1994, 121; see also Picard 1989).

Feminists were outraged that the government would place the reproduction of the nation above women's reproductive rights and equity. Their argument was that in advancing pronatal policies, the government was essentially promoting a "traditional" family structure whereby women were valued solely for their domestic role. As Sullerot has argued, a government that supports a pronatal agenda is "the most serious existing or potential threat to all that has been achieved by feminism over the years" (in King 1998, 46). Some feminists charged that the so-called fertility crisis, and the claim that the future of Québécois society was in peril if Quebec women did not produce more babies, were blatant fabrications by nationalists in an attempt to advance their own agenda (Baker 1994; Maroney 1992; Hamilton 1995). In a scathing critique of the nexus of demography and policy-making, Maroney (1992) charged that Quebec's **pronatal policies** only served to marginalize women, reducing them to objects of demographic policy. Similarly, Hamilton (1995) argued that in Quebec "loomed that aspect of nationalist ideology which linked survival to a high birth rate—that is, to women exploiting their reproductive potential in the service of the nation" (137).

Critics also pointed out that underlying these policies loomed the stereotype of the prolific Québécois woman (see Gauvreau 1991; Hamilton 1995; Lavigne 1986). Despite research that clearly negates the existence of a monolithic woman in Quebec (see Gauvreau 1991; Lavigne 1986), the assumption that historically all Québécois women desired and had large families continued to be popular among nationalists. Thus, the veiled message behind these new policies was that with a bit of incentive, women would resume their reproductive responsibilities. Ironically, as Hamilton (1995) points out, "when women in Quebec had large numbers of children, it was neither to save the nation nor foil the English" (141).

These critiques coincided with a growing awareness that Quebec's incentive policies were not producing the expected birth increases (Krull and Pierce 1997; Krull 2001). Although there was an initial increase in the late 1980s in the total fertility rate from 1.49 children per woman in 1988 to 1.72 in 1990,[6] after 1990 total births decreased and families with three or more children remained uncommon. It was becoming clear that the Quiet Revolution, having transformed the province into a modern urban industrial state, was now driven by individualistic values as reflected in the younger generation's propensities toward alternative life styles and self-actualization over the pursuit of early family formation and childbearing. "The simple slogan of the *Comité de lutte pour l'avortement libre et gratuit*—'We will have the children that we want to have'—expresses what most women appear now to be doing" (Hamilton 1995, 142). Consequently, policies favouring third and subsequent children are increasingly viewed as contrary to the needs of most families (Saint-Pierre and Dandurand 2000).

QUEBEC'S ALTERNATIVE TO PRONATAL POLICIES

Acknowledging the ineffectiveness of its pronatal policies, the provincial government created the *Ministère de la Famille et de l'Enfance* in 1997 to reassess the province's family policy needs (*Ministère de la Famille et de l'Enfance* 1999). The *Ministère's* mandate was threefold. First, a unified child allowance program was to be established to assist low-income families with children under the age of 18. The amount of family allowance is determined by the number of dependent children under the age of 18, family type (single-parent, two parents), and family income (the threshold is $15,332 for single-parent families and $21,825 for two-parent families). Next, to assist families during maternity or parental leave, a parental insurance plan was to be implemented whereby remuneration to parents is increased during and following pregnancy. Finally, a network of government-regulated childcare facilities was to be integrated, highly subsidized ($5 per day), and offer a quality educational program to children from birth to kindergarten age. Accordingly, the government promised 200,000 childcare places by 2005. According to Baril et al. (2000), "direct financial assistance would henceforth be aimed almost exclusively at low-income families, while indirect assistance, such as subsidized daycare services, would be offered gradually to all families in Quebec" (4). By September 1997, all but the parental insurance plan had been implemented, replacing previous assistance programs. The parental insurance plan has yet to be realized.

These new policy changes demonstrate the efforts being put forth by the Quebec government toward strengthening families (Krull 2001). Quebec is the only province at this time to have a universal subsidized daycare program. Moreover, the Quebec government has recently launched ten innovative pilot projects that offer evening or 24-hour daycare service, seven days a week (Dougherty and Jelowicki 2000). This trial extended-hours project will cost the Quebec government $500,000 (Peritz 2000).

It is important to note that the new policies, although a huge improvement from the previous ones, are not without their critics. The major criticism is that these policies no longer provide universal family assistance, but rather targeted assistance aimed almost exclusively at low-income families. Clark (1997) charges that middle-class families have ended up paying for the policies. In addition, the new policies inadvertently limit women's choices since they favour employed mothers over stay-at-home mothers (A9). Although the government has assured Quebecers that 95 percent of families will benefit from their new assistance programs, Baril et al. (2000) argue that the new programs ultimately create winners and losers among families.

The results show that families claiming social assistance are barely affected by the reforms. Families with an income ranging from $10,000 to $25,000 constitute the principal beneficiaries of the new programmes, while families with an income above $25,000 have become the programmes' principal contributors. This means that almost 70 percent of families have had to deal with a reduction in governmental financial assistance to facilitate the increase in levels of support for approximately 30 percent of families. The results also show that the financial loss for families increases with the number of children (4–5).

The universal daycare program has also come under attack because it "channels financial assistance primarily to families in which both parents work at regular 9-to-5 jobs and whose children are cared for in accredited centres. [As such,] it penalizes those who do not follow a particular pattern" (Vincent 2000, 3). Referring to the daycare program, the former Quebec Liberal Party leader Daniel Johnson charges that the "government is setting up structures to hide its lack of concrete support for families. [...] The government is in fact taking $300 million out of families' pockets to pay for daycares" (Clark 1997, A9). Moreover, Quebec's auditor-general Guy Breton insists that "the provincial government is ignoring infractions in some daycare centres because it is too short of daycare spaces to close any centres. ... the government has been sacrificing quality for quantity" (Thompson 1999, F7; see also Government of Quebec 1999: Sections 4.4–4.7). Thus,

> Quebec's Department of Family and Child Care has been so busy trying to create new daycare spaces to respond to the demand created by the $5-a-day daycare program, it has failed to keep tabs on the quality of care in existing centres. For example, Quebec now has one of the highest ratios of children to daycare workers, and few if any centres have filed copies of their education programs with the government. (Thompson 1999, F7)

Finally, although the new family support policies are not explicitly pronatal, anxiety over the province's low birth rates continues. For instance, the *Ministère de la Famille et de l'Enfance du Quèbec* closed its report with the following concern:

> In 1961 a woman in Quebec had an average of 3.8 children in her lifetime; today she will have less than 1.5. Thus we are seeing a considerable reduction in the size of Quebec families. [...] The questions mentioned briefly here, which are at the core of family policy, will be the subject of an overall, detailed analysis by the government in order to adapt family policy to the new situation. There is a pressing need however for the government to act on certain phenomena: the declining birth rate, [...] poverty, [...] parental responsibility, which is exercised in a context of marriage break-ups and increasing numbers of single-parent families. These serious problems represent equally serious challenges for the government and all its partners. (2)

Despite a history of endorsing a pronatal agenda, the Quebec government is currently making a conscious effort toward strengthening families. Quebec's new family policies, currently the most innovative in Canada, demonstrate this commitment to families and to facilitating women's paid employment. To realize fully the objective of strengthening Quebec families, a continued effort toward advancing women's equity is essential. Micheline Dumont, a Québécois feminist, has queried: "How can it not be recognized that henceforth the autonomy of women is an integral part of the new Quebec identity and that it can no longer be ignored? The participation of women in politics and most of all, the new conception and organization of power will be a sign of a real revolution. At the present time, it requires great faith and hope to believe that could happen" (Dumont 1995, 168). Although the tension between feminists and nationalists continues to be an integral part of Quebec's civic dialogue, the recent changes in family policies are a testimony to the influence that feminists have had in this province, especially in terms of consciousness-raising and promoting women's equity and reproductive rights.

NOTES

1. It is important to note that high fertility does not imply that all women had large families or that all births were to married women. Some women remained single, were widowed prior to having children, were involuntarily childless, or had one or two children (see Lavigne 1986; Gauvreau 1991). Moreover, as Moogk (1982) has shown, illegitimate births were not uncommon in New France.

2. It is important to point out that Quebec society was not completely immune to the modernization process prior to 1960. For example, urbanization was taking place but at a much slower pace than it did for the rest of Canada.

3. Interestingly, women in Quebec were given the right to vote in 1791 but, as Dumont (1995) points out, it was by mistake, and one that was corrected in 1834 (153). It is also important to note that women were not just handed the vote in 1940 but in fact had lobbied hard for it. As Hamilton (1995) notes, "the feminists' long campaign, which included weekly radio broadcasts, meetings, lectures, and fund-raising events paid off" (139).

4. These rates pertain to women born between 1906 and 1921 and who lived to the end of their reproductive years.

5. According to Thompson (1984, 2), the term *Quiet Revolution* is standard among Canadian academics but scholars are uncertain who created the term. He argues that the early 1960s are referred to as a "revolution" because the period marked a dramatic turning point in Quebec history. Moreover, the social and economic transformations that took place in Quebec during this time occurred unexpectedly, almost "quietly" (3).

6. Interestingly, the increase during the late 1980s is accounted for by a sharp increase in births to unmarried women. The fertility rates for married women actually decrease during this period. For example, in 1991 births to unmarried women accounted for 40.7 percent of all births in Quebec but only 26.4 percent of all births in Canada. This means that almost one out of every two births in Quebec is to an unmarried woman.

KEY TERMS

Cohabitation: The sharing of a household by an unmarried couple.

Crude birth rate: The number of births in a given year divided by the mid-year population in that year.

Divorce rate: The number of recorded divorces per 100,000 population in a calendar year.

Domestic sciences: Courses designed to prepare girls for married life, specifically concentrating on training them to be efficient housekeepers.

Dowry: The money, goods, or property that in some traditional societies a bride is required to bring to her marriage.

Fédération des femmes du Québec (FFQ): Founded by Thérèse Casgrain in 1966 for the purpose of bringing together several feminist organizations. It included representatives from all the women's associations as well as individual members. Its primary goal was to promote the interests and rights of women.

Individualism: The philosophy of individualism asserts that the value of the individual is paramount over the value of the social group.

Marriage rate: The number of marriages per 1,000 population in a given calendar year.

Neolocal: A residential pattern in which a married couple lives apart from the parents of both spouses. This pattern characterizes the nuclear family.

Nuclear family (conjugal family): A social unit composed of two (or more rarely, one) parent(s) and children.

Pronatalism: The goal of encouraging births and raising fertility in a society.

Pronatal policies: Policies aimed at maintaining or raising fertility. According to the UN, as of 1995 there are 47 countries with pronatal policies (see King 1998). Conversely, antinatalist policies are those aimed at bringing down high birthrates (i.e. "family planning policies").

Quiet Revolution: Refers to the social and economic transformations that took place in Quebec beginning in the early 1960s.

Secularization: The process in which religious thinking, practice, and institutions lose social significance; it is thought to be the consequence of the social changes brought about by urban, industrial society.

Seigneurie: Based on a land tenure system, adopted from the European feudal system and transferred to New France. It consists of dividing the land into long narrow rectangles along the river. Each rectangle of land was called a *seigneurie*. The landowner, and head of the family, was referred to as a *Seigneur*.

Sex-segregated roles: Attitudes and activities that a culture links to each sex.

Total fertility rate (TFR): The average number of children that would be born to each woman if the current birthrates remained constant.

DISCUSSION QUESTIONS

1. What factors account for the exceptionally high birth rates in New France? Who were the King's Daughters and why were they sent to New France?

2. What is meant by "the revenge of the cradles" (*la revanche des berceaux*), and what purpose did it serve?

3. Prior to the 1960s, how did the Quebec Civil Code define married women? Discuss the rights of married women according to the Civil Code. What was the significance of the Dorion Commission? Was it successful? Did obtaining the right to vote significantly change women's status?

4. What is the Quiet Revolution and what impact did it have on women's roles? On family structures?

5. Why has feminism posed such a threat to nationalists? How did nationalists react to Quebec's "fertility collapse"?

6. Describe Quebec's pronatal policies from 1988 to 1997. What criticisms were launched against these policies?

7. Do you think that Quebec's new policies go far enough to support families in Quebec?

8. In your opinion, what will be the consequences for Québécois society if birth rates remain below replacement level? Should a government attempt to intervene on such matters as reproduction? What other measures can the Quebec government take to circumvent a dwindling population and protect the vitality of its culture?

REFERENCES

Baker, Maureen. 1994. "Family and Population Policy in Québec: Implications for Women." *Canadian Journal of Women and the Law/ Revue Femmes et Droit 7*: 116–132.

Baril, Robert, Pierre Lefebvre, and Philip Merrigan. 2000. "Quebec Family Policy: Impact and Options." IRPPs *Choices: Family Policy* 6(1): 4–52.

Beaujot, Roderic, and Kevin McQuillan. 1982. *Growth and Dualism: The Demographic Development of Canadian Society*. Toronto: Gage.

Behiels, Michael D. 1986. *Prelude to Quebec's Quiet Revolution*. Kingston and Montreal: McGill–Queens University Press.

Bergeron, Leandre. 1975. *The History of Quebec: A Patriote's Handbook*. Toronto: NC Press.

Bureau de la Statistique du Quebec. 1998. *D'Une Generation a l'Autre: Evolution de Conditions de Vie*. Volumes I et II. Under the direction of Hervé Gauthier and Associates. Sainte-Foy, Quebec.

Caldwell, Gary, and Daniel Fournier. 1987. "The Quebec Question: A Matter of Population." *The Canadian Journal of Sociology 12*: 16–41.

CBC (Canadian Broadcasting Corporation). 2000. Abortions in Quebec Highest Number in Western World. www.cbc.ca/cgi-bin/templates/NWview.cgi?/news/2000/03/10/abortions000310/

Clark, Campbell. 1997. "Family Ministry Draws Fire." *The (Montreal) Gazette*, May 14: A9.

Clio Collective. 1987. *Quebec Women: A History*. Toronto: Women's Press.

Council on French Life in America. 1971. "The Fertility Crises in Quebec." Translated by Katya von Knorring. In Carl F. Grindstaff, Craig L. Boydell, and Paul C. Whitehead, eds., *Population Issues in Canada*. Toronto: Holt, Rinehart and Winston.

Dandurand, Renée B., Marianne Kempeneers, and Céline Le Bourdais. 1989. "Quel Soutien pour les familles?" *10 Options Politiques 28*.

Dougherty, Keven, and Amanda Jelowicki. 2000. "Night daycare to make debut: Pilot projects will offer $5 daily rate." *The (Montreal) Gazette* (August 31).

Drouilly, Pierre. 1980. "Les femmes et les élections." *Le Devoir* (December 17).

Dumas, Jean, and Alain Belanger. 1994. *Report on the Demographic Situation in Canada*. Ottawa: Minister of Industry (Catalogue no. 91-209-E).

Dumont, Micheline. 1995. "Women of Quebec and the Contemporary Constitutional Issue." In Fancois-Pierre Gingras, ed., *Gender Politics in Contemporary Canada*. Toronto: Oxford University Press: 153–175. Copyright © Oxford University Press, 1995. Used by permission of Oxford University Press.

Eichler, Margrit. 1988. *Families in Canada Today*, 2nd ed. Toronto: Gage.

Garigue, Philippe. 1956. "French-Canadian Kinship and Urban Life." *American Anthropologist 58*: 1090–1101.

Gauvreau, Danielle. 1991. "Destins de femmes, destins de mères: images et réalités historiques de la maternité au Québec." *Recherches Sociographiques* 32(3): 321–346.

Government of Quebec. 1999. *Report of the Auditor General to the National Assembly for 1998–1999, Summary*. Chapter 4.

Guindon, Hubert. 1988. *Quebec Society: Tradition, Modernity, and Nationhood.* Roberta Hamilton and John L. McMullan, eds. Toronto: University of Toronto Press.

Hamilton, Roberta. 1995. "Pro-natalism, Feminism, and Nationalism." In Francois-Pierre Gingras, ed., *Gender and Politics in Contemporary Canada.* Toronto: Oxford University Press: 135–152. Copyright © Oxford University Press, 1995. Used by permission of Oxford University Press.

Henripin, Jacques. 1972. *Trends and Factors of Fertility in Canada.* Ottawa: Minister of Trade and Commerce.

Henripin, Jacques. 1994. "From Acceptance of Nature to Control: The Demography of the French Canadians since the Seventeenth Century." In Frank Trovato and Carl F. Grindstaff, eds., *Perspectives on Canada's Population: An Introduction to Concepts and Issues.* Toronto: Oxford University Press: 24–34.

Henripin, Jacques, and Ives Peron. 1972. "The Demographic Transition of the Province of Quebec." In D.V. Glass and Roger Revelle, eds. *Population and Social Change.* London: Edward Arnold: 213–231.

Houle, Gilles. 1987. "Présentation/Introduction." *The Canadian Journal of Sociology* 12(1–2): 1–7.

King, Leslie. 1998. "France Needs Children: Pronatalism, Nationalism and Women's Equity." *The Sociological Quarterly* 39(1): 33–52.

Krull, Catherine. 2000. "Fertility Change in Quebec, 1931–1991." *Canadian Population Studies, Special Edition on Family Demography* 27(1): 159–180.

Krull, Catherine. 2000a. "Modernization, Fertility Decline and Pronatal Policy in Quebec, Canada", presented at the 2000 Annual Meeting of the Population Association of America, Los Angeles, California, March 24.

Krull, Catherine. 2001. "Quebec's Alternative to Pronatalism." *Population Today*, November/December. U.S. Population Reference Bureau, Washington, D.C.

Krull, Catherine, and David Pierce. 1997. "Behavior Analysis and Demographics: Government Control of Reproductive Behavior and Fertility in the Province of Quebec, Canada." In P.A. Lamal, ed., *Cultural Contingencies: Behavior Analytic Perspectives on Cultural Practices.* Westport, Connecticut: Praeger: 107–132.

Krull, Catherine, and Frank Trovato. 1994. "The Quiet Revolution and the Sex Differential in Quebec's Suicide Rates: 1931–1986." *Social Forces* 72(4): 1121–1147.

Langlois, Simon. 1992. "Women's Employment." In S. Langlois, J. Baillargeon, G. Caldwell, G. Fréchet, M. Gauthier, and J. Simard. *Recent Social Trends in Québec, 1960–1990.* Kingston and Montreal: McGill–Queen's University Press: 120–128.

Langlois, S., J. Baillargeon, G. Caldwell, G. Fréchet, M. Gauthier, and J. Simard. 1992. *Recent Social Trends in Québec, 1960–1990.* Kingston and Montreal: McGill–Queen's University Press.

Latouche, Daniel. 1988. "Quebec." *The Canadian Encyclopedia,* 2nd ed. Edmonton: Hurtig Publishers.

Latouche, Daniel. 1979. *Le systeme politique quebecois: recueil de textes.* LaSalle, Quebec: Hurtubise HMH.

Lavigne, Marie. 1986. "Feminist Reflections on the Fertility of Women in Québec." In Roberta Hamilton and Michèle Barrett, eds., *The Politics of Diversity: Feminism, Marxism and Nationalism.* London: Verso: 303–321.

Lavigne, Marie, and Yolande Pinard. 1983. *Travailleuses et féministes: Les femmes dans la société québécoise.* Montreal: Boréal Express.

Lazcko, Leslie. 1995. *Pluralism and Inequality in Quebec.* New York: St. Martin's Press.

Maroney, Heather J. 1992. "Who Has the Baby? Nationalism, Pronatalism and the Construction of a 'Demographic Crisis' in Quebec, 1960–1988." *Studies in Political Economy* 39: 7–36.

Ministère de la Famille et de l'Enfance du Québec. 1999. "Family Policy: Another Step Towards

Developing the Full Potential of Families and Their Children." Government of Québec: Les Publications du Québec.

Moogk, Peter. 1982. "Les Petits Sauvages: The Children of Eighteenth Century New France." In Joy Parr, ed., *Childhood and Family in Canadian History*. Toronto: McClelland & Stewart.

Moreux, Colette. 1971. "The French Canadian Family." In K. Ishwaran, ed., *The Canadian Family*. Toronto: Holt, Rinehart and Winston.

Nett, Emily. 1993. *Canadian Families: Past and Present*, 2nd ed. Toronto: Butterworths.

Peritz, Ingrid. 2000. "Tired of the Kids? Try 24-hour Daycare: Quebec Tests Program Aimed at Shift Workers." *The Globe and Mail* (August 31): A9.

Peters, John. 1990. "Cultural Variations: Past and Present." In Maureen Baker, ed., *Families: Changing Trends in Canada*, 2nd ed. Toronto: McGraw-Hill Ryerson: 166–191.

Picard, André. 1989. "Bourassa Pledges More Paid Leave to Parents of Three or More Children." *The Globe and Mail* (September 14): A1.

Pinard, Yolande. 1983. "Les débus du mouvement des femmes à Montréal, 1893–1902." In Marie Lavigne and Yolande Pinard, eds., *Travailleuses et féministes: Les femmes dans la société québécoise*. Montreal: Boréal Express: 177–198.

Romaniuc, Anatole. 1984. *Fertility in Canada: From Baby-boom to Baby-bust*. Ottawa: Statistics Canada.

Rousseau, Mark O. 1992. "The Politics of Language and Trade in Québec, Canada: Toward an Autonomous Francophone State." *Berkeley Journal of Sociology 32*: 163–179.

Saint-Pierre, Marie Hélène and Renée B. Dandurand. 2000. *Axes et Enjeux de la Politique Familiale Québécoise: Présentation D'Une Recension Informatisée des Écrits*. Montréal, Québec: INRS – Culture et Soceté.

Statistics Canada. 1961. *Census of Canada*. Table 103, 1:3. Ottawa: Minister of Trade and Commerce.

Statistics Canada. 1976. *Vital Statistics. Vol. 2. Marriages and Divorces*. Ottawa: Information Canada, Table 1: 3.

Statistics Canada. 1991a. *Vital Statistics, Births*. Catalogue #84-210, Annual, Births: 1921–1991.

Statistics Canada. 1991b. *Census of Canada*. Table 2, Cat. 328. Ottawa: Minister of Trade and Commerce.

Statistics Canada. 1995. *Vital Statistics. Vol. 2. Marriages and Divorces*. Ottawa: Information Canada.

Statistics Canada. 1997. *The Daily*. December 9. Ottawa.

Statistics Canada 2001. *Report on the Demographic Situation in Canada*. Ottawa: Minister of Industry.

Statistics Canada. 2002. "Therapeutic Abortions per 100 Live Births." <www.statcan/ca/english/pgdb/people/health/health42a.htm>.

Thanh Ha, Tu. 1995. "Bourchard Remarks Spark Outcry: Yes Leader Dismisses Attacks over 'White Races' Comment as Petty Politicking." *The Globe and Mail* (October 16).

Thompson, Elizabeth. 1999. "Daycare Woes Ignored: Auditor Report Blasts Lack of Supervision." *The (Montreal) Gazette*, (December 10): F7.

Thomson, Dale C. 1984. *Jean Lesage and the Quiet Revolution*. Toronto: Macmillan.

Trofimenkoff, Susan Mann. 1983. *The Dream of a Nation: A Social and Intellectual History of Quebec*. Toronto: Gage.

Turcotte, Pierre, and Alain Belanger. 1997. "Moving In Together: The Formation of First Common-Law Unions." *Canadian Social Trends* (Winter): 7–10.

Vincent. Carole. 2000. "Editors Note." IRPPs *Choices: Family Policy* 6(1): 2–3.

Wade, Mason. 1968. *The French Canadians, 1760–1967*, Volumes I and II. Toronto: Macmillan.

Wilson, S.J. 1986. *Women, the Family and the Economy*, 2nd ed. Toronto: McGraw-Hill Ryerson Ltd.

Wu, Zheng. 2000. *Cohabitation: An Alternative Form of Family Living*. Don Mills, Ontario: Oxford University Press.

12

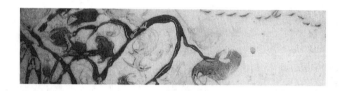

The "Culture of Making Do": Gender, Work, and Family in Cape Breton Working-Class Life[1]

Dr. Pauline T. Gardiner Barber

Department of Sociology and Anthropology
Dalhousie University

Objectives

- To highlight how history and political economy have influenced local culture in Cape Breton's old coal towns, through an ethnographic case study of Cape Breton working-class culture that adopts a structure and agency perspective.

- To show the significance of women's work to their families and communities and in local culture, here characterized as the "culture of making do," to emphasize gendered work practices.

- To highlight the differences between the families and households as social units. In Cape Breton both have fluid boundaries and are used creatively as resources to tide people over hard times.

- To illustrate that for historical reasons family and kinship relations provide Cape Bretoners with access to goods and services that are otherwise unavailable, and to demonstrate that women work hard to maintain these social ties, which are also the source of important information.

- To show that culturally specific family practices have helped Cape Bretoners accommodate themselves to persistent hard times, yet they have also facilitated expression of community and class resistance, such as strikes. Some contradictions of class and gender are suggested as particular predicaments for women.

INTRODUCTION

This essay explores the relationship between gender, work, and families on the one hand and class, culture, and community on the other. The community discussed here is an old coal mining town located on Cape Breton island, Nova Scotia. It lies a short drive from the city of Sydney, the second largest urban centre in the province. The town's population was approximately 20,000 people at the time the field study was completed in 1987. Some ten years later, the town's population had shrunk to 18,659, a decline no doubt related to the precarious state of the Cape Breton coal and fishing industries. In 1999 the closure of the last mine was announced, calling forth one last major collective effort to save the mines, the communities, and the way of life that attended them. Such a dramatic shift in livelihood and identity promises an uncertain future for the community described here; however, the following discussion should not be read as simply a historical study. The shadow of the town's formative industry will continue to frame distinctive local cultural practices and a strong sense of community and class identity for some time yet, even as globalization and new economic policies promote individualized ways of living unfettered by the strong loyalties to kin and community described here.

This study is ethnographic. My primary research methods combined participant-observation fieldwork and the collection of life and work histories from a sample of approximately 40 households located in one of several communities in the industrial area. There are some grounds for arguing that each of the communities that make up Cape Breton's old industrial area has a unique claim to community identity. Residents have remained loyal to their own particular communities, the boundaries of which are mostly invisible to outsiders. Such loyalties persist despite the demise of the founding industries and various forms of political amalgamation from the mid-20th century onward. Inter-community rivalries are played out in various ways, for example with competitive sports teams and through historical political alliances. Nonetheless, for convenience, I use the terms *local culture* and *Cape Breton culture* synonymously. This is partly to protect the exact identity of the community, and also because much of what I say about Cape Breton working-class culture also applies to the industrial region as a whole, at least as it was constituted during the research period and through the 1990s.

Culture and History: A Structure and Agency Approach

The essay has two major themes. The first part outlines a framework for understanding the relationship between culture and history: how people's ideas and experiences of "family" in a particular time and place in the Canadian landscape are shared, at least up to a point, and are shaped by local culture. *Culture,* as I use the term, takes into account both **structure** (social class relations and processes of political economy) and **agency** (how people respond individually and, more to the point, collectively to the processes that shape their lives). A structure and agency approach to culture allows us to appreciate the significance of people's responses to events in the historical development of industrial Cape Breton. Important historical moments include the arrival of several waves of European settlers whose distinctive ethnic and cultural identities were reforged in their new Canadian environment. Also significant were the harsh conditions early settlers endured, first while working the land and then later when the coal and steel industries provided difficult and dangerous jobs for men at wage rates so low that their communities reported the highest incidence of disease, poverty, and infant mortality in Canada. Throughout this history women and men have left in search of employment elsewhere in Canada and the eastern United States. It is a history marked by survival struggles and the development of strong loyalties to family and communities, a history that has generated a common set of understandings and social practices. One of the most commonly expressed approaches to daily life, voiced repeatedly in my household interviews, was the idea that families are accustomed to "getting by" during times of economic hardship and, related to this, to "making do" with what they have. Local culture in industrial Cape Breton can thus be characterized as the "culture of making do."

The "Culture of Making Do" in Cape Breton

While "making do" might also be applied to other social or spatial niches in Canadian society, for Cape Breton the history of struggle and hardship plays a central role in how people assign meaning to their lives and participate in shared community identities. In my examination of people's family practices and how they organize their time, their resources, their employment strategies, and their social networks, "making do" provides the most potent metaphor for local culture. Moreover, this concept is the best point of entry into what many Cape Bretoners themselves recognize to be distinctive about their experiences of family, workplace, and community relations. Hence, in adopting this metaphor for local culture in my analysis I apply local idioms (linguistic practices), which on the surface seem quite straightforward, to complex socioeconomic processes. The idea of the "culture of making do" is the end product of my ethnographic investigation of seemingly ordinary events and activities that, taken together, actively reproduce the social relations of work, family, and community in local culture. If, as I suspect, "making do" is structured as a cultural idiom in other parts of Canada, it will likely entail some different historical and social relationships than those described here for Cape Breton.

Families, Households, and Local Loyalties

A second set of themes in this chapter explores the differences between families (people who are related to each other through ties of kinship, marriage and sentiment, or their socially understood equivalents) and **households** (people who live together). In what sense are these two configurations of people similar in Cape Breton, and when and how do they differ? Here again, untangling these terms and the social units they refer to proves helpful to our consideration of the significance of families, gender, and work in Cape Breton culture. Gendered work practices, which sustain people and their families, rely heavily on extended-kinship networks. People's use of these networks takes us to the heart of what is highly valued in the "culture of making do." Kinship networks and how they are mobilized, therefore, play a central role in my discussion of livelihood practices in Cape Breton working-class culture.

Regardless of their family's history and point of origin Cape Bretoners commiserate—often with pleasure—about the complexities and contradictions of living with "the culture of making do." By chance, as I was writing the first draft of this chapter, I heard illustration of this in a CBC radio interview with the owner of an ice cream store in industrial Cape Breton. This family business, set up by Italian immigrants, had survived through several generations of life in Glace Bay. Despite the interviewer's pointed questions about multiculturalism, the store owner referred more to common local themes than to the family's historical origins in Italian culture. Many "Capers," as Cape Bretoners affectionately call people from Cape Breton, actively assert and define a common culture in their family, workplace, and community relations, wherever in Canada they live. They joke with visitors about needing a passport to enter Cape Breton Island when driving across the Canso Causeway. Sometimes, such arguments are convincing enough that neophytes to Cape Breton culture actually act upon the advice, or so I have been told by students who have been both on both sides of this identity-rich, boundary-marking prank. Why and how this is so, and what such assertions of common identity and culture mean across the layers of generation and travelled spaces, is what this essay sets out to answer.

The continuing loyalty to a common culture and shared identity, and the longing for "home" expressed by those who leave, presents a contradiction of sorts. Media images of the "ideal" community apply standards that equate prosperity with the desirability of a community and the loyalty of its residents. Popular sitcoms about family life are revealing in this regard. Few shows seen on Canadian television explore working-class family life. Media images of families portray a homogenized culture of consumption and affluence as the North American norm. Television families live in large, comfortable houses, drive late-model cars, dress fashionably, and live in clean, safe communities. Outside of news broadcasts, we seldom see images of people hard at work, run-down houses and neighbourhoods, or families experiencing financial hardship. The powerful media messages about the ownership of things, fashion standards, and distorted gendered social relations are seductive for young people everywhere, Cape Breton being no exception. Despite this, each generation in Cape Breton has maintained a commitment to local cultural identity and held on to their community loyalties in the face of grim economic realities. This feature of Cape Breton working-class culture invites comparison with other economically struggling Canadian contexts. Newfoundland is one Atlantic Canadian context where there are striking similarities to Cape Breton in terms of fierce loyalties to its communities and way of life. Here the similarities end, however, because the settlement of Newfoundland outports produced different patterns of class, community, and culture.

Ideas about the meaning of "family" and how people actively engage with their families in this "culture of making do," whether they are living in Cape Breton or Halifax, Toronto, Calgary, or Boston—some popular labour markets for migrant Cape Bretoners—may serve practical as well as sentimental purposes. Engaging with family members for social and economic support can help to insulate people from some broader negative trends in Canadian society. Family work practices and people's expectations of how these can, should, and actually do operate in working-class culture in Cape Breton provide the means for people both to accommodate to and to resist pressures from the combined effects of social, political, and economic changes. Persistent economic uncertainties and concern over job loss are not new to residents of the industrial communities; this is particularly true of the town discussed here. In a sense, one can argue that culturally based family practices in Cape Breton represent an adaptation to historical processes of political economy in the region. In concluding the essay, I focus upon the significance of this issue at the turn of the century as the new political agendas of globalization and economic restructuring threaten to transform the Canadian welfare state and social policies.

THE GENDERED PRODUCTION AND REPRODUCTION OF WORKING-CLASS CULTURE

The community I studied was incorporated as a town in the early 1900s after reorganization and expansion of the coal industry stimulated an influx of migrants from rural areas into the mining towns. From these early days, successive generations of residents confirmed and reconfirmed a sense of community loyalty and commitment to a common identity: a way of claiming their difference from other Nova Scotians and Canadians. Despite various government initiatives to turn the economy around, the coal towns have known more economic uncertainty than prosperity. A cultural outlook of caution whereby people are reluctant to take their economic circumstances for granted is one main legacy from these economic instabilities. Again, the idea of "making do" is one key feature of this legacy. But the idea of distinctive local culture can be further unpacked. My research reveals a number of social practices are central to the concept of "making do." As already noted, "making do" involves expressing community loyalty in the face of adversity. It also involves presenting a united front against outsiders (sometimes forcefully, but often with humour). During the 1980s, this included people from Halifax, most especially government officials who administered economic and social programs. One such person was described to me: "That one knows less than you or I have forgotten. It's pitiful." To translate, we can conclude the demeaned individual was not considered by the speaker to be very clever.

Within community relations the strongest commitment is to kinship, to one's immediate family and the often numerous spread of relatives related by birth and marriage, who are remembered vividly. One experience I had during my stay confirmed the importance of kinship, or rather its expression and emphasis, in everyday routines. On a taxi ride, I was astonished when the driver identified me (falsely, as it turned out) as one of the "MacDonald girls," his wife's second cousins. As an immigrant, I doubted I looked and spoke very much like a local but I appreciated his interest in including me in his world of familiar people. During interviews, other people also tried to trace connections between their kinship and life experiences and my own; further evidence of the important cultural practice of situating people in relationship to oneself as a means of affirming a common social position and community identity. To the extent that the production of such loyalties avoids, obscures, or even denies the negative qualities of family life in Cape Breton communities, we may speak of the loyalties as ideological. While the "culture of making do" is ideological, it also involves a set of social practices—for example, "taking care of one's own"—that provide people with access to essential and sometimes scarce goods and services such as jobs.

Local culture is also ideological inasmuch as it can mask the underlying nature of power and class inequalities in social practices. Examples would include a fish plant supervisor who hires workers on the basis of kinship and other social obligations, or a local government official who assigns short-term jobs on the same basis. In both of these cases, patronage prevails and class privileges and disadvantages are maintained. The respective merits and attributes of other potential employees are not necessarily considered, making it difficult for many young people to improve their circumstances beyond that of their parents, particularly if they wish to continue living in the community. Because of the limited number of well-paid jobs and the prevalence of kin-favouring norms, education is not necessarily rewarded either. On the other hand, there can also be advantages to employers and employees from patronage as the *modus operandi* of job recruitment. Such possibilities, played out in the gendered work routines of Cape Breton life, are shaped by interwoven historical and cultural experiences. This is particularly so when labour and class issues are at stake. Results, however, are never entirely predictable (see also Barber 1992a, 1992b, and 2002 for a further discussion of these issues).

These cultural themes, whether expressed ideologically or reflected in social practices, have produced contradictory faces to the meaning of "family" and "community" at different historical moments in Cape Breton coal communities. At the beginning of the century, feisty coal miners from Scotland and Europe joined Cape Breton coal miners (mostly from earlier waves of rural Scottish migration) to produce one of the more interesting and militant periods of Canadian labour history (see Frank 1976, 1979, 1980; Macgillivray 1973, 1974; Muise 1980). A series of major strikes through the 1920s taught Cape Breton mining families deeply felt lessons about the necessity of family support, and class and community loyalties.

The particular form of working-class culture associated with this fractious labour history necessarily includes women's experiences, although this has been less discussed in the literature. Commitment to class, community, and familial processes has been as true for women as it has been for men. Although women did not work directly for wages in the mines, they contributed significant amounts of additional labour in their household duties as a direct result of the poor wages and working conditions, and the inadequate housing and community services provided by mining companies. Even the local stores were owned by the companies, providing food to families on credit charged against a miner's meagre earnings. The stores were called "pluck me's," and Cape Breton labour historians have shown that the miners were acutely aware of the companies' opportunities to exploit them twice over, for their labour in the mines and through the profits made in the company stores (for example, Frank 1979).

If we calculate women's domestic labour, our understanding of working-class exploitation in **production** increases. Domestic labour relates to the idea of **social reproduction** and is always necessary to turn wages into food. Added to this feature of reproduction is that part of women's labour produces the next generation of workers, not just biologically but also in terms of socializing children to the social and cultural values appropriate to their class backgrounds. Here then we have social reproduction in three senses: domestic labour, reproduction as child bearing and child rearing, and socialization, all of which are essential for the continuity of society as a whole—its social and class relations. Women's reproductive labour in mining towns was all the more extensive because of miners' low wages. Hence women also contributed greatly to company profits through their socially reproductive work. During periods of layoff and strikes, miners' wives and families also proved class loyalties and laid the groundwork for the cultural knowledge and resilience that I characterize as "the culture of making do." Annie MacLeod was a woman in her 80s when I met her. She had been a teacher during the difficult early years of the industry, so I asked her to help me fill in gaps left by labour historians who mostly wrote about the heroic efforts of male miners and militant union leaders. With such dramatic and obvious labour issues to explore, domestic life and women's work usually remained in the shadows of written histories. Children in Annie MacLeod's class came to school hungry and cold despite the best efforts of their mothers to feed and clothe them. Deep poverty was the norm. Children wore patched hand-me-downs and some had clothes fashioned from sackcloth. All were underclothed during the winter months. While I cannot impute a form of class militancy to Cape Breton miners' wives, I can suggest that the mothers of children taught by Annie MacLeod must have understood, every bit as much as their mining husbands and sons, brothers, and fathers, the nature of class exploitation in the industry and the significance of collective action and the mutual support networks of union and family.

It may seem rather a large jump from the early years of the 20th century, particularly the early periods of union militancy, to Cape Breton in the late 1980s and 1990s. However, the coal towns continued in the shadow cast by the mines and the historical legacy of that earlier history. In 1987, most of the 150 or so people I came to know expressed the significance of the mining history in their family histories. Many continued to have some kind of link either directly or through kin ties to the mining industry. Local employers and small-scale tourist operators arranged their schedules around the miners' holiday period, usually in July. As well, the annual calendar in the coal towns included a public holiday to commemorate miners in general and the death of William Davis in particular. Davis was killed by company police during a particularly unpleasant phase of the miners' strike of 1925.

By the late 1980s, the service sector had outpaced the industrial sector as a source of employment in the research community. The town's major employer was a nearby fish plant where up to 300 people worked in two shifts. There had been a dramatic decline in male wage labour earlier in the 1980s, mostly through a series of industrial closures, both deliberate (an ill-conceived heavy water plant) and accidental (a fish plant fire and a mine explosion). Approximately 2,300 people, mostly men, lost their jobs through these closures. Since then, seasonal and part-time jobs for women have increased in importance in local labour markets, representing a significant shift in gendered employment. During my stay the unemployment rate in the coal towns was officially hovering around 25 percent. This figure accounts only for the recently unemployed, those actively seeking work. Government officials willingly conceded that the unofficial rate of unemployment was likely to be much closer to 50 percent. During the late 1990s, some ten years after my first study, little had changed on the employment front and the troubled coal industry was creating deep anxieties, revealing the negative side of contradictory family and community relations. With 450 miners subjected to periodic layoffs because of technical difficulties at the Phalen colliery, leaving only the Prince mine in production, the communities remained desperate for viable economic solutions. Still they imagined their futures to include coal. One municipal politician, Gerard Burke of Glace Bay, was reported in the provincial newspaper in 1998 as saying: "Somebody has to get off their fanny and do something. With the amount of suicides, marriage breakups and vandalism, Glace Bay is starting to look like Tombstone—the town depicted in old western movies" (*Mail Star*, 22 January 1998).

Along with the steady erosion of job loss in the male industrial sectors, there has been an escalating crisis in the East Coast fishery to contend with. Although less historically significant to the regional economy than the mining and steel industries, there had been a viable inshore fishery sector until the northern cod crisis struck Atlantic fisheries in August of 1992. Prior to the crisis, which saw massive reductions in the amount of cod that could be caught legally, some fish caught by Cape Breton fishers was shipped off to external markets for sale, but much of the catch was processed in plants in towns such as North Sydney, Louisbourg, and Glace Bay (see Apostle and Barrett 1992). If nothing else, young people told me, they could always try to get a job in the local fish plants. This is no longer true and the problem of declining fish stock has spread from cod to other species.

Thus, by the 1990s Cape Breton's old industrial heartland reflected the global trend of a new gendered division of labour in production, where male unemployment is on the increase and lesser-paid female employment is on the rise. However, in Cape Breton female unemployment is also an ever-present possibility because of the frail economy and its connection to service sector jobs including those in the seasonal tourism industry and, most recently, telemarketing jobs in call centres. This sets the scene for new tensions in the gender division of labour in reproductive work at home, as alluded to by Councillor Burke above. Moreover, recent history and the struggle that was waged to maintain the coal industry, or least keep it operational until younger miners could earn sufficient pension credits, has yet again called forth a sense of self-reliance in the face of collective adversity and a cynicism about the effectiveness of government programmes. Well-learned historical lessons remain in force as people produce and reproduce core themes in local culture in a context of continuing economic uncertainty. Women's labour—whether it is deployed at home or at work, and regardless of how gender ideologies constitute what is properly "women's" and "men's work"—remains central to the "culture of making do."

For Cape Bretoners today, then, there continue to be contradictory faces to the meaning of "family" and "community." Historical processes have laid the cultural foundations for both *accommodation* (coping with the adverse conditions of political economy, relying upon support networks of kinship and patronage) and *resistance* (drawing upon these same loyalties to fight back). Here again, collective expressions of resistance to the demise of the coal industry became cleaved along gender and age lines. In an effort to fight mine closures, and later in the struggle to acquire pensions for all laid-off miners, some miners' wives organized themselves under the banner of "Miners' Families," later known as "Miners' Wives," and commenced lobbying government. Tenacity and courage took them to the offices of senior politicians in Halifax and Ottawa during 1998 and 1999. Their very public, heartfelt campaign incurred the disapproval of the miners' union, which maintained that it had the singular authority to bargain on behalf of the miners who were about to lose their jobs. "Miners' Wives" disagreed with the union position on pensions (only men 48 years old by December 31, 1998, were eligible for early retirement packages), arguing that all long-serving miners, including those in their 40s, deserved full pensions. One wife told her story to the *Cape Breton Post* in January 1999. She pointed out that because her 44-year-old husband (father to her three children) had worked underground for 22 years, his legs "were shot" and no one would want to hire him. Even as she expressed her dismay at the mine's closure and the sense of abandonment felt by families like hers, she also reiterated her community loyalty. She said: "All I know is my feet are planted firmly on the ground here [in Cape Breton]."

These political struggles over strategy and the power to negotiate the conditions of industrial exit for younger miners were extremely divisive in a particularly vulnerable moment in community history. They revealed how community and union loyalties disguise gendered interests and power, despite a common cause. Moreover, discourses of community history and loyalty as reported in the local and provincial media underscore my point about the importance of history and political economy in the articulation of a community identity founded upon notions of family and collectivity, even as such relations are contested. As with families, so too with class and community.

Culture, Identity, and Political Economy

The above discussion of the culture concept links local culture to the economy and material conditions in Cape Breton. I have emphasized how working-class culture reveals both the potential for expressions of collective militancy and a commitment to community, family, and one's kith and kin. This is a more specialized notion of local culture than the everyday use of the term in Canada, which equates people's culture with ethnic heritage—for example, the multi-cultural community groups and festivals that Heritage Canada supports. The "officially" produced version of culture is problematic to the degree that the superficial symbols of a cultural group may be displayed in the absence of any clarification of the political significance people concerned may attribute to those symbols. Experiences of historical colonial subjugation (in race and/or class terms), or of present-day racism, are thereby rendered invisible through "officially" sponsored representations of cultural heritage.

Where culture is equated with "ethnic heritage" and the history that is commemorated is selectively presented, representations of culture are subject to romantic distortion. This is true in Cape Breton when Scottish culture is presented as the primary heritage shared by all, despite historically different migration flows into the region. Celtic music, popular across Canada, furthers this distorted representation—proficiency in fiddle playing is much less common than national media reports would lead one to believe. There are other forms of identity and internal differences far greater than those between the Scottish, Irish, and English. Other differences and identities are passed over by a selective tradition that portrays Cape Breton culture as Scottish (now capitalized upon by the tourist industry). In my research, the relative ethnic homogeneity I encountered should not be grounds for assuming the absence of diversity, or of racism for that matter, in industrial Cape Breton. In Sydney, the community of Whitney Pier is well known now for ethnic diversity, and there is a small population of descendants of African-Canadians in the Sterling area of Glace Bay. Nonetheless, the working-class neighbourhoods I came to know, old company-type houses clustered around what were once functioning pit-heads, were represented to me as sharing ethnic homogeneity. Short of neighbourhood census taking I could not really confirm this, but my visual impression confirmed little visible ethnic diversity at the neighbourhood level.

In any event, any divisiveness arising out of competing ethnic loyalties among male wage earners in the earlier years of the development of the coal and steel industries, and later in the industrialized fish plants, was overcome through collective struggles to unionize for improved conditions of employment. The matter of gender consciousness is more complicated but is also subsumed under class and sometimes familial loyalties, a subject I return to in concluding the essay (see also Barber 1992b and 1992c).

My use of the concept *culture* arises out of recent research on the significance of culture in social anthropology in particular and cultural studies in general. As noted earlier, such approaches seek to take account of both structure and agency. This approach developed partly in reaction to perceptions of economic determinism in Marxist theories of social structure. Some critics of structural Marxism insist upon the possibility that people have a range of subjective components to their identities. They argue that it is misleading to group people solely in terms of broad social categories, such as those of class and gender, and assume from such groupings a common set of experiences. Most people experience competing loyalties depending upon their social position and how this shapes their interpretation of the social situations they encounter. Thus, a woman who is a wife of an unemployed miner in Cape Breton, where there remains a strong notion of masculinity associated in part with being a good provider for one's family, may be unwilling to support her union's stance on affirmative action for women, or indeed for people from minority backgrounds. Yet at other times and in other social spaces she may support employment rights for women and minorities.

Acknowledgment of people's subjectivity and contradictory loyalties, while important, can also be overstated. The vagaries of political economy in Cape Breton provide a common continuing frame of reference. Moreover, a structure and agency approach to culture recognizes that social forces beyond the local context are also important. For example, the political economy generates forces that constrain the ways in which local, regional, and national cultures are articulated in relations between people and over time and space. Parents of teenaged children in a two-earner family in Cape Breton may voice as their ideal future that their children will get married and "settle down" to life in Cape Breton. Yet unemployment rates in industrial Cape Breton remain the highest in the province, and many people are compelled by circumstances beyond their control to consider moving to some distant location in search of employment. Here we see that while different kinds of individual responses to this situation are possible, patterns and processes from the political economy render people both individually and collectively vulnerable. How they respond will in part depend upon shared cultural frameworks, as well as their access to information, social, and economic resources—again, mediated through culture. Culture in this sense is reproduced by people as they negotiate meaning with each other in daily interactions. To see culture as negotiated and constituted through people's actions and interpretations represents a theoretical and conceptual innovation. Here, we allow a role for historical political economy but we avoid the determinism that has flawed earlier predictive arguments in Marxist sociology. If political economy determined local culture, culture would be monolithic, not subject to variation and change, and not at all constituted in the actions of people in a particular time and place.

Culture, in the historical and material yet negotiated sense that I am proposing here, allows us to see how people's understanding of their lives, in daily activities and in a broader historical view, cannot be detached from political and economic processes. The example above reveals the role of the coal mining and steel industries in the development of industrial Cape Breton, a feature of political economy that contributes to some key aspects of local culture. As later examples will show, local culture is closely linked to people's shared sense of how to respond to particular events in community life. Thus, local culture is a form of collectively expressed identity, drawing a boundary between "us" and "them," be it articulated in terms that have a spatial element (although the meaning goes beyond the merely spatial) such as region, community, or neighbourhood, or in more explicitly social terms, such as ethnic group membership, an age-defined grouping, or in terms of class and gender.

GENDER IN "FAMILY" AND "HOUSEHOLD"

Household and *family*, two main concepts used in this study, are not interchangeable as they are in their common everyday sense. Rather, in sociology and anthropology, family and household refer to social units that can be quite different. Technically, the concept of household refers to a residential unit: people who live together. The term itself suggests nothing about the kinds of relationships the co-residents may have with each other. Co-residence need not imply family relationships, and family relationships need not imply co-residence. Although households in Cape Breton can contain complex and changing configurations of people, not all necessarily related to each other (for example, households with boarders), family is the more meaningful concept in people's lives. As the following discussion will reveal, in Cape Breton there is a fluidity to how people use the concept of family. What people mean by family depends very much on the context of use. Sometimes people mean their kin, people whom they recognize as related to them through descent and marriage. At other times, family means the people in a person's immediate residential family. The broader meaning of family, the one that appeals to wider ties of kinship, is a vital feature of Cape Breton working-class life. Kin ties for Cape Bretoners are acted upon often.

In general, then, Cape Bretoners place a high degree of importance upon family ties, and most will speak about family in a positive sense. Of course, as with many aspects of social life, a researcher such as myself, acutely aware of familial contradictions in my own immigrant background, has only to probe a little deeper beneath the surface expressions of familial loyalty and affection to uncover ambiguities and ambivalence in some aspects of family relations. Nonetheless, I propose that the contradictions surrounding the positive sense of family relations in industrial Cape Breton are less distinctive than the high value, both symbolic and practical, associated with family. The ideal (or perhaps ideology, in the sense of distorting the contradictory aspects in favour of the positive slant) is, I suggest, very much part of historically developed local culture.

A final piece of the puzzle of working-class culture in Cape Breton concerns gender. Culture, class, and community, the critical factors that shape family relations and household economy, are all structured and experienced by gender. For instance, gender is an organizing principle for work, whether such work is carried out in the context of family life or for wages. Later in the essay there are some examples of gendered livelihood practices in industrial Cape Breton.

Gender ideologies comprise a key element of the organization of livelihood practices and projections for the future. Men's and women's work in the domestic arena of family life and in the wage labour force are circumscribed by gender ideologies and systemic patterns of gender inequality that are related to local political economy and culture. Therefore, to understand patterns of change and resistance to change, we need to analyze the interrelationships between production and reproduction. This means considering (1) gender relations in labour markets and (2) the impact of gendered labour markets on the organization of family life in Canadian society. For too long family dynamics (reproductive relations in the social sense) were treated in isolation from the dynamics of wage work (or productive relations) and political and economic processes.

My research into gender and family dynamics indicates that Cape Bretoners live in a variety of different family structures reflecting the same types of demographic features that characterize families in Canada today (see Eichler 1988). However, in industrial Cape Breton, people's views about families and the gendered division of labour, and their familial and gender ideologies (views and practices that mask and distort the nature of these social relations) have not significantly altered to keep abreast of the decline in male employment and the increased reliance on women's wage labour. As noted earlier, people remain committed to ideals of family and local community as contexts that provide social and economic support in times of need or hardship. Because of gender ideologies prescribing this kind of clear-cut gendered division of labour where men are the ideal main breadwinners, it is often the work of women, more so than men, that maintains the emotional and social networks of kin and community so critical in providing access to necessary resources. It is also women who contribute the additional labour required to extend the limited cash resources of working-class households, which the women themselves spoke of as "stretching the dollar to make ends meet."

Some of the patterns of gendered work and class culture revealed in my research are also present in comparative studies of working-class households outside of Canada. For example, Lydia Morris reviewed many studies of gendered work in households in the postwar period both in the United Kingdom and in the United States. Morris's comparative study confirms that class and locality, or regional political economy, are indeed critical factors in the organization of household resources. Her general conclusions about shifts in the shape of production and reproduction are strikingly similar to my own for Cape Breton. Morris (1990) states that in situations where there has been an increase in male unemployment and an increase in female employment,

> the evidence for both Britain and America indicates an absence of any significant change in established gender roles. Women do not, in significant numbers, take over from their unemployed husbands to become sole earners; unemployed men do not assume the house-wife role; and married women's employment does not prompt a significant rise in domestic involvement on the part of husbands. (189)

Particularly relevant is Morris's conclusion that gender ideologies are generally resistant to change, even in the face of disruptions to the gendered pattern of livelihood associated with male loss of employment in traditional industrial sectors such as steel and coal. Morris's comparative data concerning the gendered division of labour in non-wage work performed on behalf of other members of the household reveal that the appropriate question is not whether men are increasing their contributions to domestic labour. Rather, her discussion suggests, the issue is one of women's labour being reduced only when their wages are sufficiently high to allow them to purchase goods and services to replace some of their domestic labour. This process is called the *commoditization of domestic labour*. Morris proposes that where and when women's wages permit, usually when women work in professional occupations, they are likely to purchase childcare and housekeeping services. The situation in Cape Breton reflected rather more the opposite of the commoditization of household goods and services found in British and U.S. middle-class households. Women's household labour and their management of household resources involved extensive commitments of time and labour, which were less likely to take them to the market for the purchase of household goods and services and more likely to represent fluctuating levels of consumption: de-commoditization.

Not only were women in Cape Breton households more likely to expand their own labour rather than purchase things to "cut corners," people in the study were also extremely cautious about debt. Few households were carrying debts such as personal loans and mortgages, and most shied away from using credit cards. Only two households had made recent major purchases with credit cards—the purchase of household appliances through a Sears account, planned on the basis of the wives' seasonal income from a food processing plant. Instead, most women made use of lay-away schemes in local stores, or they made major purchases with extra non-wage cash payments to the household such as family allowance cheques or the child tax credit. The majority of households did not have two reliable wage incomes; nor were any significant savings being accumulated by individual family members. Most cash arriving in the household was spent on groceries, rent, utilities, clothing, and things required by children. In several households there were disagreements about the costs of entertainment, particularly cash for men to spend on beer on the weekends. I was told by the women that they resented this expense but they tolerated the beer budget as long as cash was coming into the household. The women themselves desired more cash to spend on clothes and personal items, but their purchases would depend upon their fluctuating weekly paycheques. I was told, "The basics come first, then the children."

Turning now to a closer view of the gendered division of labour in households in industrial Cape Breton, we find Lydia Morris's research again quite helpful. In both contexts new pressures occur in production and reproduction as men's and women's labour-market participation shifts. Were there any signs of change in people's ideas about the new patterns of work, or are the gender ideologies of male blue-collar employment still pervasive? Here again, Morris's research reveals the same pattern that I found in Cape Breton. In short, there is little change in the gendered domestic work patterns, nor in the ideologies that support them. Working-class gender ideologies that portray the male as the head of household and the breadwinner, and maintain that domestic labour is primarily women's work, still hold sway. The ideologies and social practices are resilient, even in the face of the high rates of male unemployment and female employment. Here is what Morris (1990) says:

> In the particular case of male unemployment there is little evidence of any renegotiation of gender roles in either the US or the UK, but rather both countries show a male defensiveness against any challenge to their traditional gender identity. This reaction is not confined to the men alone, however, and whilst there is some sign of flexibility regarding participation in domestic tasks, the woman's conventional load remains largely intact. One effect of the woman's traditional role is that she carries the main burden of budgeting, which often involves struggling not only to meet the collective needs of the household but also to control her husband's personal spending requirements. (190–91)

This is very familiar to me from my Cape Breton examples.

There have been few contemporary studies of working-class gendered work practices in Canada. Meg Luxton's (1980) earlier research on three generations of women's work and family experiences in Flin Flon, Manitoba, provides a useful comparison with Cape Breton. There are similar patterns in the gendered divisions of labour. Also relevant is the research on gender and class patterns in fishing-dependent households in Nova Scotia by Martha MacDonald and Patricia Connelly (1989) and Connelly and MacDonald (1983). None of these studies report men contributing significantly to domestic labour, nor women's work being accorded much social and economic value. One further more recent Canadian study of ideas about gender and work among Hamilton steelworkers, male and female, by Meg Luxton with David Livingstone, presents a more complex picture. Livingstone and Luxton's (1989) research reveals that gendered ideologies are being renegotiated as women enter industrial sectors like the auto industry. Nonetheless, older patterns persist and many men resist change in gendered work patterns in the workplace and at home. Ideologies about domestic labour as women's work, it would seem, are very hard to shift in working-class cultures. In this, then, Cape Breton is not unique. Again, while I found little evidence of changing expectations of the gendered division of labour, there was a great deal of evidence for resistance to change; both men and women viewed domestic labour as primarily women's work. And while women saw their wage labour as critical for the economic resources of the household budget, men and women considered a man's main contribution to the household workload to lie in the breadwinner role. Male job loss is a real threat to a man's identity from a male perspective. From a wife's point of view, a husband losing his job means more worries because of the loss of cash income. Women have to be even more creative in their work of "stretching the dollar to put bread on the table."

Moreover, the necessity of "making ends meet" and "getting by" through skillful manipulation of the available material and social resources so dominates women's orientation to family life and to waged work that what are, in effect, discussions of their economic strategies comprised the major foci of daily life for the women I met. These discussions were about such things as what items were on sale in local grocery stores, how much money to set aside for gifts for family members or workmates, how to get hold of some new curtains in exchange for left-over household paint supplies, who knows someone who needs a boarder for the spare room, whether there are any cheap supplies of coal. Such planning and questions were central in daily conversations with kin, neighbours, and co-workers. It is the centrality of these practices in daily life, plus the intense sociability that accompanies these efforts to locate necessary goods and services outside of the cash economy, that distinguishes local culture as "the culture of making do." Older studies, less mindful of gender, might associate these kinds of cultural practices with a moribund coal mining culture's adaptation to economic uncertainty. While this is certainly the case, my characterization of the "culture of making do" allows for the inclusion of gender in culture. It also highlights the role of women's contributions to the household economy and to the maintenance of close-knit ties based upon kinship and community. My research also points to the linkages between the formal economy and so-called informal economic activities, as outlined in the next section.

In this Cape Breton study, targeting production and reproduction and placing *household dynamics* as the link between political economy and labour markets on the one hand, and workplace and domestic relations on the other, proved very worthwhile. Gender and family relations permeate all arenas of daily life. For example, ideologies of family commitments and gender, which I observed in family and household contexts, were also carried over into the organization of workplace relations and class politics. This finding confirmed the significance of feminist arguments about the need to address production and social reproduction in a coherent, continuous, and consistent framework. Gendered family practices are relevant to issues of class and consciousness as well. Women workers do not stop thinking about their domestic responsibilities and their obligations to kin when they don their plant uniform or participate in union meetings. In fact, because of how these relationships are constructed in Cape Breton, women workers are quite likely to bring family concerns to union meetings.

HOUSEHOLDS, WORK, AND LIVELIHOOD: THE CULTURAL REPRODUCTION OF "MAKING DO"

> Livelihood is never just a matter of finding or making shelter, transacting money, and preparing food to put on the table or exchange in the market place. It is equally a matter of the ownership and circulation of information, the management of relationships, the affirmation of personal significance and group identity, and the interrelation of each of those tasks to the other. All these productive tasks together constitute the work of livelihood. A similarly expanded concept of work is implicit in studies of unenumerated economic organization or the informal sector. (Wallman 1984, 22)

Wallman's characterization of **livelihood** provides a useful umbrella for reflecting on household and family dynamics in industrial Cape Breton. As has been noted above, the routines of daily life allow people ample scope to apply themselves to the work of livelihood as they maintain networks of kinship and friendship for social and economic purposes. Some examples are holding benefits and celebrations, arranging housing, and operating in the informal economy.

The Benefit Dance and Life-Cycle Celebrations

Benefits serve the dual purpose of socializing and fundraising. An individual or a family with a legitimate requirement for extra cash could host a dance in a neighbourhood hall, raising money through a door fee, the sale of refreshments, and perhaps donations that people would provide for the night's entertainment. One benefit I heard about involved a mother, a miner's widow, who required additional cash for the trip to Halifax for specialized medical services for her child. In another case, a benefit was planned to assist a couple whose teenaged son had died in a tragic accident. The people attending benefits would often know the sponsor of the benefit, but the raising of funds in this manner went beyond personal ties. Empathy brought in contributions from people not known personally to sponsors. There appeared to be no social stigma attached to the staging of a benefit. Indeed, people were sympathetic to economic hardship, expecting that if they should require community support, it would be forthcoming for them also.

Similarly, occasions such as weddings, anniversaries, births, and children's educational progress were all opportunities for family, friends, and co-workers to contribute gifts and cash to the persons being honoured. The exchanges were modest in the case of co-workers, but some presents to and from kin were quite generous, involving considerable planning and saving on the part of the donor. In the case of engagements and bridal and baby showers, co-workers might invite each other to the shower they were arranging for a friend, even if the friend was not known to the co-workers. In such cases, it was appropriate to provide an excuse along with a card plus a small cash contribution. Often the gift exchanges would take place in the context of some kind of party, which would require considerable planning and a round of further donations of food and supplies. Such occasions involved people in an extensive series of reciprocal obligations that allowed for the redistribution of resources and the cementing of social ties, both of which facilitated access to further resources in the short and longer term for all the participants.

Households

Housing is a major resource in the economic strategies of Cape Breton families. During my study in 1987 people moved between households giving and receiving aid in response to changes in their own or others' circumstances. Few households in the study remained stable throughout the research period. Residence patterns also emphasized the protracted dependency of children upon their parents for shelter and for other resources. Adult children in their middle years could request to return to a parental home. Other kin also participated in shared residence arrangements. The ruling principle in such arrangements appeared to be that people contributed what they could afford to the budget of the household where they resided. The transactions were couched in terms of "helping out" those who become tenants rather than providing economic benefit from the extra cash income for the owners of the house. "Taking care of one's own" was a key element in local culture. Clearly, there may well be some mutual benefits accorded by helping kin solve their accommodation problems.

Examples from my field notes included the following:

- A woman, separating from her common-law partner, collected her two children and moved in with her widowed mother. The grandmother then provided childcare to the youngest of the two children while the mother worked and the elder child was at school. Another female relative, a niece, also received childcare from the older woman. Modest amounts of cash were exchanged for childcare services and there were contributions to the household budget on a "pay what you can afford" basis.

- A single parent with a toddler moved out of her parents' house and in with her aunt and her aunt's husband. The two women worked together in a local store, and while the aunt had no children of her own she was prepared to provide some childcare to her niece when time permitted. These arrangements were described to me as "helping each other out."

- A newly married couple took up residence in the basement of the groom's parents' house. The groom's two elder brothers had also started their married life in this accommodation. All parties viewed this arrangement as temporary but all appreciated that economic conditions might protract the arrangements far longer than the initially projected "couple of years." The arrangement was explicitly stated to be a means to provide the young couple with an opportunity to save money for a "good start" to married life.

- One couple in their mid-40s lived in a very complex family nexus. The wife's father lived with them along with one male boarder, one teenaged daughter still in school, and one out-of-work son in his 20s who had just returned home after failing to find work in Halifax that would pay sufficiently to allow him to meet his expenses and save money. The parents were predicting that a second son who had just moved to Halifax with his girlfriend would also be forced to return home because of his meagre earnings. Upon their return, the young couple might live with them also.

- An adult daughter lived with and supported her aged parents.

- An employed man and his wife and their three young children moved out of their apartment and in with the husband's parents. This couple planned to purchase a house rather than seek alternative rental accommodation.

- A retired man and his wife were raising a teenaged granddaughter without receiving any financial support from the girl's family or the "authorities."

The Informal Economy

The concept of the *informal sector* has been criticized because it suggests that there are two unrelated economic sectors, the informal one being somehow separated from the formal, officially regulated economy where goods and services are produced and consumed, and taxes are collected, all according to government regulations (see Redclift and Mingione 1985, and especially Redclift 1985). Clearly, as British sociologist R.E. Pahl (1984, 1985) has demonstrated, there are direct linkages between all forms of work, inside and outside the official marketplace. It is for this reason that Pahl suggests household work strategies, rather than the informal sector, as the most appropriate unit to study. Similarly, feminist scholars, at pains to identify the extensive forms of work that women contribute to their households and broader political and economic processes, have criticized the treatment of formal and informal sectors as discrete entities (for Canada, see Belinda Leach's work [1993], and for the global political economy, see Kathryn Ward [1990]). I use the concept *informal-sector work* in a provisional way and I emphasize how formal and informal practices can coincide, intersect, and overlap.

Processes of informal economy in industrial Cape Breton can best be described as two-tiered. For working-class people, informal exchanges often took place without cash payments, or with modest payments that allowed the service provider to be a service receiver (for example, in the case of women paying each other for hairdressing services). Middle-class people, on the other hand, could purchase the services of skilled tradespeople who (certainly in 1987 at least) operated in the informal sector, sometimes in combination with their formal-sector employment (see Spencer 1988). The lesser cost of having work done through informal arrangements suited the buyer, and tradespeople benefited from lower overheads and non-payment of taxes, unemployment insurance contributions, benefits, and so on. Alternatively, informal-sector workers could not receive state-regulated benefits such as unemployment insurance, pension credits, workers' compensation, and other health and safety programs. Nonetheless, local experts (including Spencer 1988) claimed that the informal sector in skilled trades was substantial, a form of shadow economy that some workers stuck to by choice because it offered greater economic security than their formal-sector commitments. In other words, despite the lack of regulation and benefits, the shadow informal sector in Cape Breton appeared to be in competition with formal-sector goods and services. This would be in accord with conventions of local culture that I observed, a reliance on kinship and neighbourhood networks, and, in terms of job searches, upon patronage networks of kin and community. Such networks have historical resonance and are deeply rooted; they allow pragmatic approaches to economic and social needs when the market and cash nexus are less predictable.

Class and Gender Revisited: Patterns of Informal Exchange

Most of the households in my sample were working class. In this class context, when the skills of one's kin, co-workers, and neighbours were appropriate for the job, it was customary to request aid without a direct cash payment taking place. For example, in one neighbourhood, a man who had a reputation for being "good with his hands" was called upon by his neighbours to do small plumbing and carpentry repairs. In return, he would be given some money for gas for his truck and sometimes some baked goods. Men tended to help one another out trading skills for household repairs, but it was the realm of car repairs that seemed to claim most of their attention. Knowledge about car repairs and working on cars was a great source of male pride, and I encountered several families with older-model cars containing rebuilt engines. Through trading knowledge and skills, the expenses associated with owning and operating cars were minimized. Again, working together on their cars also served to maintain male networks, as well as to produce and reproduce the cultural context of masculinity. Historically, coal mining has provided the basis for a strong masculine identity and pride associated with the nature of working "underground" (a concept now familiar to Canadians generally through the songs of Cape Breton singer Rita MacNeil). This history may well have shaped the cultural framework and influenced contemporary forms of resistance by men and women to men's domestic labour contributions (see also Yarrow 1991).

Women's activities were much more continuous with their everyday domestic labour and called for a more diverse range of skills; as noted earlier, women's work is critical to livelihood practices and "stretching the dollar to make ends meet." In addition to the domestic work women performed on behalf of their households, women's skills were also applied to informal-sector activities such as home decorating, sewing, cooking and catering, childcare, hairdressing, and major annual house-cleaning projects. Indeed, all of these activities are so well integrated into everyday domestic routines that few women were forthcoming about the range of work activities they performed on behalf of others and about the benefits they contributed to the resources of their households from their skills. Activities such as making new curtains and interior house painting were most likely to involve straight exchanges of labour—for example, between mothers and daughters, or between sisters. Catering, on the other hand, was more likely to draw in labour resources from a wider pool of contributors. Women's catering skills are a source of identity and pride for individual women, and a particularly capable cook could earn a modest cash return for catering larger gatherings upon request. More often than not, however, women's contributions of prepared food were made on the basis of reciprocal understandings of giving and receiving in times of need.

CONCLUSIONS

This case study of household economy in Cape Breton has emphasized how particular features of family and community life, including a broad range of informal economic practices, combined with conservative attitudes toward spending and saving resulted in a distinctive set of gendered cultural practices that have been produced and socially reproduced through the household economy. One result of longer-term economic insecurity has been the development of close-knit communities and delicately balanced economic and social interdependencies. It is ironic that regional development strategies oriented during the 1970s and 1980s to large-scale capital projects and more recently to entrepreneurial activities continue to be controversial. Many working-class Cape Bretoners, particularly those with ties to the old industrial sectors, maintain their commitment to the package of livelihood strategies briefly sketched above. Education is often held out as the means to economic prosperity but this is troublesome if it means young people will have to leave home to compete in external job markets. Job retraining—for example, for miners—is also viewed with suspicion, particularly where entrepreneurial activities or service sector jobs are targeted. As I was told on many occasions, what people want is "real jobs," not seasonal, part-time, or low-wage jobs in economically precarious small businesses.

As is the case elsewhere in Canada, women in Cape Breton have urgent need of services for the unique set of problems they experience all too often in the routines of daily life: sexual harassment in the workplace, battering and abuse in the family, and sexual and economic violence in their communities. The most brutalizing aspect of familial ideologies in close-knit communities is that such ideologies can obscure the forms of violence women are subjected to and must face alone in the absence of support from community-based services. Women also need assistance in improving their employment readiness through employment training, counselling, educational upgrading, and other such programs that might assist them to compensate for the disadvantages they face in sex-typed labour markets. Without such support services, women will live their lives and raise their children within households and family processes that perpetuate rather than resolve inequalities of gender and class. Within the commitment to family processes and community in Cape Breton communities there are contradictory tensions; the positive aspects involve families collaborating in their livelihood practices. By the same token, class and gendered forms of control and inequality can be masked through the familial orientation. Here, as in many other parts of the world and in many other social and ethnic niches in Canadian society, policy interventions with and on behalf of women will flounder, if not backfire, if they are not respectful of the social, cultural, economic, and personal significance of families to women's lives.

NOTE

1   The research discussed in this paper was first completed in fulfilment of the requirements for my doctoral dissertation in the Department of Anthropology at the University of Toronto. An earlier version of the second part of this paper was prepared as a discussion paper, "Household Economy and Family Work Patterns in Cape Breton," funded by the Demographic Review Secretariat's Family Research Programme, Health and Welfare Canada, 1991. The essay was revised in 2002.

KEY TERMS

Agency: How people respond to structural conditions that shape their lives. Responses might include relying on kin, family, and community networks, out-migration, political militancy, political expediency, resignation, and/or resistance.

Household: Refers to a residential unit of people who live together. They may or may not be related by ties of kinship. Families and households are not necessarily the same kind of social units.

Livelihood: The full range of work and social practices that people engage in to sustain themselves and their families in a given context. Livelihood is thus a broad term that includes but goes beyond wage work, domestic labour, and the buying, selling, and bartering of skills, goods, and services in formal and informal markets. It includes how various combinations of these sustaining activities are bundled together and accorded meaning in a particular context.

Production: The producing of goods and services for wages and/or exchange in formal and informal markets where a value is assigned to those goods and services, and, in the case of formal markets, where a value is assigned to productive labour resulting in wages.

Social reproduction: The different kinds of domestic labour undertaken, usually by women, on behalf of their families. Sometimes reduced to a biological function, social reproduction is best thought of as containing three related forms of socially necessary work: (1) the feeding of people on a daily basis, technically the reproduction of labour; (2) the bearing and nurturing of children, technically the reproduction of the labour force; and (3) the socialization of children to appropriate social values, technically the reproduction of the social system.

Structure: How relations based on social class, gender, and ethnicity intersect and are organized in a particular context. For example, structure takes account of labour markets, the sectors within which people are employed, how much they earn, who the unemployed and the underemployed are, and how these people support themselves.

DISCUSSION QUESTIONS

1. How does the "culture of making do" in Cape Breton compare with working-class culture in other parts of Canada? Select a familiar community and identify both the points of similarity and the differences. In exploring this question it will prove helpful to first identify some of the key features of working-class culture in Cape Breton.
2. Why does the author suggest that the "culture of making do" is a gendered characterization of culture?
3. Informal-sector work provides access to many goods and services in Cape Breton. What is meant by informal-sector work, and how are women and men involved in these activities? What might happen if the government sought to collect taxes from informal-sector activities? Should it?
4. What are some of the contradictory aspects of family life in Cape Breton for women, for men, and for youth?
5. Why is out-migration unlikely to provide a good solution to the current high rates of unemployment among Cape Bretoners?
6. In what sense is Cape Breton culture ideological? Do you think Cape Breton culture provides an alternative set of values about what is important in life, in contrast to the consumption-oriented lifestyles portrayed on television family sitcoms?
7. What have you learned about gender and work from reading this article? Do you think it is fair that women's work is never-ending? What are some of the ways in which future generations of working-class Canadians might reorganize their family divisions of labour to allow for greater balance between women's and men's contributions to family and wage work?

REFERENCES

Apostle, Richard, and Gene Barrett, eds. 1992. *Emptying Their Nets: Small Capital and Rural Industrialization in the Nova Scotia Fishing Industry*. Toronto: University of Toronto Press.

Barber, Pauline T. Gardiner. 1992a. "Household and Workplace Strategies in 'Northfield.'" In R. Apostle and G. Barrett, eds., *Emptying Their Nets: Small Capital and Rural Industrialization in the Nova Scotia Fishing Industry*. Toronto: University of Toronto Press.

———. 1992b. "Working through the Crisis: Resistance and Resignation in the Culture of a Deindustrialized Community." In J. Calagione, D. Francis, and D. Nugent, eds., *Worker's Expressions: Beyond Accommodation and Resistance*. Albany, NY: SUNY Press.

———. 1992c. "Conflicting Loyalties: Gender, Class and Equity Politics in Working Class Culture." *Canadian Woman Studies 12*(3): 80–85.

———. 2002. "Militant Particularism and Cultural Struggles as Cape Breton Burns Again." In W. Lem and B. Leach, eds., *Culture Economy Power: Anthropology as Critique, Anthropology as Praxis*. Albany, NY: SUNY Press.

Connelly, M. Patricia, and Martha MacDonald. 1983. "Women's Work: Domestic and Wage Labour in a Nova Scotia Community." *Studies in Political Economy* 1(10): 45–72.

Eichler, Margrit. 1988. *Families in Canada Today: Recent Changes and Their Policy Consequences.* Toronto: Gage.

Frank, David. 1976. "Class Conflict in the Coal Industry: Cape Breton 1922." In Gregory S. Kealey and Peter Warrian, eds., *Essays in Canadian Working Class History.* Toronto: McClelland & Stewart.

———. 1979. "The Cape Breton Coal Miners 1917–1929." Unpublished Ph.D. dissertation, Dalhousie University, Halifax.

———. 1980. "The Cape Breton Coal Industry and the Rise and Fall of the British Empire Steel Corporation." In Don Macgillivray and Brian Tennyson, eds., *Cape Breton Historical Essays.* Sydney, NS: University College of Cape Breton Press.

Leach, Belinda. 1993. "Flexible Work: Precarious Future." *Canadian Review of Anthropology and Sociology* 30(1).

Livingstone, D.W., and Meg Luxton. 1989. "Gender Consciousness at Work: Modification of the Male Breadwinner Norm among Steelworkers and Their Spouses." *Canadian Review of Sociology and Anthropology* 26(2): 240–75.

Luxton, Meg. 1980. *More Than a Labour of Love: Three Generations of Women's Work in the Home.* Toronto: The Women's Press.

MacDonald, Martha, and M. Patricia Connelly. 1989. "Class and Gender in Fishing Communities in Nova Scotia." *Studies in Political Economy* 30: 61–85.

Macgillivray, Don. 1973. "Cape Breton in the 1920s: A Community Besieged." In Brian Tennyson, ed., *Essays in Cape Breton History.* Windsor, NS: Lancelot Press.

———. 1974. "Military Aid to the Civil Power: The Cape Breton Experience in the 1920s." *Acadiensis* 3(2): 45–64.

Morris, Lydia D. 1990. *The Workings of the Household: A US–UK Comparison.* Cambridge: Polity Press.

Muise, Del. 1980. "The Making of an Industrial Community: Cape Breton Coal Towns 1867–1900." In Don Macgillivray and Brian Tennyson, eds., *Cape Breton Historical Essays.* Sydney, NS: University College of Cape Breton Press.

Pahl, R.E. 1984. *Divisions of Labour.* Oxford: Basil Blackwell.

———. 1985. "The Restructuring of Capital, the Local Political Economy and Household Work Strategies." In Derek Gregory and John Urry, eds., *Social Relations and Spatial Structures.* Basingstoke: Macmillan.

Redclift, Nanneke. 1985. "The Contested Domain: Gender, Accumulation and the Labour Process." In Nanneke Redclift and Enzo Mingione, eds., *Beyond Employment: Household, Gender and Subsistence.* Oxford: Basil Blackwell.

Redclift, Nanneke, and Enzo Mingione, eds. 1985. *Beyond Employment: Household, Gender and Subsistence.* Oxford: Basil Blackwell.

Spencer, Gerald. 1988. "Informal Economic Practice as Workers' Self Activity: A Case Study in an Underdeveloped Community." Paper presented to the Atlantic Association of Sociologists and Anthropologists, Saint Mary's University, Halifax.

Wallman, Sandra. 1984. *Eight London Households.* London: Tavistock.

Ward, Kathryn, ed. 1990. *Women Workers and Global Restructuring.* Ithaca: ILR Press, Cornell University.

Yarrow, Michael. 1991. "The Gender-Specific Class Consciousness of Appalachian Coal Miners: Structure and Change." In *Bringing Class Back In: Contemporary and Historical Perspectives.* Boulder, CO: Westview Press.

PART III

Emerging Issues

Part III of this text presents the findings from two studies that can be considered as indications of emerging issues in research on Canadian families, hearing the voices of family members as they reflect upon their experiences. Both of these studies contribute a refreshing change in family analysis, as they speak from the voices of adolescents.

Ellen Gee and Barbara Mitchell point out what in fact is more of a change than continuity in family households, in looking at the emergence of multi-generational households in Canada. Their research takes place in the Vancouver area and draws upon the experiences of Canadians from a variety of national and cultural backgrounds to explore these family households, which have increased by nearly 40 percent between 1986 and 1996. The impact of increased numbers of Asians and South Asians on this growth of multigenerational households is noted.

Gee and Mitchell point out a number of salient features of these family households. First of all, they are not fixed, but fluid as people move into and out of households as needs, obligations, and opportunities arise. Secondly, they are diverse in terms of who shares housing with whom; in some cases three grandparents are in the household, and in others a widowed daughter-in-law and her child live with her in-laws. Some follow the maternal line and others the paternal line; some live together because of the increase in divorce. They differ as well as to which generation is the homeowner, or host, and which is the guest, or co-resident.

As Susan McDaniel points out in her essay on the impact of aging on families, life course is a necessary point of analysis in determining why these types of family households emerge at certain times. And people do not age in a vacuum, but within particular economic, political, and cultural contexts. Health, employability, and opportunities for family immigration have an impact on when families decide to merge their living quarters. Exchange of instrumental and social-emotional services are important in these families. The role of women as caregivers emerges across various ethnocultural differences. Young

NEL   289 people in these families indicate a fresh breath of support, insight, and appreciation for older family members.

Freshness emerges as well from the recent research of Vappu Tyyskä, whose chapter provides the second one in this section and the final one in the text. As Gee and Mitchell locate their research on Canada's west coast, in urban Vancouver, Tyyskä draws upon the rich cultural diversity of central Canada, in Toronto, to look at a seldom studied group: Iranian Canadians. Again, the voices of adolescents describing their family dynamics provide insight seldom seen in sociological studies of families, especially those of adolescents of a fairly recent ethnocultural community in Canada.

Like Gee and Mitchell, Tyyskä emphasizes the fluidity of family relations, perhaps especially among those who have migrated halfway across the world to form their families in a cultural context very different from the one they left. Like other essays in this text, this research also shows single-parent families, families in which the women play a very strong economic role, and families in which the children have a decided impact on family interactions and have a sense of both their responsibilities and their entitlements.

Unlike other studies of intergenerational interaction, Tyyskä does not emphasize conflict but instead focuses upon intergenerational, functional, and consensual solidarity as the central dynamic of these families. She also emphasizes the importance of agency and subjectivity, demonstrating that young people play a central role in families, both instrumentally and social-emotionally. As their parents advise them on important issues such as education and moral choices, they advise their parents on where to live, what to buy, and learning the English language.

Outside of our grounding in the rich culture of First Nations peoples, Canada is a country of immigrants, and a nation in which cultural heritage and memories play an important role, both at the community and national levels. Immigration stories indicate that many people come to Canada to provide a better life for their children, in some cases at substantial sacrifice to their own work and status. The adolescents in Tyyskä's study indicate an appreciation of this pattern. They understand that their education and concentration on doing well are important for the entire family. They understand, as well, that they have both opportunities and many freedoms in Canada that they would not have had in Iran. This is particularly the case with young women. As Tyyskä illustrates in this important piece of research, the complexities of intergenerational family dynamics are framed by these goals on the part of both generations in the family.

13

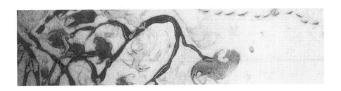

One Roof: Exploring Multi-Generational Households in Canada[1]

Ellen M. Gee and Barbara A. Mitchell

Department of Sociology and Anthropology
Simon Fraser University

Objectives

- To provide an examination of multi-generational households in Canada—a type of family living that has received little research attention.

- To present the voices of persons living in multi-generational households in the Vancouver area, with a focus on Canadians of European, Chinese, and Indian ethnic origins.

- To describe the diversity and fluidity of Canadian multi-generational households.

- To examine financial exchanges across generations in multi-generational households and assess the role of financial hardship in their formation.

- To examine patterns of instrumental assistance and emotional support across generations.

- To discuss patterns of intergenerational conflict and assess the *generational stake hypothesis* with our data.

INTRODUCTION

Most Canadians throughout history have lived in family units consisting of parent(s) and dependent children—that is, in nuclear families. Despite myths about large, extended households in bygone times, demographic realities—particularly high mortality and short life expectancy—meant that three generations were not likely to be alive at the same time. Also, Western-origin families have a traditional cultural ideal of family nuclearity. As life expectancy increased dramatically over the course of the 20th century, making multi-generational living feasible, Canadian families did not opt to live in **multi-generational households** in large numbers. Indeed, one of the major changes in family life in Canada, especially in the latter half of the 20th century, has been a large increase in older women, largely widows, living alone (Gee 1995)—a trend shared by all Western industrialized countries (Wolf 1995). Of course, most Canadians have **multi-generational families,** but they are not typically co-resident units. It is sometimes said that people in societies like ours prefer *intimacy at a distance*; we want to interact with our relatives, but we do not want to live with them (spouse and dependent children excluded).

In part because of their relative rarity, there is little statistical information on multi-generational households in Canada. However, 1996 Canadian census data reveal 208,000 Canadian families in which three generations are living "under one roof" (Che-Alford and Hamm 2000). This translates into approximately three-quarters of a million Canadians living in a three-generational arrangement. Especially noteworthy, however, is that three-generational households in Canada *increased by nearly 40 percent* over the period 1986–96 (Che-Alford and Hamm 2000). This increase has been attributed, at least in part, to increasing immigration of persons from Asia; most Asian cultures stress kin relationships and favour multi-generational living arrangements.

The composition of three-generational households in Canada in 1996 is as follows (Che-Alford and Hamm 2000)[2]:

- 1 grandparent, 2 parents: 31 percent
- 2 grandparents, 2 parents: 21 percent
- 1 grandparent, 1 parent: 24 percent
- 2 grandparents, 1 parent: 24 percent

Thus, multi-generational households in Canada take diverse forms. It is noteworthy that nearly one-half of these households contain one parent (in the middle generation) only; this suggests that divorce may be a factor leading to the formation of multi-generational living arrangements.

This chapter provides an in-depth exploration of 15 multi-generational households. We cannot claim that these households are representative of all multi-generational units. However, they form a starting point for an understanding of the ways in which multi-generational households form and function. Our goal is to provide some initial insights into the characteristics and interactive context of a type of household that has rarely been studied in Canada.[3] In so doing, we foreground the voices of the people who live multi-generationally, believing that their words provide the strongest evidence on the experience of living in a multi-generational household.

METHODS

The data for this chapter are from semi-structured interviews with two members (dyads) of 15 families living multi-generationally in the Vancouver area.[4] These in-depth interviews constitute supplementary research to a major study entitled Culture and Co-residence. In the main study, a random sample of 1,907 young adults aged 19–35 from four ethnocultural groups (British, Southern European, Chinese, and [East] Indian) residing in the Greater Vancouver area were interviewed by telephone on aspects of their home leaving (and home returning) behaviour, current living arrangements, and intergenerational relationships. We had hoped to draw upon these young adults (and their family members) to form a subsample for a more in-depth analysis of multi-generational living. This was not successful, in part because of the complexities of getting two family members to agree to be interviewed and in part because of the time lag between the telephone interviews and the in-depth interviews. In the end, we used snowball sampling to obtain the 15 families (and 30 individuals) for this exploration on multi-generational living. The criteria for inclusion in this supplementary study were that one of the family members had to be aged 19 to 35 (for comparability with the main study); the family had to fit into one of the four ethnocultural groups noted above; and both members of the interviewed dyad had to be living in a household containing at least three generations.

The interviews took place in respondents' homes between autumn 2000 and autumn 2001, with each person providing informed consent and being promised confidentiality. Each interview was conducted privately; that is, no other family members were present. The interviews lasted one hour and ten minutes on average. Twelve of the interviews were conducted in the respondent's home language—one of the adult children (Chinese-Canadian) and all of the older-generation persons of Chinese and Indian origins preferred to be interviewed in their native language; indeed, many were not fluent in English. In the Indo-Canadian case, all interviews were conducted in the Punjabi language (all of the Indo-Canadian families identified as being Punjabi Sikh); for the Chinese-Canadians, interviews were conducted in either Cantonese or Mandarin. With permission, all interviews were tape-recorded and later transcribed verbatim. Persons fluent in English and the other language translated the non-English transcriptions into English. Our ability to "tap into" the experiences of non–official language speakers adds an important dimension to this research, capturing the voices of persons typically excluded from Canadian research findings.

The ages of the dyad members, their family relationships to one another, and their ethnocultural origins are presented in Table 13.1. As shown, the majority of family members interviewed were parent–child dyads (daughter and mother, son and mother, son

Table 13.1: Characteristics of Sample

Dyad (and ages)	Ethnic Origin
granddaughter (27) and grandmother (75)	Irish
granddaughter (22) and grandmother (71)	Chinese
granddaughter (21) and grandmother (67)	Indian
daughter (22) and mother (47)	Greek
daughter (25) and mother (55)	Greek
daughter (35) and mother (late 50s)	Chinese
daughter (22) and mother (60)	Indian
daughter (34) and mother-in-law (56)	Indian
son (21) and mother (60)	Greek/Italian
son (22) and mother (46)	Chinese
son (22) and mother (47)	Chinese
son (21) and mother (47)	Indian
son (24) and mother (51)	Indian
son 30) and mother (late 50s)	Indian
son (22) and father (51)	Chinese

and father [one case only]). However, three granddaughter–grandmother pairs were interviewed, as well as one daughter and mother-in-law combination. Also, it should be noted that we have information—in varying degrees of detail—about the other adults (that is, other than the dyads who were interviewed) in these households. Our 30 interviews yielded data on approximately 60 adults living in these 15 multi-generational households.

Of the 15 adult children who were interviewed, 10 were born in Canada; of the remaining 5, 2 were born in India, and one each were born in Hong Kong, Taiwan, and the People's Republic of China. Of the 15 older relatives, all but one (the Irish-origin grandmother) were born overseas—in Europe, India/Pakistan, and the PRC/Taiwan/Hong Kong. Although our sample is small and non-random, these data support the importance of immigration to the growing incidence of multi-generational living arrangements in Canada.

Data from the 30 interviews were analyzed for themes related to multi-generational living, especially with regard to intergenerational exchanges and interdependence. Qualitative data analysis software was used in part, but most of the themes were identified and explored through careful reading and re-reading of the transcripts.

RESULTS

Dimensions of Diversity

Our first observation relates to the *high degree of diversity* in the composition of the multi-generational households in our sample (see Table 13.2). First, two of the households are four-generational (one Chinese-Canadian and one Indo-Canadian family), a phenomenon that has not been explored in Canada to date. While these families are similar with regard to number of generations present, they vary along a number of dimensions. Probably the most important difference is the marital status of the adult child. In the Chinese case, the adult child is a widow whose husband was killed in the Tiananmen Square protests in Beijing in the early 1990s. She was living with her husband and child only (as a nuclear family) in China and it is unlikely she would even be in Canada were it not for her husband's death. (Her parents had immigrated to Canada in the 1970s and it does not appear that she had any wish to emigrate prior to her widowhood.) In the Indian case, the adult

Table 13.2: Composition of Multi-generational Households

Three Generations		Four Generations	
1 grandparent 2 parents* AC	8	1 grandparent 2 parents AC (and spouse) children	1
1 grandparent 1 parent (divorced) AC	1	2 grandparents 2 parents AC (widow) child	1
2 grandparents 2 parents AC	2		
3 grandparents 2 parents AC	1		
1 grandparent 1 non-parent (uncle) AC (and spouse)	1		

* one set of parents consists of a step-mother and father
AC = Adult Child

child is a married woman. Another difference lies in the lineal context of the two families. The Chinese-Canadian woman is living with her own parents and grandparents; the Indo-Canadian woman is living with her husband's ascendant relatives.

The 13 three-generation households do not closely resemble the national data presented above. First, there are two "new" types here: a household (Chinese-Canadian) in which there are three grandparents, and a family (Irish-Canadian) in which the middle generation is not a parent (the unmarried uncle of the adult child). Second, the distribution of household types differs quite significantly from the Canadian data. On the one hand, a close match between our data and the national data is not to be expected given our selection criterion for "child" being an adult child aged 19 to 35—thus eliminating three-generation households with young children only.[6] On the other hand, a certain degree of similarly would be expected. The major axis of difference relates to multi-generational households in which there is only one parent. Whereas such families account for nearly one-half of three-generational families in the national sample, we have only one case (a divorced mother in a Greek/Italian household). We suspect that this difference relates to the ethnic origins of our sample—that is, that Canadian immigrants of southern European, Chinese, and Indian origins have relatively low divorce rates (Jeng and McKenry 2000; Mullatti 1995). This then raises the possibility that within Canada as a whole a not-unsubstantial portion of three-generation families are from "mainstream" Western origins (with higher rates of divorce), and even suggests that among them divorce may be a factor leading to the creation of multi-generational households.

The multi-generational households in our sample can be divided into three main types, depending on **lineage** or blood line. Lineage is an important dimension to explore, given that traditional cultural preferences and ideals regarding co-residence in non-Western societies fall along this axis. Six families are *maternal-line-only* households; in all cases the adult child is living with his/her maternal grandmother. However, the middle generation varies from parents to a divorced parent to an uncle. Notably, three of the four European-origin families are of this type, suggesting that the emotional tie between mother and daughter may be especially important in determining multi-generational living arrangements among families of European descent.[7] Given the strong patrilineal character of traditional China, it is noteworthy that three of the five multi-generational Chinese-Canadian households in our sample are maternal-line. For example, one of the Chinese-Canadian respondents, a 46-year-old woman, stated: "Parents are supposed to stay with their son, not daughter. That's the norm." This woman is correct—that is the norm in traditional Chinese society; however, that norm appears to be renegotiated in the Canadian context. Eight families are *paternal-line-only* households; in all cases, the adult child is living with a paternal grandparent—although it may be a grandmother, a grandfather, or both. This is the most homogeneous variant of multi-generational living arrangement, both in terms of form and ethnic profile. The only variations from the adult child–parents–paternal grandparent(s) form are that (a) one parent is a step-parent and (b) in the adult child generation, one child is married and one has a co-resident sister-in-law. Five of the six Indo-Canadian households in our sample are of this paternal-line-only type. As noted above, only two of the five Chinese-Canadian households are of the paternal-line-only form, despite traditional Chinese **patrilocal** preference. The third type of three-generation household type, represented by one Chinese-Canadian family, is the *combined-maternal-paternal line*. Here, the adult child is living with both maternal and paternal grandparents.

Another dimension of difference in multi-generational living arrangements relates to household maintenance—that is, who is living in whose home? Several years ago, Canadian sociologist Carolyn Rosenthal (1986) pointed out the important difference between multi-generational households headed or maintained by the elder generation (the parent) versus those headed by the middle generation (the adult child). However, sociologists in Canada have not taken up the call to study these different types of multi-generational households. A recent U.S. study (Cohen and Casper 2002) examines this dimension of multi-generational living, using the (odd) terms "hosts" to refer to the household maintainers and "guests" to refer to the co-resident household members who are not household maintainers. Overall, they report that "hosting" is most common among persons in their 50s and 60s, and that "guesting" is more typical of young adults in their 20s and elderly persons over 70. In general, the households in our sample follow this pattern. In 12 of the households, the household maintainer(s) is of the middle generation and in mid-life. However, in two households (both Indo-Canadian), the distinction between maintainer/non-maintainer is rather blurry. In these households, the house is owned by the grandparent(s), but they do not contribute significantly to household expenses. And, in one household (Irish-Canadian), the 75-year-old grandmother is clearly the homeowner and household maintainer. Our findings parallel those of Kamo (2000), who reports that within the United States Asians in mid-life are more likely to bring the elder generation into their homes. In other words, the question of "who lives in whose home?" has a definite ethnocultural component to it. However, why this is the case is not clear, and begs for further research attention.

Fluidity within Multi-generational Households

We also observe a *high level of fluidity* in the multi-generational households in our sample. This fluidity takes two forms. One is "rotational" living arrangements in the grandparent generation. That is, the grandparent or grandparents live in the homes of various children—or at least one other child—throughout the year. Five of the families here exhibit this pattern (three Chinese-Canadian, one Indo-Canadian, and one Greek-Canadian family). For example, one Chinese-Canadian grandmother (aged 71) rotates, on no fixed schedule, between her son's home in Vancouver and the homes of her other children in Australia. In another Chinese-Canadian family, the paternal grandparents live in their son's home in Vancouver for six months of the year and in Hong Kong for the other six months, "when it is warmer"; a similar six-month rotation occurs for an Indo-Canadian grandfather. In another variation, a Greek-Canadian grandmother lives in her daughter's home for six months of the year, in two-month blocks. Members of the elder generation often prefer this type of arrangement; as one Chinese-Canadian grandmother says:

I do not always live with them. In my opinion, it is better to live around rather than living in one place permanently. The elderly might give some troubles to the young adult and I do not like to bother people all the time... There is no fixed schedule ... it depends on my preference.

A second aspect of the fluidity of multi-generational households concerns their duration. It is sometimes assumed that multi-generational households "age in place"; that is, they are formed early in the life course and remain multi-generational (except for dissolution due to death). In our sample, only five families fit this pattern (three Chinese-Canadian,[8] one Indo-Canadian, and one Greek-Canadian). More typically, the families in our sample have been formed as multi-generational household units in relatively recent years only. An important life-course transition often acts as a stimulus to multi-generational living. Sometimes, major illness is a precipitating factor:

My grandmother joined us four years ago. My grandmother had developed Alzheimer's, so we brought her from Greece to live with us. (22-year-old female adult child)

Before when her [mother-in-law] health was good, she used to live by herself in India. Then she came here. (Mother, aged late 50s)

This finding accords with research (for example, Daniewicz 1995; Pendry et al. 1999) showing that health declines can play a significant role in the moves of elderly persons to the households of relatives. However, it is important not to overemphasize the role of age-related health deterioration in multi-generational household formation. Our data suggest that other life course changes can facilitate multi-generational living. One such life course event is widowhood. An Indo-Canadian grandmother (aged 67) states:

It was only after my husband's death [six years ago] that we started living all together. I feel better now living with my son and his family. (The son and his family had lived in Calgary, but moved in with his mother after she was widowed.)

Also, retirement can lead to multi-generational living. A 24-year-old Indo-Canadian male adult child explains:

My grandparents were living in India, and after they retired, they were getting bored and wanted to be around family and, though they felt a strong connection with India, they felt a stronger connection with the family. So they decided to move to Canada; they did so in '93 and have been living with us ever since.

Another life-course transition leading to a (short-term) multi-generational household formation is a grandson's wedding. A 30-year-old Indo-Canadian male adult child says:

[My grandparents] came from India in 1999, September, for my wedding and they've lived here [in this house] since then. They are expected to go back to India next May.

The Irish-Canadian young adult woman has lived with her grandmother (and uncle) for six years, following a move from Edmonton to Victoria to attend school. She and her husband expect to move out on their own soon, but the granddaughter is quick to point out that her departure is contingent on her mother's planned move to Victoria. Her mother will help out with the grandmother, although not live with her. These last two examples highlight the impermanence and (relatively) short duration of some multi-generational living arrangements.

Financial Exchanges

In most of the households in our sample, the middle generation (that is, the parents of the adult child) carries the majority of the financial load in the home. An extreme example is a 51-year-old Chinese-Canadian father who says: "Except expenses, we do not share. I pay for everything for the household." It is important to emphasize that many of the 22 elders in these 15 multi-generational families lack the financial means to live independently, or at least to live out of poverty. Most do not have a pension; many are from countries in which public pensions are non-existent and many have not lived in Canada long enough to collect even a pro-rated amount of Old Age Security. For example, one Greek-Canadian 55-year-old mother says: "My mom has no income."

However, even when the elder generation has a pension, it may not be used to contribute much to household living expenses. A 46-year-old mother originally from Taiwan says of her co-residing parents-in-law:

> We [self and husband] are the major income earners for the household. We cover about 90 percent. Ten percent depends on them—but only if they want to ... They have a pension, but we don't ask them to pay for household items.

This same woman goes on to say, with reference to her children:

> If they have a family, we'll help financially—help them to buy a house, et cetera.

It thus appears that significant financial assistance from parents to children occurs when the children and their parents are relatively young; when parents are elderly, their financial contribution to the younger generation is not substantial. Typical financial assistance from the elder generation is captured in the following quotes:

> My grandma doesn't really need to put that much money out for the family. Usually, the money that she does spend is when she goes to Chinatown by herself and she buys BBQ chicken or duck to bring home for dinner. (Chinese-Canadian adult child, aged 22)

> My mother-in-law sometimes gives money for food. (Indo-Canadian parent, aged late 50s)

> They do not expect me to spend any money or incur any expenses. But I spend money as I wish—I buy them [other household members] gifts and sometimes clothes. (Indo-Canadian grandmother, aged 67)

> My mom only pays the Hydro. (Greek-Canadian mother, aged 60)

Our finding that elderly grandparents tend not to contribute a lot to household finances conflicts somewhat with Che-Alford and Hamm's (2000) research on Canadian three-generation households that reports a relatively high level of income-pooling. Part of the difference in findings relates to the "old" nature of our sample. We suspect that most financial intergenerational transfers from parents to children occur when the older generation is not yet elderly (or later, after the death of the parents). In addition, our findings highlight that a high proportion of immigrant-headed families in Canada are not well-off. This is important to emphasize given current stereotypes of Asian families (and Chinese families in particular) as wealthy.

Virtually all of the parent generation helps their adult children, the majority of whom are students. All 11 of the unmarried adult children in this sample live rent-free. To varying degrees, the children receive other financial support such as help with tuition fees and car insurance. The Chinese-Canadian families are especially supportive of helping out their children while they are students. A typical comment is:

> I expect to support them financially while they [my children] are still in school. (Chinese-Canadian mother, aged 46)

One Chinese-Canadian father goes so far as to say of his UBC-student son:

> As long as my son does not need a tutor, it already is a great [financial] help to me.

One Chinese-Canadian daughter states:

> They view education as such a big thing that when I do want to work, they [parents] tell me not to. They tell me to focus on school.

In only two of the families in our sample—one Indo-Canadian and one Chinese-Canadian—does the adult child make an important financial contribution to the household.

U.S.-based research suggests that multi-generational living is a response to economic hardship (for example, Angel and Tienda 1982; Hogan et al. 1990). In part, this is based on the premise that North Americans prefer to live independently in nuclear units (Ruggles 1996; Wister and Burch 1987). Other research suggests that cultural ideals play a more important role, pointing to Asians and Latinos in the U.S. as more likely to live multi-generationally, holding constant individual variables such as resources, need, and demographic variables (Kamo 2000; Wilmoth 2001). In the Canadian case, Pacey (2002) finds that, with regard to Chinese-Canadian immigrants, cultural preferences outweigh economic predictors of multi-generational living arrangements. However, it is difficult to disentangle economic (need) and cultural (preference) factors, given that most of our sample consists of immigrants from cultural settings in which household extension is viewed as ideal. What do our data have to offer on this issue? We see a complex picture in which more questions are asked than answered. First, only two of the households in our sample appear to be financially needy. It is interesting that in one case (Greek household) it was the formation of the multi-generational household that *led to* financial difficulties; when the elderly grandmother joined the household, her daughter-in-law was forced to quit her job to attend to elder-care responsibilities, and her son retired early because of depression associated with his mother's declining health (due to Alzheimer's). This case indicates that, at least sometimes, multi-generational living creates economic hardship rather than being a response to it. With de-institutionalization trends and a lack of home-care supports, we may see more examples of social policy–created multi-generational households facing financial problems. More research is needed on which families/households are at risk of financial hardship created in this manner.

Second, the hypothesis that multi-generational households form as a way to cope with limited finances does not take into account that different generations within the household may economically benefit to different degrees. In our sample, all of the unmarried adult children have their basic needs (particularly, housing and food) taken care of and all but one attend post-secondary educational institutions (often with parental assistance with tuition fees). As a whole, they would not be better off if they lived independently, especially if we assume that these "dependants" were to continue their education (which is in part a financial investment for the future, for which they are not accruing significant student loan debt). But it is difficult to say whether they would be worse off than their age peers in Canadian society who do live independently. The grandparent generation in our sample is better off than if they were living on their own—as noted above, many lack pensions. The one exception is the Irish-Canadian grandmother, who has the means to maintain her own home, regardless. Notably, she is the only Canadian-born grandparent in our sample. The middle generation is the one bearing the financial brunt in most all of these households. In almost all cases, they would probably be better off financially if not living in a multi-generational setting; that is, they would have more disposable income—if it is assumed that they would not be paying for their "dependants" to live elsewhere. Overall, these households do not seem to have formed as a way to cope with poverty—a dominant theme in the U.S. research literature on multi-generational living that has focused on black households (Jarrett 1994; Roschelle 1999; Trent and Harlan 1994).

Instrumental Assistance/Support

Almost all members of the grandparent generation in these 15 households provide instrumental assistance with household tasks, albeit strongly gendered. This is important to note, since it counters the all-too-prevalent ageist stereotype that seniors are frail dependants in need of assistance from their children (or the health-care system). These examples also illustrate how elders who lack direct financial resources may nevertheless contribute to the operation of the household.

> My grandma is always there to provide me with ... things like breakfast, lunch, dinner, etc. If I'm going to take the bus, she'll always be there and have a pocketful of change. (Chinese-Canadian female, aged 22)

Her 71-year-old grandmother states:

> I make dinner for them (daughter, son-in-law, and two grandchildren) during the week.

Other comments include:

> My parents-in-law share my housework. There are many advantages [of living multi-generationally] for me. (Chinese-Canadian mother, aged 46)

> My grandma, she's really active, she cooks the evening meal, for example, when before she was living with us my mom would have to come and cook. So now, she [grandmother] takes care of that responsibility. As well, during the day, she tidies up and cleans the washrooms or whatever. (Indo-Canadian male, aged 24)

My husband, daughter, and I work [for pay] but my parents help looking after my grand-daughter. My mother-in-law takes care of the cooking and my father-in-law takes care of the garden. (Chinese-Canadian mother, aged late 50s)

This latter example highlights how multi-generational living can facilitate the working-for-pay of parents with young children, thus contributing to the overall financial status of the household. This represents a traditional response to a modern-day problem—working mothers' need to find adequate childcare.

This is not to minimize that some of these families face elder-care responsibilities. The most extreme case in our sample is a Greek-Canadian household containing a recently arrived grandmother with Alzheimer's disease. The parents in this household are clearly stressed with caregiving. The 47-year-old mother says of her mother-in-law:

She requires total care from the time she wakes up ... It is not easy ... My husband cannot support me psychologically as he is suffering from depression because of his mother ... Of course I do all the cooking, cleaning but my husband does help me with his mother's feeding and cleaning as much as he can.

In addition, this family is not able to access social services:

We have been unable to access any support systems here in Canada because my mother-in-law is not a legal landed immigrant.... We did look into some program where they come into your house for five hours a day, but they want $17.00 an hour, and we just don't have the finances for this.

This woman was forced to quit her job as a data-entry clerk in order to be "a caregiver 24 hours a day," and her husband "took early retirement due to health problems." These parents also financially support their 22-year-old daughter,. who is a part-time student and part-time worker. The mother says that she desperately needs **respite care**, so that she and her husband could get away for a few days, but does not see this as a real possibility.

A less extreme situation exists with the Irish-Canadian 27-year-old granddaughter, who has gradually found herself taking on more household responsibilities in her 75-year-old grandmother's house. The granddaughter says:

I do a lot of work around the house ... And Mama—sorry, I should mention that I call my grandmother Mama—she may start something, but then she sort of starts a task and then becomes tired or just sort of rests and then I just pick up from there and take over. Household chores—a lot of things, especially in the last couple of years. She can't really do any heavy lifting anymore and she started to not reach as high.

The grandmother agrees that her granddaughter does a lot of housework, but her description has a bit of a different spin to it. For example, she states:

My granddaughter supports me the most in chores and help around the house. I don't even have to ask her. She just sees things that have to be done and she whips in and does them up very quick and very well.

The married granddaughter wants to live on her own (with her husband), but cried when asked a question about how she felt about leaving her grandmother's house; she is not leaving until her mother moves nearby and will be able to assist the grandmother.

The other adult children in our sample also provide instrumental assistance, although not to the degree of this young woman above. Overall, the four married adult children in our sample provide much more instrumental assistance than do the unmarried children. The unmarried for the most part seem to be continuing in a more "adolescent-type" role with regard to housework and household chores, especially the ten who are students (either full-time or part-time). Examples of the instrumental assistance given by unmarried children are provided below.

> I do, in terms of helping around the house, or helping with mainly manual stuff, like if something breaks or needs to be fixed. Also, helping with my dad's business stuff, if he needs some research done on the Internet. (Chinese-Canadian male, aged 22)

> I don't feel like I do too much. I just help out with the little things like driving or picking up something, or just keeping my room clean, or helping out with household chores. (Chinese-Canadian female, aged 22)

> I support [mother] by cleaning around the house and doing yard work. (Greek-Canadian male, aged 20)

> My mom does pretty much all. I am a bad cook. I am away from the house from 10 to 12 hours a day. I go to school full-time and have two part-time jobs too. My mom takes care of the household work. (Greek-Canadian female, aged 22)

Emotional Support

The multi-generational households in our sample provide evidence of a high level of emotional support across generations. In terms of the grandparent–grandchild tie, the Chinese-Canadian adult children in particular express a warm and close relationship—as illustrated in the three verbatims below. It can also be noted in the first two quotations that the grandparent–grandchild tie can act as a buffer between adjacent generations. In the first case below, the grandmother–grandchild tie works to counter frustration in the mother–daughter relationship; in the second case, the grandmother's relationship with her daughter is buffered by her bond with her granddaughter.

> I find a lot of different support, especially with my grandma. A lot of times, I can just go and talk to my grandma, and I know she will be there to listen to me. My mother, she's very busy.... If I'm frustrated with my mom, I'll talk it out with her [grandmother]. She'll listen. (Chinese-Canadian female, aged 22)

> Emotionally, I think I support my grandma the most. Because at times—if she is not getting along with my mom, or if she just wants someone to talk to. I feel she looks to me as a best friend. (Chinese-Canadian female, aged 22)

> My grandfather used to bring me everywhere with him. Now we play chess and other games like 'Go' together. He makes my life more exciting. He supports me almost every day. (Chinese-Canadian male, aged 22)

These young adult children also receive emotional support from their parents. The first three quotes below suggest that the mother–adult child emotional relationship is particularly strong. It can also be noted that, with regard to the first two verbatims, fathers tend not to be able to establish such intense emotional ties with their daughters, although these father–daughter relationships do not appear to be especially problematic.

> For emotional support, it is my mom. My dad also tries to provide emotional support, but he really ends up annoying me. (Greek-Canadian daughter, aged 22)

> [My mother] provides me with emotional support. I can tell her what is going on and I really do not have to censor ... because we think a lot alike. My father—he is not so good at the emotional side of things. But I know I can count on him if the chips are down. (Greek-Canadian daughter, aged 24)

> When I first came here [after being widowed in China], my mother was a big help emotionally and helping me fit into a new country. (Female, aged 35)

Some sons have a strong tie with their fathers:

> My dad [provides me with the most support]. I always ask for his opinion. (Indo-Canadian male, aged 21)

However, in general sons also are more emotionally close to their mothers than their fathers. The Chinese-Canadian father (aged 51) says:

> I would say my son is closer to my wife. If there is a matter that needs to be solved, I confront my wife and she will talk to my son regarding the matter.

Similarly, a Chinese-Canadian son (aged 22) does not mention his father at all when asked about emotional support. He states:

> I am most supported by my mom and grandfather. My mom is a great help. She gives great advice.

A Greek-Canadian mother (aged 60) states: "We have a close relationship—my son and I."

The emotional tie between parents (of the adult child) and their co-resident parent(s) (grandparent(s) of the adult child) varies considerably in our sample of households. In general, closeness of tie depends on biological relatedness. That is, middle-aged children are close to their parents, but not necessarily their in-laws. Sometimes there is a very close tie, as is evident in the two quotes below (notably, the first quote is from a woman in the only Indo-Canadian maternal-line household in our sample):

> [My father and I] are very close. He tells me everything and I tell him everything. (Female, aged 47)

> We have a good relationship, especially with my mom ... I'm her favourite ... Even now I am married and have a grandchild, she wants to protect me. (Greek female, aged 55)

The tie between an adult child and a co-resident (biological) relative in the parental generation (maternal uncle) is close in the one case we have of this type:

> He (uncle) knows when I am stressed out, so we'll take out the dogs for a walk and talk.... (Irish-Canadian female, aged 27)

However, the situation is more mixed with regard to in-laws. In the following three cases, the emotional bond is close.

> With my mother-in-law, [our relationship] is very close. I treat her like my own mom and she treats me like her own daughter.... My father-in-law and I aren't close. But we are polite with each other … we are distant. (Chinese-Canadian female, aged 46)

> As to my mother-in-law, we have a good relationship. (Chinese-Canadian male, aged 51)

> They have never treated me like their daughter-in-law—especially Dad. I have never felt they were my in-laws. (Indo-Canadian female, aged 34)

However, there is also evidence of daughter-in-law/mother-in-law tension, as illustrated in the following three verbatims.

> If there's an argument between my parents-in-law and me, it won't be like with my mom. We will always have unhappy feelings and remember what happened in the past. (Chinese-Canadian female, aged 47)

> She [mother in-law] usually spends time and talks with her son [the informant's husband]. Sometimes she talks with me. (Indo-Canadian female, aged late 50s)

> Sometimes it happens like my mother-in-law thinks she owns my husband … you know, they came from India and they think daughters-in-law are a bit lower. (Indo-Canadian female, aged 51)

The last quotation above makes reference to the more general issue of daughter-in-law/mother-in-law-tension in traditionally patrilineal and patriarchal societies such as northern India and China. Cross-cultural studies of family structure and organization have often noted the prevalence of such tension in societies in which the status of women is low (Stephens 1965). Recent work by Chen (2000) shows that, in contemporary times, this tension is not inevitable and is in large part conditioned by the attitudes and behaviours of other family/household members, particularly the husband/son.

It is probably not surprising that we capture daughter-in-law/mother-in-law tension among relatively recent immigrants to Canada from traditionally patriarchal societies. The Chinese-Canadian woman says she "tolerates" living with her in-laws but "we have no choice because it is our responsibility to take care of the elderly"; the two Indo-Canadian women are much happier with multi-generational living (while also expressing a duty to co-reside with their husband's parents). Overall, these tensions are not bad enough to cause significant disruption in household functioning; they appear to be accepted as inevitable, or at least not unexpected, by these daughters-in-law. This cultural expectation is expressed by one of the Chinese-Canadian adult sons, who says he would never live with his in-laws because of "all of the stories I have heard that it puts both yourself and your wife in a very difficult position." He has no reservations about living with his parents later on; presumably his wife would learn to adjust to her in-laws.

Intergenerational Conflict

While we find strong evidence of intergenerational exchange and support of both emotional and instrumental types in these multi-generational households, there are also signs of tension, especially regarding in-law relationships as discussed above. Of course, members of any household will experience conflicts from time to time; in multi-generational households there are, however, more possibilities and more axes for discord. Here, we do not deal with trivial irritants (like someone leaving dirty dishes in the sink), but with indications of severe disruption. One Indo-Canadian intergenerational household is experiencing much higher conflict than any of the other households in our sample. The 24-year-old male child says:

> I personally feel my father is not living up to that obligation of taking care, of being supportive, and fulfilling his roles, for example, tuition fees. Every time I have asked for money, he's refused. (This son does not contribute to the household finances.) Me and my father don't speak to each other, so that is kind of rough. I've laid down the foundation of the dynamic in my family. Now, there's problems. There's that implicit assumption that the younger, the kids will take care of the parents, right? Now my grandparents are also feeling like my parents are not living up to their obligations.

His 51-year-old mother does not mention any of this conflict—in fact, she does not appear to be aware of any problems with her in-laws. However, she broke down in tears during the interview because one of her daughters left home at 18, after feeling pressured to get married. She says: "I couldn't sleep for almost two years. I would wake up and see if she was here." This mother is still chastising herself for not better handling the cultural conflict with her daughter, even though her daughter is doing well on her own. All the conflicts in this household relate to unmet expectations; the son (and perhaps the grandparents) do not feel the parental generation is meeting its obligations; the daughter failed to meet cultural expectations regarding marriage; the mother feels she did not meet maternal standards in dealing with her daughter. Yet, this mother–son dyad does not point to the same set of problems—they focus on differing perceived conflicts. This may be a conflict-diffusion technique in conflicted multi-generational households. If all household members are bothered by the same problem, it may escalate to a point that the continued existence of the unit is threatened. This is only speculation; what we can say with more certainty is that perceptions may vary considerably among members of the same household.

Conflicting Values?

The **generational stake hypothesis** holds that young adult children and their parents will have different values because they have a different stake in their relationship (Bengtson and Kuypers 1971). The children have a stake in establishing their own lives and doing things their own way; the parents have a stake in preserving what they have built. The result is a purported *generation gap*, in which the two generations hold different and often conflicting values. This hypothesis has garnered some empirical support (Lynott and Roberts 1997; Giarrusso et al. 1995), but it has not been examined with regard to ethnic minorities, and particularly ethnic minorities in which the two generations co-reside. We assessed this hypothesis by asking the adult children the following question: "If there were an important thing that your parents (and grandparents) would want you to learn from them, what would it be? How do you feel about this?" The same question was asked of the older generation, but reworded to their point of view.

Our data reveal a high degree of congruence between parents and young adult children in basic values, especially among the Asian-origin groups. Among the Chinese-Canadians, all interviewees invoked the value of respect for others (especially elders). Other values, in addition to respect, are mentioned by some—for example, politeness, the importance of family, retention of the mother tongue, the importance of cultural festivities such as Chinese New Year. Among the Indo-Canadians, the values of retaining the Sikh religion and marrying within the culture predominate for both adult children and their elders. Within the European-origin subsample, responses to these questions are less monolithic. However, an emphasis on the importance of family and the retention of religion emerges. Within this group, two of the adult children indicate a resistance to the religious heritage that is so important to their parents. However, the intrinsic value of family is shared by the generations.

Overall, our data show very little support for the generational stake hypothesis within multi-generational households. Among the Chinese and Indo-Canadians, the generations strongly agree on basic values (although what is valued differs in the two ethnocultural groups). Among those of European origin, there is some rejection of religion by young adults, but a high degree of congruence with parents on the value of family. We do not have a large enough sample to provide a definitive conclusion on the generational stake hypothesis, but our data strongly suggest that it has differential applicability depending on living arrangements and cultural background.

CONCLUSION

While multi-generational households are not common in Canada, they are increasing at a fast rate. As with other types of household, however, it is important not to homogenize them; they display a considerable amount of diversity. Also, we have seen that they are fluid over time; this means that longitudinal data are necessary to capture their dynamics. Some general patterns that emerge—from an admittedly small and cross-sectional study—include the following:

- Financial exchanges favour young adults and elders.
- Financial hardship does not appear to be a major determinant of multi-generational household formation in Canada.
- While some households are coping with significant elder-care responsibilities, the majority of elders contribute in a significant way to the daily running of the households.

- The instrumental assistance of young adults to the household depends on their marital status.

- Overall, emotional support across the generations is high, and women (of any generation) both give and receive more emotional support than men.

- There is some evidence of the traditional mother-in-law/daughter-in-law tension in households from cultural backgrounds that are patriarchal and patrilinea.

- There is a high level of congruence in basic values between young adults and their elders in these co-resident households.

The members of the households studied here shed light on one way in which reciprocity can function in families. *Reciprocity* means a balance in social (exchange) relations; that is, persons in social relationships must give as much as they receive.[9] Because of the age-related dependencies in family relationships, reciprocity cannot necessarily be accomplished at one point in time. Rather, families are engaged in relations involving **global reciprocity**. That is, exchanges are balanced over time. The classic example is the woman who looks after her frail mother, "making up" for being looked after by her mother when she was a child. In these households, global reciprocity is accomplished through co-residence. One of the Chinese-Canadian adult children (male, aged 22) summed it up better than we can, and so we give him the last word:

> After they [my parents] support me, I will support them. It's an obligation. It's essential. And I don't mind that. For example, in the future, I will support them financially and morally and care for their health—no different from how they support me now.

NOTES

1. The support of the Social Sciences and Humanities Research Council of Canada is gratefully acknowledged.

2. All households contain at least one child/grandchild.

3. More research has been done in the United States (e.g., Alwin 1996; Cohen and Casper 2002; Kamo 2000; Ruggles 1996). However, this research has tended to focus on ethnic groups—such as Hispanics and African Americans—that have less relevance in the Canadian context.

4. One family resides in Victoria, British Columbia.

5. One of these adult children, although born in Canada, lived in Hong Kong as a young child for seven years.

6. However, the four two-generational households in our sample do contain minor children.

7. Emotional closeness to mother has been found to be an important determinant of "mature co-residency"; that is, adult children aged 25 to 34 living with parents, within the Canadian population as a whole (Mitchell, Wister, and Gee 2002).

8. In two of these three Chinese-Canadian families, there were periods of time when the multi-generational family was separated due to the different timing of immigration of generations.

9. What is given and received in social relationships is often intangible, and does not lend itself to strict measurement. However, it is important that people feel that, overall, they are not giving (or receiving) more than they are receiving (or giving).

KEY TERMS

Generational stake hypothesis: An explanation for differing values between young adults and their parents, focusing upon the different things that each generation has "at stake" in their relationship.

Global reciprocity: Exchange relations that are balanced over time.

Lineage: The tracing of descent through a blood line; worldwide, the most common lineage type is patrilineal, in which descent is traced through the paternal blood line.

Multi-generational family: A group of persons related together by blood and/or marriage, consisting of three or more generations.

Multi-generational household: A co-residing group of persons related by blood and/or marriage, consisting of three or more generations. Sometimes, two adult generations co-residing (for example, a married couple and the wife's mother) are considered to comprise a multi-generational household. The terms "extended family" and "multi-generational household" are often used synonymously.

Patrilocal: A rule of residence that states that relatives on the paternal side only should reside together. When sons marry, their wives live in the household of the husband's parents. When daughters marry, they move to the household of their husband's family.

Respite care: Arrangements in which persons who have heavy caregiving duties in the home are provided with time off. The care recipient may be taken to a different location for a few days, or alternative caregivers may come into the home.

DISCUSSION QUESTIONS

1. In what ways are multi-generational households in Canada diverse?
2. What factors might lead to an increase in multi-generational living arrangements in Canada over the next few decades?
3. What is gained by living multi-generationally? What is lost? From whose point of view?
4. How would you design a study to learn more about multi-generational households in Canada?

REFERENCES

Alwin, Duane F. 1996. "Coresidence Beliefs in American Society: 1993–1991." *Journal of Marriage and the Family* 58: 393–403.

Angel, Ronald, and Marta Tienda. 1982. "Determinants of Extended Household Structure—Cultural Pattern or Economic Need?" *American Journal of Sociology* 87: 1360–1383.

Bengtson, Vern L. and Jon A. Kuypers. 1971. "Generational Differences and the Developmental Stake." *Aging and Human Development* 2: 246–260.

Che-Alford, Janet, and Brian Hamm. 2000. "Under One Roof: Three Generations Living Together." In *Canadian Social Trends, Volume 3*. Toronto: Thomson Educational Publishing.

Chen, Man-Hua. 2000. The Relationship of Mothers and Daughters-in-Law in Urban Chinese Families. Unpublished doctoral dissertation. Texas Woman's University.

Cohen, Philip N. and Lynne M. Casper. 2002. "In Whose Home? Multigenerational Families in the United States, 1998–2000." *Sociological Perspectives* 45: 1–20.

Daniewicz, Susan C. 1995. "When Parents Can't Live Alone: Choosing Multi-generational Households." *Journal of Gerontological Social Work* 23: 47–63.

Gee, Ellen M. 1995. "Families in Later Life." In R. Beaujot, E.M. Gee, R. Fernando, and Z. Ravanera, *Family Over the Life Course*. Ottawa: Statistics Canada. Catalogue No. 91-543E.

Giarrusso, R., M. Stallings, V.L. Bengtson, A.S. Rossi, and V.W. Marshall. 1995. "Intergenerational Stake Hypothesis Revisited: Parent–Child Differences in Perceptions of Relationships 20 Years Later." In V.L. Bengtson, K.W. Shaie, and L. Burton, eds., *Adult Intergenerational Relations: Effects of Societal Change*. New York: Springer.

Hogan, Dennis P., Ling-Xin Hao, and William L. Parish. 1990. "Race, Kin Networks, and Assistance to Mother-Headed Families." *Social Problems* 41: 797–812.

Jarrett, Robin L. 1994. "Living Poor: Family Life among Single-Parent, African-American Women." *Social Problems* 41: 30–49.

Jeng, Wei-Shiuan, and Patrick C. McKenry. 2000. "A Comparative Study of Divorce in Three Chinese Societies: Taiwan, Singapore, and Hong Kong." *Journal of Divorce and Remarriage* 34: 143–161.

Kamo, Yoshinori. 2000. "Racial and Ethnic Differences in Extended Family Households." *Sociological Perspectives* 43: 211–229.

Lynott, P.P. and R.E.L. Roberts. 1997. "Development Stake Hypothesis and Changing Perceptions of Intergenerational Relations, 1971–1985." *The Gerontologist* 37: 394–405.

Mitchell, Barbara A., Andrew V. Wister, and Ellen M. Gee. 2002. "There's No Place Like Home: An Analysis of Young Adults' Mature Coresidency in Canada." *International Journal of Aging and Human Development* 54: 57–84.

Mullatti, Leela. 1995. "Religious and Ideological Orientations and Characteristics." *Journal of Comparative Family Studies* 26: 11–25.

Pacey, Michael A. 2002. "Living Alone and Living with Children: The Living Arrangements of Canadian and Chinese-Canadian Seniors." *SEDAP Research Paper No. 74*. Hamilton, ON: McMaster University.

Pendry, Elizabeth, Geraldine Barrett, and Christina Victor. 1999. "Changes in Household Composition among the Over Sixties: A Longitudinal Analysis of the Health and Life Surveys." *Health and Social Care in the Community* 7: 109–119.

Roschelle, Anne R. 1999. "Gender, Family Structure, and Social Structure: Racial Ethnic Families in the United States." In M.M. Ferree, J. Lorber, and B.B. Hess, eds., *Revisioning Gender*. Thousand Oaks, CA: Sage.

Rosenthal, Carolyn J. 1986. "The Differentiation of Multigenerational Households." *Canadian Journal on Aging* 5: 27–42.

Ruggles, Steven. 1996. "Living Arrangements of the Elderly in America: 1880–1990." In T. Hareven, ed., *Aging and Generational Relationships: Historical and Cross-Cultural Perspectives*. New York: Aldine de Gruyter.

Stephens, William N. 1965. *The Family in Cross-Cultural Perspective*. New York: Holt, Rinehart and Winston.

Trent, K. and S.L. Harlan. 1994. "Teenage Mothers in Nuclear and Extended Households: Differences by Marital Status and Race Ethnicity." *Journal of Family Issues* 15: 309–337.

Wilmoth, Janet M. 2001. "Living Arrangements among Older Immigrants in the United States." *The Gerontologist* 41: 228–238.

Wister, Andrew W. and Thomas K. Burch. 1987. "Values, Perceptions, and Choice in Living Arrangements of the Elderly." In E.F. Borgatta and R.J.V. Montgomery, eds., *Critical Issues in Aging Policy*. Newbury Park, CA: Sage.

Wolf, Douglas A. 1995. "Changes in the Living Arrangements of Older Women: An International Comparison." *The Gerontologist* 35: 724–731.

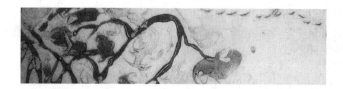

14

Solidarity and Conflict: Teen–Parent Relationships in Iranian Immigrant Families in Toronto[1]

Vappu Tyyskä

Department of Sociology
Ryerson University

Objectives

- To shed light on the family relationships of Iranian-Canadians, one of the least studied immigrant communities.

- To illustrate young people's views of their relationships with parents.

- To challenge prevailing ideas about a necessary "generation gap" and intergenerational conflict between parents and their adolescent children, particularly as they pertain to the negative imagery associated with immigrant families as inherently conservative and particularly prone to intergenerational conflict.

- To demonstrate the prevalence of both intergenerational conflict and solidarity in teen–parent relations.

- To demonstrate that intergenerational relations are subject to change in the process of immigrant settlement.

INTRODUCTION

There are a number of tendencies and gaps in Canadian research of parent–adolescent relationships. First, there is a preoccupation with the negative aspects of teen–parent relationships, present in the assumption of the prevalence of **intergenerational conflict** and a **generation gap.** Second, there is a particular emphasis on these negative elements in relation to immigrant families. Third, this is associated with a lack of attention to social change and the concomitant changes in the attitudes and behaviours of immigrant family members, particularly as they pertain to parental and paternal/patriarchal power in families. Finally, there is an overemphasis on the adult and parental perspective (manifest in literature on parenting practices, parents as socializers) at the expense of attention to young people's perceptions of their relationships with their parents.

Intergenerational Conflict and the Generation Gap

Some life-course researchers (Bengtson et al. in Koller 1974, 224; also see Nett 1993, 199–201) suggest that parents have a greater **developmental stake** or investment in their children's lives because children represent intergenerational continuity to their parents. At the same time, children need to distance themselves from their parents as they develop a separate identity on their way to maturity. For example, adolescents tend to report less openness and more problems in intergenerational familial relations than their parents (Noller and Fitzpatrick 1993, 267), and young people's satisfaction with their family life decreases with age (Holmes and Silverman 1992, 31–32).[2]

It is also widely accepted that parental attempts to control their children are met with rebellion on the part of young people who strive toward independence. This expectation of a generation gap and resultant intergenerational conflict is reinforced by popularized versions of **psychoanalytic theories** and **developmental stage theories.** The former conceptualize adolescence as a period of identity confusion that can be resolved only by adolescents becoming autonomous from their parents, and the latter see the problems of adolescence solved through a series of steps that take them from one life stage to another in an orderly fashion (Tyyskä 2001, 13).[3] Meanwhile, it's worth noting that the idea of youth in conflict with adult-led institutions is primarily rooted in the 1960s and 1970s analysis of widespread student and youth rebellions (for example, Duncan 2000). However, the concept of a generation gap and associated conflict has been less clearly demonstrated empirically in the post-1970s era (Nett 1988, 175).

Nevertheless, it is commonplace to expect intergenerational conflict and a generation gap between parents and adolescents, given the decades separating young people from their parents' age group. It is taken for granted that there is so much social change taking place in those few decades that it would be quite abnormal if there were not any areas of disagreement about values and expectations between parents and adolescent children. As it is, the logic of parental control leading to rebellion is generally culturally accepted in North America. For example, Canadian sociologist Anne-Marie Ambert (1992, 131–149) explored the perceptions of 109 university students of their effect on their parents as teenagers. Notably, all but seven reported having had either a negative effect or a more negative effect on their parents as teenagers than in any other age group. They linked this factor to having been more "rebellious/difficult," or to parental styles that they experienced as challenging.

Adolescents and Parents in Immigrant Communities

The tendency to focus on intergenerational conflict is particularly pronounced where parenting and socialization of adolescents in immigrant communities is concerned. Much is made of the generation gap between "old world" parents and their "new world" children, including issues related to peer relations and social behaviour, dating and spouse selection, educational and career choices, and cultural retention.[4]

In research of Canadian immigrant communities, intergenerational conflict can be directly related to the prevailing **acculturation thesis,** which sees a natural progression whereby each successive generation adopts more of the "behaviours, rules, values, and norms of the host society" (Boyd and Norris 2000: 138; Tyyskä 2001, 103–105), with resultant friction between generations.

Notably, Isajiw (1990, in Isajiw 1999: 189–191) and Boyd and Norris (2000, 140–141) have shown that there is variation between ethnic and immigrant groups in the acculturation or assimilation process. However, there is still an unfortunate tendency to lump different immigrant groups together. More research is required to counter generalizations based on studies of selected immigrant communities. Further, there are significant differences not only between different immigrant groups but also within immigrant communities.

Generalizations about immigrants lead to an unjustified overemphasis on the generation gap in immigrant families. An **old world vs. new world stereotype** prevails, depicting all immigrant parents as conservative throwbacks to "old world" values and behaviours. In contrast, as representatives of "new world" values, adolescent immigrants are seen in a particularly problematic light, as potentially more rebellious, troubled, and prone to delinquency. They supposedly work out their confusions between their ethnic heritage and North American values and valiantly struggle to throw away the shackles of parental oppression rooted in the simple-minded ways of their retrograde parents.

Also of note is the issue of female children's oppression by patriarchal, religious, and cultural practices. Indeed, research into specific immigrant communities suggests that gender differences may be heightened in some immigrant communities, with adolescent girls having much less freedom of movement and decision making power than their brothers (Arruda 1993, Dhruvarajan 1996).[5] However prevalent these practices may be in specific communities, research in this area pays little attention to changes brought on by immigration; that is, whether there are changes in parents' (or children's) opinions, values, attitudes, and practices through the immigration and settlement experience.

Among immigrant groups, those of racialized and religious minorities tend to be particularly subject to representation based on negative stereotypes. Living in a racist society is generally a challenge for members of minority populations. For example, Calliste (2003, 262–264) has addressed problems of raising black children to be physically and emotionally healthy in an anti-black racist society. There is a process of **racial socialization** that children and youth are subjected to as they mature. This process involves an internalization of the messages that one is exposed to in the social environment, including schools, workplaces, peer groups, and all other social institutions.[6] Immigrants from Muslim backgrounds are subjected to similar processes, based on the general anti-Islamic sentiments among the population.

What About Young People's Views?

Further, where North American researchers address intergenerational relations, it is usually in terms of parenting practices.[7] The focus is on what parents do, what they expect from their children, and what kinds of parenting practices produce the best outcomes for children. The points of view of children or adolescents on their relationship with their parents or their expectations from those relationships are rarely examined. Anne-Marie Ambert's (1992, 131–149) study of university students' perceptions of their impact on their parents is a rare study on this topic in Canada. Ambert reports that children of immigrants hold a wider variety of perceptions of their impact on their parents than children of non-immigrants. However, differences arise in relation to the specific immigrant group. Contrary to the generalized "immigrant family" stereotype, children of immigrants from the Caribbean, British Isles, or Israel did not generally link any impact they had on their parents to their parents' immigrant status. In comparison, responses by children of Italian, Greek, and Portuguese immigrants were in line with the old world/new world intergenerational gap, which was particularly acute for girls whose parents were Southern European. Their parents were seen to be more restrictive and protective and even more coercive than they would be toward sons. The girls also described a significant impact they had on their parents, including their rebellion against parental control.

The youth in Ambert's (1992) study mentioned their contributions to their parents because of their better ability to speak English. Other research also suggests that, because immigrant children often learn the language more quickly than their parents, there is a tendency for parents to rely on their children, thus reversing the normative patterns of dependency. It is suggested by some that this may initially be good for parent–child cooperation, but that it may result in producing more gaps. For example, children may feel embarrassed or ashamed of their parents, or develop feelings of inferiority because of them (Isajiw 1999, 103). Arruda's (1993) research among Portuguese immigrant families confirms that parents rely on their children in dealing with the social institutions, schools, and hospitals of the host society. Adolescents may also contribute in tangible ways to family finances. These elements may both enhance and create difficulties in families, depending on the ethnic group in question and other background variables including social class or urban/rural differences.

THE CASE STUDY: IRANIAN-CANADIAN TEENAGERS IN TORONTO

In order to start shedding light on these gaps and problems in existing research, I conducted a small qualitative study in the summer of 2000. Individual interviews were conducted with 16 adolescents in the Toronto Iranian community, regarding their views of their relationships with their parents.[8]

Of the 16 teens, 8 are males and 8 are females, between the ages of 13 and 19. The oldest respondent was a college student, and the rest attended school in grades 9 to 11. Five of the youth held part-time jobs. All respondents indicate Farsi as their first language, this being the majority language in Iran. Given a choice of language in the interview, 5 were conducted in English only, 4 in Farsi only, and 7 in a combination of English and Farsi.[9]

The majority of these young people were landed immigrants, with three refugees and another three who were born in Canada. All except one had arrived in Canada with both parents. The families of all of the immigrant and refugee respondents had arrived in Canada between 1986 and 2000. This time frame marks the period of the influx of most of the approximately 30,000 Iranians who came to Canada following the 1979 Iranian revolution. About 50 percent of them live in Ontario, and more than two-thirds of this group live in Toronto (Pajouhandeh 1999, 3). That means that the Toronto Iranian population numbers around 10,000.

Most of the respondents are now Canadian citizens. About half indicate that their religion is Muslim, while the other half reported no religious affiliation. Again, this matches with the general population of Iranian-Canadians, most of whom are Muslim (Dilmaghani 2001). Also like the general Iranian immigrant and refugee population, the youth form a relatively diverse group in terms of demographic characteristics, such as family structure and parents' education and occupation.

Most of the subjects of this research live in intact families; seven males and two females reported that their parents are married. One male reported that his parents are separated, while six females reported that their parents are divorced. The majority (seven males and three females) lived with both parents, while four (one male and three females) lived with their mother, and another two females lived with mother and another relative. Almost all (seven males and five females) have siblings. Family sizes are small; respondents are either only children or have only one sibling. Notably, immigrant families in Canada tend to have fewer children than the Canadian-born population.

The parents of these youth come from diverse educational and occupational backgrounds. However, most fathers (12) were reported to have post-secondary education, either a university degree (10) or a college diploma (2). The rest had high school education; only one had an elementary-level education. Among the mothers, 13 had either college (6) or university (7) education. The rest had completed high school.

Before coming to Canada as refugees (3) or immigrants (12), the fathers had a variety of occupations, including steelworker, social worker, teacher, engineer, mechanic, businessman, professor, and artist. One father was a student. All except one father were employed, most of them (11) full-time, and another three part-time. The teens commented that their fathers have a different occupation in Canada than in Iran, including two journalists, two university professors, a social and community worker, two businessmen, and a caretaker.

Among the mothers, 3 had arrived in Canada as refugees and 13 as landed immigrants. In Iran, 9 mothers (5 of the teenage males' and 4 of the females' mothers) had no occupation. The remaining 7 mothers were in traditional female occupations, including nursing, social work, and teaching. One was a lab technician and another one was an artist. The majority (11) are employed full-time in Toronto, and another one is employed part-time; the remaining three are not employed. The teens report a change in their parents' employment in Canada compared to Iran. The range of jobs includes typical female-dominated occupations, such as teacher, nurse, social and community worker, banker, city clerk, system analyst, fashion designer, insurance company worker, and customer service representative.

These general educational and occupational features correspond to the Iranian immigrant population in Canada, the majority of whom are from urban and middle- and upper-class backgrounds. More recently, as the Iran–Iraq war was waged from 1980–88, there were immigrants and refugees from a more diverse population. Generally, Canadian immigration favours professionals with high levels of education, with the end result that there tends to be more of this element among Iranian immigrants as well (Behjati-Sabet 1990; Dilmaghani 2001).

Analytical Framework

The main goal of the study is to explore specific aspects of young Iranian-Canadians' relationships with their parents. I asked general questions about family settlement and adjustment to life in Canada, overall relationship with parents, and differences in teens' relationships with mothers and fathers. I also asked more specific questions of the teens in three different areas, explained below. All questions asked both what the teens think and do themselves, and what they see their parents as thinking and doing in their family relationships.

My focus here is on the elements that are indicative of **solidarity**, the sharing of aims and interests between generations. A point of strong caution is necessary here. Fundamentally, the notion of solidarity, in its sociological usage, evokes a **structural-functionalist** analysis, characterized by an emphasis on the harmonious elements in social relationships and the acceptance of power relationships as normative. Applied to intergenerational relationships, structural-functionalists would suggest that the life stages of childhood, adolescence, and youth are a time of preparation for adult life, and by necessity involve the submission of pre-adults to adult power and control (Tyyskä 2001, 11–14). This is definitely not my intent in using the concept here. In no way do I want to dismiss the elements of conflict and power in parent–child relationships. As a response to the long-term neglect of youthful views of adult–offspring relationships, I am specifically emphasizing both **agency** and **subjectivity** of the adolescents I interviewed. First, I am critical of an overemphasis on the power of adults at the expense of *agency* of young people, defined as the ways in which young people act on and contest adult power and control. Young people are not passive recipients of socialization; they actively engage in a socializing relationship with their parents, each influencing the other. Likewise, in contrast to the standard adult-oriented parenting research, it is important to pay attention to *subjectivity*, defined as the ways in which young people interpret and communicate about their relationships with their parents. In this study, agency and subjectivity are two sides of the same coin, resulting in a youth-oriented approach that overcomes the confines of structural-functionalism and traditional family research and builds on our understanding of power, influence, and solidarity in teen–parent relationships.

My analytical approach also follows and builds on categories developed by American researcher Vern Bengtson in the 1970s and beyond (see, for example, Rosenthal 1987), and are related to the concept of **intergenerational solidarity**, or shared and agreed-upon elements in family relationships between parents and their children. Bengtson as well as Canadian researcher Carolyn Rosenthal (1987) used this framework to explore the relationships between aging parents and their adult children. I have adapted these categories to the relationships between teens and their parents.

One of the aspects of research is the question of mutual support in family between teens and parents (Bengtson's **functional solidarity**). This refers to general practical support by parents toward teens and vice versa, and in my research I asked specific questions about money issues, housework, giving and getting advice, and parents' help with schoolwork and activities. In this chapter, I focus on financial and emotional support and giving and getting advice.

A second set of questions has to do with general values and opinions of parents and teens (Bengtson's **consensual solidarity**); that is, the kinds of values that are central to both the teens and parents, including areas of agreement and disagreement. This has to do with values such as the importance of family and friends and educational and vocational choices.

A third area has to do with expectations of family members from one another (Bengtson's **normative solidarity**); that is, what do parents expect from teens and vice versa as members of the family, again including areas of agreement and disagreement. This taps into elements such as the degrees and types of supportiveness expected from family members, and the degrees of freedom seen as appropriate by different family members.

Further, in all these three areas (functional, consensual, and normative solidarity), I also asked this important question: Do you think your family's patterns in this area have changed as a result of immigration to Canada? Explain and give examples.

RESULTS

Functional Solidarity: A Question of Support

Both the male and female teens perceive their parents as generally supportive, particularly when it comes to education and career plans. Most also think there is a good balance of support in their families, and some say their parents support them more than they are able to support their parents. Parental financial support is the most obvious way; most of these young people do not have jobs, and many get an allowance and other money from their parents toward both their daily necessities and their entertainment.

The teens also speak about parents' emotional support. Both males and females note that mothers and fathers give different types of support. For example, one 15-year-old female says:

> I think my parents support me differently, like my dad supports with my education and my mom supports with how I can make myself a better person and makes me more confident in how I am thinking. (F2)

And a 13-year-old male says:

> My mom supports me more. Like when I am wrong about something, she talks to me and guides me with a good reason. If I need some money, she gives [it to] me or helps me with other stuff. My dad supports me whether I am right or wrong, he talks to me and tells me why I was wrong or if I did something right. I feel he is proud of me even when I make mistakes. (M5)

The teens also think of themselves as generally supportive of their parents, although they acknowledge that there is an imbalance in that they get more support from their parents than vice versa. The areas identified as teen support of parents range from *emotional support* to *practical help* such as doing housework and looking after younger siblings. A few teens (3 female, 1 male) comment that their parents do not welcome their support because they think that they are too young, and do not have respect for their attempts at support. This is more obvious for the females.

In one extreme example, a 16-year-old female says:

> I support my family as much as I could. I would like to support them emotionally because I feel my father needs it but he does not take it seriously. He believes that I'm still a kid and it is too soon for me to get involved emotionally. But I think the opposite. (F8)

One significant area of specific support is giving and getting advice.

Parental Advice to Teens

Of all respondents, only one teenaged girl indicates that she does not accept any advice from her parents. She is 19, and feels she is old enough to make her own decisions. The others indicate a wide range of advice, mostly about friends, peers, and school. There are some gender differences in this, in that more of the females get advice about their friends specifically from their mothers (recall that most of these girls live with their mothers only). However, some of the males also comment on getting slightly different kinds of advice from their fathers and mothers, or the different manner in which mothers and fathers give advice. For example, a 17-year-old male says:

> My father when he wants to give me some instructions, he usually raises his voice because he thinks I might understand better... This is hard for me but I do not have any other choice than to sit down and look at him while he is talking to me and I also I have to follow his rule to do whatever he says. My mother understands me better in this situation and she tries to help me and guides me with the best of her knowledge. (M1)

And a 15-year-old male says:

> My father usually does not come to my business but my mother expects me to obey some rules around the house. (M6)

Teen Advice to Parents

Five of the teens (2 males, 3 females) do not generally give advice to their parents. They do not get asked for their advice and they do not volunteer it because it is not their place and the parents would not listen to them. One 16-year-old said:

> I cannot communicate about anything specific or consult them because they think I am a child. (F8)

And a 17-year-old male says:

> I think I do not advise them about their problems or even give them advice about my own problems because they are mature enough to solve problems and usually they don't ask for any advice. The way I have grown up in this family, I never allow myself to interfere and/or discuss their needs, issues, or problems. (M7)

However, the majority of teenagers do give advice to their parents. Both males and females identify issues such as questions about where to live and household purchases. In addition to these, the male teens indicate giving advice about travel and vacation plans, and how the parents should look after their health and well-being. One male indicates advising parents about the English language.

Impact of Immigration on Functional Solidarity

Only a minority of the teens (1 female, 3 males) thought their family's pattern of support has not changed upon immigration. For example, one 15-year-old male says:

> I think if we lived in Iran, I would still have the same support because I see it very deeply from both of them and it would not change them no matter where we live. (M4)

The rest indicate that their families have become more supportive of one another upon immigration. Many of the comments of the teenage girls had to do with their parents allowing them more freedoms and supporting their ventures to doing more. For example, one 15-year-old female says:

I think if we were in Iran, I've got to use every day as a girl to do cooking, cleaning, and washing but in Canada I do it because I want to, not because of our culture and I want to make both my parents happy. My mom has her own mind like her opinions and her thinking and I think she has not really changed them when she came to Canada. My dad believes in lots of Iranian things, but both of them think that I did not grow in Iran so they believe that they should not expect or treat me the same as an Iranian girl who grows up in Iran. (F2)

Consensual Solidarity: Values and Opinions

Generally, the teens indicate a very close agreement about values with their parents. The most common shared values are the importance of family, education, future occupational success, and the value of having friends. In line with other research discussed above, where the teens and their parents disagree, these disagreements are commonly in the areas of choice of friends or dating and how they spend their spare time, as well as about how much they should focus on their education.

There is a distinct gender difference in this area between the male and female teens. Whereas the young males do not identify specific differences between their parents, some of the girls talk about more agreement with their mothers than with their fathers. And they indicate that their fathers are stricter or more distant, while their mothers are closer and more lenient. Consequently, there is more distance and more disagreement with Dad. One 13-year-old female says:

My mom and me are alike but my dad and me aren't alike a lot. Me and my dad agree when he treats me in a good way, and when he is nice I like it a lot but when I disagree about him being so lazy to spend time with me, he usually argues with me and tells me that he is right and I should not expect too much from him. I disagree in the situation that he talks too much on the phone and he does not put enough time for me. As I said before me and my dad don't have communication that much and he doesn't even try to build up our relationship between each other. Me and my mom don't have lots of disagreement. I don't know why. We mostly are agreeing with one another. I am very pleased with our relationship and I think only my mom helps me to handle the problems that I have with my father in our relationship. (F6)

Impact of Immigration on Consensual Solidarity

Only 3 teens (1 male and 2 females) think their families' values have not changed upon immigration. The rest think that there has been some change in parental values. The young males focus on how the external environment is something the whole family learned from, to change their values and opinions. For example, one 17-year-old says:

Because Canada is a new country for us and we are experiencing a new life style here which is different from Iran, we are facing new values, experiences, and issues every day which for sure have an impact on our lives and on our relationship. For example, our communication with others and our education have been changed. We have learned how we can support each other in different aspects of life and how can we share our opinions and transfer them to one another. (M7)

Once again, the value of more freedoms is seen to be a significant area, and particularly the teenage girls talk about the issue of more opportunity for freedoms for girls. For example, one 13-year-old female says:

> I think if I lived in Iran it would be way worse because mostly we don't have freedom that we have in here like I would not be able to have different friends either boys or girls but in Canada I have this opportunity to have these kinds of freedoms. I think these different kinds of things bring more disagreement between Iranian parents and their children who live in Iran. But in Canada, children have chances to talk about their different points of views or different opinions about their values to the parents. I would not be happy if I was there but I am happy to be here because there are lots of open doors for me and other Iranian teenagers. (F4)

Normative Solidarity: Expectations from Family

Generally, the teens expect a balance of support, parental involvement, and personal freedoms from their parents. This group of expectations is verbalized by one 13-year-old girl as follows:

> I expect them to ask questions about where I am. I know they care but do not ask too many questions that they want for every detail of my life. I expect them to watch me and to help me out but not too much. I expect them to care about my schoolwork. I expect them to let me decide what I want to do and don't judge until something that is bad happened. For example, don't judge my friends that they are not good or they are good. I expect them to give me advice but they should let me pick the advice if I want to because sometimes I don't want to take their advice. (F4)

Some of them get this type of respect and freedoms. However, the biggest complaints from the teenagers are that they should have more freedoms, more understanding, and more respect. This is particularly notable for the teen males. One 13-year-old male says:

> I expect them to give more freedom and that's all. (M8)

Another 15-year-old male says:

> I expect them to understand me. I understand they get mad about my studying but they should be more supportive and understanding which they are but it won't happen all the time. (M4)

When asked what parents expect of them, the teens identify respect of parents, listening to them, and doing well in school as the major points. Many of the teens say they work hard to meet their parents' expectations and most think they actually meet them and their parents recognize their efforts. One 19-year-old female says:

> I respect and obey their rules because we live under the same roof. (F1)

Impact of Immigration on Normative Solidarity

Most of the teens' comments have to do with how their parents expect more from them in Canada because there is a wider range of opportunities. Many of the teens comment that they have an ability to say no to their parents here, which is something they did not have in Iran. The answers are similar for males and females. Their ideas are the same, but they are expressed differently by the young males and females. Some of the males say that their parents expect more from them here than in Iran because male children are treated more leniently in Iran. In Canada, there is more opportunity, and more pressure from parents. But when their parents push, they have the right to resist. From the teen females' side, some of them say that too much is expected of girls in Iran, but here in Canada they have an ability to say no—they have rights, and can refuse to be pushed here. For example, one 13-year-old female says:

> If I didn't come to Canada, I did not have ability to say no, but in Canada I have this ability to say yes and no. I think if I lived in Iran I did not have another option to say a word of my own opinion and my own expectations but in Canada the expectation is way less than in Iran because in Iran, Iranian parents have too many expectations from their children, especially their daughters and I think all of us, either me or my parents, our expectations become less and less. (F4)

This is echoed by a 17-year-old male:

> Their expectations from me have changed since we came to Canada. They have more expectations. Like sometimes I believe that I am right but my father disagrees with me. I did not think that my father could be wrong in Iran but I do here. Recently their expectations have reduced, because I have expressed my disagreement about different issues and we discuss it. I think it has been the result of our settlement in Canada. I am very happy for being here because... I got some rights for my own life so it makes life easier for me. (M1)

A SUMMARY OF GENERAL PATTERNS

Teens and Parents Generally Get Along

The teenagers talk about their relationships with their parents as a balance of positive and negative features. In fact, the study suggests that there is a range or a continuum in teen–parent relationships, from those that are more conflict-ridden to those that are relatively conflict-free. Although all teens identify some things that really bother them, they conclude that their relationship with their parents is generally good, and that they are able to sort out most disagreements with their parents reasonably. Many have only minor disagreements with their parents, over issues such as how they spend time and with whom, or how much schoolwork they should do. In comparison, there is only one teenage female who indicates that she is quite detached from her parents and the rest of her immediate family. She has lived apart from them for many years, having been raised by an aunt in the United States. As she is now reunited with her parents, she is having difficulties with them about expectations. For example, she describes her home as more like a hotel to her where she comes to sleep at night. The rest of the teens have a range of positive and negative experiences. One 15-year-old male says about his relationship with his parents that

It is very good and we don't have many problems. But I am old enough to be heard more. It is my right that my parents should understand me better because they have had these kinds of expectations when they were teenagers. (M6)

Relations with Mothers and Fathers

Second, some of the teens indicate that both of their parents treat them the same, and that their relationships with both parents are similar. However, many others comment on some differences, most notably of being more distant with fathers who are stricter, and closer to mothers who often act as allies in dealing with fathers. They also indicate getting different types of advice and support from mothers and fathers. In this regard, many of the young women think that they get treated fairly, and have a good relationship with both their fathers and their mothers.

However, whereas more of the teenage males talk about either parent being the strict one, more of the teenage females identify their father as the stricter and more distant one. Three of the young women have a big problem around fathers whom they see as uncaring, not spending any time with them, and showing no respect for them. Two of these young women indicate major problems around the treatment of girls and women. They feel quite desperate about their situation, and about the lack of respect for girls and women, the unfairness of the division of household labour, and their limited freedoms compared to their brothers and other young men. Here we have to note that six of these eight teenage females live with their mothers, their parents having divorced. They do not see or spend as much time with their fathers as with their mothers.

Therefore, that daughters would find their fathers more distant is not surprising given that many of these girls live with their divorced mothers and see their fathers only once a week and on the weekends. What is striking is that these young women want to develop a closer relationship with their fathers; they want to have their attention and love. Meanwhile, there is a wider range of reactions to mothers and fathers by the teen males than by the females. Some of the teen males comment on the caring and loving aspect of their relationship with their mothers. One of them is bothered by his mother's excessive "adoration" of him. Others think their mothers are more strict, and they could communicate better with their fathers. But many teen males as well as teen females see their mothers as allies in their relationships with their fathers; that is, they could have their mother listen to them and influence their father's opinion.

Wishes from Parents

Many of the teens want more freedoms and for their parents to listen to them more and be open and communicative. Another wish is for equal treatment of children by parents. For example, one 16-year-old female says:

I think parents should listen to their kids and treat them equally. Why some people like me who [is a] girl and younger should do everything at home but my brother should not. (F8)

Finally, the notion of "freedom" that emerges from the interviews is most interesting. Almost unanimously, all of these teens, males and females alike, perceive that they have a claim to more freedoms in Canada than they did or would in Iran. This comes out particularly in the end, when these young people are given a chance to add or change something to what they had said. All except two of them not only wanted to add something but also to say similar things, related to the ideas of more freedoms and more say in their families. And their point of reference is Iran compared with Canada. For example, one 17-year-old male says:

> As an Iranian teenager, I would like to mention that youth are living in a closed environment in Iran. In Canada, there is lots of opportunity for youth to grow and become successful, especially for girls. I know some Iranian parents who are very strict with their children. I know they have lots of restrictions and limitations toward their children, especially teenagers, but I have this suggestion to them that they could let their children breathe and feel some freedom of being in Canada. It is good for them to have a healthy life and safe environment so that they can have a bright future. (M7)

What is interesting here is that most of these teens do not find themselves to be oppressed in their families, by their parents, or by their fathers, yet they come to the issue of freedoms in the end of the interview. It has been suggested that there is a sense of protectiveness about families among Iranian youth.[10] This means that they are more comfortable when talking in generalities about families than answering specific questions about their own families. This is in line with the expectation in Iranian families that children should "safeguard the good name of the family" (Behjati-Sabet 1990).

CONCLUSIONS

First, this study finds that there are both positive and negative aspects in the relationships between adolescents and their parents in Iranian-Canadian families in Toronto. Although there is evidence of intergenerational conflict and a generation gap, these are not extreme and appear to be subject to constant negotiation. The relationships are best conceptualized along a continuum, from extreme conflict and little or no solidarity to little or no conflict and a lot of solidarity. The reasons for conflict vary, the most common ones being disputes over schoolwork and the use of social time.

Second, there is little reason to suggest that the degree of intergenerational conflict is either more or less severe among Iranian-Canadians than among the general population. Although this study lacks a comparison group, the main point is that existing research, discussed above, suggests a range of intergenerational behaviour patterns among different ethnic and racialized minorities. It is more important to expand this research than to assume any behaviours on the part of specific groups, immigrants or otherwise.

Third, the interviews confirm that there are changes in family relationships as a result of immigration. This goes counter to the prevailing stereotype about "old world" parents and "new world" children locked in combat. Most of the respondents indicate that their parents have gradually changed in their approach to their children in all three main areas under investigation: functional, consensual, and normative solidarity. In the area of *functional solidarity*, many of the teens perceive that family members have become more supportive of one another. Significantly, although some of the teens do not give or are not expected or allowed to give advice, most of the teens give advice to their parents. This heightened focus on family supportiveness may be, among other things, a reaction to the lowered occupational and economic status of Iranian immigrants in Canada, compared to their lives in Iran (Behjati-Sabet 1990). In the area of *consensual solidarity*, the value of freedoms is seen to be central to the parents' approach to their teens. Many teens think that their parents allow them more freedoms than they would or did in Iran. In the area of *normative solidarity*, the teens think their parents expect more of them in terms of educational and occupational pursuits than they would or did in Iran, because of the wider range of opportunity in Canada. This conclusion is supported by a general emphasis on education among Iranian-Canadians found in other studies (Behjati-Sabet 1990).

Fourth, there are significant gender differences both on the part of the parents (mothers and fathers) and between the male and female teens. Notably, almost all of the girls are more emphatic about the positive changes on the part of their parents through immigration. In all three areas of solidarity, the girls indicate that their parents allow them more freedoms and more say about their lives than they would or did in Iran. That being said, there are three female teens but only one teen male who indicate serious problems with their parents, particularly their fathers. Mothers are generally seen to be warmer and more supportive than fathers by both male and female teenagers.

Behjati-Sabet (1990, 97–99) suggests that Iranian families can be classified into "traditional" and "modern" varieties. In the **traditional family**, children's lives are governed by the male head of the household and wives submit to husbands and mediate the relationships between fathers and children. In the **modern family**, parental authority over children is weakened, as is the husband's role as the only wage-earner and head of household. However, although women are more likely to engage in wage work, they still carry the burden of nearly all household labour.

It is suggested that Iranian immigrants in Canada represent the modern family category (Behjati-Sabet 1990, 98). My study supports this conclusion where most of the parent–adolescent relationships are concerned. However, there seems to be a small but significant traditional element, particularly as it pertains to the situation of daughters. What is evident here is that despite the many changes brought on by immigration, fathers continue to be a more distant parental figure particularly to teen girls, and mothers continue to mediate the relationship between the fathers and children while maintaining their own warmer and closer relationship with their teenagers. This seems to be evidence of a continuation of patriarchal patterns of family relationships. However, many of the female respondents also come from divorced families where they have less contact with their fathers than their mothers. Although this aspect requires more analysis and future research, my study suggests that there are major shifts in many family relationships upon immigration, including marital relations and parent–offspring relations. Insofar that teens, and particularly female teens, report distant relationships, it may be that Iranian immigrant adult husbands/fathers are more resistant to changes than adult wives/mothers, and may continue to hold on to traditional ideas about their power and status in relation to women and children. Meanwhile wives/mothers regardless of their employment or marital status continue their traditional domestic roles, part of which maintain their closer relationships with their offspring.

Finally, hearing young people's views about their relationships with their parents shows that more of this kind of research is required to illuminate processes that take place in families as well as in society at large. In terms of family life, as suggested above some suspect that many of these teens may have—out of **filial obligation**—presented their parents in an unrealistically positive light. However, their answers cover a lot of ground and indicate a balance of positive and negative features.

Significantly, there is room for negotiation, challenges, and complaints by teens. In most cases, as these teens push the limits of their freedoms, they also indicate that their parents do change somewhat. Having said that, the teenagers' continued preoccupation with and complaints about the lack of freedoms in Iranian families indicate that parental power over teen children is still a fact of life in most of these families. Of final and important note are the general social forces at work. Family relationships evolve in a specific social context. As indicated in the introduction, negative images and stereotypes about ethnic and racialized minorities abound in Canada. Particularly, Muslim countries and immigrants from predominantly Muslim areas of the world are subject to anti-Islamic prejudice from their immediate communities and popular media in Canada. The young people in this study talk about their notion of freedoms for teenagers by making a contrast between Canada and Iran. This contrast is likely to be rooted both in their parents' experiences and accounts and the generally anti-Muslim and anti-Iranian media reports. Thus, the idea of "Canadian freedoms" contrasted with their parents' "Iranian attitudes" reflects a process of both primary and secondary racial socialization in which images of freedom are central.

Listening to young people's views is an important gateway toward understanding family relationships as well as general social processes. In fact, it is a necessary element in understanding the issues and challenges that particularly immigrant families face as they settle in their new environment.

NOTES

1. I gratefully acknowledge financial support to this study from the start-up funds of the Social Sciences and Humanities Federation of Canada, granted by Ryerson University, 2000–2001, and Research Assistant funding from the Office of Research Services, Ryerson University, under the Ontario Work-Study Program. This chapter is based on a paper entitled "In the Eye of the Beholder: Views of Iranian-Canadian Adolescents of Their Relationships with Their Parents," presented at the Conference of the European Sociological Association, University of Helsinki, Finland, August 28, 2001.

2. Even though most adolescents, male and female, are satisfied with their family relationships, there is a decrease between ages 13 and 16, from 87 percent to 80 percent for girls, and from 92 percent to 85 percent for boys (Holmes and Silverman 1992, 31–32).

3. See also Koller 1974, esp. see 208–209; Seltzer 1989: 227; Beaumont 1996.

4. For literature on peer relations, see Wong (1999), Wade and Brannigan (1998); dating and spouse selection patterns, see Chimbos (1980, 34–35), Dhruvarajan (1996), Arruda (1993), Isajiw (1999, 103); educational and career choices, see Li (1988, 74–83), Fuligni (1997), Dhruvarajan (1996), Arruda (1993, 16–18), Christensen and Weinfeld (1993, 32–35): retention of culture/ethnicity, see James (1999, 95), Pizanias (1996, 350), Ambert (1992, 236, 241–245), Isajiw (1990 in Isajiw 1999, 189–191).

5. This has been noted, for example in the Vancouver Portuguese community in Canada (Arruda 1993), and the Winnipeg Hindu Indo-Canadian community (Dhruvarajan 1996).

6. Also see James 1999; Kelly 1998.

7. For a good summary, see Paulson and Sputa 1996; also see Tyyskä 2001, 92–96.

8. I thank Shokofeh Dilmaghani from the Family Service Association of Metropolitan Toronto for her help in recruiting the research participants and for providing helpful feedback on many aspects of the research project.

9. I thank my research assistant Fariba Davani, a social work student at Ryerson University, who conducted the interviews in the summer of 2000, translated the Farsi interviews into English, and transcribed all interviews.

10. Shokofeh Dilmaghani, Iranian community worker, Family Service Association of Metropolitan Toronto, personal communication, July 23, 2001.

KEY TERMS

Acculturation thesis: A theory that suggests that each successive immigrant generation increasingly adopts the behaviours, rules, values, and norms of the host society. Also referred to as the *process of assimilation.*

Agency: The ways in which people act on and contest power and control. The young people in this study are seen to exhibit their agency in their relationship with their parents, resulting in changes.

Consensual solidarity: Shared values and opinions. This study examined the agreement between teens and parents about the importance of family and friends and educational and vocational choices.

Developmental stage theories: Exemplified by the work of Erik Erikson and Jean Piaget, these theories propose a sequence of life stages in human development, driven by biology. The stage of adolescence is seen as particularly crucial for the development of self/identity.

Developmental stake: Parental investment of time and energy on their offspring because they represent intergenerational continuity to their parents.

Filial obligation: The obligation of offspring to show respect to their parents based on a culturally specific pattern. In this study, there is a sense that Iranian teens must present their parents in a positive light in order not to shame them and their family.

Functional solidarity: Mutual practical support between people. In my study, the focus was on patterns of giving and getting advice between parents and teens.

Generation gap: The idea that because parents and their offspring are subjected to historically different experiences in their formative years, there is a gap between these generations in understanding and getting along with one another.

Intergenerational conflict: The idea that there is conflict between parents and their offspring because of a generation gap.

Intergenerational solidarity: The idea that relationships between different generations are characterized by mutual pathways of support and sharing of aims and interests.

Modern family: A type of contemporary family in which parental authority over children is weakened, as is the husband's role as the only wage-earner and head of household.

Normative solidarity: Expectations from other people in a social relationship. This study examined what is expected from members of the family, including degrees and types of support and the degrees of freedom seen as appropriate by different family members.

Old world vs. new world stereotype: A prevailing idea that all immigrant parents cling to the traditional values and behaviours of their countries of origin, while their offspring represent more modern North American values. This is assumed to result in an enhanced generation gap in immigrant communities.

Psychoanalytic theory: Developed by Sigmund Freud, this theory proposes that human development is driven by a psycho-sexual drive toward maturity. The stage of adolescence is marked by a conflict between dependence and independence, which is resolved when the adolescent internalizes the new expectation of independent behaviour.

Racial socialization: Raising children of racialized minorities in a context that gives them negative or mixed messages about their history and heritage. In this study, the Iranian youth are seen to be recipient of anti-Islamic sentiments from Canadian society, and both pro- and anti-Iranian sentiments from their parents.

Solidarity: The sharing of aims and interests.

Structural-functionalism: A theoretical tradition in sociology that puts emphasis on the harmonious elements in social relationships and accepts power relationships as normative. Applied to intergenerational relationships, structural-functionalists would suggest that the life stages of childhood, adolescence, and youth are a time of preparation for adult life and by necessity involve the submission of pre-adults to adult power and control.

Subjectivity: The ways in which people interpret and communicate about their lives.

Traditional family: A type of family in which children's and wives' lives are governed by the male head of the household, who is the sole wage-earner.

DISCUSSION QUESTIONS

1. Teen–parent relations in North America are generally presented as conflict-ridden. Is this an accurate portrayal? What do you think explains the emphasis on intergenerational conflict and the generation gap?

2. Most of the literature on immigrant families presents them as conservative and prone to intergenerational conflict. Discuss the ways in which this chapter challenges that view.

3. In your experience, what are the kinds of issues that are likely to result in conflict between teens and parents? What are issues that teens and parents are likely to have agreement about?

4. How important is the gender of adolescents in teen–parent relationships? In what ways does it matter? Are there areas where it makes no difference?

5. How important is the gender of parents in teen–parent relationships? In what ways does it matter? Are there areas where it makes no difference?

6. Teens may see their parents as not being able to change. How does this chapter challenge that view?

7. As a person in his/her teens or twenties, how does (or did) the theme of "freedoms" enter into your relationship with your parents?

REFERENCES

Ambert, A-M. 1992. *The Effect of Children on Parents.* Binghamton, NY: The Haworth Press.

Arruda, A.F. 1993. "Expanding the View: Growing Up in Portuguese-Canadian Families, 1962–1980." *Canadian Ethnic Studies* 25(3): 8–25.

Beaumont, S.L. 1996. Adolescent Girls' Perceptions and Conversations with Mothers and Friends. *Journal of Adolescent Research* 11(3): 325-340.

Behjati-Sabet, A. 1990. "The Iranians." In J.M. Anderson and E. Richardson, eds., *Cross-Cultural Caring: A Handbook for Health Professionals in Western Canada.* Vancouver: University of British Columbia Press.

Boyd, M., and D. Norris. 2000. "The Crowded Nest: Young Adults at Home." *Canadian Social Trends.* Vol. 3. Toronto: Thompson Educational Publishing.

Calliste, A. 1996. "Black Families in Canada: Exploring the Interconnections of Race, Class and Gender." In M. Lynn, ed., *Voices: Essays on Canadian Families.* Toronto: Nelson Canada.

Chimbos, P.D. 1980. The Greek-Canadian Family: Tradition and Change. In K. Ishwaran, ed., *Canadian Families. Ethnic Variations.* Toronto: McGraw-Hill Ryerson.

Christensen, C.P., and M. Weinfeld. 1993. The Black Family in Canada: A Preliminary Exploration of Family Patterns and Inequality. *Canadian Ethnic Studies* 25(3): 26-44.

Dhruvarajan, V. 1996. "Hindu Indo-Canadian Families." In M. Lynn, ed., *Voices: Essays on Canadian Families.* Toronto: Nelson Canada.

Dilmaghani, S. 2001. *We Are Listening. Harfat Ra Mishenavam.* Toronto: Family Service Association of Toronto.

Duncan, S. 2000. "Is There a Generation Gap?" Montana State University. Communication Services. <www.montana.edu/wwwpb/home/gap.html>.

Fuligni, A.J. 1997. The Academic Achievement of Adolescents from Immigrant Families: The Roles of Family Background, Attitudes, and Behaviour. *Child Development* 68(2): 352-363.

Holmes, J., and E.L. Silverman. 1992. *We're Here, Listen to Us! A Survey of Young Women in Canada.* Ottawa: Canadian Advisory Council on the Status of Women.

Isajiw, W. 1999. *Understanding Diversity: Ethnicity and Race in the Canadian Context.* Toronto: Thompson Educational Publishing.

James, C.E. 1999. *Seeing Ourselves: Exploring Race, Ethnicity and Culture.* 2nd ed. Toronto: Thompson Educational Publishing.

Kelly, J. 1998. *Under the Gaze: Learning to be Black in a White Society.* Halifax, N.S.: Fernwood.

Koller, M.R. 1974. *Families: A Multigenerational Approach.* Toronto: McGraw-Hill.

Li, P.S. 1988. *Ethnic Inequality in Class Society.* Toronto: Thompson Educational Publishing.

Nett, E. 1988. *Canadian Families: Past and Present.* Toronto: Butterworths.

Nett, E. 1993. *Canadian Families: Past and Present,* 2nd ed. Toronto: Butterworths.

Noller, P., and M.A. Fitzpatrick. 1993. *Communication in Family Relationships.* New York: Prentice Hall.

Pajouhandeh, P. 1999. Young Iranian Immigrant Women and the Process of Acculturation. Master's research project. Toronto: OISE, University of Toronto.

Paulson, S.E. and C.L. Sputa. 1996. Patterns of Parenting During Adolescence: Perceptions of Adolescents and Parents. *Adolescence* 31(122): 369-382.

Pizanias, C. 1996. "Greek Families in Canada: Fragile Truths, Fragmented Stories." In M. Lynn, ed., *Voices: Essays on Canadian Families.* Nelson Canada.

Rosenthal, C.J. 1987. "Aging and Intergenerational Relations in Canada." In V. Marshall, ed., *Aging in Canada,* 2nd ed. Toronto: Fitzhenry and Whiteside.

Seltzer, V.C. 1989. *The Psychosocial Worlds of the Adolescent: Public and Private.* Toronto: Wiley & Sons.

Tyyskä, V. 2001. *Long and Winding Road: Adolescents and Youth in Canada Today.* Toronto: Canadian Scholars' Press.

Wade, T. and A. Brannigan. 1998. "The Genesis of Adolescent Risk-Taking: Pathways Through Family, School and Peers." *The Canadian Journal of Sociology* 23(1): 1-20.

Wong, S.K. 1999. "Acculturation, Peer Relations, and Delinquent Behaviour of Chinese-Canadian Youth." *Adolescence* 34(133): 107-119.